THE EXERCISE PROFESSIONAL'S GUIDE TO GROUP FITNESS INSTRUCTION

Deliver memorable movement experiences that build healthier communities

AMERICAN COUNCIL ON EXERCISE®

EDITORS

SABRENA JO, PhD

CHRISTOPHER S. GAGLIARDI, MS

JAN SCHROEDER, PhD

DANIEL J. GREEN

ACE

Library of Congress Control Number: 2021924491

ISBN 978-1-890720-91-9

Printed in the United States of America

A B C D

Distributed by:
American Council on Exercise
4933 Paramount Drive
San Diego, CA 92123
(858) 576-6500
(858) 576-6564 FAX
ACEfitness.org

Project Editor: Daniel J. Green
Technical Editors: Sabrena Jo, PhD, Christopher S. Gagliardi, MS, & Jan Schroeder, PhD
Review of Equity, Diversity, and Inclusion Content: Jessica Jackson, MBA, Med, TorranceLearning – Racial Equity Strategist
Art Direction and Production: Devon Browning
Cover Design: Rick Gray
Photography: Vertex Photography
Anatomical Illustrations: James Staunton
Stock images: Adobe Stock and Getty Images
Index: Kathi Unger
Exercise models: Rebekah Abrahim, Rachel Browning, Klinton Buechele, David Burnell, Angel Chelik, Jacque Crockford, Makeba Edwards, Morgan Frazier, Christopher S. Gagliardi, Noreen Gentry, Chris Kiepfer, Sydney Jack Stevens, Jessica Talbi, & Monique Vargas
Production services provided by Westchester Education Services of Dayton, Ohio—A U.S. Employee-owned Company

Acknowledgments:
Thanks to the entire American Council on Exercise staff for their support and guidance through the process of creating this textbook.

NOTICE
The fitness industry is ever-changing. As new research and clinical experience broaden our knowledge, changes in programming and standards are required. The authors and the publisher of this work have checked with sources believed to be reliable in their efforts to provide information that is complete and generally in accord with the standards accepted at the time of publication. However, in view of the possibility of human error or changes in industry standards, neither the authors nor the publisher nor any other party who has been involved in the preparation or publication of this work warrants that the information contained herein is in every respect accurate or complete, and they are not responsible for any errors or omissions or the results obtained from the use of such information. Readers are encouraged to confirm the information contained herein with other sources.

DISCLAIMER
Moving forward, ACE will use "they" and "their" in place of "he/she" and "his/her." This change eliminates gender biases associated with these pronouns and is more inclusive of all individuals across the gender spectrum. Note that all ACE content moving forward will reflect this update, and previous content will be updated as needed. It is ACE's goal to share our mission to Get People Moving with all people, regardless of race, gender, gender identity, sexual orientation, physical or intellectual abilities, religious beliefs, ethnic background, or socioeconomic status.

ACE's Mission Is to Get People Moving.

P22-03

ACE STATEMENT ON INDUSTRY GUIDELINES

ACE Certification exams assess if candidates are qualified to enter the job role associated with the certification they seek. This includes evaluating a candidate's knowledge and application of the most current evidence-based professional standards and guidelines. The dynamic nature of this field requires that ACE Certification exams be regularly updated to ensure that they reflect the latest industry findings and research. Therefore, the knowledge and skills required to pass these exams are not solely represented in this or any industry text. In addition to learning the material presented in this textbook and study program, ACE strongly encourages all exam candidates and certified professionals to keep abreast of new developments, standards, and guidelines from a variety of valid industry sources.

To help ensure that candidates can stay up to date on industry standards and guidelines, ACE provides a list of the latest edition of the key sources referenced in our textbooks and study materials, which can be accessed at www.ACEfitness.org/Industry-Guidelines. These include commonly cited materials such as the *Physical Activity Guidelines for Americans*, *Dietary Guidelines for Americans*, the latest guidelines on conditions such as hypertension and cholesterol, and physical activity–related documents from organizations like the World Health Organization and the American College of Obstetricians and Gynecologists.

Whenever these sources are cited in this textbook, you will see a call-out indicating which edition of the source is being discussed with a reminder to visit the website above. It is important to note that ACE Certification exams assess your ability to apply guidelines in your interactions with clients and class participants. Therefore, exam candidates can be successful with their studies if they prepare by using the ACE study materials and reviewing the website above when prompted to do so.

TABLE OF CONTENTS

SECTION III

Elements of Leading Group Fitness Classes

SECTION IV

Professional and Legal Considerations

FOREWORD

In 1989, when I first read the ACE group fitness textbook (then called the *Aerobic Dance-Exercise Instructor Manual*), I knew I had to get certified! I was already a certified instructor and Registered Fitness Leader in Australia, but upon reading that manual I knew there was much more I needed to learn. I had a hunger for knowledge and wanted to continue my education so I could be a more effective instructor. At that time (long before the internet), the certification wasn't available in Australia. So, if I wanted to take the exam, I had to come the United States, so I saved up and flew to Los Angeles to get ACE Certified. That was in 1990.

From the very beginning of my career, I had a passion for fitness. This was my reason for becoming an instructor: I loved being fit, I loved group exercise (back then, it was called aerobics), and I loved the music and the whole room moving together. Ultimately, though, I wanted to make a difference. It was clear that through teaching classes I could do just that!

As a fitness instructor, I'm acutely aware of the need for education and the responsibility to learn. I love my role in helping improve the health and well-being of the people in my classes. Over the years, I've seen the positive changes participants experience in my classes and this is highly motivating. However, I also see how critical my role is in creating safe, effective classes that provide participants with memorable and positive experiences. This is something I take seriously, as that experience can change a person's life, whether that individual is a life-long exerciser or brand new to movement.

I'll never forget a participant who started coming to my beginner's aerobics class in 1986. David had morbid obesity, was in poor health, and had never exercised. I took great care to provide him with a safe workout, but just as importantly, a fantastic experience. David kept coming back and, with growing confidence, he was smiling and enjoying movement. In the following months, David graduated to my intermediate and then advanced level classes. After a year or so, he met with me and brought a before-and-after picture, as well as his old jeans. He stepped both of his legs into one pant leg and pulled the waist of the jeans out to the side to demonstrate how much smaller he was. He was half his size! He told me that I'd made these changes possible. He thanked me for helping change his life. After wiping my tears, I knew then I would dedicate myself to making a difference through fitness.

To this day, I remember that feeling and that decision, which eventually led me to the United States a few years later to earn my ACE certification. That decision ultimately changed the whole direction of my life. Having the ACE certification makes such a difference in how employers see me. It sets me apart and assures the people I work for that I am qualified and that my education marks a level of expertise they can trust. It's clear to me that the ACE certification sets the gold standard in the fitness industry.

Today, group fitness classes are not what they were 35 years ago. Thank goodness there's more than high-impact aerobics! You have so many more opportunities to offer a wide variety of classes in diverse settings. Now, I'm teaching fitness classes in live and online settings and found a whole new skillset. With such a wide variety of programs to consider, this textbook is an invaluable resource. As you grow in your career, you will find *The Exercise Professional's Guide to Group Fitness Instruction* an invaluable tool to come back to again and again.

I was so proud when I passed my exam! So much has changed in the industry since then, but my pride has not. Thirty years later, I have maintained my certification through continuing education and when I renew every two years, I still feel that same sense of accomplishment. As you study this textbook, you will find a rich resource that provides you with the science and art of group fitness instruction to move you beyond competence and into greatness.

Keli Roberts

ACE Certified Group Fitness Instructor, Personal Trainer, and Health Coach; ACE Master Trainer and continuing education provider

2007 Inductee into the National Fitness Hall of Fame

INTRODUCTION

The American Council on Exercise is proud to introduce *The Exercise Professional's Guide to Group Fitness Instruction*. This textbook teaches the instructional techniques, leadership skills, and professional responsibilities that instructors need to lead safe, effective, and enjoyable group fitness classes.

In response to an evolving fitness industry, this textbook addresses teaching classes in environments outside the traditional fitness facility, from outdoors to online. In addition to offering cueing and leadership strategies specific to these environments, this text includes coverage of legal considerations that are vital to the success of the ACE Certified Group Fitness Instructor (GFI), such as shared-use agreements to ensure that you are using public land in a safe and legal way and considerations for the proper, legal use of music when livestreaming classes or offering prerecorded sessions.

In addition, features are included throughout—including Apply What You Know, Think It Through, Expand Your Knowledge, and the ACE Mover Method™—that bring theoretical concepts to life and ask you to pause to gauge your understanding of the topic being discussed, as well as your comfort level with utilizing that knowledge when teaching classes. We encourage you to take advantage of these application-based tools so that you will be better prepared to thrive in real-world situations.

GFIs can apply the ACE Mover Method—a behavior-change philosophy that centers on the needs, goals, and values of participants—both before and after class using the ACE ABC Approach™ when privately engaging with participants. This textbook introduces the ACE RRAMP Approach™, on the other hand, as a unique way to implement the ACE Mover Method by engaging with participants as a group while leading a group fitness class. The ultimate goal is to use these approaches and other behavior-change strategies to create a caring and task-involving environment that allows participants to progress through the stages of learning and experience the intended outcome of the class while also having a positive experience.

This textbook is organized into four sections:

- **Section I: Group Fitness Fundamentals** explains the role and scope of practice of the GFI, exercise and behavior-change principles, and the foundations of movement and healthy eating.
- **Section II: Preparation and Design for Group Fitness Classes** explains choreographic methods and the basic components of a group fitness class; key considerations regarding apparel, equipment, and music; program design, including structuring and sequencing movements and developing a class blueprint; and onsite procedures and responsibilities.
- **Section III: Elements of Leading Group Fitness Classes** focuses on participant-centered instruction, including participant learning styles and the teaching of multilevel classes; teaching techniques and styles, including cueing strategies and leadership considerations; the specific considerations stemming from teaching

classes outdoors and online; and working with participants with health considerations ranging from cardiac conditions to low-back pain.

- **Section IV: Professional and Legal Considerations** covers participant safety, including injuries and medical emergencies, as well as the legal and professional guidelines that all GFIs must consider.

Finally, in response to cultural shifts both inside the fitness industry and in the world at large, this textbook emphasizes the importance of equity, diversity, and inclusion (EDI). In addition to features explaining the current state of the fitness industry and how you as a GFI can help the industry move forward in a more inclusive way, EDI considerations are included throughout in the context of participant motivation and adherence, as well as the ability of the GFI to provide a welcoming and empowering climate for all participants.

Along with serving as a study aid for the ACE Group Fitness Instructor Certification Exam, *The Exercise Professional's Guide to Group Fitness Instruction* is a valuable resource for both new and veteran instructors that not only provides the critical knowledge you will need to effectively lead a class, but also application-based tools to help you master that content and then utilize it to create memorable movement experiences and empower your participants through person-centered instruction and behavior-change strategies.

We wish you luck as you prepare for a rewarding career as an ACE Certified Group Fitness Instructor and sincerely hope that this textbook serves you well as you prepare for the certification exam and remains a trusted resource throughout your career.

Sabrena Jo, PhD
Senior Director of Science and Research

Daniel J. Green
Senior Project Manager and Editor for Publications and Content Development

STUDYING FOR THE ACE GROUP FITNESS INSTRUCTOR CERTIFICATION EXAM

TO HELP YOU ON YOUR JOURNEY TO BECOMING AN ACE CERTIFIED GROUP FITNESS INSTRUCTOR, WE HAVE PUT TOGETHER A COMPREHENSIVE SET OF RESOURCES YOU CAN USE WHILE YOU STUDY.

ACE University contains online study materials that include videos, learning activities, and quizzes for each corresponding chapter of *The Exercise Professional's Guide to Group Fitness Instruction*, as well as a summary review of each chapter to help you focus your studies. ACE University also includes an end-of-course exam review and practice tests with annotated responses to enhance learning.

For Textbook and ACE University

If you purchased an ACE Group Fitness Instructor (GFI) study program that includes ACE University, you will use our online program to guide you through your studies.

If you are utilizing ACE University, log in to your My ACE Account at www.ACEfitness.org/MyACE to access your online study program, and then take the following steps to best prepare for the exam:

- **STEP 1:** Read Chapters 1–4 of this book, *The Exercise Professional's Guide to Group Fitness Instruction*. These chapters cover the fundamentals of becoming an ACE Certified Group Fitness Instructor—from the role of the GFI in the health and fitness industry to an introduction to behavior-change principles, human movement, healthy eating, and exercise principles.

  After reading each chapter, watch the videos and complete the learning activities and quiz questions in ACE University.

  Also, review the ACE Code of Ethics, which can be found in the Appendix of the textbook.

- **STEP 2:** Read Chapters 5–8 of this book. This material covers the key design considerations and preparation for creating and leading memorable group fitness classes, including class blueprints and group exercise facility and equipment considerations.

  After reading each chapter, watch the videos and complete the learning activities and quiz questions in ACE University.

- **STEP 3:** Read Chapters 9–12 of this book, which cover the essential elements of leading group fitness classes, participant-centered instruction, and working with participants with health considerations.

  After reading each chapter, watch the videos and complete the learning activities and quiz questions in ACE University.

- **STEP 4:** Read Chapters 13 and 14 of this book, which cover professional and legal considerations for group fitness instructors, including participant safety and legal guidelines and professional responsibilities.

After reading each chapter, watch the videos and complete the learning activities and quiz questions in ACE University.

At this point, we also recommend that you register for the ACE Group Fitness Instructor Certification Exam by visiting www.ACEfitness.org. Setting a date will give you a clear goal to work toward while you complete your studies.

- **STEP 5:** Complete the Exam Preparation module and the practice test(s) in ACE University. The results of your practice test will help you assess your level of preparation and plan your remaining study time as your exam date approaches. Be sure to review the feedback to each practice test question to help you gain a better understanding of competency-based assessments and the professional role of the ACE Certified Group Fitness Instructor.

IMPORTANT TIPS

- To register for your exam, do not forget that you must be at least 18 years old, have completed high school (or the equivalent), and hold a current certificate in adult cardiopulmonary resuscitation (CPR), and, if living in North America, proper use of an automated external defibrillator (AED). You may obtain this certificate through a variety of local providers. However, for more information on how to meet this requirement through ACE, please visit https://www.acefitness.org/cpr.
- As you make your way through you study materials, be sure to keep an eye out for the boldface terms in the chapters, which are defined in the glossary.
- As a general rule, ACE recommends that candidates allow approximately three months of study time on average to adequately prepare for the ACE Group Fitness Instructor Certification Exam.
- For additional tips and resources, check out the ACE Answers web page at www.acefitness.org/fitness-certifications/ace-answers. ACE Answers offers a wide range of study support resources, including answers to commonly asked study questions, exam preparation blog articles, video demonstrations and lectures, and optional virtual education sessions. You can also connect with ACE Answers and your peers at www.facebook.com/ACEFitnessAnswers.

EXAM CONTENT OUTLINE

The ACE Group Fitness Instructor Exam Content Outline is a valuable tool for candidates preparing for the Certification Exam. It is the result of an in-depth job analysis, which is validated via an industry-wide survey and then used in assembling each ACE Group Fitness Instructor exam.

Candidates are encouraged to refer to this document as they study, as it details key concepts and competencies assessed by the exam.

The ACE Group Fitness Instructor Exam Content Outline can be found at www.ACEfitness.org/GFIexamcontent.

A KEY TO THE FEATURES AND ICONS IN THIS TEXTBOOK

Throughout this book, you will see features that highlight certain content within the chapters. In some cases, these features are meant to broaden your knowledge or apply what you've learned, while others provide an opportunity to reflect on the content just presented. Here is a description of the features you will see in this book:

ACE→ MOVER™ METHOD

This feature explains how to use the ACE Mover Method™ philosophy, the ACE→ ABC APPROACH™, and the ACE→ RRAMP APPROACH™ to help participants change health-related behaviors and establish positive relationships with exercise.

EQUITY, DIVERSITY, AND INCLUSION

This feature highlights the importance of equity, diversity, and inclusion in a changing fitness industry—and a changing world. Here, readers will learn how they can help every participant, regardless of background, feel welcomed and empowered and have a positive group fitness experience.

LEGAL CONSIDERATIONS

This feature highlights often-overlooked legal issues that group fitness instructors should be mindful of throughout their careers, such as proper use of music and copyright law, as well as shared-use agreements and other legal considerations associated with leading outdoor classes.

APPLY WHAT YOU KNOW

This feature gives truly practical advice on how something just learned might be applied in daily practice. For example, a discussion on exercise considerations for participants with asthma might include a feature on how to perform various breathing techniques.

EXPAND YOUR KNOWLEDGE

This feature presents cutting-edge research that readers might not be aware of, but that impacts the daily work of exercise professionals. For example, a discussion on what to include during the warm-up might include a feature discussing research on whether participants should perform static stretches during that portion of class.

THINK IT THROUGH

This feature asks the reader to pause and consider a question that includes a real-world scenario. For example, in a discussion on common injuries, you might be asked to think of appropriate ways to support a participant who is returning to physical activity after a serious injury.

ACE-SPONSORED RESEARCH

This feature explains the results derived from ACE-sponsored research into topics of interest to group fitness instructors (e.g., rates of detraining or the proper sequencing of exercises).

In addition to the features just described, you will see the following icons in the margins beside the associated text:

Safety

This icon appears whenever there is discussion of in-class participant safety (e.g., signs and symptoms of potential injuries or fatigue) or when safety-related responsibilities are covered (e.g., sequencing movements to prevent rapid changes in body position).

Emergency Procedures

This icon appears alongside content about how to handle in-class emergencies (e.g., what to do when a participant has a stroke or hypoglycemia).

Legal Considerations

This icon appears alongside valuable legal considerations or concerns that are mentioned in the text.

ACE-sponsored Research

This icon appears whenever ACE-sponsored research is cited in the text, as well as in the reference list at the end of each chapter.

AUTHORS

CHRISTOPHER S. GAGLIARDI, MS, is the Scientific Education Content Manager of the American Council on Exercise, where he creates, reviews, edits, and updates educational resources and serves as a key contributor to the development and revision of written, audio, and video content. He also serves as a subject matter expert for video and photoshoots and for media requests. Gagliardi is an ACE Certified Personal Trainer, Health Coach, Group Fitness Instructor, and Medical Exercise Specialist, NSCA Certified Strength and Conditioning Specialist, National Board Certified Health and Wellness Coach (NBC-HWC), and NASM Certified Personal Trainer who loves to share his enthusiasm for fitness with others and is committed to lifelong learning. He holds a bachelor's degree in kinesiology from San Diego State University, a master's degree in kinesiology from A.T. Still University, and a certificate in orthotics from Northwestern University Feinberg School of Medicine.

SABRENA JO, PhD, is the Senior Director of Science and Research for the American Council on Exercise and ACE Liaison to the Scientific Advisory Panel. Jo has been actively involved in the fitness industry since 1987. As an ACE Certified Group Fitness Instructor, Personal Trainer, and Health Coach, she has taught group exercise and owned her own personal training and health-coaching businesses and is a relentless pursuer of finding ways to help people start and stick with physical activity. Jo is a former full-time faculty member in the Kinesiology and Physical Education Department at California State University, Long Beach. She has a bachelor's degree in exercise science, a master's degree in physical education/biomechanics, and is pursuing a PhD in exercise psychology from the University of Kansas.

AMBER LONG, MEd, currently serves as the Executive Director of Wellness & Recreation Services at the University of Colorado, Denver, where she led the charge in opening the new, holistic-wellness focused Salazar Student Wellness Center. She is an ACE Certified Group Fitness Instructor, Personal Trainer, Health Coach, and Medical Exercise Specialist, and views exercise as a means to prepare the body and mind for living life more fully. Long holds a master's degree in higher education leadership and a bachelor's degree in community and public health education from Iowa State University. She remains active in the industry as an author, consultant, instructor, trainer, and coach.

MARK S. NAGEL, EdD, teaches in the Sport and Entertainment Management Department at the University of South Carolina. He is also an adjunct professor at Saint Mary's College of California and the University of San Francisco. Dr. Nagel has published extensively in a variety of areas of sport management, including law, finance, marketing, and college sport. He has co-authored nine books and has given dozens of research presentations. Prior to becoming a professor, Dr. Nagel worked in campus recreation and intercollegiate athletics.

JAN SCHROEDER, PhD, is a professor in the Department of Kinesiology at California State University, Long Beach. She is the coordinator of the Bachelor of Science degree in fitness as well as past department chair. Dr. Schroeder holds more than 20 licenses and certifications, from ACE Certified Group Fitness Instructor to Certified Exercise

Physiologist to X-Ray Technician – Bone Densitometry, and she has published more than 60 research and applied articles and prepared more than 40 presentations. She also owns Garage Girls Fitness, both an online and in-person training platform. Her degrees include a bachelor's degree in Movement and Exercise Science from Chapman University, a master's degree in Physical Education/Exercise Physiology, and a doctorate in Physical Education/Exercise Physiology with a specialization in Gerontology from the University of Kansas.

SECTION

I

Group Fitness Fundamentals

CHAPTER 1

The Role of the Group Fitness Instructor

SABRENA JO, PhD | Senior Director, Science and Research; American Council on Exercise; ACE Certified Group Fitness Instructor, Personal Trainer, and Health Coach

CHRISTOPHER S. GAGLIARDI, MS | Scientific Education Content Manager, American Council on Exercise; ACE Certified Group Fitness Instructor, Personal Trainer, Health Coach, and Medical Exercise Specialist

IN THIS CHAPTER

LEARNING OBJECTIVES

Upon completion of this chapter, the reader will be able to:

- Explain how group fitness continues to evolve
- Describe the group fitness instructor's role in the healthcare continuum
- Differentiate between professional certification, certificates, and continuing education
- Describe the role and scope of practice for the ACE Certified Group Fitness Instructor

ACE UNIVERSITY

If your study program includes ACE University, visit www.ACEfitness.org/MyACE and log in to your My ACE Account to take full advantage of the ACE Group Fitness Instructor Study Program and online guided study experience.

A variety of media to support and expand on the material in this text is provided to facilitate learning and best prepare you for the ACE Group Fitness Instructor Certification exam and a career as a group fitness instructor.

Group fitness has its origins in cardiorespiratory exercise via classes inspired by dance. In his 1968 best-selling book *Aerobics*, Kenneth Cooper, MD, promoted various modalities of aerobic exercise as a means to help prevent **coronary heart disease.** Shortly thereafter, participating in activities such as walking, running, cycling, and swimming became popular as a way to improve health. Included in this trend was a new form of exercise that combined traditional calisthenics with popular dance styles, aptly called dance aerobics. These types of classes were popular throughout the 1970s and early 1980s and consisted mostly of high-impact movements. By the late 1980s, low-impact aerobics and step aerobics gained popularity because of the less-jarring movements used in the classes.

In the 1990s, classes began to emerge that incorporated more than just aerobic exercise, often with specific types of equipment, such as dumbbells, resistance tubing, and stability balls. Hence, the term "aerobics" was replaced by the term "group fitness." Currently, a large number of varied formats exist, including equipment-based modalities, such as indoor cycling, group strength training, suspension training, kettlebell classes, and ballet barre classes; specialty classes focused on aquatic exercise and fall prevention; martial arts and combat sports–inspired classes; as well as mind-body formats, such as yoga and Pilates. Additionally, classes that serve a specific niche for participants who desire a more vigorous workout, such as boot camp–style training and **high-intensity interval training (HIIT),** have become popular.

As the general public continues to access more and more fitness information via the Internet and social media, it is imperative that ACE Certified Group Fitness Instructors (GFIs) provide sound, evidence-based instruction to keep participants safe. With innovation in exercise equipment and programming, GFIs have a responsibility to stay up to date with current standards and established teaching techniques to provide their participants with safe and effective classes.

Over the past several decades, awareness has heightened about the opportunities for helping people improve their lives through healthy behavior change, sound exercise programs, and strategies for nutritious eating. Accordingly, the profession has continued to develop its **standard of care** and refine its **scope of practice** with the help of education and certification organizations, such as the American Council on Exercise (ACE).

EXPAND YOUR KNOWLEDGE

Standards of Practice and Organizations Advocating for Industry Best Practices

Common standards of practice for exercise professionals include:

- Assurance that the professional has been accurately assessed and maintains documented qualifications to practice in the specific professional role [e.g., earning a certification that is accredited by the **National Commission for Certifying Agencies (NCCA)**]
- Evidence that the professional has completed appropriate education and training
- Practicing in accordance with standards and guidelines within the defined scope of practice for the profession

- Commitment to continued professional development
- Protecting client/participant privacy by not disclosing information to third parties unless required by law
- Maintenance of appropriate filing systems and documentation of all professional activity
- Implementing proper screening and assessment, and requiring medical clearance when recommended for the safety of the client or participant
- Referral of clients or participants to appropriate healthcare practitioners when needed
- Implementing risk-management strategies and services in accordance with business, industry, and legal standards and guidelines
- Avoiding conflicts of interest, improper distribution of information, or any other false representation
- Calling attention to unethical, illegal, and unsafe behaviors by other professionals

The International Confederation of Registers for Exercise Professionals (ICREPs), Europe Active, and, in the United States, the Coalition for the Registration of Exercise Professionals (CREP) are serving exercise professionals and the public through standards setting, professional advocacy, and national registries of well-qualified exercise professionals. CREP is currently made up of the American Council on Exercise (ACE), American College of Sports Medicine (ACSM), Collegiate Strength and Conditioning Coaches association (CSCCa), National Council on Strength and Fitness (NCSF), National Strength and Conditioning Association (NSCA), and the National Pilates Certification Program (NPCP).

Group Fitness Instructors Help Improve Health through Physical Activity

The content in Table 1-1 is based on the 2018 *Physical Activity Guidelines for Americans.* Please visit www.ACEfitness.org/Industry-Guidelines to confirm that this is the latest edition. If a newer set of guidelines is available, exam candidates should study that version to ensure they are up to date with the latest industry guidelines.

There are many reasons why people choose to participate in an exercise program. The evidence-based health-related benefits associated with regular participation are often mentioned, as individuals look for ways to maintain or improve a specific aspect of their health. GFIs are perfectly positioned to help individuals work toward these health-related goals by creating and delivering safe, effective, and enjoyable exercise experiences that provide an appropriate amount of movement to elicit a training response that may result in the desired benefit. Table 1-1 offers a list of some of the many evidence-based benefits associated with regular physical activity. GFIs can empower participants to pursue goals that align with their personal values and lifestyles. Taking an evidence-based approach to fitness will help bolster the GFI's professionalism and help build **rapport.**

TABLE 1-1

Health Benefits Associated with Regular Physical Activity

Children and Adolescents
- Improved bone health (ages 3 through 17 years) - Improved weight status (ages 3 through 17 years) - Improved cardiorespiratory and muscular fitness (ages 6 through 17 years) - Improved cardiometabolic health (ages 6 through 17 years) - Improved cognition (ages 6 to 13 years)* - Reduced risk of depression (ages 6 to 13 years)

TABLE 1-1 (*continued*)

Adults and Older Adults
▸ Lower risk of all-cause mortality
▸ Lower risk of cardiovascular disease mortality
▸ Lower risk of cardiovascular disease (including heart disease and stroke)
▸ Lower risk of hypertension
▸ Lower risk of type 2 diabetes
▸ Lower risk of adverse blood lipid profile
▸ Lower risk of cancers of the bladder, breast, colon, endometrium, esophagus, kidney, lung, and stomach
▸ Improved cognition*
▸ Reduced risk of dementia (including Alzheimer's disease)
▸ Improved quality of life
▸ Reduced anxiety
▸ Reduced risk of depression
▸ Improved sleep
▸ Slowed or reduced weight gain
▸ Weight loss, particularly when combined with reduced calorie intake
▸ Prevention of weight regain following initial weight loss
▸ Improved bone health
▸ Improved physical function
▸ Lower risk of falls (older adults)
▸ Lower risk of fall-related injuries (older adults)

Note: The Advisory Committee rated the evidence of health benefits of physical activity as strong, moderate, limited, or grade not assignable. Only outcomes with strong or moderate evidence of effect are included in this table.

*See Table 2-3 of the *Physical Activity Guidelines for Americans* (2nd ed.) for additional components of cognition and brain health.

Reprinted from U.S. Department of Health & Human Services (2018). *Physical Activity Guidelines for Americans* (2nd ed.). https://health.gov/paguidelines/second-edition/pdf/Physical_Activity_Guidelines_2nd_edition.pdf

In addition to the many health benefits related to physical activity mentioned in Table 1-1, there are several benefits of being physically active that are specific to group exercise:

- Group exercise results in decreased perceived stress levels beyond reductions observed during individual workouts (Yorks, Frothingham, & Schuenke, 2017).
- Regular group exercise contributes to balanced health (i.e., health in the physical, mental, and social domains) in older adults, including improved or maintained functional health and life enjoyment (Komatsu et al., 2017).
- Regular group exercise contributes to expanding communities through social connectedness and mutual support in older adults and leads to a sense of security in the community through caring for others and supporting each other (Komatsu et al., 2017).
- Group exercise drives improved perceived quality of life beyond improvements experienced during individual workouts (Yorks, Frothingham, & Schuenke, 2017).

The Healthcare Continuum

The healthcare continuum is composed of health practitioners and professionals who are credentialed through certifications, registrations, and/or licensure and provide services to identify, prevent, and treat diseases and disorders (Figure 1-1). Physicians and nurse practitioners are the "gatekeepers" for entry into the continuum, evaluating patients to diagnose ailments and implement treatment plans that can include medication, surgery, rehabilitation, or other actions. Physicians are assisted in their efforts by nurses, physician assistants, and a number of other credentialed technicians. When ailments or treatment plans fall outside their areas of expertise, physicians refer patients to specialists for specific medical evaluations, physical or occupational therapy, psychological counseling, dietary planning, and/or exercise programming.

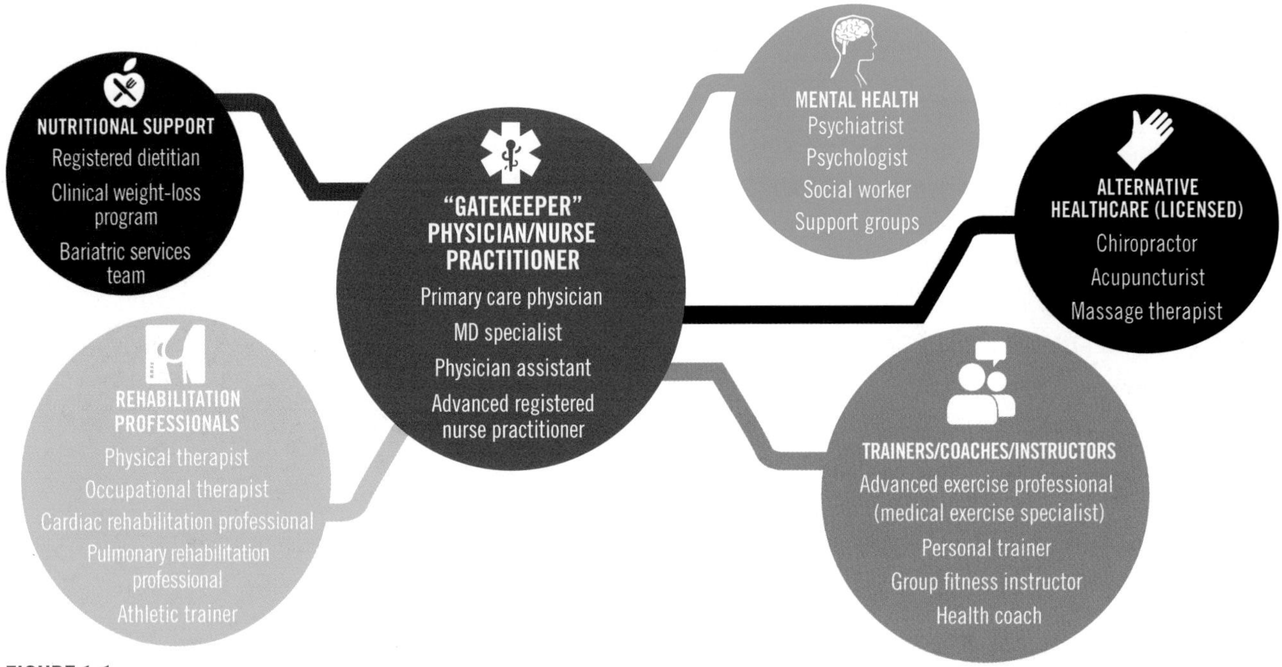

FIGURE 1-1
Who is the ACE Certified Group Fitness Instructor?

Physicians and nurses teach patients the importance of implementing their treatment plans. **Physical therapists** and **occupational therapists** lead patients through therapeutic exercises and teach them to perform additional exercises at home to facilitate rehabilitation. **Athletic trainers** help athletes prevent injuries and take them through therapeutic exercises following injury. **Registered dietitians** teach clients proper nutrition through recipes, meal plans, food-preparation methods, and implementation of specialized diets, often as a component of **medical nutrition therapy.** While these professionals might also give patients or clients guidelines for general exercise (e.g., "try to walk for up to 30 minutes per day on most days of the week"), few of them actually teach clients how to exercise effectively. This is where exercise professionals, including GFIs, hold a unique position in the healthcare continuum.

The majority of GFIs will work with apparently healthy participants, helping them to improve fitness and health. Not only do well-qualified GFIs lead safe and effective exercise classes, they also foster an environment wherein participants develop camaraderie and engage in social experiences that potentially strengthen their **motivation** and **adherence** to exercise. The community aspect of participating in group fitness classes is a strong draw for exercisers who enjoy socializing while being physically active.

EXPAND YOUR KNOWLEDGE

Initial Insights into Raising Exercise Professional Competency

An international movement focused on raising the level of professional competency and skill attainment among exercise professionals is currently underway. This movement began gaining momentum in 2003 when the board of directors of the International Health, Racquet and Sportsclub Association (IHRSA) recognized the need for legitimate professional credentialing. Following an assessment of credible accrediting organizations, the board made a recommendation that personal fitness trainers seek exercise professional certifications from only those organizations that have been accredited by the NCCA, the accrediting body for what was then called the National Organization for Competency Assurance (NOCA) and is now the Institute for Credentialing Excellence (I.C.E.). IHRSA later updated the recommendation to include accrediting organizations recognized by the U.S. Department of Education, creating significant confusion, as education program accreditation is very different from, and not comparable to, certification accreditation. The crucial point to understand is that an accredited education program (which offers narrowly focused content about a specific topic) is distinctly different than an accredited certification program (which provides a competency-based assessment of an individual's knowledge, skills, and abilities related to performing a job).

EXPAND YOUR KNOWLEDGE

Important Terminology Related to Credentialing

There are several important terms related to credentialing that the GFI should understand:

- *Professional certification:* This is a voluntary process by which a nongovernmental body, such as ACE, grants a time-limited recognition and use of a credential to individuals who have demonstrated that they have met the criteria for required knowledge, skills, and/or competencies for safe and effective practice in a specific job role. This is typically demonstrated by passing one or more competency-based assessments that are independent from any single or specific education or training program. A renewal process is associated with certification that requires the **certificant** to obtain continuing education or, in some fields, pass a recertification exam in order to retain the credential. The credential awarded by the certifier denotes that the individual possesses particular knowledge, skills, and/or competencies to practice in the profession.
- *Certificates*: This involves completion of an education or training program on a specific topic for which participants receive a certificate after attendance and/or completion of the coursework. Some programs also require successful demonstration of attainment of the course objectives, such as a post-course assessment of knowledge or practical demonstration. One who completes a certificate program is known as a certificate holder. Importantly, completing an education or training program does not result in the granting of a professional certification (or license).

- *Licensure*: This is a mandatory process by which a governmental agency grants a time-limited permission to an individual to engage in a given occupation after verifying that they have met standardized criteria and offers title protection for those who meet the criteria.
- *Registration*: This involves either the professional designation defined by a governmental entity in professional regulations or rules, or to a listing, or registry, of practitioners who meet designated standards. Depending on the profession, there may or may not be educational, experiential, and/or competency-based requirements. Registration also may give a time-limited status, thereby authorizing those individuals to practice, similar to licensure. The United States Registry of Exercise Professionals (USREPS) is an internationally recognized registry of certified exercise professionals in the United States that is maintained by CREP. All currently ACE Certified GFIs are listed on www.USREPS.org.

Defining "Scope of Practice"

A scope of practice defines the legal range of services that professionals in a given field can provide, the settings in which those services can be provided, and the guidelines or parameters that must be followed. Many factors go into defining a scope of practice, including the education, training, and certifications or licenses required to work in a given field, the laws and organizations governing the specific profession, and the laws and organizations governing complementary professions within the same, or adjunct, field. Most laws defining a profession are determined and regulated by state regulatory agencies, including licensure. As a result, the scope of practice for licensed practitioners in a given profession can vary from state to state. In addition, most professions have organizations that serve as governing bodies within the profession that set eligibility requirements to enter educational programs or sit for certification exams, set requirements for certification to practice in the field, and establish codes for professional conduct and disciplinary procedures for professionals who break these codes.

The laws, rules, and regulations that govern a profession are established for the protection of the public. The laws governing a GFI's scope of practice and the ramifications faced by instructors who provide services that fall outside the defined scope are detailed in Chapter 14. The eligibility and certification requirements to work within this legal scope of practice are defined by the professional organizations that offer group fitness instructor certifications. These organizations also establish codes of ethical conduct and mandate that they are upheld by certified professionals and applicants for certification in all actions related to group fitness instruction. It is crucial for practitioners in every industry to be aware of the scope of practice for their given profession to ensure that they practice within the realm of the specific education, experience, and demonstrated competency of their credential.

SCOPE OF PRACTICE FOR ACE CERTIFIED GROUP FITNESS INSTRUCTORS

The ACE Certified Group Fitness Instructor scope of practice is presented in Figure 1-2. ACE Certified Group Fitness Instructors must work within this defined scope of practice to provide effective exercise leadership for their class participants, gain and maintain support from the healthcare community, and avoid the legal ramifications of providing services outside their professional scope.

FIGURE 1-2
ACE Certified Group Fitness Instructor Scope of Practice

The ACE Certified Group Fitness Instructor is an exercise professional who has met all requirements of the American Council on Exercise to prepare and lead safe, effective, and enjoyable fitness classes to promote and support a healthy, active lifestyle. In addition to possessing knowledge of exercise science, the ACE Certified Group Fitness Instructor motivates and leads by using teaching techniques suitable for multiple stages and styles of learning, and adapts workouts based on the diverse needs of the participants. The ACE Certified Group Fitness Instructor realizes that group fitness instruction is a service focused on helping people enhance fitness and modify risk factors for disease to improve health. As members of the healthcare continuum with a primary focus on prevention, ACE Certified Group Fitness Instructors have a scope of practice that includes:

- Developing and leading exercise classes that are safe, effective, and appropriate for individuals who are apparently healthy or have medical clearance to exercise
- Conducting pre-class assessments of participants, and where appropriate, conducting health screenings with participants in order to determine the need for referral and identify contraindications for exercise
- Constructing group exercise classes that are appropriate for the intended audiences and goals for the class format using evidence-based and published protocols
- Assisting participants in setting and achieving realistic fitness goals
- Teaching correct exercise methods and progressions through demonstration, explanation, and proper cueing and exercise leadership techniques
- Instructing class participants in how to properly monitor exercise intensity using heart rate, rating of perceived exertion, and/or ventilatory response
- Empowering individuals to begin and adhere to their exercise programs using guidance, support, motivation, lapse-prevention strategies, and effective feedback
- Assessing the class environment by evaluating/monitoring the room and equipment before and during each class session
- Educating participants about fitness- and health-related topics to help them in adopting healthful behaviors that facilitate long-term success
- Protecting participant confidentiality according to the Health Insurance Portability and Accountability Act (HIPAA) and related regional and national laws
- Always acting with professionalism, respect, and integrity and providing inclusive exercise classes for all participants
- Recognizing what is within the scope of practice and always referring participants to other healthcare professionals when appropriate
- Being prepared for emergency situations and responding appropriately when they occur

GFIs should never provide services that are outside their defined scope of practice. For example, a GFI may be asked nutrition questions by participants wanting to reduce weight and/or **body fat.** GFIs can help participants with their weight-loss goals by leading effective exercise classes that bring about positive **body composition** changes and helping them to adopt more healthful behaviors. This can include showing participants how to utilize the tools available at www.myplate.gov or educating them about the recommendations in the *Dietary Guidelines for Americans* to help them gain a better understanding of healthful foods and make better choices (U.S. Department of Agriculture, 2020). Participants who are looking for more detailed nutritional programming, such as specific meal plans or recommendations for nutritional supplements, should be referred to a registered dietitian, as these services are beyond the scope of practice for GFIs or other exercise professionals and are in the legal domain of services provided by registered dietitians in most states.

THINK IT THROUGH

Respecting Scope of Practice

How would you handle a situation in which a participant specifically asks you to make a recommendation that you know is outside your scope of practice? For example, consider a scenario in which a participant asks which medication you find more effective for post-workout soreness, ibuprofen or acetaminophen. Draft a standard response you can use in these situations.

Knowledge, Skills, and Abilities of the ACE Certified Group Fitness Instructor

The ACE Group Fitness Instructor Certification is designed for exercise professionals wanting to provide general exercise leadership to apparently healthy individuals in a group setting. The certification program is continually evaluated to ensure that it is consistent with the most current research and industry standards. In addition, every five years a group of industry experts analyzes the specific job requirements for GFIs to update the outline of tasks, knowledge, and skills required to perform the job of group fitness instruction effectively. After being validated by several thousand ACE Certified Group Fitness Instructors, this outline is published as the ACE Group Fitness Instructor Exam Content Outline (www.acefitness.org/fitness-certifications/certification-exam-content), which serves as the blueprint for the ACE Group Fitness Instructor Certification Exam and provides a template for candidates preparing for the exam. It is also a written job description of the knowledge, skills, and abilities required to be an effective Group Fitness Instructor.

Professional Responsibilities and Ethics

The primary purpose of professional certification programs is to award credentials to individuals who meet the requirements to practice in the professional role and to protect the public from harm (e.g., physical, emotional, psychological, and financial). Professionals who earn an ACE Group Fitness Instructor Certification validate their capabilities and enhance their value to employers, class participants, and other healthcare providers. This does not happen simply because the individual has a new title. This recognition is given because the ACE certification itself upholds rigorous standards established for assessing an individual's competence in making safe and effective exercise-programming decisions. ACE has established a professional ethical code of conduct and disciplinary procedures, and ACE certifications have all received third-party accreditation from the NCCA.

To help ACE Certified Professionals understand the conduct expected from them as health and exercise professionals in delivering group exercise classes and protecting the public from harm, ACE has developed the ACE Code of Ethics (see the Appendix). This code serves as a guide for ethical and professional practices for all ACE Certified Professionals and is enforced through the ACE Professional Practices and Disciplinary Procedures (www.ACEfitness.org/getcertified/certified-code.aspx). All ACE Certified Professionals and candidates for ACE certification exams must be familiar with, and comply with, the ACE Code of Ethics and ACE Professional Practices and Disciplinary Procedures.

ACE CODE OF ETHICS

The ACE Code of Ethics governs the ethical and professional conduct of ACE Certified Professionals when working with clients/participants, the public, or other health and exercise professionals. Every individual who registers for an ACE certification exam must agree to uphold the ACE Code of Ethics throughout the exam process and as a professional, should they earn an ACE certification. Exam candidates and ACE Certified Group Fitness Instructors must have a comprehensive understanding of the code and the consequences that can come from violating each of its principles.

EQUITY, DIVERSITY, AND INCLUSION

Introduction to Equity, Diversity, and Inclusion

Alex McLean, international fitness presenter, 25+ year fitness professional, ACE Certified since 2008

Companies and industries have responded to growing racial and social unrest throughout the world that has been largely fueled by health and social disparities that disproportionately impact marginalized communities. **Equity, diversity,** and **inclusion** (EDI) help businesses and industries enter these conversations and facilitate change.

There is often an emphasis on EDI as it relates to racial and ethnic differences, but health disparities also occur across lines of gender, sexual identity, age, disability, socioeconomic status, and geographic location.

To fully engage in this conversation and in social change making, a clear depiction of EDI is necessary. Equity is often erroneously equated to equality. Figure 1-3 illustrates how equality provides the same opportunities to all, regardless of each person's circumstances. Equity takes a more nuanced look at opportunities by recognizing that individuals do not start at the same place, acknowledging social imbalances that may exist, and then making the necessary adjustments to level the playing field.

While they are related, diversity and inclusion are not the same. Diversity is the reflection of a group of people's many unique characteristics and differences. Inclusion focuses on the collective as a whole. While differences continue to exist within inclusive environments, inclusion creates opportunities for connection across these differences (Figure 1-4). The common denominator in a diverse population is

FIGURE 1-3
Equality vs. equity

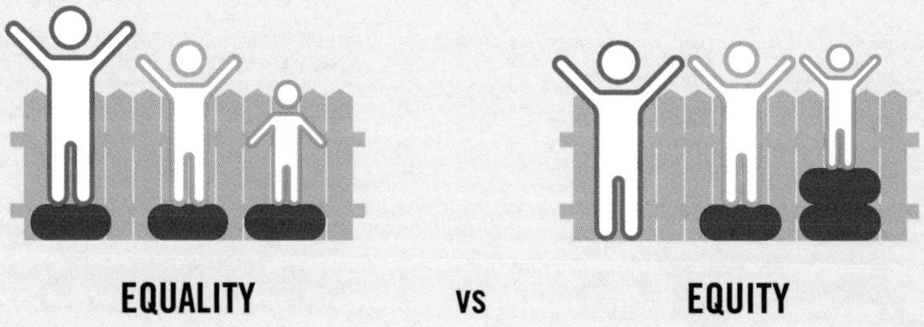

FIGURE 1-4
Diversity vs. inclusion

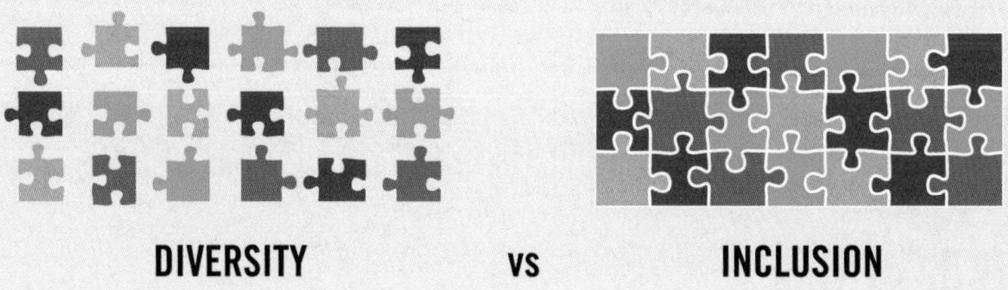

its humanity. Inclusion creates a space where individuals feel truly welcomed, valued, and celebrated for who they are across our diverse differences.

The Importance of EDI Initiatives on Business

While EDI has ethical implications, there is evidence that EDI initiatives positively impact companies across profitability and human indicators. Across industries, companies with diverse environments experience higher performing and more collaborative teams, which can lead to better business outcomes (Padamsee et al., 2017).

In addition to the positive outcomes EDI has on business, employees working in diverse companies may feel more appreciated, which could potentially lead to higher levels of engagement and satisfaction. This type of culture leads to lower levels of employee turnover and better engagement, and engaged employees often offer new insights that results in more innovation and creativity.

EDI also affects relationships with the public and consumers. Ostensibly, from the end-user standpoint, consumers may prefer to buy from companies that employ people who look like them. EDI is a win-win for all parties involved and may be a competitive advantage for businesses.

State of the Fitness Industry

From a broad perspective, the fitness industry appears diverse. However, as the lens narrows, it becomes clear that some segments in fitness are more diverse than others.

The ground floor of a building features multiple entry points and, as a result, has the highest number of people and the most foot traffic. To reach higher floors, entry is limited to the stairs, escalators, and elevators, each of which is able to accommodate only a few select people.

Similarly, the ground floor of the fitness industry has the largest percentage of exercise professionals and reflects the most diversity. This is due to the many entry points, such as group exercise, personal training, sports and conditioning, mind-body disciplines, and the like. However, as people climb the corporate ladder, or climb to higher floors, the amount of diversity drastically diminishes.

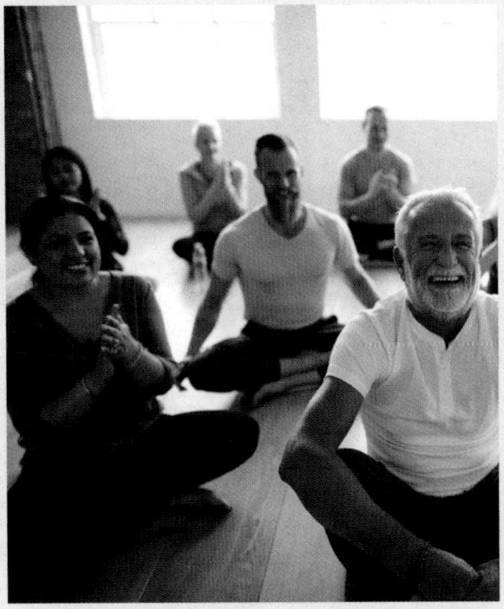

These higher-floor opportunities, such as the selection process for presenters at fitness conferences, reflect less diversity due to bias and barriers to access. Fitness facilities have many qualified people of color in group fitness and personal training, but presenters for sessions at fitness conferences are typically sponsored by brands, and those brands choose presenters from their master trainer teams. On most brand master trainer teams, there may be one or two people of color. In addition, brands may be more likely to select presenters who are on multiple teams and who are already attending the conference to share expenses and save money. This creates barriers to access and can make it that much harder to have a diverse group of presenters, thereby creating a situation in which presenter lineups on the national and international scenes often lack diversity. Finally, new, non-sponsored presenters are rare. Typically, they are not offered pay or expense reimbursement. Instead, they receive a complimentary registration to the conference in exchange for the opportunity.

Impact on the Fitness Industry

EDI initiatives have helped start many discussions on the state of the fitness industry, which reflects society's prevalent and structural racism and bias. EDI serves as both a mirror to life and as a measuring stick to analyze progress.

How can group fitness instructors impact EDI efforts? GFIs should create experiences that are welcoming to all. To accomplish this:

- Learn the first names and appropriate pronouns for participants.
- Use words, analogies, and imagery people understand.
- Offer exercise options for both challenge and success.
- Cater programming to the health and fitness levels of participants.
- Choose music that matches the interests and preferences of participants.
- Use words that foster community and camaraderie.

Conclusion

Inequities cannot be overturned with good intentions and promises. To move forward, we must purposefully take the first step. As exercise professionals, GFIs often ask participants to get physically uncomfortable so they can create change to reach fitness goals. Similarly, the fitness industry must do the same and ask its constituents to do the hard, sometimes uncomfortable work to transform the industry into a more welcoming and inclusive one.

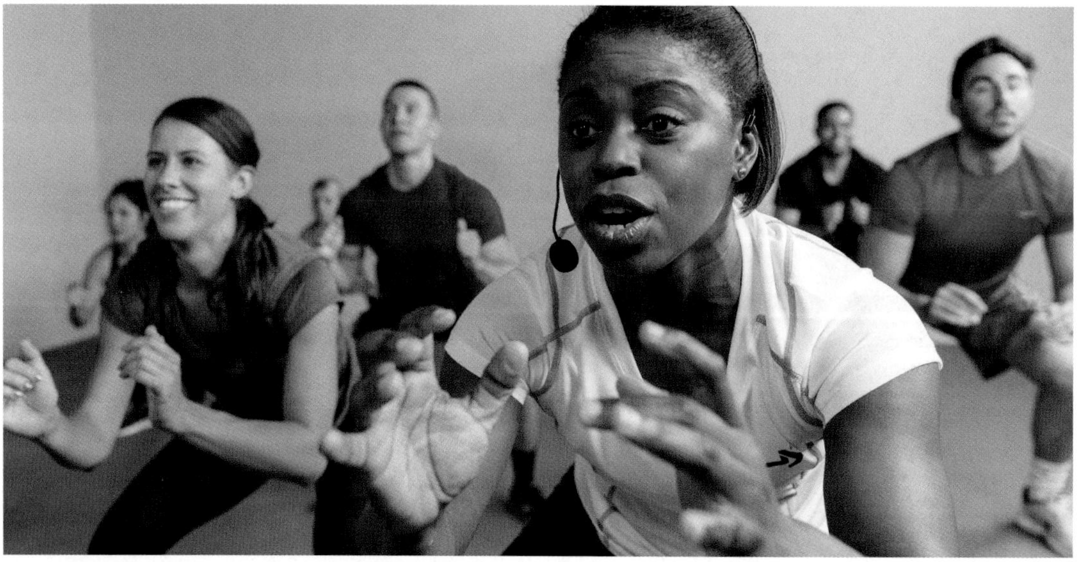

Qualities of an Effective Group Fitness Instructor

Teaching group fitness classes is a rewarding experience because GFIs serve as agents of change, facilitating activities that improve both physical health and state of mind. Leadership abilities and first impressions affect participants' perception of the type of class they are about to experience. It is often thought that leadership is an innate trait, but leadership skills can be developed even by those not considered "born leaders." Some of the qualities of a GFI that produce an effective, adherence-boosting class experience include punctuality, dependability, professionalism, and dedication.

PUNCTUALITY AND DEPENDABILITY

GFIs must be respectful of class start and end times. A class that starts late or does not end as scheduled is disruptive to both participants and other group fitness classes. As such, GFIs should plan on arriving early to greet participants and ensure a punctual class start. Additionally, participants like to know that their regular instructor, not a parade of substitutes, will be there consistently to lead their fitness experience. Whenever possible, absences should be planned in advance, allowing substitutes to be scheduled accordingly and participants to be well informed of changes.

PROFESSIONALISM

All participants should be treated with respect. Gossiping about class members or fellow instructors is inappropriate and should not occur in the group fitness environment. Negative comments about other class formats or fitness programs adversely affect the fitness industry and diminish the credibility of a GFI. All facility staff members are on the same team and have the same goal—to improve exercise adherence and instill excitement and enjoyment for exercise among class participants.

As a team player, a GFI will often offer to substitute teach classes for other instructors when needed. Teaching another GFI's regular class is always an adjustment for everyone.

However, the substituting GFI should teach the class as if it were their own, offering the same level of service and attention they would give to regular classes. A GFI should always refrain from language, opinions, or actions that may undermine the regular instructor.

Professionalism extends beyond communication to also include choice of attire. Although a GFI may wish to be stylish by following popular fashion trends, it is not professional to be dressed in a provocative manner when leading group fitness classes, as doing so may make participants feel uncomfortable.

DEDICATION

Part of being an effective leader involves ongoing dedication to one's work. Participants will often approach GFIs before and after class with health- and fitness-related questions. Obtaining and maintaining a professional certification demonstrates commitment to one's profession and enables a GFI to best serve class participants. Additionally, efforts should be made on a continual basis to keep fitness classes inclusive, diverse, fun, and enjoyable for participants. This means GFIs must continually seek out continuing education opportunities to keep up with the latest exercise trends and to obtain evidence-based information to appropriately address questions participants may have on health-related topics. GFIs should use discretion when referring participants to online sources (and help them identify the more credible sites) and refer them to healthcare providers when the topic is beyond a GFI's scope of practice.

Professional Conduct

The decision to pursue certification as a GFI is an important step in being a recognized and respected professional in the field of health and fitness. Those who earn the ACE Group Fitness Instructor Certification demonstrate competency in designing and delivering safe, effective, and engaging group exercise class experiences that enhance the general well-being and movement abilities of class participants. While the newly certified GFI has proven their ability to appropriately apply broad-based knowledge of various subjects in a variety of practical situations, this credential should be viewed as the foundation of professional development. Ongoing education and training are both necessary and required, as is a thorough understanding of one's professional boundaries and scope of practice in order to protect and best serve participants.

CONTINUING EDUCATION

GFIs are encouraged to pursue continuing education in areas of personal interest as well as those that best serve the needs of participants. Factors that should be considered when evaluating continuing education courses include identifying courses with level-appropriate content, selecting educational opportunities that are offered in a preferred learning format (e.g., live workshop or home study course), verifying that the instructor has the appropriate qualifications to teach the course, understanding if the course is ACE-approved or will have to be petitioned for continuing education credits (CECs), and determining if the education provided is within the GFI's scope of practice.

While completing continuing education in more than one area of interest can be beneficial in terms of diversifying the GFI's career path options, focusing on a specific modality (e.g., indoor cycling) or participant demographic (e.g., older adults) can prove helpful in establishing the GFI as a recognized and sought-after expert in a given discipline.

BEST PRACTICES FOR STAYING CURRENT ON RESEARCH AND GUIDELINES

The dynamic nature of the health and fitness industry requires professionals to understand the latest research and professional standards and guidelines, and how they impact the design and delivery of movement-based classes. To stay abreast of the most current information and best practices, GFIs must make time to regularly review a variety of credible industry resources such as professional journals, position statements, guidelines from leading professional organizations [e.g., United States Department of Agriculture (USDA) and American College of Obstetricians and Gynecologists (ACOG)], and trade and lay periodicals. GFIs should also attend professional meetings, conferences, and workshops, and complete web-based courses and online educational offerings (e.g., webinars) whenever possible.

Visit ACEfitness.org/Industry-Guidelines to review a list of key guidelines that GFIs should be aware of, along with information and links to the most recent edition of each.

REFERRALS

GFIs must have a clear understanding of their professional qualifications and boundaries, and always refer participants who require services and guidance outside of their scope of practice to the appropriate qualified fitness, medical, or health professionals. It is prudent for GFIs to network and develop rapport with other health professionals in their local area first before referring participants, as doing so demonstrates a strong commitment to the safety and well-being of participants while also conveying respect for the expertise and services of these important professionals, many of whom may provide reciprocal referrals. GFIs must also be well-versed in the scope of practice for various professionals in order to ensure referrals are appropriate so that participants are promptly provided with the attention and care that they need. Knowing both when and how to refer participants enhances the GFI's credibility, while also providing clarity about the services the GFI does and does not have the legal standing to offer.

EXPAND YOUR KNOWLEDGE

Developing a Referral Network

It is important for a GFI to develop a network of referral sources to meet the varying needs of their participants. Instructors should identify allied health professionals who are reputable and aspire to the same professional standards as an ACE Certified Group Fitness Instructor. Potential referral sources include, but are not limited to:

- Instructors of classes outside a GFI's expertise (e.g., tai chi, aquatic exercise, or sports conditioning)
- Personal trainers
- Health coaches
- Certified medical exercise specialists
- Licensed psychologist or professional counselor
- Support groups (e.g., bariatric surgery, cancer survivors, and Overeaters Anonymous)
- Massage therapists
- Registered dietitians
- Physical therapists
- Diabetes prevention programs

As the GFI develops a referral network, it is important to research instructors, programs, and/or organizations before recommending any programs or services to a participant. Pertinent questions to ask include: (1) Do they have the proper licensure or certification? (2) Can they provide a list of references? (3) How many years of experience do they have? and (4) Is the program evidence-based?

The GFI does not want to jeopardize their reputation by referring participants to unqualified health and exercise service providers. With proper networking, the GFI may also gain referrals from the other health and exercise professionals within the network.

ACE UNIVERSITY

If your study program includes ACE University, visit www.ACEfitness.org/MyACE and log in to your My ACE Account to take full advantage of the ACE Group Fitness Instructor Study Program and online guided study experience.

A variety of media to support and expand on the material in this text is provided to facilitate learning and best prepare you for the ACE Group Fitness Instructor Certification exam and a career as a group fitness instructor.

SUMMARY

Since its origins in the 1970s and 1980s, group exercise has been a mainstay in the fitness industry. With innovation in exercise equipment and programming, group fitness will continue to evolve. Successful GFIs will continue to evolve as well, as they pay heed to the standard of care and scope of practice associated with the safe and effective practice of group fitness instruction. Well-qualified GFIs hold current NCCA-accredited certifications in group fitness instruction, place an emphasis on furthering their education, and are able to provide safe, effective, and enjoyable exercise experiences for their class participants.

REFERENCES

Cooper, K.H. (1968). *Aerobics*. New York: M. Evans.

Komatsu, H. et al. (2017). Regular group exercise contributes to balanced health in older adults in Japan: A qualitative study. *BMC Geriatrics*, 17, 190.

Padamsee, X. et al. (2017). *Unrealized Impact: The Case for Diversity, Equity, and Inclusion.* https://www.promise54.org/wp-content/uploads/2020/10/Unrealized_Impact-ExecSummary-Final-072017.pdf

U.S. Department of Agriculture (2020). *2020-2025 Dietary Guidelines for Americans* (9th ed.). www.dietaryguidelines.gov

U.S. Department of Health & Human Services (2018). *Physical Activity Guidelines for Americans* (2nd ed.). https://health.gov/paguidelines/second-edition/pdf/Physical_Activity_Guidelines_2nd_edition.pdf

Yorks, D.M., Frothingham, C.A., & Schuenke, M.D. (2017). Effects of group fitness classes on stress and quality of life of medical students. *The Journal of the American Osteopathic Association*, 117, 11, e17.

SUGGESTED READING

The United States Registry of Exercise Professionals Mission Statement and Website http://usreps.org

CHAPTER 2

Behavior-change Principles

SABRENA JO, PhD | Senior Director, Science and Research; American Council on Exercise; ACE Certified Group Fitness Instructor, Personal Trainer, and Health Coach

CHRISTOPHER S. GAGLIARDI, MS | Scientific Education Content Manager, American Council on Exercise; ACE Certified Group Fitness Instructor, Personal Trainer, Health Coach, and Medical Exercise Specialist

IN THIS CHAPTER

LEARNING OBJECTIVES

Upon completion of this chapter, the reader will be able to:

- Identify factors that influence exercise adherence
- Define rapport and apply strategies for effectively connecting with participants
- List and describe the five stages of behavior change
- Explain the difference between extrinsic and intrinsic motivation
- Instruct participants on how to formulate SMART goals

ACE UNIVERSITY

If your study program includes ACE University, visit www.ACEfitness.org/MyACE and log in to your My ACE Account to take full advantage of the ACE Group Fitness Instructor Study Program and online guided study experience.

A variety of media to support and expand on the material in this text is provided to facilitate learning and best prepare you for the ACE Group Fitness Instructor Certification exam and a career as a group

Exceptional ACE Certified Group Fitness Instructors (GFIs) not only instruct classes, but also serve as leaders and coaches who empower participants to develop a positive association with exercise by experiencing physical activity in enjoyable and meaningful ways. While it is imperative for a GFI to possess skill in safely and effectively cueing movements, as covered in Chapter 9, they must also be well-versed in the art of constructing and delivering enjoyable and meaningful classes in order to reach and retain participants. From building **rapport** with participants and understanding the basics of behavior change, to implementing strategies that enhance **motivation,** improve **adherence,** and develop camaraderie, the GFI can create a positive, caring, and inclusive environment in which all participants can thrive.

Factors Influencing Participation and Adherence

Much research has examined the factors related to physical-activity participation, including an understanding of potential determinants for physical activity, which are those factors that influence a person's decision to engage in exercise behavior. The potential determinants for physical activity can be broken down into three categories (Dishman & Buckworth, 1997):

- Personal attributes
- Environmental factors
- Physical-activity factors

GFIs should have a general understanding of these factors in order to better address the challenges participants may face with regards to attending group fitness classes.

PERSONAL ATTRIBUTES

Demographics

Adherence to physical-activity programs has been consistently associated with education, income, age, and sex [Armstrong et al., 2018; Centers for Disease Control and Prevention (CDC), 2013]. Specifically, lower levels of activity are seen with increasing age, fewer years of education, and low income. Age, however, has been shown to be unrelated to adherence levels when examined in supervised exercise settings, such as the group fitness environment. This is of importance to GFIs who lead structured movement-based classes, because when exercise sessions are conducted under the guidance of health and exercise professionals, adherence levels are increased among participants of various ages (Lowry et al., 2013; Dorgo et al., 2011). Regarding differences between the sexes, males tend to adhere more to exercise than females (Hallal et al., 2012), and females tend to find the psychological benefits, physical conditioning, and physical appearance to be among their most important reasons for exercising (Ley, 2020).

Health Status

Physical activity and exercise are preventive measures for reducing the risk of **chronic disease** and **mortality** and, when physical activity and exercise are incorporated into a medical management plan after a diagnosis of chronic illness, a better treatment outcome can be expected. In other words, exercise is an important aspect of both chronic disease prevention and treatment (Anderson & Durstine, 2019). However, individuals who suffer from chronic illness, such as **diabetes** and heart disease, typically exercise less than those who are apparently healthy (Newsom et al., 2012). While physical limitations might be a mitigating factor, it is likely that the misconception that individuals with chronic diseases should not exercise plays a role in the reduced physical-activity levels. According to the CDC (2021), 60% of American adults have one chronic disease and 40% have two or more (Figure 2-1). Meanwhile, chronic diseases represent most causes of death worldwide (Figure 2-2), killing 41 million people each year [World Health Organization (WHO), 2021]. Modifiable behaviors increase the risk of **noncommunicable diseases (NCD),** with 7.2 million deaths each year stemming from tobacco use and exposure to second-hand smoke, 4.1 million deaths attributed to excess salt/sodium intake each year, 1.65 million alcohol-related NCD deaths each year, and 1.6 million deaths attributed to physical inactivity each year (WHO, 2021).

Exercise can improve both quality of life and longevity for individuals living with chronic disease. As a GFI, it is important to create an environment in which all participants are able to engage in exercise safely and successfully, through the incorporation of **progressions** and **regressions** of exercises (thereby increasing or decreasing the intensity or complexity of an exercise) and a general understanding of the needs of various participants. See Chapter 12 for more information on working with participants with various health considerations.

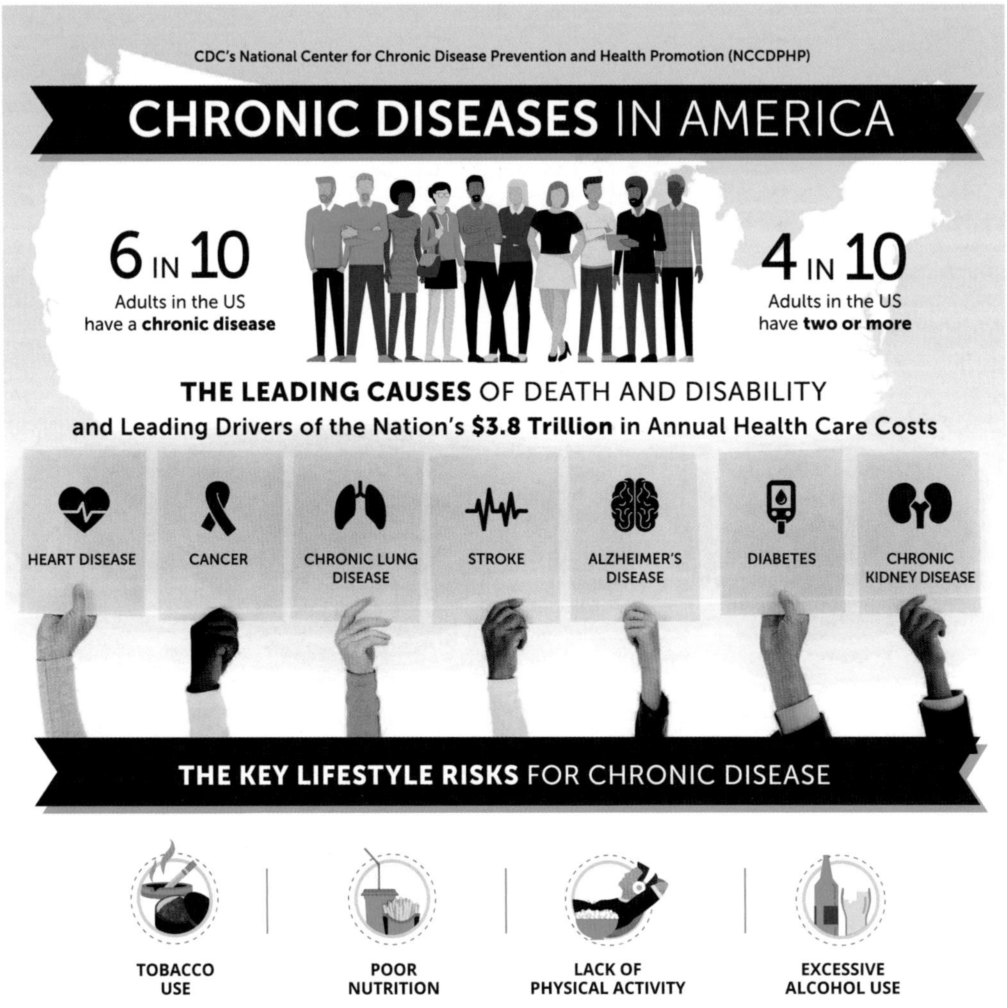

FIGURE 2-1
Chronic diseases in America

Source: Centers for Disease Control and Prevention (2021). *Chronic Diseases in America*. https://www.cdc.gov/chronicdisease/resources/infographic/chronic-diseases.htm

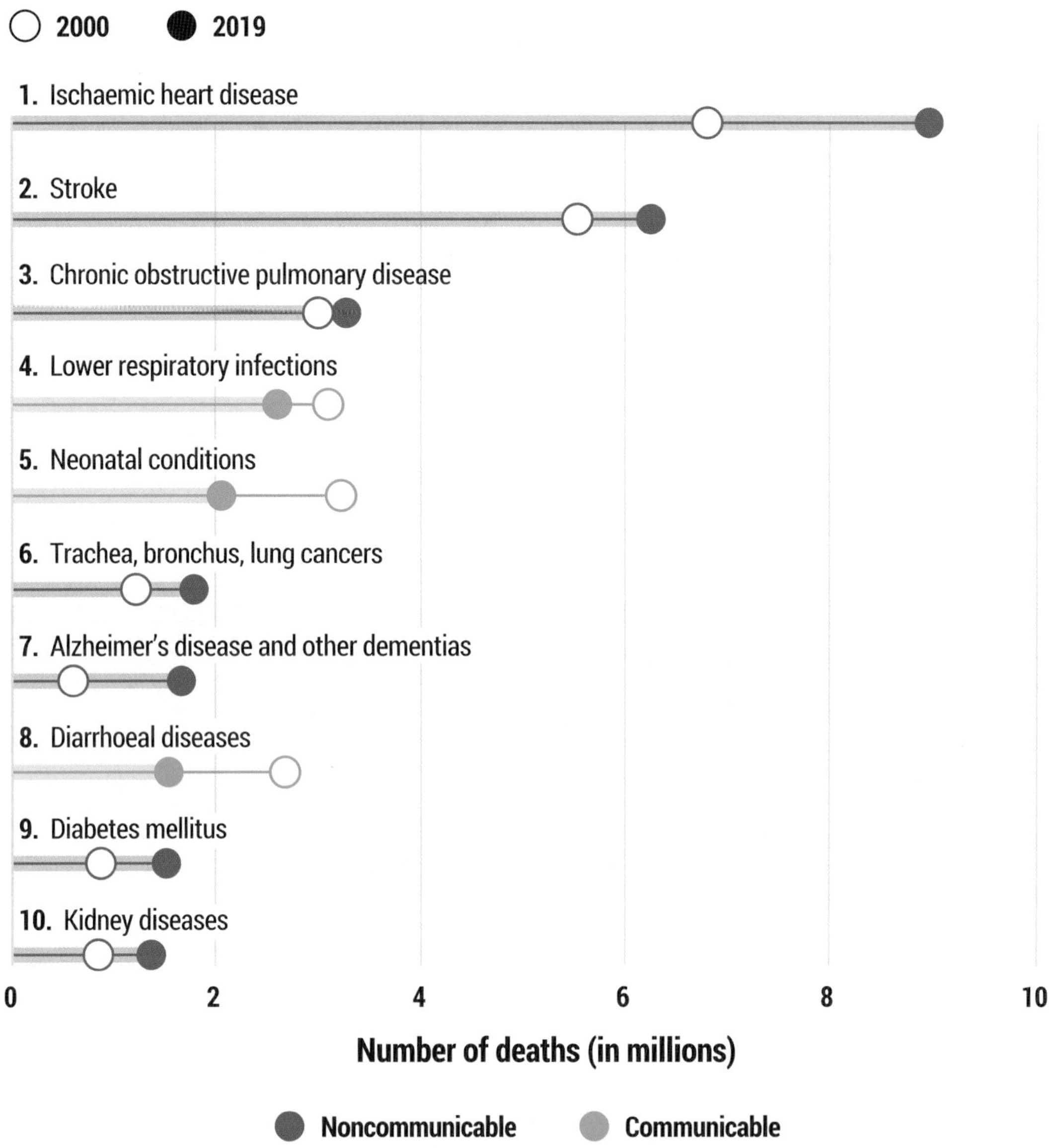

FIGURE 2-2
Leading causes of death globally

Source: World Health Organization (2020). *The Top 10 Causes of Death.* https://www.who.int/news-room/fact-sheets/detail/the-top-10-causes-of-death

Physical Activity History

Arguably one of the most important and influential personal attribute variables is physical activity history (Rodrigues et al., 2020). In supervised exercise programs, past program participation is the most reliable predictor of current participation. This relationship between past participation and current participation is consistent regardless of sex, **obesity,** and **coronary heart disease** status (Dishman & Buckworth, 1997). Therefore, it is important that GFIs take time to get to know participants as part of the onsite pre-class preparation in order to garner physical activity history information from participants while also developing rapport.

Psychological Traits

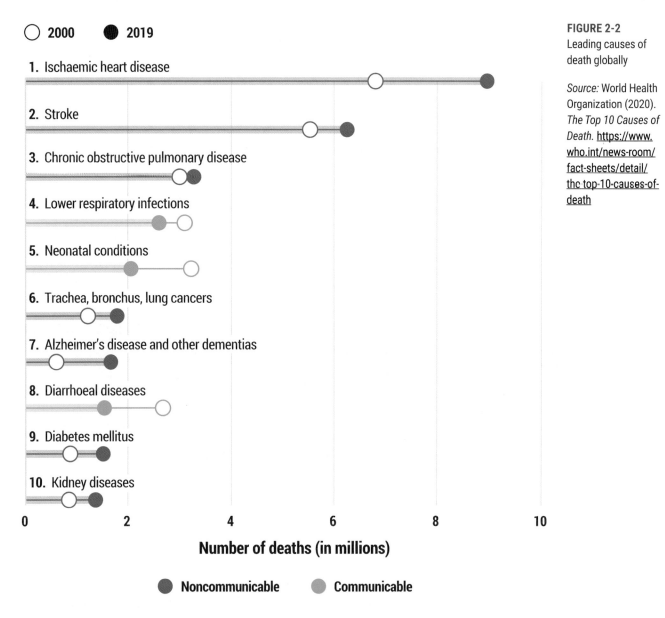

General personality tendencies and psychological traits among participants, while often difficult to define and measure, can influence adherence to physical activity. For example, self-motivation, which is reflective of one's ability to set goals, monitor progress, and self-reinforce, has been shown to have a positive relationship with physical-activity adherence (Teixeira, Silva, & Palmeira, 2018; Dishman, 1982).

Knowledge, Attitudes, and Beliefs

Individuals have a wide variety of knowledge, attitudes, and beliefs about starting and maintaining a consistent routine of physical activity. Modifying the way a participant thinks and feels about exercise, as well as their physical perceptions of their own ability, has been shown to influence their intentions regarding being physically active (Sales, Levinger, & Polman, 2017). **Health perception** has been linked to adherence, as individuals who perceive their health to be poor are unlikely to be physically active or adhere to an activity program (Forechi et al., 2018; Alkerwi et al., 2015). Furthermore, if they do participate, it will likely be at a low intensity and frequency (Dishman & Buckworth, 1997). The use of appropriate teaching techniques (see Chapter 9), self-monitoring methods (see Chapter 4), and effective communication strategies can prove helpful in positively influencing how a participant feels about attending group fitness classes.

EQUITY, DIVERSITY, AND INCLUSION

The Role of EDI in Exercise Participation and Adherence

Alex McLean, international fitness presenter, 25+ year fitness professional, ACE Certified since 2008

From health status and activity history to access to facilities and the intensity of the exercise class, there are countless factors that impact a person's ability to participate in and adhere to an exercise program. Should social identity be one of them? Health disparities that exist across social identities—things like race, gender, sexual identity, and gender identity—can impact one's ability to engage in exercise programs. As a GFI, it is essential that you remain mindful of not only how these differences impact exercise adherence, but also what you can do to help participants manage their concerns and overcome any barriers to participation.

Starting an exercise program can be daunting for anyone, as there are challenges to overcome before the first fitness class experience. For example, a person may have doubts about whether they can perform certain exercises, be nervous about entering the facility for the first time, or have questions about how to choose the right class for their fitness level and goals. These concerns may be amplified for members of marginalized social identity groups.

As you reflect on the barriers that participants can experience, this feature presents several considerations for addressing barriers that could stem from socio-economic status, religion, culture, race, gender identity, and sexual identity. While this list is non-exhaustive, the questions, considerations, and solutions presented can serve as a model when supporting the needs of any social identity group.

The design of a fitness facility, from locker room layouts to signage and marketing pieces, are often guided by a cisgender mentality. A cisgender person is one whose gender identity and expression match the sex assigned at birth, while a transgender person is one whose gender identity and expression do not match their birth sex. Common questions that a transgender person may have before walking into a facility include the following:

- Does this facility welcome and cater to people who are transgender?
- Are people who are transgender represented in the marketing images of the facility?

- Is inclusive and gender-neutral language and signage visible?
- Will the staff acknowledge the person's chosen name, pronouns, and gender identity?
- What changing room, restroom, and showers will the person use? Are the rooms gender-neutral or designated by gender?

As an exercise professional, you might consider whether there are outside partners and resources to which you can refer participants and members who are transgender, if necessary.

Another common concern related to long-term exercise adherence is the convenience of the location of the facility. This may be a major hurdle in some communities, as there are often no physical fitness facilities in lower socio-economic areas. In addition, public transportation may be the main means of travel, which can limit participants' ability to attend classes at certain times and can sometimes lead to participants being late for class or having to leave early. As a GFI, solutions may involve bringing fitness to the community in creative ways, including the following:

- Partnering with a community center in the area to offer live classes
- Teaching in non-traditional outlets such as outdoor settings, churches, senior citizen centers, and schools
- Designing a gospel-based movement session, such as a praise dance in conjunction with church services, meetings, or other events
- Creating at-home workouts with minimal equipment requirements
- Scheduling classes with bus or train schedules in mind
- Offering shorter classes that better suit the transportation needs of participants

Regular exercise participation is also impacted by the convenience of the schedule. For some participants, religious needs may play a key role in their ability to attend classes. Possible considerations to accommodate religious needs include:

- Providing preprogrammed classes that can be done on-site with little to no supervision
- Setting up the group fitness studio when not in use to host preprogrammed classes, whether live or recorded
- Changing the schedule or providing alternative class options based on religious celebrations or observances
- Offering proprietary digital solutions for at-home workouts

Intensity is another key variable to achieving fitness results. Intensity intersects with culture as it relates to those who may want to avoid intense workouts to prevent sweating profusely. Potential solutions include:

- Offering a variety of classes that focus on lower intensities, such as yoga, Pilates, and tai chi
- Keeping the group exercise room at a cool, climate-controlled temperature while providing ample air circulation
- Cueing alternative forms of movement that provide options for various levels of intensity

In some cultures, the importance and financial cost of hair care can impact decision making when it comes to exercise. For example, many African-American women opt not to exercise before or during the workday due to these concerns. Potential solutions include:

- Offering classes later in the day so they can be attended on the way home from work
- Offering lower-intensity activities such as yoga and Pilates before and during the workday

- Leading classes in non-heated rooms
- Providing shower caps that protect hair

Every individual has their own set of challenges when it comes to starting and adhering to an exercise routine, so it is vital that GFIs educate themselves on potential obstacles that may not seem obvious to them due to ethnic, religious, or gender-identity differences. Finally, GFIs should be sure to approach these situations with care and with a spirit of open dialogue and a participant-centered approach. Never lose sight of the fact that the goal should be for the GFI to further their education in this area and empower participants to succeed.

ENVIRONMENTAL FACTORS

Access to Facilities

The location of a fitness facility influences participant adherence. When facilities are conveniently located near a person's home or work, the individual is more likely to adhere to a physical-activity program. Specifically, when facility access is measured objectively (i.e., true access and availability of a facility), it is a consistent predictor of physical-activity behavior, such that people with greater access are more likely to be physically active than people with less access (Lee et al., 2016). GFIs should ask their participants about access issues and understand how convenient or inconvenient it is for each individual to reach the facility during the specific day and time of the class they are teaching. If a GFI finds that an individual is struggling to regularly attend class due to factors such as distance of the facility from home or work, traffic conditions during that time, and/or a varying work schedule, the instructor should discuss alternative class options with the participant that will enable them to attend class more consistently, even if the other class option is taught by another instructor. While attending group fitness classes in person may be the preferred and ideal option for many people, a growing number of online class options may lead to a variety of new ways to overcome the challenge of having limited access to facilities (see Chapter 11). If online group classes are an option, attendance via online presence should be discussed as a possible solution for attending class more consistently.

Time

Lack of time is often a reason provided for not exercising and for dropping out of an exercise program, as some people perceive that they simply do not have time to be physically active. The perception of not having enough time to exercise could be a result of not valuing or enjoying the activity, or not being committed to the activity program. GFIs can help shift participant perception of time availability by listening without judgment, sharing information and resources when appropriate, and collaborating to set goals. If an individual considers health and physical activity top priorities, they may be more willing to devote time to exercise.

Social Support

Social support refers to having accessible support through social ties to other individuals, groups, and the community. Social support can encourage optimism and self-esteem, reduce stress and depressive symptoms, and may influence exercise adherence. It is difficult for an individual to maintain an exercise program if they do not have support at home. While the presence of social support may provide many benefits, a perceived lack of social support is related to reduced adherence and physical-activity levels, lower mental health and life expectancy, more stress, a higher risk for developing certain diseases, and poorer resilience (Collado-Mateo et al., 2021). Social support is a critical topic that GFIs should discuss with their classes, and instructors should be proactive in creating and establishing a support network for participants by building group camaraderie within the class.

PHYSICAL-ACTIVITY FACTORS

Intensity

The intensity of an exercise program can influence a person's emotions and mood, as well as their adherence level. For some, as exercise intensity increases, enjoyment declines. When this happens, program adherence rates may also decrease. However, this is not always the case. For example, one study comparing high- and moderate-intensity exercise for enjoyment and adherence showed that participants performing high-intensity exercise reported higher levels of enjoyment compared to those who performed moderate-intensity exercise (Heinrich et al., 2014).

This same study elucidates another important element related to a person's preparticipation perceptions of exercise enjoyment, suggesting that if baseline exercise enjoyment levels are lower, a moderate-intensity program may lead to greater initial exercise adherence (Heinrich et al., 2014). In other words, baseline exercise enjoyment levels can help determine appropriate class intensity and format recommendations.

Exercise adherence is also related to intensity through the class duration. Typically, higher-intensity classes are of a shorter duration than moderate-intensity classes, which may be appealing to participants who cite a perceived lack of time as a reason for not adhering to exercise. For the GFI, it is important to understand that the intensity of exercise can influence exercise enjoyment and adherence.

Injury

When it comes to physical activity and injury, there is an interesting paradox to consider. On one hand, higher levels of physical activity and intensity may put the participant at a higher risk for developing an activity-related injury (Rynecki et al., 2019). On the other hand, not training enough for the expected demands of an activity may also increase the risk for injury (American College of Sports Medicine, 2019; Gabbett, 2016). This relationship between intensity, overtraining, and undertraining should be considered because, no matter their cause, injuries that occur as a result of program participation are directly related to program dropout. Therefore, it is imperative that

GFIs do everything they can to mitigate the potential for injury, be prepared to help participants determine if the benefits of regular physical activity outweigh the potential risk of injury, and provide education on minimizing the risk of preventable injuries (see Chapter 13).

APPLY WHAT YOU KNOW

Strategies to Promote Positive Participant Experiences Related to Physical-activity Factors

- Stress the sense of **relatedness** (building authentic social connections with others).
- Incorporate participants into the decision-making process when choosing exercises.
- Provide a sense of achievement through positive feedback.
- Allow for self-regulation of intensity.
- Increase transparency by preannouncing the contents of future classes.
- Increase the diversity of training options (i.e., new and challenging exercises that enhance the acquisition of new skills) (Lakicevic et al., 2020; Jekauc, 2015).
- Anticipate strength adaptations and incorporate changes in workload, which may enhance enjoyment despite the need for more physically strenuous activity (Heisz et al., 2016).

Understanding Behavior Change

To create impactful group fitness experiences, GFIs must have a strong understanding of the foundational components associated with adopting and adhering to healthful behaviors such as physical activity. From learning how to establish meaningful relationships with participants by using effective communication strategies, to understanding a participant's readiness for change and the specific strategies that will help ensure ongoing success and motivation, GFIs must be well-versed in more than just selecting exercises and building movement sequences.

ESTABLISHING RAPPORT

When attending a group fitness class for the first time or taking a class taught by a new instructor, participants may have feelings of insecurity and apprehension. A GFI can help combat these feelings of uncertainty by developing rapport with individuals. Rapport can be defined as a relationship of trust and mutual understanding. While developing rapport is an ongoing process that continues to grow throughout the relationship between instructor and participant, GFIs should take great care to set the foundation for rapport when first meeting new participants. This is done through positive and thoughtful interactions rooted in **empathy,** which involves the sharing of experiences, desires, and needs among individuals, the ability to perceive the perspective and emotions of others and then cognitively and emotionally resonate with them, and the ability to distinguish between our own and others' emotions to promote behaviors intended to help others (Riess, 2017). When GFIs use strategies such as **active listening,** effective communication, respect for cultural differences, and professionalism to create a climate of trust and respect, participants can feel confident knowing that their needs are understood and their involvement in class is valued.

Learning Names

While it can be challenging to get to know each participant individually, GFIs should make it a point to learn as many participant names as possible to further assist in building rapport. Using names before class when greeting participants, during class while offering positive **feedback,** as well as after class to provide praise for a job well done can help GFIs commit names to memory while creating strong, lasting relationships with participants. GFIs may also wish to consider using ice-breaker activities at the start of each class (see Chapter 10) to personally become acquainted with new participants while also allowing individuals in the class to get to know one another.

EFFECTIVE COMMUNICATION STRATEGIES

Rapport evolves over time and is enriched through effective communication between the GFI and participants. Research suggests that the time spent establishing a good working relationship enhances adherence (Ryan et al., 2011). The capabilities of the GFI, including their knowledge and skills, are only important to participants if they feel that the GFI truly cares about their success and enjoyment in the class.

To communicate effectively with participants, GFIs must send clear messages and accurately interpret messages they receive through active listening. Essential components of active listening include, but are not limited to, asking **open-ended questions** at appropriate times and using verbal and nonverbal communication techniques such as body language to appropriately demonstrate attentiveness, empathy, and genuine concern for the content, intent, and feelings of a message.

Core Communication Skills

When engaging in one-on-one discussions with a participant, a GFI can utilize several different approaches to demonstrate good listening and effective communication (Miller & Rollnick, 2013). The acronym **OARS** (open questions, affirming, reflecting, and summarizing) represents four foundational person-centered communication skills that can be used to open a door to sharing information; demonstrating respect, understanding, and empathy; developing rapport; and engaging with participants in a meaningful way. OARS skills include:

- *Asking open-ended questions:* Open-ended questions invite people to think before responding and commonly begin with the words “what,” “why,” and “how.” This questioning technique is useful for initiating a conversation with a participant, learning more details about what is being communicated, developing a better understanding of the participant’s views, or simply keeping the conversation going.
- *Affirming:* Affirming is a process of “accentuating the positive,” recognizing and acknowledging the good and inherent worth of a fellow human being, and offering support and encouragement. Offering affirmations is not the same as praise.

When the GFI is the source of affirmation, they are commenting on something that is good about the person while avoiding the word "I" and focusing on the use of "you" statements.

- *Reflective listening:* This approach helps the GFI empathize, reflect, and clarify the main points and feelings a participant is expressing. Using reflective statements allows the GFI to deepen their understanding by seeking clarification on what they think they heard a person say. This is an opportunity to make a "best guess" at what the GFI thinks a person is saying, giving them a chance to confirm the GFI understood what they meant or provide more information. This strategy allows participants to hear the thoughts and feelings they are expressing in different words and encourages people to continue talking, exploring, and considering.
- *Summarizing:* At appropriate points in the conversation, the GFI should try to synthesize what they have heard in one or two concise sentences, helping to keep the topic of the conversation focused and on track in a way that encourages a person to continue speaking and inviting further exploration. A summary is essentially a long reflection that pulls together what a person has been saying.

Nonverbal Skills

While the words spoken verbally during a class are important, they constitute only a portion of the complete message that participants receive. Nonverbal skills that convey genuine care, concern, and undivided attention include:

- *Voice quality:* A weak, hesitant, or soft voice does not inspire participant confidence. On the other hand, a loud, tense voice tends to make people nervous. Developing a voice that is firm and confident communicates professionalism.
- *Eye contact:* Direct, friendly eye contact shows participants they are the center of attention, whether the GFI is listening or talking. When a listener looks away while a person is speaking, the speaker feels as though they are not being heard. Similarly, when a speaker looks away, the listener does not feel important, as the speaker does not seem to care about the listener's reaction.
- *Facial expression:* Facial expressions convey emotion but work best when the emotion is sincere (most people can sense an artificial smile). As GFIs work with participants, their faces should display the concern, thoughtfulness, and/or enjoyment they are feeling.
- *Hand gestures:* Use of hand gestures varies from culture to culture. In general, people are most comfortable when a speaker uses relaxed, fluid hand gestures while explaining something. When listening, a GFI's hands should be comfortably resting. Fidgeting hands, clenched fists, abrupt gestures, and finger pointing may be distracting.
- *Body position:* An open, well-balanced, erect body position communicates confidence and symbolizes professional expertise. A body posture that is leaning or stooped suggests fatigue and boredom, while a rigid, hands-on-hips stance may be interpreted as aggressive. Keeping arms uncrossed and relaxed indicates that the GFI is receptive to, and interested in, engaging in discussion.

THINK IT THROUGH

Practicing Communication Skills

Practice using verbal and nonverbal skills when conversing casually with friends and family members. Afterward, think of ways in which you can incorporate these active listening strategies into your interactions with participants before, during, and after your classes.

EQUITY, DIVERSITY, AND INCLUSION

Increasing Your Cultural Competence

Alex McLean, international fitness presenter, 25+ year fitness professional, ACE Certified since 2008

When you look at this illustration, what is the first thing you see? Several families? People of various ages? Diverse races? What physical marker did you use to create distinct groups?

Now that you have assigned groups in this illustration, reflect on the characteristics that informed these choices. What perspectives do you have about them? What shapes these perspectives? Was this informed by past personal experiences? Stories from friends? Social media? News and other media outlets?

It is human nature to notice differences and make generalizations that compartmentalize these differences into categories. While using a familiar framework to categorize individuals simplifies the process of understanding the people one encounters, it could also expose biases hidden within the assumptions used to classify people. Could you unknowingly be sabotaging your personal and professional relationships due to your preconceived notions and unconscious bias about people?

Cultural competence is the ability to understand and interact effectively with people from other cultures. To be successful, a GFI must connect the reason they became an exercise professional in the first place—that is, their "why"—to their relationships with a variety of people. To connect with others, you first have to self-evaluate.

The first step in increasing cultural competence is to understand yourself, and to acknowledge personal biases and the root of those assumptions. Biases may hinder your ability to respectfully and positively interact with people of other backgrounds, including those of a different ethnic background, age, sexual orientation, physical ability, socioeconomic level, size, race, sex, gender, and other **diversity** factors. The following are examples of how a lack of cultural competence may manifest in your fitness instruction:

- Assigning dumbbell weights by gender as opposed to ability
- Assuming regular participants are more advanced than non-regular attendees and providing progressions and regressions accordingly without considering the needs of the individuals in your class
- Describing modified push-ups as "girl push-ups"
- Assuming age correlates to frailty and a lack of ability
- Assuming fitness level is directly linked to motivation
- Assuming a participant's diet is based solely on willpower

The second step to increasing cultural competence is to open your mind and actively learn about new cultures. Identifying misconceptions and addressing them by learning more about participants' beliefs, attitudes, and lifestyles through the use of effective communication skills will help ensure that each participant is treated with the dignity and respect they deserve. The key is to use open-ended questions that foster detailed explanations, give your utmost attention to the person, and be fully present and invested in the discussion. Commit to learning more about people different from yourself, no matter the source of that difference. Consider the following ways to learn more:

- Research online.
- Watch documentaries.
- Attend special events and go to museums.
- Ask friends from diverse backgrounds if they are willing to engage in cultural exchange conversations with you.
- Dissect the storytelling in the music, literature, performing arts, and theater of the culture.

After understanding the root of personal bias and appreciating the differences among cultures, the last step to increasing cultural competence is to apply your learning. Once you know better, act better. As a GFI, there are elements you can control in your classes. For example, what types of modifications could support those from diverse religious backgrounds? Consider the following suggestions for modifying your offerings based on participants' religion:

- Adjust the workout intensity during fasting rituals for religious celebrations.
- Offer additional classes at different times during religious holidays when participants must be home by sunset.
- Recommend at-home workout options such as digital programming and the use of apps.
- Create take-home workouts that require no or limited equipment when electricity is unavailable during religious holidays.

The process of increasing one's cultural competence is a continual work in progress and will evolve as you continue to consider others. Take the following steps to develop strong cultural competence:

- Focus on self-awareness.
- Actively learn about different cultures in an effort to grow.
- Apply and act on what you have learned.

HEALTH BELIEF MODEL

The **health belief model** states that people's ideas and underlying emotions about illnesses, prevention, and treatments may influence health behaviors and decisions about changing (or not changing) health behaviors (Rosenstock, 1966). The outcome variable of interest is the decision to change, so the model is especially applicable to people in the early stages of change, where they are still weighing the pros and cons. The model states that at least four variables influence a person's decision to change. The first two involve a person's beliefs about a health threat. The second two reflect the person's beliefs about the health behavior that could reduce the threat (Sears, Brehm, & Bell, 2014) (Figure 2-3).

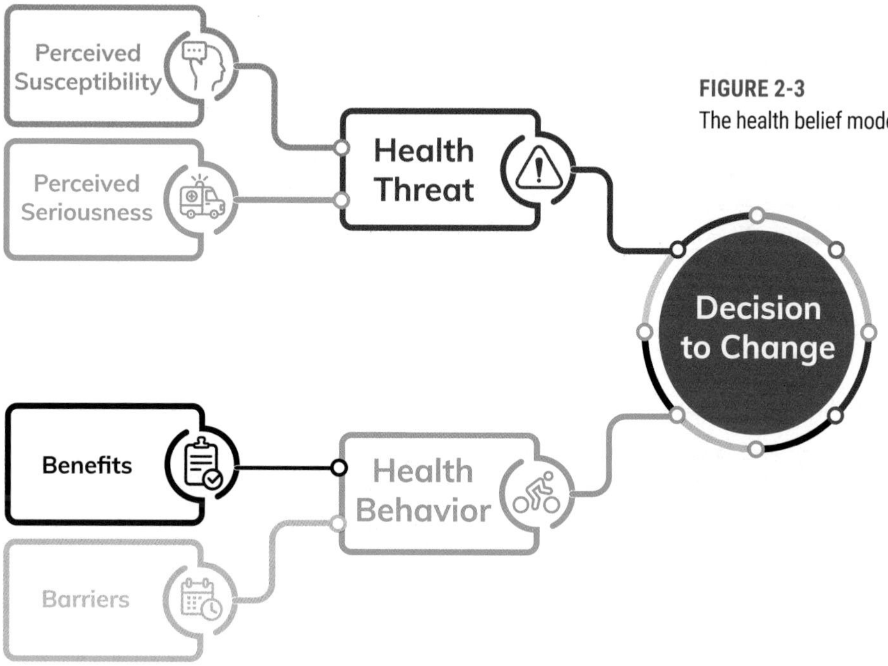

FIGURE 2-3
The health belief model

The belief in the health threat has two components, **perceived susceptibility** to an illness and **perceived seriousness** of the illness. Perceived susceptibility refers to people's perceptions of how likely they are to develop the illness. Perceived seriousness refers to people's perceptions regarding the short- and long-term severity of the illness. Health screenings that indicate a potential problem sometimes motivate behavior change because they may alter people's perceptions of susceptibility. For example, people who have not thought much about what they eat may become more aware of their eating habits if they hear their **blood pressure** is high. They may suddenly feel more susceptible to **hypertension** and feel motivated to prevent its development through beneficial health-behavior change, perhaps by improving their food choices and exercising.

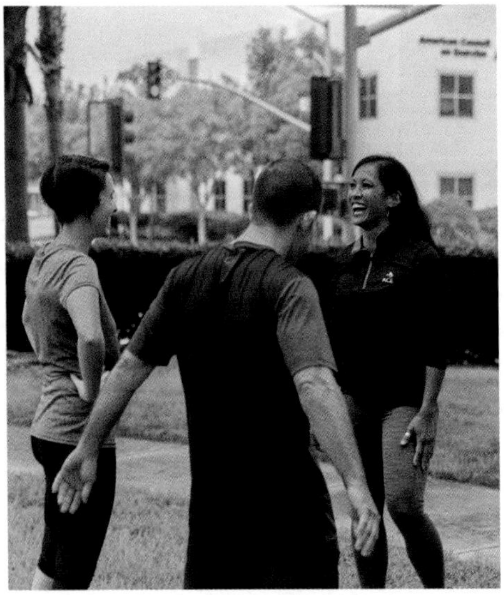

The second set of variables relates to perceptions of the health behavior. People may perceive both benefits and barriers to taking action with a specific health behavior. Beliefs about benefits may include how effective the person thinks a health behavior would be in preventing or treating an illness. Beliefs about barriers or drawbacks of a health behavior might include how difficult implementing the new behavior would be and the negative effects associated with doing so. If people feel susceptible to high blood pressure, but do not believe that limiting fast-food intake would help very much or be easy enough to do long-term, they would be unlikely to change the amount of fast food they eat. Addressing health beliefs is especially important for participants in the early stages of behavior change. GFIs may find themselves in a position to discuss with class participants their beliefs about health concerns and behavior change and correct misperceptions with accurate information that will help participants weigh the pros and cons of behavior change and hopefully form intentions to modify their lifestyles.

TRANSTHEORETICAL MODEL OF BEHAVIOR CHANGE

An important factor in the successful adoption of any routine of physical activity is the individual's readiness to make a change. This individual readiness for change is the focus of a well-accepted theory examining health behaviors called the **transtheoretical model of behavior change (TTM)** (Prochaska & DiClemente, 1984). More commonly called the **stages-of-change model,** the TTM is important for GFIs to understand when promoting group fitness participation.

The TTM is made up of five stages of behavior change (Figure 2-4). These stages can be related to any health behavior, but in the exercise context the stages are as follows:

- The **precontemplation** stage is the stage during which individuals are physically inactive and are not intending to begin an activity program. They do not see physical activity as relevant in their lives and may even discount the importance or practicality of being physically active.
- The **contemplation** stage consists of people who are still inactive, but are thinking about becoming more active in the near future (within the next six months). They are starting to consider physical activity as important and have begun to identify the implications of being inactive. However, they are ambivalent about change and are still weighing the pros and cons of becoming physically active.
- The **preparation** stage is marked by some engagement in physical activity, as individuals are mentally and physically preparing to adopt an activity program. Activity during the preparation stage may be a sporadic walk, or even a periodic visit to the gym, but it is inconsistent. People in the preparation stage are getting ready to adopt and live an active lifestyle.

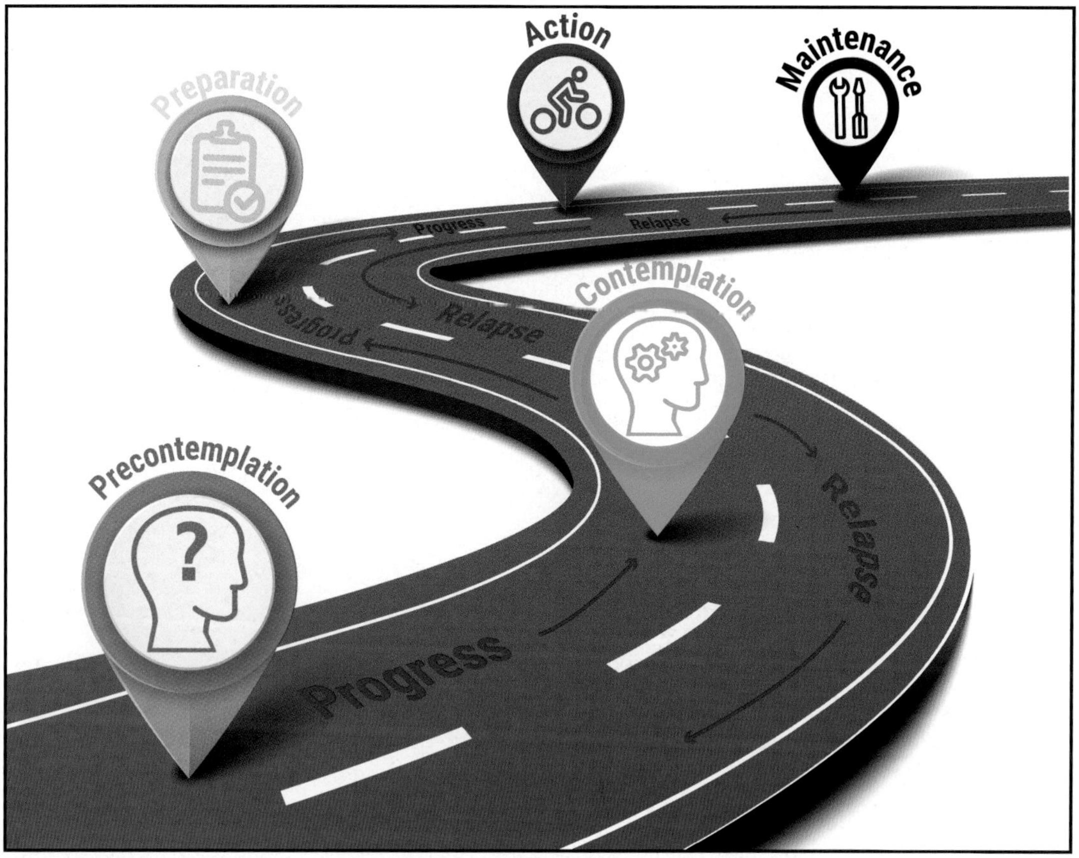

FIGURE 2-4
Stages of behavior change

- The **action** stage is comprised of people who are engaging in regular physical activity but have been doing so for less than six months.
- The **maintenance** stage is marked by regular physical-activity participation for longer than six months.

Some participants in group fitness classes may be in the preparation stage of change and their motivation and self-confidence may be quite fragile. Individuals in this stage of change need plenty of support and reassurance in the form of positive feedback that they are doing well in the class. Ongoing feedback is also important for participants in the action stage, as even though they are regularly participating in physical activity, they have been doing so for less than six months and need continued positive reinforcement to ensure long-term adherence.

GFIs may also encounter individuals in the contemplation stage of change, such as a currently **sedentary** individual who comes in to tour the facility to gather information about the types of classes offered. The GFI should make it a point to emphasize the fun and social aspects of exercising in the group fitness environment and extend an invitation to the individual to attend a group fitness class, such as by providing a free guest pass or information about an upcoming open house that will feature demo classes.

Table 2-1 presents the identifying traits commonly observed in individuals within each stage of change, goals to work on at each stage of change, as well as effective strategies that can be utilized to help advance from one stage of change to the next.

TABLE 2-1

The Stages of Behavior Change

Stage	Traits	Goals	Strategies
Precontemplation	▸ Unaware or under-aware of the problem, or believe that it cannot be solved	▸ Increase awareness of the risks of maintaining the status quo and of the benefits of making a change ▸ Focus on addressing something relevant to them ▸ Have them start thinking about change	▸ Validate lack of readiness to change and clarify that this decision is theirs ▸ Encourage reevaluation of current behavior and self-exploration, while not taking action ▸ Explain and personalize the inherent risks ▸ Utilize general sources, including media, Internet, and brochures, to increase awareness ▸ Explore the participant's personal values
Contemplation	▸ Aware of the problem and weighing the benefits versus risks of change ▸ Have little understanding of how to go about changing	▸ Collaboratively explore available options ▸ Support cues to action and provide basic structured guidance upon request from the participant and with permission	▸ Validate lack of readiness to change and clarify that this decision is theirs ▸ Encourage evaluation of the pros and cons of making a change ▸ Identify and promote new, positive outcome expectations and boost self-confidence
Preparation	▸ Seeking opportunities to engage in the target behavior	▸ Co-create an action plan with frequent positive feedback and reinforcements on their progress	▸ Verify that the individual has the underlying skills for behavior change and encourage small steps toward building self-efficacy ▸ Identify and assist with problem-solving obstacles ▸ Assist the participant in identifying social support and establishing goals
Action	▸ Desire for opportunities to maintain activities ▸ Changing beliefs and attitudes ▸ High risk for lapses or returns to undesirable behavior	▸ Establish the new behavior as a habit through motivation and adherence to the desired behavior	▸ Use behavior-modification strategies ▸ Empower participants to restructure cues and social support toward building long-term change ▸ Increase awareness of inevitable lapses and bolster self-efficacy in coping with lapses ▸ Support participants in establishing systems of accountability and self-monitoring
Maintenance	▸ Empowered, but desire a means to maintain adherence ▸ Good capability to deal with lapses	▸ Maintain support systems ▸ Maintain interest and avoid boredom or burnout	▸ Reevaluate strategies currently in effect ▸ Plan for contingencies with support systems, although this may no longer be needed ▸ Reinforce the need for a transition from external to internal rewards ▸ Plan for potential lapses ▸ Encourage reevaluation of goals and action plans as needed

Building Self-efficacy

An important component of the TTM is **self-efficacy,** which refers to the belief in one's perceived ability to successfully achieve a particular goal or perform a specific task. An individual's self-efficacy is related to whether they will participate in physical activity, and a person's participation in physical activity in turn influences their self-efficacy level. Therefore, self-efficacy is both a determinant and an outcome of behavior change.

There is also a relationship between self-efficacy and the stages of behavior change, as individuals in the precontemplation and contemplation stages of change often report significantly lower levels of self-efficacy than those in the action or maintenance stages. There are six sources of self-efficacy that help influence participant self-efficacy levels.

- **Past performance experience** is an influential source of self-efficacy information. GFIs may ask participants about their previous experiences with exercise, fitness facilities, and working with exercise professionals. These previous experiences will strongly influence their current self-efficacy levels.
- **Vicarious experience** is important for participants who are new to exercise and who have little previous personal experience with group exercise. The observation or knowledge of someone else who is successfully participating in a similar class—or has done so in the past—can increase one's self-efficacy. This is particularly true if the person being observed is perceived by the participant to be similar to themself (e.g., age, chronic illness status, sex, and/or fitness level).
- **Verbal persuasion** typically occurs in the form of feedback and encouragement from GFIs. Statements from others are most likely to influence self-efficacy if they come from a credible, respected, and knowledgeable source. Different participants will require different amounts of verbal encouragement and statements of belief. Being aware of how much feedback a person needs and then providing that verbal support is an important motivational tool for GFIs.
- **Physiological state appraisals** related to exercise participation are important because participants may experience emotional arousal, pain, or fatigue. The types of appraisals people make about their physiological states may lead to judgments about their ability to participate successfully. It is important to help participants evaluate appraisals of their physiological states to create positive interpretations. By teaching people to appropriately identify muscle fatigue, soreness, and tiredness, as well as the implications of these states, GFIs can help participants view the "feelings" of working out in a more positive light.
- **Emotional state and mood appraisals** of program participation can also influence self-efficacy. Negative mood states and emotional beliefs associated with exercise, such as fear, anxiety, anger, and frustration, are related to reduced levels of self-efficacy and lower levels of participation. On the other hand, positive mood states and emotional beliefs, including mastery, are related to higher levels of self-efficacy. Hence, giving encouraging coaching cues and tailoring group exercise experiences that are sufficiently challenging, yet simply mastered, contribute to elevated moods and positive emotional states.
- **Imaginal experiences** refer to the imagined experiences (positive or negative) of exercise participation. It is important to understand a person's preconceived notion

of what exercise will be like, as this information will influence actual self-efficacy levels. The GFI may encourage positive imagined experiences by asking open-ended questions such as, "How do you imagine you'll feel when you reach your goal of attending all the aquatic exercise classes on this week's schedule?"

One of the most powerful predictors of self-efficacy is past performance experience. Therefore, participants with little to no exercise experience may have lower self-efficacy regarding their ability to engage in a consistent routine of physical activity. In light of this, GFIs should focus on creating positive, meaningful, and inclusive classes in which all participants experience feelings of success and accomplishment. GFIs should consider how to use these sources of self-efficacy to enhance their class offerings, because the group exercise environment may be the perfect setting for drawing on multiple sources over the course of a single class.

Decisional Balance

Another important aspect of TTM is **decisional balance,** which refers to the evaluation of the pros and cons an individual perceives regarding adopting and/or maintaining an activity program. Individuals in the precontemplation and contemplation stages of change perceive more cons (e.g., time, sore muscles, cost, and sweating) related to being regularly active than pros. It is important to note that newcomers to exercise may not be accustomed to the feeling of increased breathing, heart rate, and sweating associated with physical activity. Therefore, GFIs should acknowledge these minor discomforts associated with exercise and reassure participants that they are normal responses and should be expected. GFIs should then focus on emphasizing the wide variety of benefits of being physically active. Incorporating verbal and nonverbal cues that emphasize enjoyment of movement and feelings of accomplishment will help participants experience a greater sense of satisfaction during each class, which over time can help individuals identify more pros than cons associated with regular physical activity.

Emergency Procedures

In addition to being aware of the discomforts participants who are new to exercise may experience, GFIs must also be able to recognize the warning signs of potential injuries and emergency situations that warrant immediate attention. Instructors may find it helpful to regularly check in with participants throughout the class by asking them how they are feeling. Participants can respond verbally or nonverbally (i.e., thumbs up or down). Instructors can also incorporate specific methods for monitoring intensity [e.g., **rating of perceived exertion (RPE)** and **talk test**] (see Chapter 4). Refer to Chapter 13 for detailed information on the **signs** and **symptoms** that warrant activation of emergency medical services (EMS).

MOTIVATION

People generally do not like to be told what to do. People like to feel that they have choices, and that they can make decisions about behavior according to their own wishes and in accordance with their own values and goals. **Self-determination theory** examines two basic types of motivation: **autonomous motivation** and **controlled motivation.** Autonomous motivation means that people feel as if they are behaving of their own free will. They are doing something because they want to do it. To be autonomously motivated to the fullest extent is known as having **intrinsic motivation.** Controlled motivation, on the other hand, means people are doing something because they feel pressured by demands from external forces.

Autonomous motivation and controlled motivation feel very different to people. It is critically important that GFIs respect a person's **autonomy** and start from the understanding that, while the GFI may be an expert on group exercise program design and implementation, ultimately the participant is the expert on themself, and lasting change will happen only when the individual is ready and has decided that it should.

In the exercise context, to be intrinsically motivated means that a person is engaged in an exercise activity for the inherent pleasure and experience that comes from the engagement itself. Having more intrinsic participation motives or goals associated with exercise, such as social engagement, challenge, and skill development, is associated with greater exercise participation (Teixeira et al., 2012). People who are intrinsically motivated report being physically active because they truly enjoy it. Such involvement in an activity is associated with positive attitudes and emotions (e.g., happiness, freedom, and relaxation), maximal effort, and persistence when faced with barriers (Ryan & Deci, 2000).

While many people truly enjoy being physically active, very few (if any) adults are completely intrinsically motivated. Fundamental goals of exercise professionals include maximizing participant enjoyment and engagement, while also being careful not to expect that people will always demonstrate intrinsic motivation.

The reality is that most adults experience some amount of controlled motivation, which involves the engagement in exercise for any benefit other than for the joy of participation. Controlled motivation often results in people being physically active because of some external factor (e.g., lose weight, be healthy, make their spouse happy, look good, or meet new people) and may lead to feelings of tension, guilt, or pressure related to participation (Ryan & Deci, 2000). Most individuals fall somewhere on the continuum between controlled and autonomous motivation. Instead of feeling like they need to make their participants more intrinsically motivated, GFIs strive to enhance the feelings of enjoyment and accomplishment that come with program participation.

In their work in developing self-determination theory, researchers Ryan and Deci (2000) reported that people have innate, basic psychological needs, and when those needs are met, the conditions are favorable for supporting intrinsic motivation. The three needs they identified are autonomy, **competence,** and relatedness. A sense of autonomy is important for intrinsic motivation such that an individual must feel that their behavior is self-determined and not coerced or controlled. Competence relates to the self-perception that a person can successfully perform a task, which is enhanced when they receive positive performance feedback (see Chapter 8). Receiving negative feedback, on the other hand, diminishes the perception of competence and may thwart intrinsic motivation. Lastly, social environments that promote relatedness, or a belongingness and connectedness with others, are contexts in which intrinsic motivation may flourish.

GFIs can create environments wherein their participants' basic psychological needs are met by (1) including the participant in aspects of goal setting and program design (promoting autonomy), (2) creating opportunities for mastery experiences through offering appropriately challenging exercises and consistent positive feedback (promoting competence), and (3) encouraging a sense of camaraderie among the group of participants and others in the fitness setting (promoting relatedness) (Figure 2-5). Encouraging participant ownership and continued involvement in the group exercise program design will further facilitate the development of intrinsic motivation by enhancing a person's self-sufficiency.

FIGURE 2-5
Creating an environment that supports intrinsic motivation

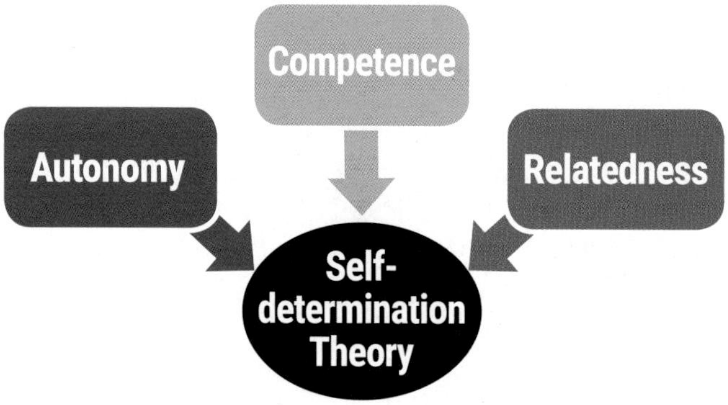

Creating a Motivational Climate in the Exercise Setting

Research on creating a motivational climate in the exercise setting indicates that an exerciser's self-determination for physical activity is low when motivated by external factors (e.g., to please others or gain a reward) and, conversely, is high when motivated by internal factors (e.g., enjoyment and self-care) (Ng et al., 2012). Further, it has been shown that supportive others, such as GFIs, can play a critical role in fostering the development of increased self-determined motivation (Ryan & Deci, 2000).

Similar to how individuals' perceptions influence their belief about the actions they take for health, so too do perceptions about their environment affect the efforts they put forth in the exercise setting. Seminal research suggests that environments can be perceived by participants as either task-involving or ego-involving (Nicholls, 1984). Task-involving climates promote a focus on individual effort and improvement where everyone is made to feel valued and welcomed and cooperation is fostered among everyone in the setting. Ego-involving climates, on the other hand, highlight the most skilled or fit participants among a group and rivalry is encouraged to the point where members may feel embarrassed if they do not know how to use a piece of equipment or perform an exercise correctly.

Perhaps not surprisingly, participants who exercise in task-involving climates report having higher self-esteem, feeling more competent and autonomous, feeling a greater sense of relatedness to others, and experiencing more enjoyment, versus ego-involving climates where they report greater physical exhaustion and higher anxiety (Moore & Fry, 2017; Hogue et al., 2013). Research on a separate aspect of climate—the extent to which it is perceived as caring—has also shown psychological benefits. That is, a caring climate wherein physical-activity participants perceive the setting to be a safe and supportive environment that fosters a sense of belonging and where participants feel their exercise leaders have genuine concern for their well-being is associated with higher enjoyment, greater commitment to the activity, and higher empathic concern for others (Brown, Fry, & Moore, 2017; Brown & Fry, 2014; Brown & Fry, 2013; Brown & Fry, 2011).

APPLY WHAT YOU KNOW

Creating a Caring, Task-involving Climate

In combination, the research just described suggests that creating a caring and task-involving climate may provide significant psychological benefits to participants through increased enjoyment, social interactions, and feelings of competence. The following describes strategies that may be used specifically by group fitness instructors.

- GFIs may foster a caring, task-involving climate by emphasizing **process goals** (e.g., making it to the gym four times this week) rather than **outcome goals** [e.g., losing 10 pounds (0.45 kg)]. Further, encouraging participants to focus on the intrinsic rewards associated with exercise (e.g., feeling better and having more energy) versus extrinsic rewards (e.g., getting in shape for swimsuit season) will help put the focus more on process goals. Deemphasizing outcome goals may also be helpful because individuals have less control over the rate at which their bodies respond to exercise (e.g., pounds or kilograms lost per week). However, the improved mood that goes along with being physically active may happen immediately.
- Being careful not to compare participants to others is another important aspect of creating a caring, task-involving climate. Instead of offering information such as, "Compared to people your age, you should be completing 20 push-ups," a GFI may reframe the conversation to, "Over the next four weeks, we could aim to increase your push-ups by one repetition per set at each class. How does that sound to you?"
- GFIs have a unique opportunity to celebrate the accomplishments of their participants each time they meet. For example, a GFI could make positive, encouraging remarks about milestones such as completing more repetitions, lifting heavier weights, performing an exercise with greater ease, moving more efficiently, or making it into the gym more frequently. Positive feedback is critical, as individuals may not be aware of their progress, especially if their focus has been on outcome goals that surface more slowly. These types of statements demonstrate that participants are cared for and valued by the GFI, bolstering the caring environment.

- To promote feelings of belonging and relatedness, GFIs may consider introducing participants to other members of the group before or after their classes. Going a step further and encouraging people to cheer each other on when physical-activity and fitness milestones are reached is another effective option for fostering a caring, task-involving climate. Lastly, one of the most important roles of the GFI is to provide genuine warmth and acceptance to all participants, taking extra steps to enhance rapport and help individuals to feel supported. In this way, GFIs may fulfill the "supportive others" role, which is critical in the development of self-determined motivation.

ACE MOVER™ METHOD

Introducing the ACE Mover Method™ Philosophy, the ACE ABC Approach™, and the ACE RRAMP Approach™

The greatest impact that GFIs can regularly have on the lives of class participants is to help them to positively change health-related behaviors and establish positive relationships with exercise. For this reason, the participant–GFI relationship is the foundation of the ACE Integrated Fitness Training® (ACE IFT®) Model, which is built upon rapport, trust, and empathy, with the GFI serving as a "coach" to all class participants throughout their physical-activity and health behavior-change journey (see Chapter 4 for more on the ACE IFT Model). This approach starts with realizing that the "participant" is the first person in the participant–GFI relationship.

A key element of using the ACE IFT Model to empower class participants to make behavior changes to improve their health, fitness, and overall quality of life is the adoption of the ACE Mover Method, which is founded on the following tenets:

- Each professional interaction is participant-centered, with a recognition that participants are the foremost experts on themselves.
- Powerful open-ended questions and active listening are utilized during every interaction with class participants.
- Each class participant is genuinely viewed as resourceful and capable of change.

Group fitness Instructors can apply the ACE Mover Method both before and after class using the ACE ABC Approach when privately engaging with participants. The ACE RRAMP Approach, on the other hand, is used to empower participants when communicating with the class as a whole when leading a group exercise class.

ACE ABC APPROACH™

The ACE ABC Approach is used when communicating one-on-one with participants and consists of three steps:

- Ask open-ended questions
- Break down barriers
- Collaborate

Every time a GFI interacts with a class participant before, during, and after class, there is an opportunity to utilize coaching skills to help build rapport while positioning the participant as an active partner in their behavior-change journey. Asking questions leads to the identification of goals and options for breaking down barriers, which in turn leads to collaborating on next steps. The ACE Mover Method provides the foundational skills for communicating effectively with class participants, but it is not the equivalent of a health coaching certification. GFIs should work in concert with other professionals, such as health coaches and **registered dietitians** and other allied health professionals, whenever appropriate, to take a team approach to improving each class participant's health and wellness.

Step 1 of this process involves asking powerful questions to identify what the participant hopes to accomplish by attending group exercise classes and what, if any, physical activities they enjoy. Open-ended questions are the key to sparking this discussion.

Step 2 involves asking more questions to discover what potential barriers may get in the way of the participant reaching their specific goals. Questions like "What do you need to start doing now to move closer to your goals?" and "What do you need to stop doing that will enable you to reach your goals?" can be very revealing.

Step 3 is all about collaboration as the participant and exercise professional work together to set **SMART goals** and establish specific steps to act toward those goals. Allowing the participant to lead the discussion of how to monitor and measure progress empowers them to take ownership of their personal behavior-change journey.

ACE RRAMP APPROACH™

Empowering participants to make behavior changes to improve their health, fitness, and overall quality of life is optimized by creating a caring and task-involving climate in every class. A caring and task-involving climate has the following characteristics, which can be used when communicating with a class as a whole:

R	Respect	Each class participant feels valued.
R	Recognition	Effort and improvement are prioritized and honored.
A	Alignment	Cooperation is fostered and valued.
M	Mistakes	Mistakes are a part of learning.
P	Participant	Each person's uniqueness contributes to the overall experience that cannot be replicated.

The ACE RRAMP Approach helps to build an environment that recognizes and serves everyone who shows up to participate in class, and its tenets can be weaved into pre-class interactions, introductions, programming, cues, class closings, and post-class interactions.

To begin, consider all aspects of a class and reflect on the following questions:

R	Respect	How can I create a kind and respectful environment?
R	Recognition	How can I create opportunities for recognition that are beyond going harder, faster, bigger, or better?
A	Alignment	How can I create the feeling that me and my participants are in this together?
M	Mistakes	How can I ensure that mistakes are an acceptable part of the learning experience?
P	Participant	How can I ensure each individual understands their important role in the class?

Every class offers an opportunity to add RRAMP-inspired language, actions, and interactions and, in doing so, partner with participants in their behavior-change journey. The skills employed in the ACE RRAMP Approach lay the groundwork for creating a caring and task-involving climate, which promotes group-participation adherence, thereby bolstering behavior-change efforts.

Throughout this textbook, look for ACE Mover Method features to learn more about effective strategies for employing a participant-centered approach to group fitness leadership. For practical examples of implementing the ACE RRAMP Approach, see Chapter 10.

Group class participants want to know that the GFI cares about them. This is similar to what individuals seek when hiring the services of other professionals who have an impact on their quality of life, and it is at the heart of a participant-centered approach to group fitness leadership. From physicians to financial planners, people will continue to work with the same professional if they can see that the professional truly cares about them and their health, whether it be physical or financial. Class participants should have a belief that the GFI has the knowledge, skills, and abilities to help them reach their goals. With rare exception, they do not care to hear all the science, training methods, and other health-related information that the exercise professional knows. Instead, they want to hear that the GFI is invested in them. Successful GFIs keep conversations focused on the participant. A primary goal of every GFI should be to have every class participant wanting to return for the next class.

Goal Setting

When an individual joins a group fitness class, it is important that they take the time to develop realistic, flexible, and individualized short-term goals that build off of the objectives of the class (see Chapter 7). Realistic goals are important to not only avoid injury, but also to help maintain interest and manage expectations.

GFIs can teach participants goal-setting strategies by applying the SMART goal guidelines. This catchy acronym includes the key components for developing effective goals. Goals should be:

S SPECIFIC	M MEASURABLE	A ATTAINABLE	R RELEVANT	T TIME-BOUND
What will you do, when, where, and with whom?	How will you know when you have reached your goals?	Can you really do this? Can you do it at this time?	Are your goals relevant to your particular interests, needs, and abilities?	How soon, how often, and for how long?
Example: Instead of, "I will go to the gym for a workout," a more specific goal may be, "I will go to FitWell gym with my wife for a cycling class on Monday, Wednesday, and Friday at 6:30 p.m. after work."	*Example:* Instead of, "I will exercise at a moderate intensity today," a more measurable goal may be, "I will row at an RPE of 6 for 10 minutes."	*Example:* Instead of, "I will do a three-minute plank," a more attainable goal may be, "I will perform a plank with proper form for 30 seconds."	*Example:* Instead of, "I will train to run a marathon in under three hours," a more relevant goal may be, "I will increase the amount of physical activity I do by going to a boot-camp class twice per week."	*Example:* Instead of, "I will lose at least 10% of my body weight in an effort to improve my appearance," a time-bound goal may be, "I will lose 20 pounds in the next four months at a reasonable rate of 1 to 2 pounds per week."

Often, class participants want to incorporate health- and skill-related components of physical fitness into their SMART goals to focus on both the process of making health-related changes and the desired outcomes toward which they are working. Fitness indicators can be incorporated into SMART goal setting because they are measurable and help to connect specific process goals to specific outcomes. For example, you may help a class participant to shape an effective SMART goal that looks like this: "To decrease my resting heart rate from 80 beats per minute to 75 beats per minute (outcome health indicator), I will attend your group exercise class twice per week on Tuesday and Thursday and will perform cardiorespiratory exercise on my own twice per week for 30 minutes at a moderate intensity (process goal) for the next three months." Table 2-2 provides examples of other fitness indicators that may be used as part of setting SMART goals.

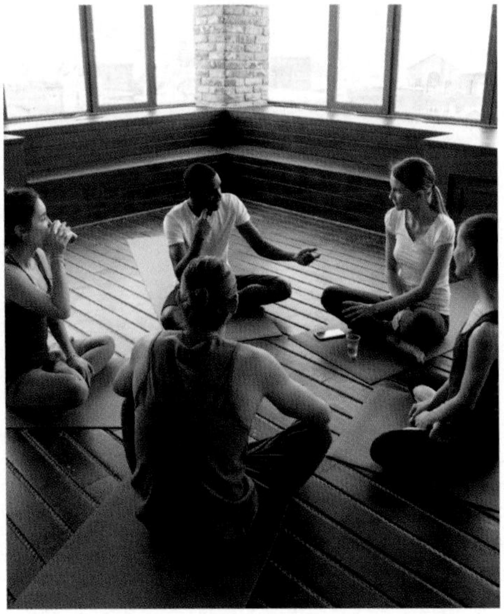

Goals can be specific to the exercise process, such as attending a certain number of classes in the coming weeks or supplementing group fitness classes with physical activity performed outside of the gym. Participants can also choose to set goals related to making new friends or developing a new social network. It is useful to encourage goals related to enjoyment and pleasure from moving and being active rather than only focus on physical goals such as weight loss.

TABLE 2-2

Fitness Indicators for SMART Goal Setting

Fitness Indicator	Notes for Goal Setting
Emotional health indicators	Participants may have measurable improvements in mood, energy level, and sleep quality, and fewer feelings of stress and irritability following exercise.
Resting heart rate	Many group fitness instructors have class participants measure their resting heart rate, either first thing in the morning or before falling asleep at night. Individuals new to exercise often experience a decrease in resting heart rate after a few months of regular exercise participation.
Heart rate at a given submaximal workload	Participants are likely to experience a decrease in exercise heart rate during exercise performed at a standard workload after several weeks of consistent training.
Muscular fitness	Gains in muscular fitness occur quickly during the first few months of an exercise program. These changes are easily measured by observing the amount of resistance used and the number of repetitions performed.
Cardiorespiratory fitness	Measuring cardiorespiratory fitness improvements with some sort of timed walking, running, cycling, or step test usually yields positive results if participants have been performing cardiorespiratory exercise for several weeks.
Flexibility	Flexibility is very slow to improve and should only be included as a goal if regular stretching or range-of-motion exercise is taking place.
Balance	Balance measures show the most improvement for adults participating in some sort of balance-training program, which are becoming increasingly popular, especially among older adults.
Skill level	Class participants will be pleased to see improvements in skill-related components of physical fitness (e.g., agility, coordination, power, reaction time, and speed), as well as improvements in activities that require skill, such as rock climbing, tennis, and golf. These improvements can be measured via specific tests or based on activity/game performance.
Medical indicators, such as resting blood pressure, blood lipid levels, or blood sugar levels	If any of these are the focus of a participant's motivation to exercise, they should have these measures taken at regular intervals as established by their healthcare providers. These variables may be affected by many factors besides exercise participation, including diet or changes in body weight, and these factors should be taken into consideration when evaluating exercise results.
Body weight	Body weight is easily measured but is a poor indicator of body-composition changes. Body weight may remain unchanged even though positive changes in body composition are occurring, or it may change by several pounds or kilograms due to changes in hydration. Nevertheless, participants following a weight-reduction program with more than a few pounds or kilograms of overweight will probably see a decrease in weight with regular participation. Participants should work for slow and consistent weight loss, which is more likely to yield long-term weight-loss maintenance.
Body size	Participants who have a goal to lose only a few pounds may not see much change in scale weight. Body-composition changes (fat loss with an increase in muscle mass) may still lead to a change in body size. Lean tissue, because of its greater density, takes up less space than fat tissue. Many people are happy when a waistband on a skirt or pair of pants fits more loosely. Many exercise professionals encourage participants to watch for changes in the way their clothes fit.
Body composition	If body composition is measured, the same test should be used consistently. Some exercise professionals record circumferences or skinfolds without predicting body composition. Changes in these measures may be indicative of fat loss or increases in muscle size.

EXPAND YOUR KNOWLEDGE

The Importance of Personalized Goal Setting

The importance of setting personalized goals with group fitness participants should not be underestimated. One study showed that the implementation of a monthly small-group coaching session with group fitness participants can significantly increase exercise behavior and that this additional support may be needed to maintain adherence to regular exercise (Middelkamp et al., 2016). Compared to a control group, the group fitness participants who received a monthly small-group coaching session decreased drop-out rates by 50% over 12 weeks and participated in four times as many exercise classes. During the monthly small-group coaching sessions, which lasted 30 minutes, participants used a coaching form to discuss self-efficacy expectations to determine which class may be best for their level of fitness and perceived self-efficacy. They also discussed six-month outcome expectations, breaking down six-month goals into monthly goals that considered both product and process goals, the participant's values, and the importance of outcomes to the participant, as well as each participant's current level of confidence for reaching process goals and ways to increase that confidence (Middelkamp et al., 2016). Although this type of small-group coaching outside of group exercise classes may not be commonplace, GFIs may want to consider the opportunities to introduce this type of offering for their participants to promote positive experiences and improve adherence.

Preparing for Setbacks

It is important that participants realize there will be times when they will not be able to attend class, such as during vacations, holidays, or times of increased work or family obligations. How these lapses in an exercise routine are handled determines if they will be temporary or permanent. When participants must miss a regular class, GFIs should encourage them to engage in physical activity outside of the group fitness environment, such as by performing home-based exercises and/or engaging in other modes of physical activity, such as walking, swimming, or hiking, perhaps with a friend, family member, or coworker. When a participant successfully exercises on their own, the foundation for long-term exercise adherence is reinforced.

COGNITIONS AND BEHAVIOR

As reflected in self-determination theory and TTM, a person's exercise behavior is influenced by how they think about exercise and about succeeding in an exercise program. Not only should GFIs understand what their participants think about exercise participation, but they should also support them in becoming more aware of their own thoughts, or cognitions.

Replacing Irrational Thoughts

Each person has a unique way of viewing the world and interpreting events. Most people understand this concept on a basic level but may sometimes operate on the assumption that their personal judgments are an accurate perception of reality without realizing that they may not be perceiving the whole picture. Some people may suffer from **cognitive distortions** (Figure 2-6) that reinforce irrational and potentially harmful thought patterns that interfere with their well-being (Burns, 1999). The GFI may help individuals recognize and replace irrational cognitions with healthier, more productive and factual thinking by asking them to answer questions such as the following:

- What is the evidence for and against this thought?
- What would I tell a friend in this same situation (as opposed to what I tell myself)?
- What is the worst that could realistically happen? How bad would that be?
- Is it really true that I must, should, ought to, have to...?
- Are there any other possible responses besides blaming myself?
- Is there any conceivable way to look at this positively?
- Is thinking this way helping the situation, myself, or others, or only making it worse?
- How have I effectively managed or tolerated these situations in the past?

FIGURE 2-6
Common cognitive distortions

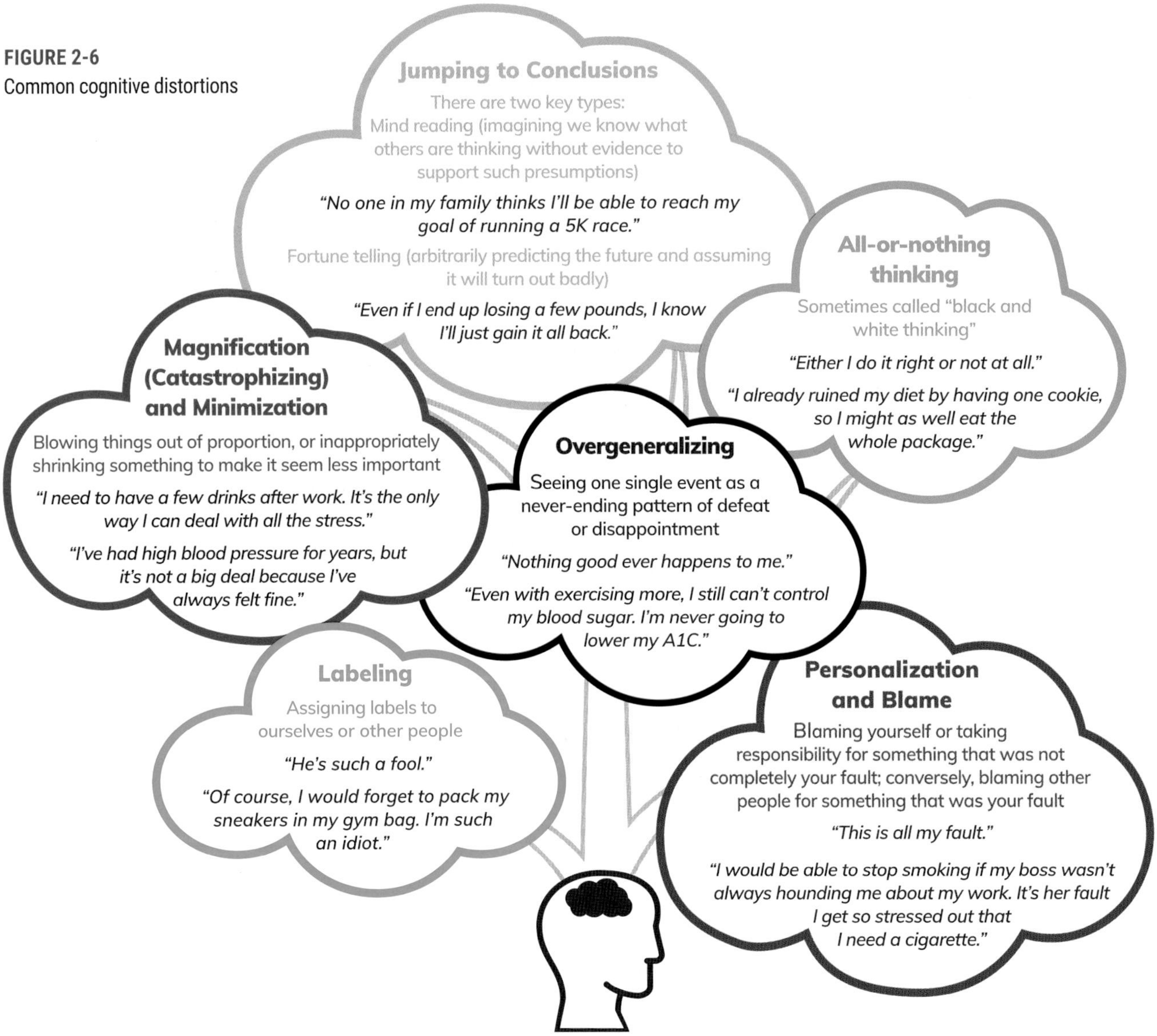

Going through the process of answering these questions may help participants to check, challenge, and change their own words, through which they are better able to understand why their irrational thoughts may be impeding progress or unnecessarily skewing their perceptions about physical activity in a negative way.

THINK IT THROUGH

Reflecting on Your Own Behavior-change Strategies

Think about your own daily routine and how you may already be using principles of behavior change in your own life. Are there any techniques you can encourage your participants to use to improve their chances for success at sustained healthy lifestyle change?

ACE UNIVERSITY

If your study program includes ACE University, visit www.ACEfitness.org/MyACE and log in to your My ACE Account to take full advantage of the ACE Group Fitness Instructor Study Program and online guided study experience.

A variety of media to support and expand on the material in this text is provided to facilitate learning and best prepare you for the ACE Group Fitness Instructor Certification exam and a career as a group fitness instructor.

SUMMARY

An outstanding GFI possesses skill in designing and leading safe and effective classes while also demonstrating cultural competence, the ability to create a motivational, caring and task-involving climate, and a thorough understanding of how to develop rapport and connect with participants in a meaningful way. Through the use of effective communication strategies rooted in behavioral science and additional considerations beyond what is outlined in basic class programming, GFIs can create unique and memorable movement experiences that build participant self-efficacy, guide participants toward appropriate goals, ensure participant success, and enhance motivation and adherence.

REFERENCES

Alkerwi, A. et al. (2015). Adherence to physical activity recommendations and its associated factors: An interregional population-based study. *Journal of Public Health Research*, 4, 1, 406.

American College of Sports Medicine (2019). Load, overload, and recovery in the athlete: Select issues for the team physician—a consensus statement. *Current Sports Medicine Reports*, 18, 4, 141–148.

Anderson, E. & Durstine, J.L. (2019). Physical activity, exercise, and chronic diseases: A brief review. *Sports Medicine and Health Science*, 1, 1, 3–10.

Armstrong, S. et al. (2018). Association of physical activity with income, race/ethnicity, and sex among adolescents and young adults in the United States: Findings from the National Health and Nutrition Examination Survey, 2007-2016. *JAMA Pediatrics*, 172, 8, 732–740.

Brown, T.C. & Fry, M.D. (2014). Motivational climate, staff members' behaviors, and members' psychological well-being at a national fitness franchise. *Research Quarterly for Exercise & Sport*, 85, 208–217.

Brown, T.C. & Fry, M.D. (2013). Association between females' perceptions of college aerobics class motivational climates and their responses. *Women & Health*, 53, 843–857.

Brown, T.C. & Fry, M.D. (2011). Helping members commit to exercise: Specific strategies to impact the climate at fitness centers. *Journal of Sport Psychology in Action*, 2, 70–80.

Brown, T.C., Fry, M.D., & Moore, W.G. (2017). A motivational climate intervention and exercise-related outcomes: A longitudinal perspective. *Motivation Science*, 3, 4, 337–353.

Burns, D.D. (1999). *Feeling Good: The New Mood Therapy* (revised edition). New York: Wm. Morrow & Co.

Centers for Disease Control and Prevention (2021). *Chronic Diseases in America*. https://www.cdc.gov/chronicdisease/resources/infographic/chronic-diseases.htm

Centers for Disease Control and Prevention (2013). Adult participation in aerobic and muscle-strengthening physical activities— United States, 2011. *Morbidity and Mortality Weekly Report*, 62, 17, 326–330.

Collado-Mateo, D. et al. (2021). Key factors associated with adherence to physical exercise in patients with chronic diseases and older adults: An umbrella review. *International Journal of Environmental Research and Public Health*, 18, 4, 2033.

Dishman, R.K. (1982). Compliance/adherence in health-related exercise. *Health Psychology*, 1, 237–267.

Dishman, R.K. & Buckworth, J. (1997). Adherence to physical activity. In: Morgan, W.P. (Ed.). *Physical Activity & Mental Health* (pp. 63–80). Washington, D.C.: Taylor & Frances.

Dorgo, S. et al. (2011). Comparing the effectiveness of peer mentoring and student mentoring in a 35-week fitness program for older adults. *Archives of Gerontology & Geriatrics*, 52, 3, 344–349.

Forechi, L. et al. (2018). Adherence to physical activity in adults with chronic disease: ELSA-Brasil. *Revista de Saúde Pública*, 52, 31.

Gabbett, T.J. (2016). The training–injury prevention paradox: Should athletes be training smarter *and* harder? *British Journal of Sports Medicine*, 6, 50, 273–280.

Hallal, P.C. et al. (2012). Global physical activity levels: Surveillance progress, pitfalls, and prospects. *Lancet*, 380, 247–257.

Heinrich, K.M. et al. (2014). High-intensity compared to moderate-intensity training for exercise initiation, enjoyment, adherence, and intentions: An intervention study. *BMC Public Health*, 14, 489.

Heisz, J.J. et al. (2016). Enjoyment for high-intensity interval exercise increases during the first six weeks of training: Implications for promoting exercise adherence in sedentary adults. *PLoS One*, 11, 12, e0168534.

Hogue, C.M. et al. (2013). The influence of a motivational climate intervention on participants' salivary cortisol and psychological responses. *Journal of Sport and Exercise Psychology*, 35, 1, 85–97.

Jekauc, D. (2015). Enjoyment during exercise mediates the effects of an intervention on exercise adherence. *Psychology*, 6, 48–54.

Lakicevic, N. et al. (2020). Make fitness fun: Could novelty be the key determinant for physical activity adherence? *Frontiers in Psychology*, 15.

Lee, A.L. et al. (2016). The relationship between sports facility accessibility and physical activity among Korean adults. *BMC Public Health*, 16, 1, 893.

Ley, C. (2020). Participation motives of sport and exercise maintainers: Influences of age and gender. *International Journal of Environmental Research and Public Health*, 17, 21.

Lowry, R. et al. (2013). Obesity and other correlates of physical activity and sedentary injuries among U.S. high school students. *Journal of Obesity*, Article ID 276318.

Middelkamp, J. et al. (2016). The effects of two self-regulation interventions to increase self-efficacy and group exercise behavior in fitness clubs. *Journal of Sports Science & Medicine*, 15, 2, 358–364.

Miller, W.R. & Rollnick, S. (2013). *Motivational Interviewing: Helping People Change* (3rd ed.). New York, N.Y.: The Guildford Press.

Moore, E.W.G. & Fry, M.D. (2017). National franchise members' perceptions of the exercise psychosocial environment, ownership, and satisfaction. *Sport, Exercise, and Performance Psychology*, 6, 2, 188–198.

Newsom, J.T. et al. (2012). Health behavior change following chronic illness in middle and later life. *The Journals of Gerontology*, 67B, 3, 279–288.

Ng, J.Y.Y. et al. (2012). Self-determination theory applied to health contexts: A meta-analysis. *Perspectives on Psychological Science*, 7, 325–340.

Nicholls, J.G. (1984). Achievement motivation: Concepts of ability, subjective experience, task choice, and performance. *Psychological Review*, 91, 328–348.

Prochaska, J.O. & DiClemente, C.C. (1984). *The Transtheoretical Approach: Crossing Traditional Boundaries of Therapy*. Homewood, Ill.: Dow Jones/Irwin.

Riess, H. (2017). The science of empathy. *Journal of Patient Experience*, 4, 2, 74–77.

Rodrigues, F. et al. (2020). Understanding exercise adherence: The predictability of past experience and motivation determinants. *Brain Sciences*, 10, 2.

Rosenstock, I.M. (1966). Why people use health services. *Milbank Memorial Fund Quarterly*, 44, 94–127.

Ryan, R.M. et al. (2011). Motivation and autonomy in counseling, psychotherapy, and behavior change: A look at theory and practice. *The Counseling Psychologist*, 39, 2, 193–260.

Ryan, R.M. & Deci, E.L. (2000). Self-determination theory and the facilitation of intrinsic motivation, social development, and well-being. *American Psychologist*, 55, 68–78.

Rynecki, N.D. et al. (2019). Injuries sustained during high intensity interval training: Are modern fitness trends contributing to increased injury rates? *The Journal of Sports Medicine and Physical Fitness*, 59, 7, 1206–1212.

Sales, M., Levinger, P., & Polman, R. (2017). Relationships between self perceptions and physical activity behaviour, fear of falling, physical function among older adults. *European Review of Aging and Physical Activity*, 14, 17.

Sears, S.R., Brehm, B.A., & Bell, K. (2014). Understanding behavior change: Theoretical models. In: Brehm, B.A. *Psychology of Health and Fitness*. Philadelphia: F.A. Davis.

Teixeira, D.S., Silva, M.N. & Palmeira, A.L. (2018). How does frustration make you feel? A motivational analysis in exercise context. *Motivation and Emotion*, 42, 419–428.

Teixeira, P. et al. (2012). Exercise, physical activity, and self-determination theory: A systematic review. *International Journal of Behavioral Nutrition and Physical Activity*, 13, 78.

World Health Organization (2021). *Noncommunicable Diseases*. https://www.who.int/news-room/fact-sheets/detail/noncommunicable-diseases

World Health Organization (2020). *The Top 10 Causes of Death*. https://www.who.int/news-room/fact-sheets/detail/the-top-10-causes-of-death

SUGGESTED READINGS

American Council on Exercise (2019). *The Professional's Guide to Health and Wellness Coaching*. San Diego: American Council on Exercise.

American Council on Exercise (2014). *Coaching Behavior Change*. San Diego: American Council on Exercise.

Bandura, A. (1986). *Social Foundations of Thought and Action: A Social Cognitive Theory*. Englewood Cliffs, N.J.: Prentice-Hall.

Dishman, R.K. (1994). *Advances in Exercise Adherence*. Champaign, Ill.: Human Kinetics.

Duncan, T.E. & McAuley, E. (1993). Social support and efficacy cognitions in exercise adherence: A latent growth curve analysis. *Journal of Behavioral Medicine*, 16, 199–218.

Hagger, M.S. & Chatzisarantis, N. (2007). *Intrinsic Motivation and Self-Determination in Exercise and Sport*. Champaign, Ill.: Human Kinetics.

Miller, W.R. & Rollnick, S. (2013). *Motivational Interviewing: Helping People Change* (3rd ed.). New York, N.Y.: The Guildford Press.

Uchino, B. (2004). *Social Support and Physical Health: Understanding the Health Consequences of Relationships*. New Haven, Conn.: Yale University Press.

CHAPTER 3

Foundations of Movement and Healthy Eating

CHRISTOPHER S. GAGLIARDI, MS | Scientific Education Content Manager, American Council on Exercise; ACE Certified Group Fitness Instructor, Personal Trainer, Health Coach, and Medical Exercise Specialist

IN THIS CHAPTER

LEARNING OBJECTIVES

Upon completion of this chapter, the reader will be able to:

- Apply human movement principles to group fitness instruction
- Describe which joints in the human body favor stability over mobility and which favor mobility over stability
- Apply the concept of planes of motion to movements performed at all joints
- Demonstrate a basic understanding of gross anatomy, specifically bones and muscles, as required for successful exercise instruction
- Apply anatomical alignment concepts to common body positions seen in group exercise classes
- Apply anatomical terminology in the group fitness setting
- Explain how the *Dietary Guidelines* and MyPlate can be used to help participants improve dietary behaviors

ACE UNIVERSITY

If your study program includes ACE University, visit www.ACEfitness.org/MyACE and log in to your My ACE Account to take full advantage of the ACE Group Fitness Instructor Study Program and online guided study experience.

A variety of media to support and expand on the material in this text is provided to facilitate learning and best prepare you for the ACE Group Fitness Instructor Certification exam and a career as a group fitness instructor.

To design and deliver cutting-edge fitness classes, ACE Certified Group Fitness Instructors (GFIs) must have a working knowledge of the human body. They also must have a thorough understanding of how to practically apply general movement principles within various class formats in order to enhance the activities participants perform in the group fitness environment and in everyday life.

In addition, proper nutrition is a vital element of overall health and a means of providing adequate fuel to perform physical activity. GFIs should be prepared to respond to participants' questions about nutrition while staying within their **scope of practice.** This chapter includes nutritional guidelines, as well as practical resources that GFIs can share with their participants.

Exercise Based on Human Movement Principles

The human body is designed to move and develops in response to stresses placed on its individual systems. Exercise enhances the movements and activities that people perform on a daily basis. Hence, the best way to functionally prepare the body is to train the same way in which it moves, favoring integration over isolation—that is, training movements, not solely muscles.

STABILITY AND MOBILITY THROUGHOUT THE KINETIC CHAIN

Movement is the result of muscle force, where actions at one body segment affect successive body segments along the **kinetic chain.** While an individual produces forces to move, the body must also tolerate the imposed forces of any external load, gravity pulling down on the body, and reactive forces pushing upward through the body. Consequently, the ability of an individual to move efficiently requires that their body maintains appropriate levels of **stability** and **mobility,** both of which are achieved by the structures of the joints (e.g., muscles, **ligaments,** and **joint capsules**) and the **neuromuscular system.**

- Joint stability is the ability to maintain or control joint movement or position.
- Joint mobility is the range of uninhibited movement around a joint or body segment.

While all joints demonstrate varying levels of stability and mobility, they tend to favor one over the other, depending on their function within the body (Figure 3-1). For example, while the lumbar spine demonstrates some mobility (approximately 10 to 15 degrees of rotation), it is generally stable, protecting the low back from injury. On the other hand, the thoracic spine is designed to be mobile to facilitate a variety of movements in the upper extremities. The scapulothoracic joint is a more stable joint formed by collective muscle action attaching the scapulae to the rib cage. This joint provides a solid platform for pulling and pushing movements at the glenohumeral joint and must tolerate the reactive forces transferred into the body during these movements. The foot is unique, as its level of stability varies during the **gait** cycle. Given its need to provide a solid platform for force production against the ground during push-off, it is stable. However, as the foot transitions from heel strike to accepting body weight, it moves into **pronation** and forfeits some stability in exchange for increased mobility to help absorb the impact forces. As the foot prepares to push off, the ankle moves back

FIGURE 3-1
Mobility and stability of the kinetic chain

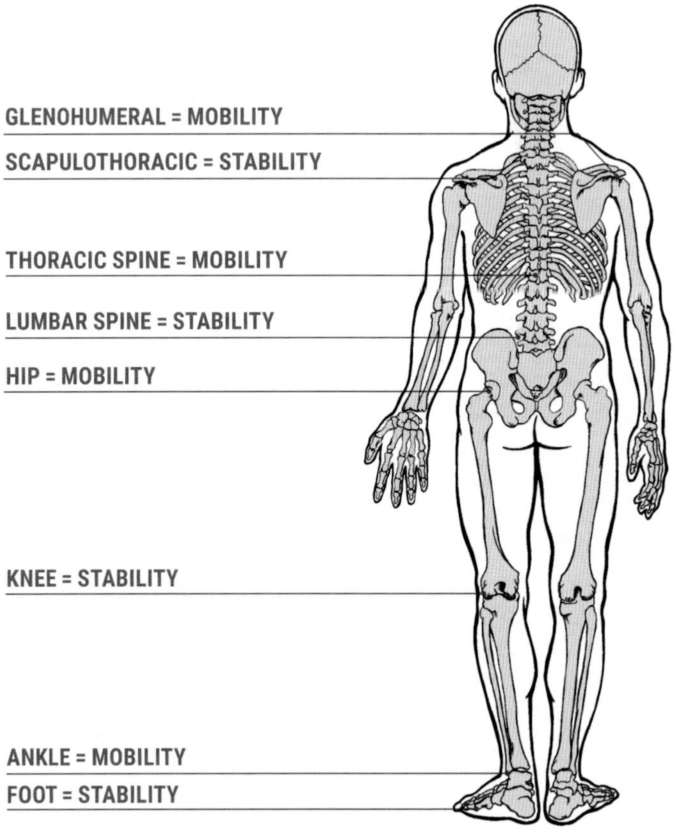

into **supination,** becoming more rigid and stable again to increase force transfer into motion. Refer to Table 3-1 for definitions of the anatomical and movement terminology used in this section.

KINETIC CHAIN MOVEMENT

Drawing on the kinetic chain principle, exercises may be described as either open-kinetic-chain exercises or closed-kinetic-chain exercises. In a closed-chain movement, the end of the chain farthest from the body is fixed, such as during a squat where the feet are fixed on the ground and the rest of the chain (i.e., ankles, knees, and hips) moves. Other examples of closed-chain exercises include push-ups and pull-ups. In an open-chain exercise, the end of the chain farthest from the body is free to move and not fixed on a surface, such as when performing a bench press. Other examples of open-chain movements include hamstrings curls, biceps curls, and shoulder presses.

The arms and legs can each be thought of as a kinetic chain, with the farthest end of each chain being the hands or the feet. If performing an upper-body exercise during which the hands are not fixed, it is an open-chain exercise. On the other hand, if the feet are fixed to a surface during a lower-body movement, this would be considered a closed-chain exercise.

Another way to understand the concept of closed- and open-chain exercises is to consider what is happening to the body when a force is applied. During closed-chain movements, a force is applied to a surface and the body moves instead of a weight or piece of equipment (e.g., push-up). In contrast, when a force is applied during an open-chain movement, not only is the part of the limb farthest from the body free to move, but the weight or piece of equipment is also moving (e.g., bench press).

Closed-chain exercises tend to emphasize compression of joints, which helps to stabilize the joints, whereas open-chain exercises tend to involve more **shearing forces** at the joints (these are forces that work in opposite directions, causing slippage). Furthermore, closed-chain exercises involve more muscles and joints than open-chain exercises, which leads to better neuromuscular coordination and overall stability at the joints.

MOVEMENT IN THREE PLANES

Human movement can be described as taking place in one of three **planes of motion**—the **sagittal plane, frontal plane,** and **transverse plane** (Figure 3-2). GFIs can better understand proper alignment and body mechanics as it applies to effective exercise program design when they have a good grasp on how the body moves in these three planes. While movements and positions are sometimes multiplanar, understanding each plane individually is critical to designing effective exercise classes, teaching movement, and recognizing safe and effective movement patterns (Table 3-1).

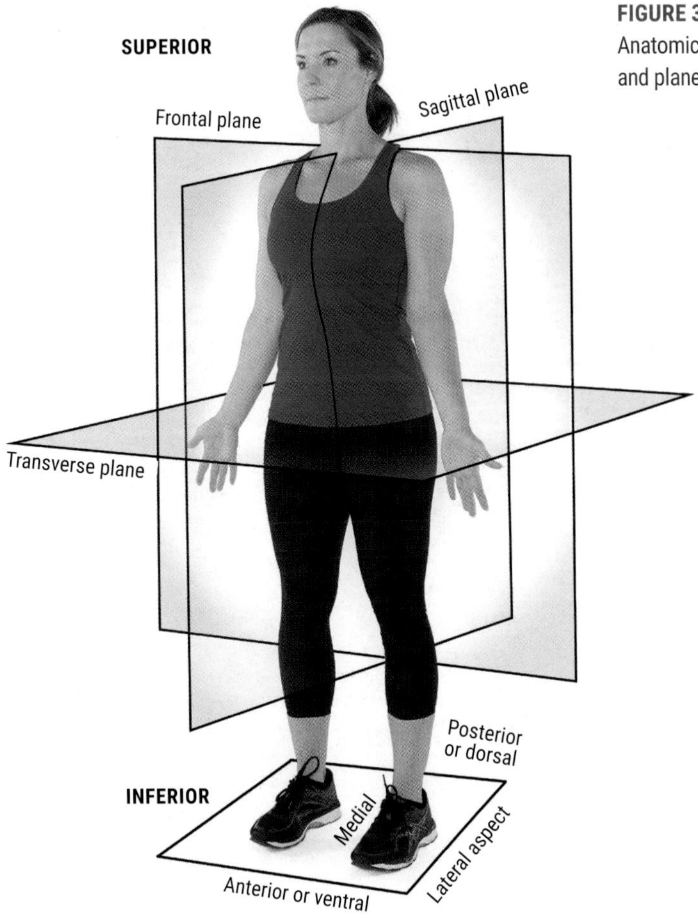

FIGURE 3-2
Anatomical position and planes of motion

TABLE 3-1

Fundamental Movements (from Anatomical Position)

Plane	Movement	Definition	Exercise Examples
Sagittal			
Separates the body into right and left halves	Flexion	Decreasing the angle between two bones	Squat, lunge, crunch, biceps curl, mambo, basic step, front kick, chair pose (yoga) (Figure 3-4)
Forward and backward movements (Figure 3-3)	Extension	Increasing the angle between two bones	
Think of standing in a doorway and moving away from the frame forward and backward.	Plantar flexion	Moving the sole of the foot downward	
	Dorsiflexion	Moving the top of the foot toward the shin	

FIGURE 3-3
Movements in the sagittal plane

TABLE 3-1 *(continued)*

Plane	Movement	Definition	Exercise Examples
Sagittal			

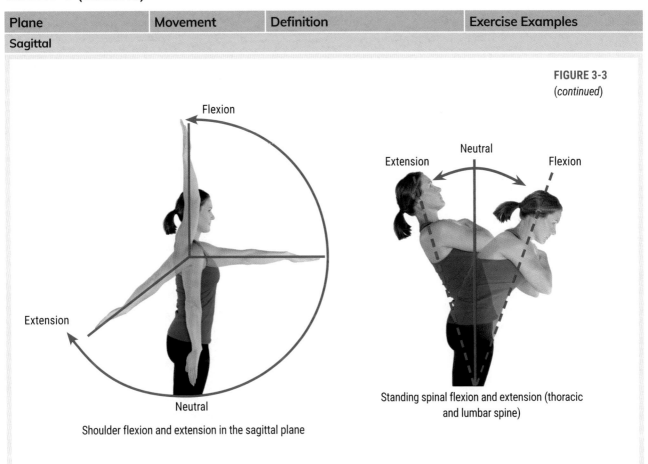

FIGURE 3-3
(continued)

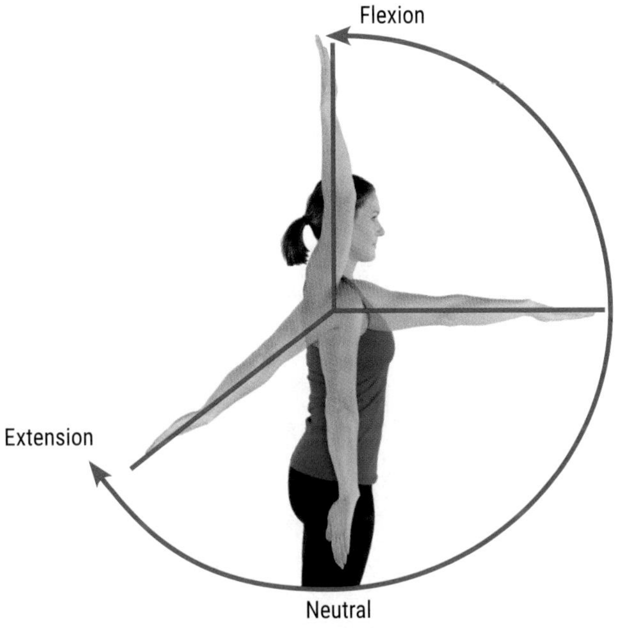

Shoulder flexion and extension in the sagittal plane

Standing spinal flexion and extension (thoracic and lumbar spine)

FIGURE 3-4
Sagittal plane movement: Chair pose

Continued on the next page

TABLE 3-1 (*continued*)

Plane	Movement	Definition	Exercise Examples
Frontal			
Separates the body into anterior and posterior halves Lateral movements (Figure 3-5) Think of moving sideways between two planes of glass while trying not to touch them.	Abduction	Motion away from the midline of the body (or body segment)	Jumping jack, lateral lunge (Figure 3-6), lateral raise, side step, side kick, over-the-top (step)
	Adduction	Motion toward the midline of the body (or body segment)	
	Lateral flexion	Bending of the neck or trunk to the left or right side	
	Elevation	Moving to a superior position (scapula)	
	Depression	Moving to an inferior position (scapula)	
	Inversion	Lifting the medial border of the foot (subtalar joint*)	
	Eversion	Lifting the lateral border of the foot (subtalar joint)	

FIGURE 3-5
Movements in the frontal plane

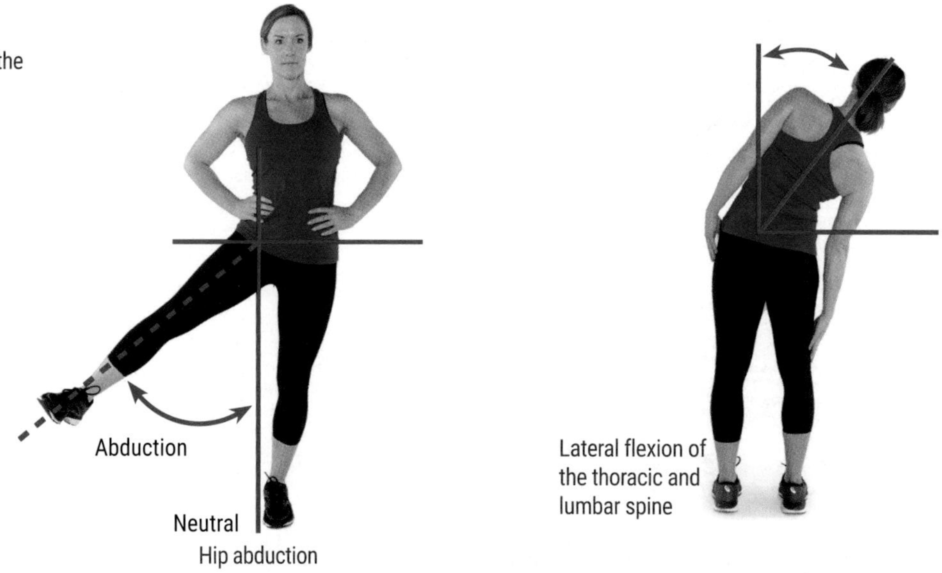

FIGURE 3-6
Frontal plane movement: Lateral lunge

*The subtalar joint is the articulation of the talus and the calcaneus and serves as the connection between the foot and the ankle.

TABLE 3-1 *(continued)*

Plane	Movement	Definition	Exercise Examples
Transverse			
Divides the body into upper and lower parts	Rotation	Inward or outward turning about the vertical axis of a bone	Supine bicycle crunch, medicine ball trunk rotation, cross punch (Figure 3-8)
Rotational or twisting movements (Figure 3-7)	Pronation (hand)	Rotating the hand and wrist medially (palm down)	
Think of rotating the rib cage in one direction while the pelvis moves in the opposite direction.	Supination (hand)	Rotating the hand and wrist laterally (palm up)	
	Horizontal flexion (adduction)	From a 90-degree horizontally abducted shoulder or hip position, the humerus or femur, respectively, is flexed (adducted) in toward the midline of the body	
	Horizontal extension (abduction)	From a 90-degree (horizontally) flexed shoulder or hip position, the humerus or femur, respectively, is extended (abducted) out away from the midline of the body	

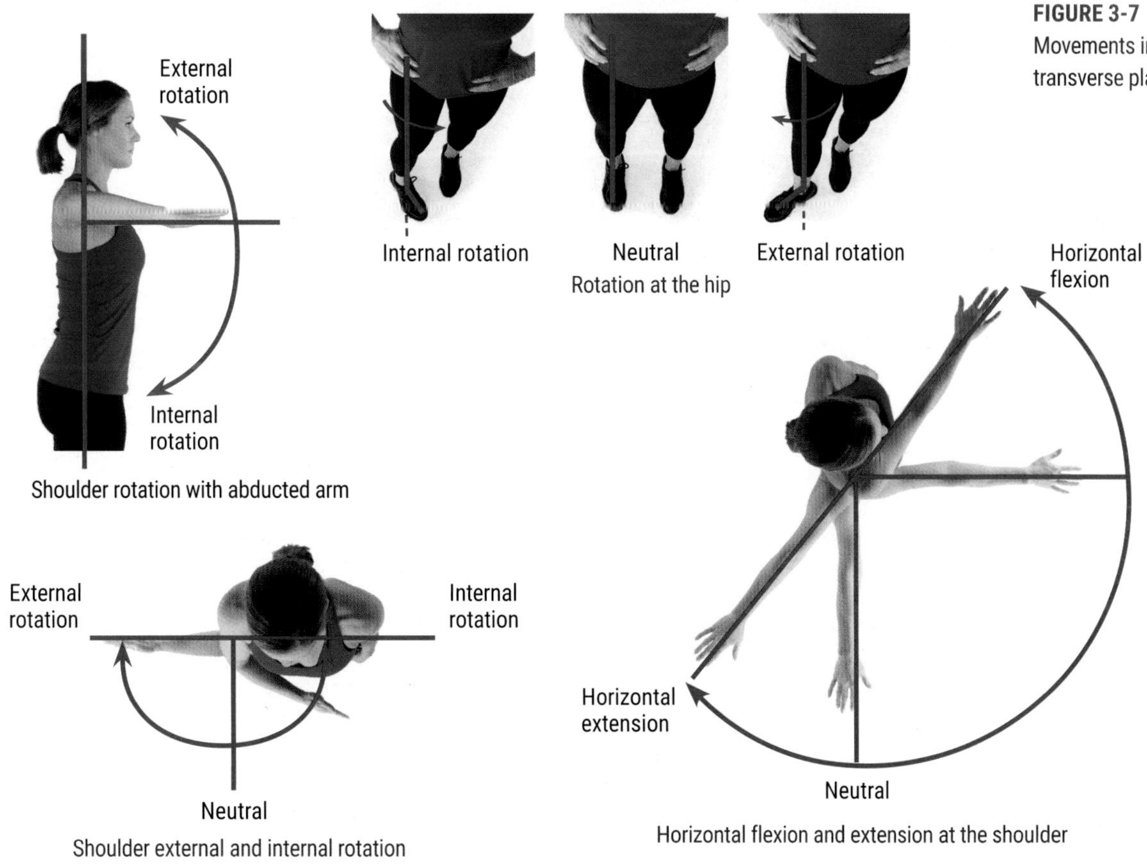

FIGURE 3-7
Movements in the transverse plane

Continued on the next page

TABLE 3-1 (*continued*)

Plane	Movement	Definition	Exercise Examples

FIGURE 3-8
Transverse plane movement: Cross punch

Plane	Movement	Definition	Exercise Examples
Multiplanar			
Combined movements that occur in multiple planes of motion (Figure 3-9) Think of combining two or more movements described above to create one, integrated whole movement.	Circumduction	"Cone" shaped movements combining flexion, extension, and adduction in sequential order	Lunge with trunk rotation (Figure 3-10), squat with a lateral raise, step touch with a front raise, triangle pose (yoga)
	Opposition	Thumb movement unique to humans and primates	
	Pronation (foot)	Combined eversion, abduction, and dorsiflexion (weight on the medial border of the foot and raising the lateral edge of the foot)	
	Supination (foot)	Combined inversion, adduction, and plantar flexion (weight on lateral border of foot and raising the medial edge of the foot)	

FIGURE 3-9
Multiplanar movement

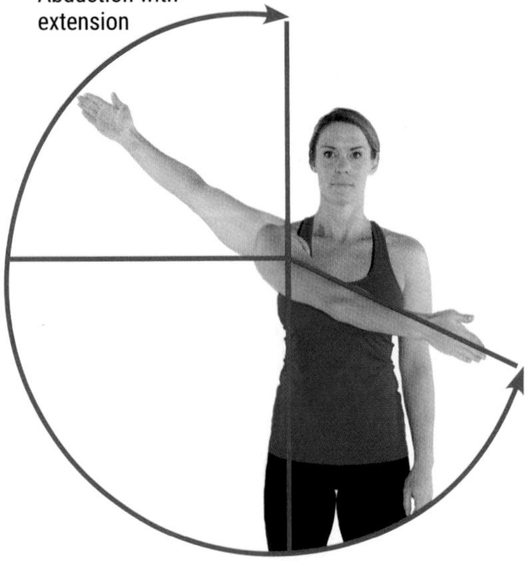

TABLE 3-1 (*continued*)

Plane	Movement	Definition	Exercise Examples

FIGURE 3-10
Multiplanar movement: Lunge with trunk rotation

THINK IT THROUGH

Multiplanar Movements

Review Table 3-1 and develop multiplanar exercises that combine movements that take place in the sagittal, frontal, and transverse planes into a single exercise. See the "multiplanar" row of that table for examples.

FIVE PRIMARY MOVEMENT PATTERNS

In addition to understanding movement in terms of the planes of motion, it is beneficial to think of exercises in terms of their application to **activities of daily living (ADL).** Specifically, activities of everyday life can be broken down and described by five primary movements (Figure 3-11):

- Bend-and-lift (raising and lowering) movements (e.g., squatting down to pick an object off of the floor, or standing up from a chair)
- Single-leg movements (e.g., walking, lunging, or climbing stairs)
- Pushing movements (e.g., pushing open a door, putting something away on a tall shelf, or propping oneself up from a side-lying position)
- Pulling movements (e.g., opening a car door)
- Rotational movements (e.g., turning to throw something away behind you or reaching across the body to buckle a seatbelt)

GFIs should incorporate a variety of exercises from each plane of motion into classes to help participants effectively train these important movements in order to enhance how they move both inside and outside of the group fitness environment.

FIGURE 3-11
Five primary movement patterns

a. Bend-and-lift movement

b. Single-leg movement

c. Pushing movement

d. Pulling movement

e. Rotational movement

THINK IT THROUGH

Activities of Daily Living

Considering the many different movements performed as part of the activities of daily living, create a list of additional daily activities and determine if they are a push, pull, single-leg, bend-and-lift, or rotational movement. Take this a step further by categorizing each movement according to the plane of motion in which it is performed.

Anatomy Overview

GFIs do not need to be expert anatomists to teach safe and effective exercise classes. However, a basic understanding of gross anatomy, specifically the structures and functions of bones and muscles, is required for successful exercise instruction.

SKELETAL SYSTEM

Becoming familiar with the names of the major bones of the body can be helpful, as a GFI can reference them when providing verbal anatomical and alignment cues (see Chapter 8). Using the correct names of anatomical structures not only makes instructors

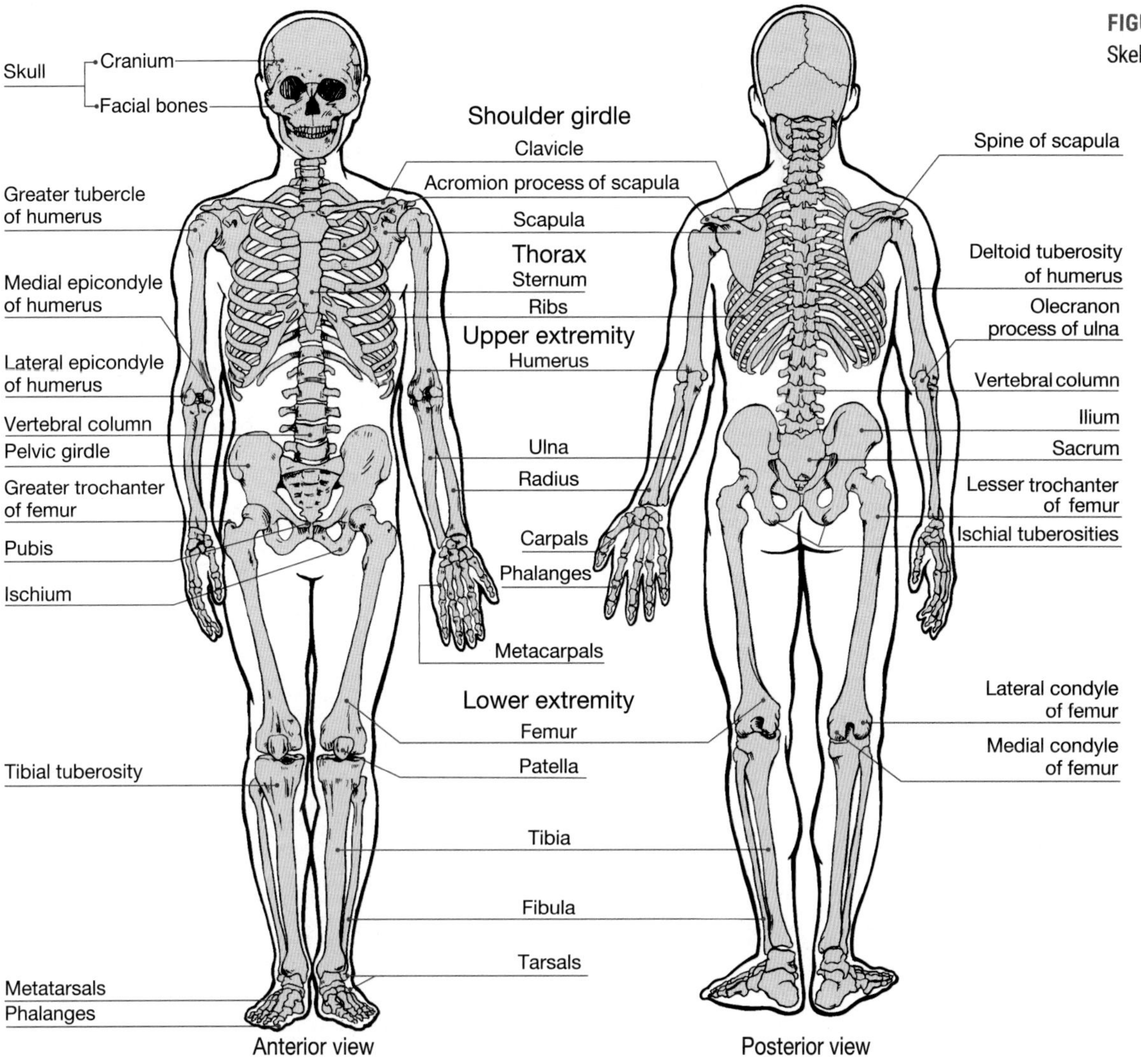

FIGURE 3-12
Skeletal system

more credible, but also helps to educate participants about their bodies. Figure 3-12 illustrates the major bones of the skeletal system, while Figure 3-13 illustrates the bones of the spine.

While not an exhaustive list, Table 3-2 presents a series of practical examples of what types of cues instructors from various disciplines can use when referencing bones.

During verbal instruction, GFIs should seek to use a variety of cues, not just anatomical, to appeal to a larger audience. Some participants may be interested in the technical aspects of anatomy and physiology during class and others may not. For example, teaching a muscle conditioning class at a university recreation center comprised largely of medical school students might prompt a GFI to use more anatomical cues, rather than lay-person language. The appropriate mix of technical and colloquial language to use may be determined by the GFI's knowledge of and confidence in using technical terms, as well as the participants' preferences to communicate using those terms.

FIGURE 3-13
Vertebral column (lateral view)

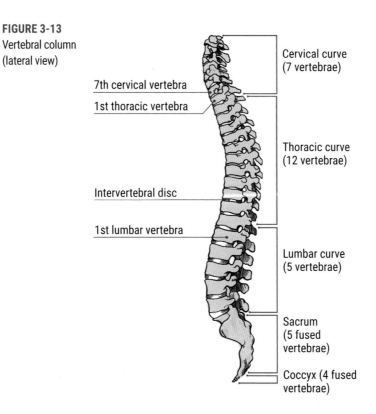

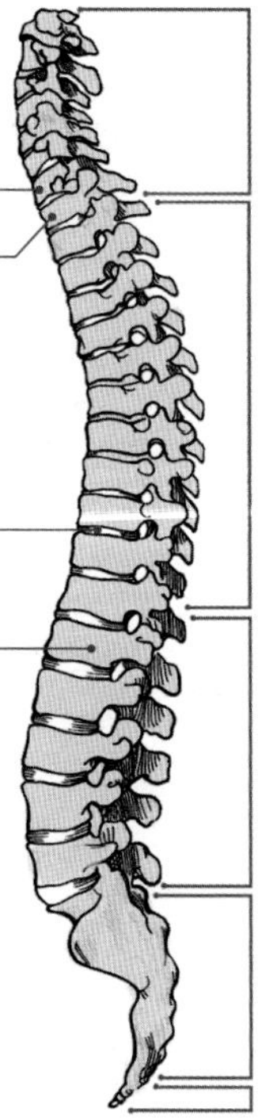

TABLE 3-2
Examples of Anatomical Cues

Discipline	Sample Cue
Cycling	"When placing the ball of your foot on the pedal, ensure that your *patella* remains aligned with your second toe as your knee flexes slightly."
Stretching	"When lying supine in the dead bug position, make sure your *tibia* and *fibula* are parallel with the floor."
Latin-based class	"Concentrate on moving your *pelvic girdle* from side to side as we do the merengue dance."
Yoga	"Find balance in boat pose by sitting on your *ischial tuberosities* instead of the *gluteus maximus* muscle."
Core conditioning	"When setting up in the side-plank position, be sure the *radius* and *ulna* are perpendicular to the spine."
Aquatic exercise	"Keep the *humerus* stable in the water while you flex and extend the elbow for those biceps curls."
Muscular conditioning	"Drop the *scapulae* back and down as you lower the *patella* toward the ground during your lunge."
Step training	"During the basic right step, make sure your *patella* is tracking to the front of the room."

MUSCULAR SYSTEM

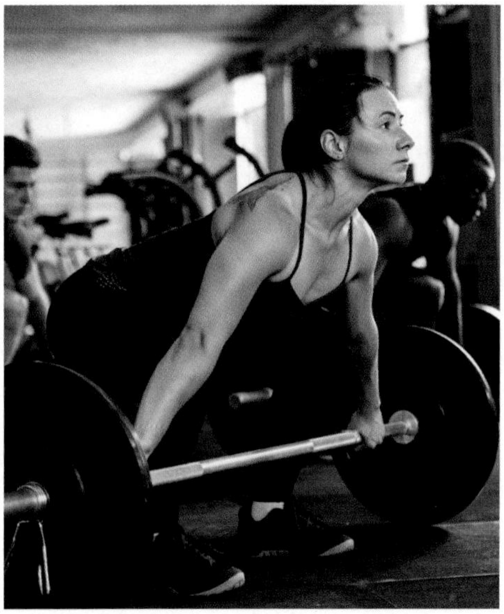

In general, GFIs should know where a muscle is located and what functions it serves. When the angle between any two bones decreases, it is called joint **flexion.** This typically occurs as a result of a muscle pulling on its attachments and shortening. Conversely, when the angle between joints increases, it is called joint **extension** and is usually the result of the muscle on the flexed side of the joint lengthening while the opposing muscle on the other side of the joint pulls and shortens. The prefix "hyper" means "excessive," so **hyperflexion** occurs when a limb or part of the body is flexed beyond its normal **range of motion (ROM).** Similarly, **hyperextension** occurs when there is movement at a joint into a position beyond the joint's normal range of extension in the anatomical position. Two important examples of these concepts occur at the elbows and knees. In indoor cycling, many participants hyperextend their elbows as they prop themselves up on the handlebars, producing tension and instability throughout the core. In muscular training, many participants hyperextend their knees when they return to the top position of a squat.

Figure 3-14 illustrates the muscular system.

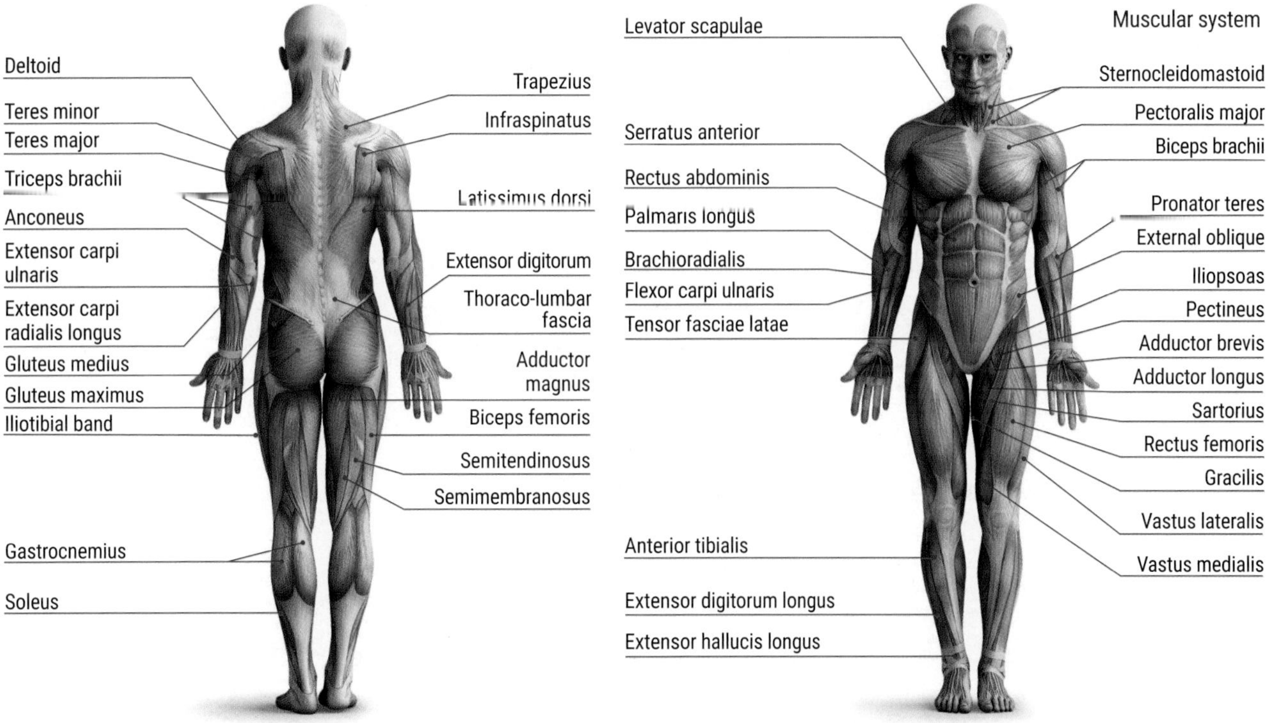

FIGURE 3-14
Muscular system

Tables 3-3 through 3-10 list the major muscles of the body, along with their primary functions and selected exercises that target each muscle.

TABLE 3-3
Major Muscles That Act at the Ankle and Foot

Muscle	Primary Function(s)	Selected Exercises
Anterior tibialis	Dorsiflexion at ankle; inversion at foot	Cycling with toe clips, resisted inversion (with dorsiflexion)
Peroneus longus	Plantar flexion at ankle; eversion at foot	Resisted eversion of foot
Peroneus brevis	Plantar flexion at ankle; eversion at foot	Resisted eversion of foot
Gastrocnemius	Plantar flexion at ankle; flexion at knee	Hill running, jumping rope, calf raises, cycling, stair climbing
Soleus	Plantar flexion at ankle	Virtually the same as for gastrocnemius; bent-knee toe raises with resistance
Posterior tibialis	Plantar flexion at ankle; inversion at foot	Resisted inversion of foot with plantar flexion
Extensor hallucis longus	Dorsiflexion and inversion of the foot; extension of the great toe	Resisted inversion with dorsiflexion
Extensor digitorum longus	Dorsiflexion and eversion of foot; extension of toes 2 through 5	Resisted eversion with dorsiflexion
Peroneus tertius	Dorsiflexion and eversion of the foot	Resisted eversion with dorsiflexion
Plantaris	Flexion of the knee; plantar flexion of the ankle	Same as gastrocnemius
Flexor hallucis longus	Flexion of the great toe; plantar flexion of the ankle; inversion of the foot	Resisted inversion with plantar flexion
Flexor digitorum longus	Flexion of toes 2 through 5; plantar flexion of the ankle; inversion of the foot	Resisted inversion with plantar flexion

TABLE 3-4
Major Muscles That Act at the Knee

Muscle	Primary Function(s)	Selected Exercises
Rectus femoris	Extension (most effective when the hip is extended)	Cycling, leg press machine, squats, vertical jumping, stair climbing, jumping rope, plyometrics
Vastus lateralis, intermedius, and medialis	Extension	Same as for rectus femoris, resisted knee extension
Biceps femoris	Flexion and external rotation	Cycling, lunging, hamstring curls
Semitendinosus	Flexion and internal rotation	Same as biceps femoris
Semimembranosus	Flexion and internal rotation	Same as biceps femoris
Gracilis	Flexion	Side-lying bottom-leg raises, with a flexed knee, resisted adduction with a flexed knee
Sartorius	Flexion and external rotation of the hip; flexion of the knee	Knee lift with hip external rotation, wide stance onto bench
Popliteus	Knee flexion; internal rotation of the lower leg to "unlock the knee"	Same as biceps femoris

TABLE 3-5

Major Muscles That Act at the Hip

Muscle	Primary Function(s)	Selected Exercises
Iliopsoas: Iliacus and psoas major and minor	Flexion and external rotation	Straight-leg sit-ups, running with knees lifted up high, leg raises, hanging knee raises
Rectus femoris	Flexion	Running, leg press, squat, jumping rope
Gluteus maximus	Extension and external rotation; Superior fibers: abduction	Cycling, plyometrics, jumping rope, squats, stair-climbing machine
Biceps femoris	Extension, abduction, and slight external rotation	Cycling, hamstring curls with knee in external rotation
Semitendinosus	Extension, adduction, and slight internal rotation	Same as biceps femoris
Semimembranosus	Extension, adduction, and slight internal rotation	Same as biceps femoris
Gluteus medius and minimus	All fibers: abduction Anterior fibers: internal rotation Posterior fibers: external rotation	Side-lying leg raises, walking, running
Adductor magnus	Adduction	Side-lying bottom-leg raises, resisted adduction
Adductor brevis and longus	Adduction	Same as for adductor magnus
Tensor fasciae latae	Flexion, abduction, and internal rotation	Hanging knee raises, side-lying leg raises, running
Sartorius	Flexion and external rotation of the hip; flexion of the knee	Knee lift with hip external rotation, wide stance onto bench
Pectineus	Flexion, adduction, and external rotation	Hanging knee raises, side-lying bottom-leg raises, resisted external rotation of the thigh
Six deep external (lateral) rotators: Piriformis, obturator internus, obturator externus, superior gemellus, inferior gemellus, and quadratus femoris	External rotation	Resisted external rotation of the thigh
Gracilis	Adduction	Side-lying bottom-leg raises, resisted adduction

TABLE 3-6

Major Muscles That Act at the Spine

Muscle	Primary Function(s)	Selected Exercises
Rectus abdominis	Flexion and lateral flexion of the trunk	Bent-knee sit-ups, partial curl-ups, pelvic tilts
External oblique	Contralateral rotation, lateral flexion, and forward flexion (both sides)	Twisting bent-knee curl-ups (rotation opposite) and curl-ups

Continued on the next page

TABLE 3-6 *(continued)*

Muscle	Primary Function(s)	Selected Exercises
Internal oblique	Ipsilateral rotation, lateral flexion, and forward flexion (both sides)	Twisting bent-knee curl-ups (rotation same side) and curl-ups
Transverse abdominis	Compresses abdomen	Prone plank, abdominal bracing
Erector spinae	Extension (both sides) and lateral flexion	Squat, dead lift, prone back extension exercises
Multifidi	Contributes to spinal stability during trunk extension, rotation, and side-bending	Bird dog

TABLE 3-7
Major Muscles That Act at the Shoulder Girdle

Muscle	Primary Function(s)	Selected Exercises
Trapezius	Upper: upward rotation and elevation of scapula Middle: upward rotation and adduction of scapula Lower: depression of scapula	Upright rows, shoulder shrugs
Levator scapulae	Elevation of scapula	Shoulder shrugs
Rhomboid major and minor	Adduction, downward rotation, and elevation of scapula	Chin-ups, supported dumbbell bent-over rows
Pectoralis minor	Stabilization, depression, downward rotation, and abduction of scapula	Push-ups, incline bench press, regular bench press, cable crossover chest flys
Serratus anterior	Stabilization, abduction, and upward rotation of scapula	Push-ups, incline bench press, pull-overs

TABLE 3-8
Major Muscles That Act at the Shoulder

Muscle	Primary Function(s)	Selected Exercises
Pectoralis major	Flexion, extension, adduction, internal rotation, and horizontal adduction	Push-ups, pull-ups, incline bench press, regular bench press, climbing a rope, all types of throwing, tennis serve
Deltoid	Entire muscle: abduction Anterior fibers: flexion, internal rotation, and horizontal adduction Posterior fibers: external rotation and horizontal abduction	Lateral raise (abduction) exercises; anterior deltoid has similar functions to the pectoralis major
Latissimus dorsi	Extension, adduction, horizontal abduction, and internal rotation	Chin-ups, rope climbing, dips on parallel bars, rowing, any exercise that involves pulling the arms downward against resistance (e.g., lat pull-downs on exercise machine)

TABLE 3-8 *(continued)*

Muscle	Primary Function(s)	Selected Exercises
Rotator cuff	Infraspinatus and teres minor: external rotation Subscapularis: internal rotation Supraspinatus: abduction All contribute to the stability of the humeral head	Exercises that involve internal and external rotation (e.g., tennis serve and throwing a baseball)
Teres major	Extension, adduction, and internal rotation	Chin-ups, seated rows, lat pull-downs, rope climbing

TABLE 3-9
Major Muscles That Act at the Elbow and Radioulnar Joints

Muscle	Primary Function(s)	Selected Exercises
Biceps brachii	Flexion at elbow; supination at forearm	Arm curls, chin-ups, rock climbing, upright rowing
Brachialis	Flexion at elbow	Same as for biceps brachii
Brachioradialis	Flexion at elbow; supination at forearm	Same as for biceps brachii
Triceps brachii	Extension at elbow; arm extension (long head)	Push-ups, dips, bench press, overhead press
Pronator teres	Flexion at elbow and pronation at forearm	Pronation of forearm with dumbbell
Pronator quadratus	Pronation at forearm	Resisted pronation
Supinator	Supination at forearm	Resisted supination

TABLE 3-10
Major Muscles That Act at the Wrist

Muscle	Primary Function(s)	Selected Exercises
Flexor carpi radialis	Flexion	Wrist curls; grip-strengthening exercises for racquet sports
Flexor carpi ulnaris	Flexion	Same as flexor carpi radialis
Extensor carpi radialis longus	Extension	"Reverse" wrist curls; racquet sports, particularly tennis
Extensor carpi ulnaris	Extension	Same as extensor carpi radialis longus
Palmaris longus	Flexion	Wrist curls

Posture and Anatomical Alignment

The term **posture** refers to the position of the body in space, or the orientation of the body to the environment in reaction to the force of gravity. Posture, which is controlled by anatomical structures, can be further defined as a position that maintains balance with maximum stability, minimal anatomical stress, and minimal energy consumption. During physical activity, the body experiences movement changes that trigger a set of interactions among the **musculoskeletal system, visual system, vestibular system, integumentary system,** and **central nervous system** that work together to control and maintain posture (Carini et al., 2017). The role of this interactive postural system is to protect the supporting structures of the body from progressive deformity and injury by keeping the body in a state of musculoskeletal balance (Carini et al., 2017). Because of the body's dynamic nature, people are constantly activating their muscles to maintain posture and balance.

When any muscle or muscle group pulls too strongly or becomes tight relative to its functional **antagonist** (i.e., the muscle that works in opposition to the contraction of the **agonist,** or **prime mover,** muscle that is responsible for the observed movement), this can create an imbalance that leads to an altered posture because of faulty anatomical alignment. Similarly, when a muscle or muscle group becomes lengthened or is too weak relative to its functional agonist, it may not pull with enough force to properly execute its intended function or have the appropriate amount of tension to maintain a neutral joint position. Each muscle must be in balance with all other muscles exerting both force and stiffness when stabilizing the body. If too much or too little force is applied, optimal balance and posture are not achieved.

A unique aspect of the trunk is how it functions as the "tunnel" through which all systems connect. The center of the core is the pelvic floor, and core training involves a general **isometric** tightening of these muscles in addition to activating the transverse abdominis, which compresses and protects the core and stabilizes the spine.

One way to describe the fitness-related function of the transverse abdominis is to think about cinching a belt around the waist, drawing in the core muscles almost as if to appear slimmer through the midsection. The technique of bracing (which involves lightly co-contracting all layers of the core musculature), performed in conjunction with pelvic floor maneuvers (such as Kegel exercises), activates the core and can enhance overall core function during classes, whether they focus on cardiorespiratory, muscular, neuromotor, or flexibility training.

Neutral posture involves an equal amount of static, isometric tension on the **lateral, anterior,** and **posterior** muscles of the core. There is a natural relationship between the ribs and the hips where there is no exaggeration in either direction. The spine has seven cervical vertebrae, 12 thoracic vertebrae, five lumbar vertebrae, five fused vertebrae called the sacrum, and four fused vertebrae at the bottom, called the coccyx (see Figure 3-13).

Because the natural, aligned spine is neither straight nor flat, instructors can use the words "natural," "neutral," "aligned," "lengthened," "tall," and "proud," instead of terms that do not adequately describe the way the vertebrae should align. While some spinal curvature is natural, deviations in the spine are common and occur when someone has an exaggeration of these curves.

FAULTY POSTURE EXAMPLES

Lordosis and Flat Back

When standing tall in an erect posture, all joints are in a neutral or extended position (Figure 3-15). When someone's pelvis tilts forward, this is called an anterior pelvic tilt

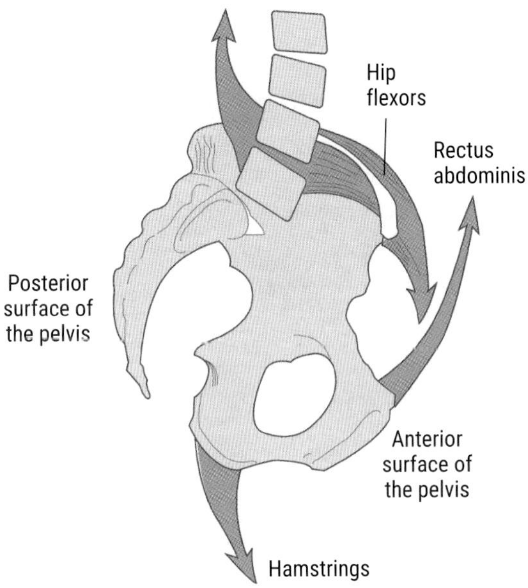

FIGURE 3-15
Muscular control of the pelvis by the abdominals and hip flexors (iliopsoas and rectus femoris) anteriorly and the spinal extensors (erector spinae) and hamstrings posteriorly

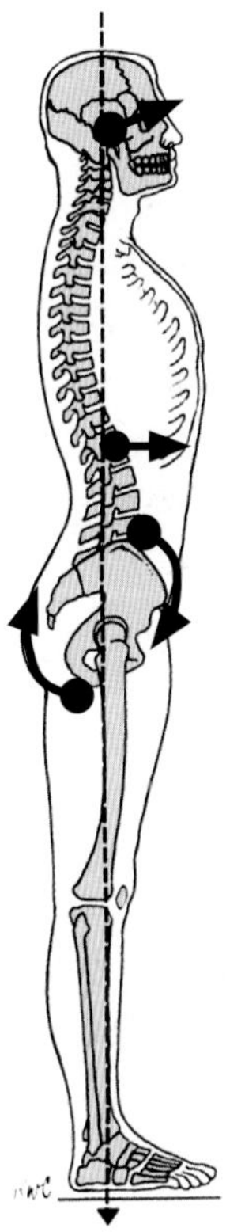

FIGURE 3-16
Lordosis

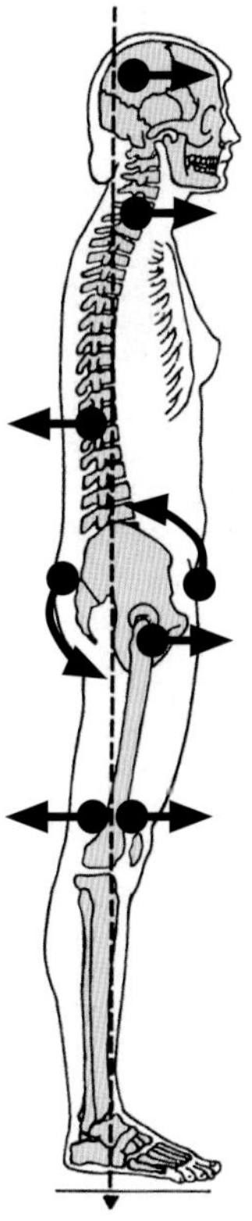

FIGURE 3-17
Flat back

and usually denotes an exaggerated lumbar curve, called **lordosis** (Figure 3-16). Often, the lumbar extensors and hip flexors are either **hypertonic,** tight, or shortened, while the hip extensors and abdominal muscles (rectus abdominis and external obliques) are in a lengthened position or are weak relative to their functional antagonists, which are the hip flexors and lumbar extensors. Individuals most likely will need to focus on strengthening their abdominal muscles (rectus abdominis and external obliques) and hip extensors (gluteus maximus and hamstrings), in addition to stretching the lumbar extensors and hip flexors (Table 3-11).

Another common postural deviation occurs when the anterior lumbar curve is decreased. This posture is called flat back (Figure 3-17). Unlike lordosis, when a person presents with a flat-back posture, the pelvis is rotated posteriorly, which causes the lumbar spine to flatten. In other words, when the pelvis rotates anteriorly, the lumbar curve increases (lordosis) and when the pelvis tilts posteriorly, the lumbar curve decreases (flat back). This change in lumbar spine alignment can be observed by standing with the back against a wall or when lying **supine** on the ground. Rotate the

TABLE 3-11
Muscle Imbalances Associated with Lordosis Posture

Facilitated/Hypertonic (Shortened)	Inhibited (Lengthened)
Hip flexors	Hip extensors
Lumbar extensors	External obliques
	Rectus abdominis

TABLE 3-12

Muscle Imbalances Associated With Flat-back Posture

Facilitated/Hypertonic (Shortened)	Inhibited (Lengthened)
Rectus abdominis	Iliacus/psoas major
Upper-back extensors	Internal obliques
Neck extensors	Lumbar extensors
Ankle plantar flexors	Neck flexors

pelvis anteriorly and feel the gap between the lumbar spine and the ground or wall increase and then rotate the pelvis posteriorly and feel the lumbar spine press against the ground or wall. Individuals with flat-back posture will most likely need to focus on strengthening their inhibited or lengthened hip flexors (iliacus and psoas major), internal obliques, lumbar extensors (erector spinae), and neck flexors, in addition to stretching their hypertonic or shortened rectus abdominis, upper-back extensors, neck extensors, and the ankle plantar flexors (Table 3-12).

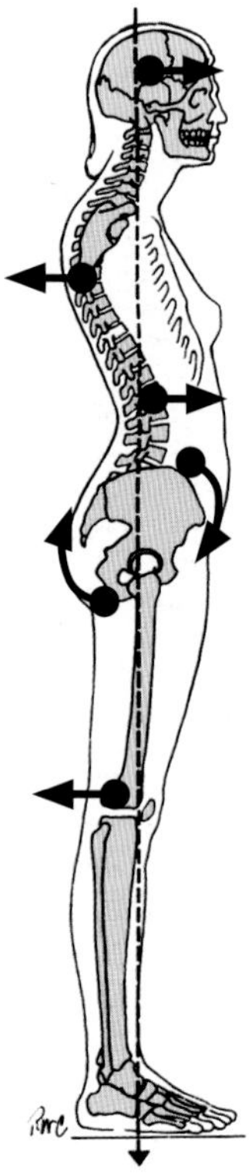

FIGURE 3-18
Kyphosis

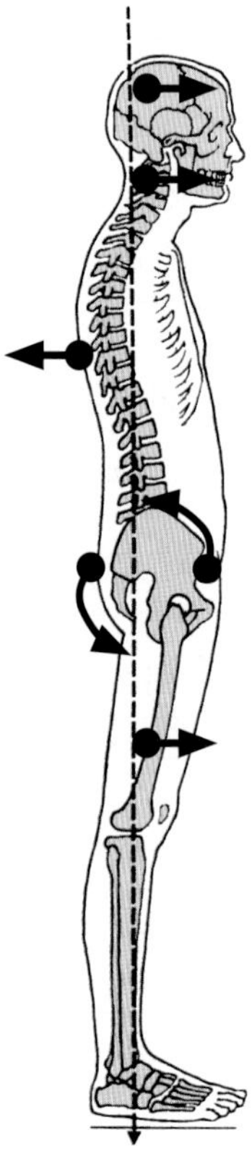

FIGURE 3-19
Sway-back posture

Kyphosis and Sway-back Posture

Excessive posterior curvature of the thoracic spine—referred to as **kyphosis** (Figure 3-18)—is marked by rounding of the upper back, often accompanied by an anterior pelvic tilt. A **sway-back** posture (Figure 3-19) also presents with an increase in the rounding of the thoracic spine along with forward-head position and rounded shoulders, but is accompanied by a posterior, or backward, pelvic tilt. In both instances, individuals will likely need to strengthen the inhibited upper-back extensors, the scapular stabilizers that pull the shoulder blades back, and the neck flexors, as well as stretch the anterior chest and shoulder muscles and neck extensors to address the increased posterior thoracic curve and forward-head position. Individuals presenting with kyphosis and lordosis (Tables 3-11 and 3-13) will need to also stretch the hip flexors and lumbar extensors and strengthen the inhibited hip extensors and abdominal muscles to address the anterior pelvic tilt. On the other hand, individuals with a sway-back posture will need to address both thoracic kyphosis and a posterior pelvic tilt by also stretching the hamstrings and abdominals and strengthening the inhibited hip flexors (iliacus/psoas major and rectus femoris) and upper-back extensors (Table 3-14). Notice that the musculature in need of stretching and strengthening is opposite for an anterior or posterior pelvic tilt. In other words, the shortened muscles in need of stretching with an anterior pelvic tilt become the inhibited or underactive muscles in need of strengthening for a posterior pelvic tilt (Table 3-15).

TABLE 3-13

Muscle Imbalances Associated with Kyphosis Posture

Facilitated/Hypertonic (Shortened)	Inhibited (Lengthened)
Anterior chest/shoulders	Upper-back extensors
Latissimus dorsi	Scapular stabilizers
Neck extensors	Neck flexors

TABLE 3-14

Muscle Imbalances Associated with Sway-back Posture

Facilitated/Hypertonic (Shortened)	Inhibited (Lengthened)
Hamstrings	Iliacus/psoas major
Upper fibers of internal obliques	Rectus femoris
Lumbar extensors	External oblique
Neck extensors	Upper-back extensors
	Neck flexors

TABLE 3-15
Pelvic Tilt

	Anterior Tilt	Posterior Tilt
Rotation	ASIS tilts downward and forward	ASIS tilts upward and backward
Muscles suspected to be tight	Hip flexors, erector spinae	Rectus abdominis, hamstrings
Muscles suspected to be lengthened	Hamstrings, rectus abdominis	Hip flexors, erector spinae
Plane of view	Sagittal	Sagittal

Note: ASIS = Anterior superior iliac spine

FIGURE 3-20
Scoliosis

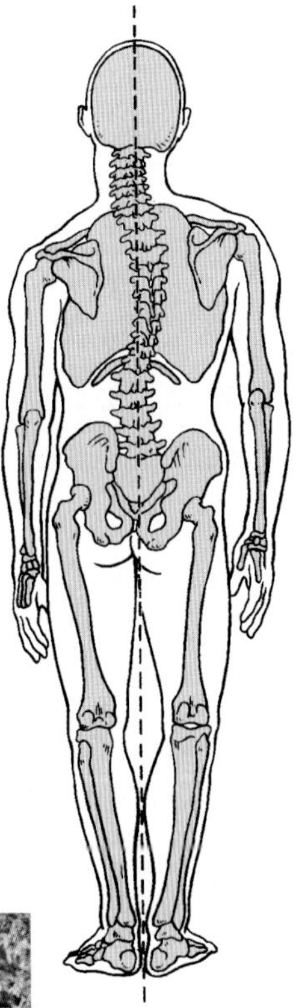

Scoliosis

When a participant's spine has a lateral curvature or an "S" shape, where the pelvis and shoulders appear uneven when looking at them from the front or back, it may be **scoliosis** (Figure 3-20). If this individual has pain and cannot assume a neutral spine position, they should be referred to an appropriate medical professional.

Muscle imbalance and postural deviations can be attributed to many factors that are both correctible and non-correctible, including the following:

- Correctible factors:
  - Repetitive movements (muscular pattern overload)
  - Awkward positions and movements (habitually poor posture)
  - Side dominance
  - Lack of joint stability
  - Lack of joint mobility
  - Imbalanced muscular-training programs
- Non-correctible factors:
  - Congenital conditions (e.g., scoliosis)
  - Some pathologies (e.g., **rheumatoid arthritis**)
  - Structural deviations (e.g., tibial or femoral **torsion,** or **femoral anteversion**)
  - Certain types of trauma (e.g., surgery, injury, or amputation)

When joints are correctly aligned, they function efficiently. This facilitates proper joint mechanics, allowing the body to generate and accept forces throughout the kinetic chain, and promotes joint stability and mobility and movement efficiency.

APPLY WHAT YOU KNOW

Feeling the Pelvic Tilt

Using your own body, experiment with tilting your pelvis anteriorly and posteriorly. Perform this activity while lying supine on the ground or with your back against a wall and notice what happens to your low back as you transition from an anterior to posterior tilt. Also, pay attention to how your back, abdominal muscles, hip flexors, and hamstrings feel as you change the position of your pelvis. To add another layer to this activity, see if you can achieve lumbar lordosis and thoracic kyphosis. Use a mirror to see how your body positioning changes as you move into a kyphotic and lordotic posture. Figures 3-21 and 3-22 illustrate neutral pelvic position, as well as an anterior and posterior pelvic tilt.

FIGURE 3-21
Anterior and posterior tilting of the pelvis—sagittal (side) view

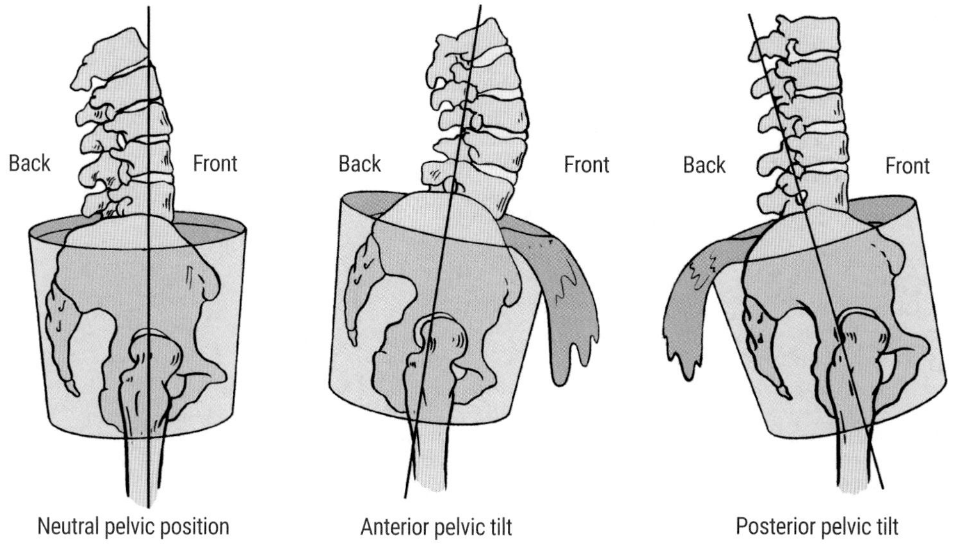

FIGURE 3-22
Alignment of the anterior superior iliac spine (ASIS) and pubic bone

Source: LifeART image copyright 2008 Wolters Kluwer Health, Inc., Lippincott Williams & Wilkins. All rights reserved.

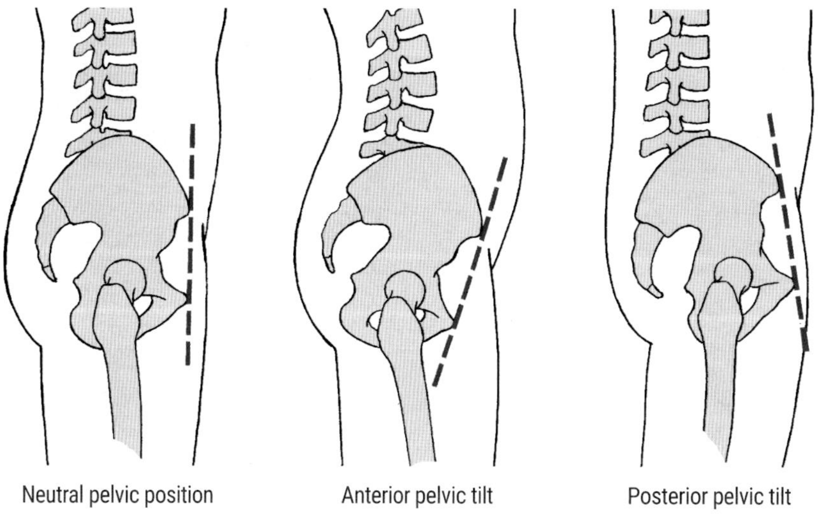

APPLY WHAT YOU KNOW

Cueing for Postural Alignment during Common Body Positions

The most practical way to apply the structural concepts of anatomy is to relate them to how the body moves and functions. GFIs must have an understanding of what neutral position of the spine and pelvis both look and feel like in a variety of positions.

Instructors must also understand what the extremities, or **distal** body parts, both look and feel like. Figures 3-23 through 3-32 present names and cues for each of the major positions of the body. Pictured are common movements from a variety of group exercise disciplines to illustrate some common exercises and a neutral spine in each position.

FIGURE 3-23
Bilateral standing

Ankles under soft knees, under neutral hips; abdominals engaged; shoulders back and down and eyes forward with chin down

FIGURE 3-24
Unilateral standing

Ankles under soft knees, under neutral hips; abdominals engaged; shoulders back and down and eyes forward with chin down

FIGURE 3-25
Kneeling (high or low)

Knees under hips, abdominals engaged; shoulders back and down; neutral spine, head, and hips

FIGURE 3-26
Quadruped (hands-and-knees position)

Palms under gently flexed elbows below shoulders; knees under hips, neutral spine, head, and hips; feet pointing in the same direction; fingers pointing forward

FIGURE 3-27
Plank

Palms under gently flexed elbows under shoulders, with fingers pointing forward (for plank or triceps push-ups) or toward each other (for triangle push-ups); neutral spine, head, and hips; feet pointing in the same direction

FIGURE 3-28
Prone (lying on stomach)

Fix the gaze on the ground slightly ahead; feet pointing in the same direction

FIGURE 3-29
Side bridge, side lying

Neutral spine and head; supported on elbow or hand

FIGURE 3-30
Supine (lying on back)

Neutral spine, head, and hips; often at least one knee flexed to support the spine

FIGURE 3-31
Reverse plank

Neutral spine; short- or long-lever legs; palms or forearms on floor with fingers spread and pointing toward feet

FIGURE 3-32
Seated

Neutral spine; knees flexed or extended; this includes indoor cycling

Nutritional Guidelines

In addition to understanding how the body moves, it is important for GFIs to understand how to fuel the body for physical activity and to achieve health-related goals. Many participants aspire to improve their fitness and optimize their health, but on a day-to-day basis struggle to maintain a healthful dietary pattern and commit to an exercise program. GFIs are uniquely positioned to help translate the federal government's nutrition advice into easily understood action items for individual participants and groups of participants.

ACE POSITION STATEMENT ON NUTRITION SCOPE OF PRACTICE FOR EXERCISE PROFESSIONALS AND HEALTH COACHES

It is the position of the American Council on Exercise (ACE) that exercise professionals and health coaches not only can but should share general nonmedical nutrition information with their clients/participants.

In the current climate of an epidemic of **obesity,** poor nutrition, and physical inactivity, paired with a multibillion dollar diet industry and a strong interest among the general public in improving eating habits and increasing physical activity, exercise professionals and health coaches are on the front lines in helping the public to achieve healthier lifestyles. Exercise professionals and health coaches provide an essential service to their clients/participants, the industry, and the community at large when they are able to offer credible, practical, and relevant nutrition information to clients/participants while staying within their professional scope of practice.

Ultimately, an individual exercise professional's or health coach's scope of practice as it relates to nutrition is determined by state policies and regulations, education and experience, and competencies and skills. While this implies that the nutrition-related scope of practice may vary among exercise professionals, there are certain actions that are within the scope of practice for all exercise professionals.

For example, it is within the scope of practice for all exercise professionals to share dietary advice endorsed or developed by the federal government, especially the *Dietary Guidelines for Americans* (www.dietaryguidelines.gov) and the MyPlate recommendations (www.myplate.gov).

Exercise professionals and health coaches who hold a current certification from a program with accreditation from the National Commission for Certifying Agencies (NCCA), or the International Organization for Standardization (ISO)/International Electrotechnical Commission (IEC) ("ISO/IEC 17024"), such as those provided by ACE, and those who have undertaken nutrition continuing education, should also be prepared to discuss:

- Principles of healthy nutrition and food preparation
- Food to be included in a balanced daily diet
- Essential nutrients needed by the body
- Actions of nutrients on the body
- Effects of deficiencies or excesses of nutrients
- How nutrient requirements vary through the lifecycle
- Information about nutrients contained in foods or supplements

Exercise professionals and health coaches may share this information through a variety of venues, including cooking demonstrations, recipe exchanges, development of handouts and informational packets, individual or group classes and seminars, or one-on-one encounters.

Exercise professionals and health coaches who do not feel comfortable sharing this information are strongly encouraged to undergo continuing education to further develop nutrition competency and skills and to develop relationships with **registered dietitians** or other qualified health professionals who can provide this information. It is within the exercise professional's scope of practice to distribute and disseminate information or programs that have been developed by a registered dietitian or medical doctor.

The actions that are outside the scope of practice for exercise professionals and health coaches include, but may not be limited to, the following:

- Individualized nutrition recommendations or meal planning other than that which is available through government guidelines and recommendations, or has been developed and endorsed by a registered dietitian or physician
- Nutritional assessment to determine nutritional needs and nutritional status, and to recommend nutritional intake
- Specific recommendations or programming for nutrient or nutritional intake, caloric intake, or specialty diets
- Nutritional counseling, education, or advice aimed to prevent, treat, or cure a disease or condition, or other acts that may be perceived as medical nutrition therapy
- Development, administration, evaluation, and consultation regarding nutritional care standards or the nutrition care process
- Recommending, prescribing, selling, or supplying nutritional supplements to clients/participants
- Promotion or identification of oneself as a "nutritionist" or "dietitian"

Engaging in these activities can place a client's/participant's health and safety at risk and possibly expose the exercise professional or health coach to disciplinary action and litigation. To ensure maximal client/participant safety and compliance with state policies and laws, it is essential that the exercise professional or health coach recognize when it is appropriate to refer to a registered dietitian or physician. ACE recognizes that some fitness and health clubs encourage or require their employees to sell nutritional supplements. If this is a condition of employment, ACE suggests that exercise professionals and health coaches:

- Obtain complete scientific understanding regarding the safety and efficacy of the supplement from qualified healthcare professionals and/or credible resources. Note: Generally, the Office of Dietary Supplements (ods.od.nih.gov), the National Center for Complementary and Alternative Medicine (nccam.nih.gov), and the Food and Drug Administration (FDA.gov) are reliable places to go to examine the validity of the claims as well as risks and benefits associated with taking a particular supplement. Since the sites are from trusted resources and in the public domain, exercise professionals and health coaches can freely distribute and share the information contained on these sites.

- Stay up to date on the legal and/or regulatory issues related to the use of the supplement and its individual ingredients.
- Obtain adequate insurance coverage should a problem arise.

This content is based on the 2020-2025 *Dietary Guidelines for Americans.* Please visit www.ACEfitness.org/Industry-Guidelines to confirm that this is the latest edition. If a newer set of guidelines is available, exam candidates should study that version to ensure they are up to date with the latest industry guidelines.

DIETARY GUIDELINES FOR AMERICANS

While the following sections outline the key content provided in the 2020-2025 *Dietary Guidelines for Americans* [U.S. Department of Agriculture (USDA), 2020], all GFIs should take the time to read the *Guidelines* in full and familiarize themselves with the many tools offered at www.dietaryguidelines.gov. Note that the *Guidelines* are updated every five years, so it is essential that all health and exercise professionals visit the website periodically to ensure their knowledge is up to date.

The 2020-2025 *Dietary Guidelines for Americans* offer four big-picture recommendations that are key to good nutrition, making every bite count, making healthy choices one day at a time, and making nutrient-dense choices one meal at a time. The key components of the guidelines, how they pertain to GFIs, and how this information can be best used to offer support in achieving nutrition-related goals are described here.

Key Guideline 1: Follow a Healthy Dietary Pattern at Every Life Stage

At every life stage, it is important to eat healthfully and almost everyone can benefit from making food and beverage choices that better support healthy dietary patterns. It is never too early or too late to follow a healthy dietary pattern.

The 2020-2025 *Dietary Guidelines for Americans* make a point to emphasize overall dietary patterns more so than individual nutrients, recognizing that the overall nutritional value of a person's diet is more than "the sum of its parts." A healthy dietary pattern should not be viewed as a rigid prescription, but rather as a customizable framework featuring core elements that individuals can personalize to make affordable choices that meet traditional and cultural preferences. The main components of a healthy eating pattern include:

- Vegetables of all types—dark green; red and orange; beans, peas, and lentils; starchy; and other

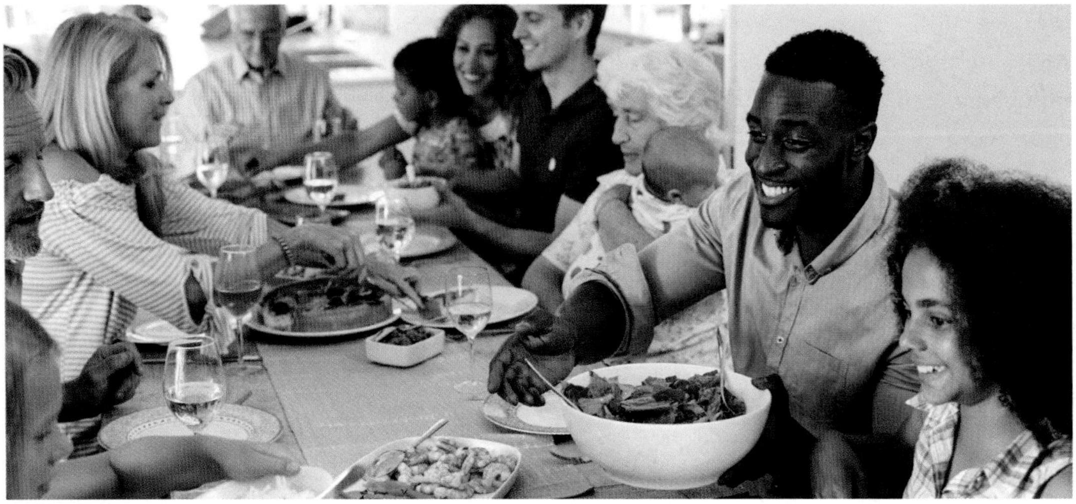

- Fruits, especially whole fruit
- Grains, at least half of which are whole grains (replacing refined grains with whole grains)
- Dairy, including fat-free or low-fat dairy, including milk, yogurt, cheese, and/or fortified soy products
- **Protein** foods, including seafood; lean meats and poultry; eggs; beans, peas, and lentils; nuts; seeds; and soy products
- Oils, including vegetable oils and oils in foods, such as seafood and nuts

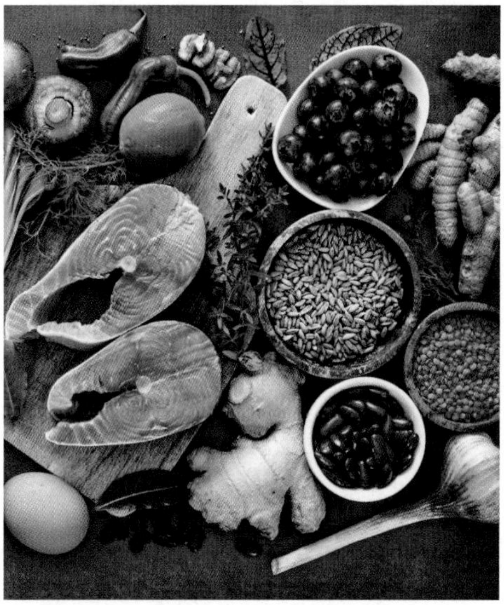

The three types of healthy dietary patterns discussed at most length in the *Dietary Guidelines* are the **Healthy U.S.-Style Dietary Pattern,** the **Healthy Mediterranean-Style Dietary Pattern,** and the **Healthy Vegetarian Dietary Pattern.** The Healthy U.S.-Style Dietary Pattern is based on the types and proportions of foods Americans typically consume, but in nutrient-dense forms and appropriate amounts. It is a framework for healthy eating that all Americans can follow.

The Healthy Mediterranean-Style Dietary Pattern is adapted from the Healthy U.S.-Style Dietary Pattern, modifying amounts recommended from some food groups to more closely reflect eating patterns that have been associated with positive health outcomes in studies of Mediterranean-style diets. The Healthy Mediterranean-Style Dietary Pattern contains more fruits and seafood and less dairy, meats, and poultry than does the Healthy U.S.-Style Dietary Pattern. The pattern is similar to the Healthy U.S.-Style Dietary Pattern in nutrient content, with the exception of providing less calcium and vitamin D.

The Healthy Vegetarian Dietary Pattern is adapted from the Healthy U.S.-Style Pattern, modifying amounts recommended from some food groups to more closely reflect eating patterns reported by self-identified **vegetarians** in the National Health and Nutrition Examination Survey (NHANES). Based on a comparison of the food choices of these vegetarians to nonvegetarians in NHANES, amounts of soy products (particularly tofu and other processed soy products); beans, peas, and lentils; nuts and seeds; and whole grains were increased, and meat, poultry, and seafood were eliminated (USDA, 2020). Dairy and eggs were included because they were consumed by the majority of these vegetarians. This pattern can be **vegan** if all dairy choices are comprised of fortified soy beverages (soy milk) or other plant-based dairy substitutes. This pattern is similar in meeting nutrient standards to the Healthy U.S.-Style Dietary Pattern, but somewhat higher in calcium and **fiber** and lower in vitamin D.

Each of these patterns provides notable health benefits and can be consumed at varying calorie levels based on individual needs. They can also be adapted to meet cultural and personal preferences. In fact, moderate to strong evidence shows that these healthy dietary patterns are associated with reduced risk of chronic diseases such as

cardiovascular disease, type 2 diabetes, obesity, and some cancers (USDA, 2020). In all, the most important components of a healthy dietary pattern include high intakes of vegetables and fruits and low intakes of processed meats and poultry, sugar-sweetened beverages (e.g., soda), and refined grains (e.g., processed "junk food" like chips).

Key Guideline 2: Customize and Enjoy Food and Beverage Choices to Reflect Personal Preferences, Cultural Traditions, and Budgetary Considerations

Following a healthy dietary pattern should be enjoyable at all life stages and across all ages, racial and ethnic backgrounds, and socioeconomic statuses.

The *Dietary Guidelines* provide a framework intended to be personalized to meet individual, household, and federal program participants' preferences, in addition to the foodways of the diverse cultures in the United States. Recommendations are made at the food-group level to avoid being prescriptive and to allow people to "make it their own" by selecting the meals, beverages, snacks, and healthy foods they prefer and that are specific to their needs.

- *Begin with personal preferences:* From a young age, it is important to expose children to different types of food to develop an interest in, and willingness to eat, a variety of foods. Progressing through each life stage, it is important to ensure that individual and family preferences—in nutrient-dense forms—are built into everyday choices to establish and maintain a healthy dietary pattern.
- *Include cultural traditions:* To help communities across the country to eat and enjoy a healthy dietary pattern, it is important to customize the dietary guidelines framework to respect specific traditions and cultures.
- *Be mindful of budget considerations:* Eating healthfully does not have to be expensive, as a healthy dietary pattern can be affordable and fit within individual or family budgetary constraints. Employing a wide range of strategies, including using a variety of fresh, frozen, dried, and canned options; considering seasonal and regional food availability; and planning ahead, can make it possible to follow a healthy dietary pattern that fits within any budget.

Key Guideline 3: Focus on Meeting Food Group Needs with Nutrient-dense Foods and Beverages, and Stay within Calorie Limits

Adhere to a dietary pattern that meets the recommendations for vegetables, fruits, grains, dairy, oils, and protein foods consumed at an appropriate calorie level with limited amounts of added sugars, saturated fats, and sodium. Cut back on foods and beverages higher in these components to amounts that fit within healthy dietary patterns.

The *Dietary Guidelines* urge Americans to meet nutritional needs by consuming nutrient-dense foods and beverages, which provide **minerals, vitamins,** and health-promoting elements with no or little added sugars, sodium, or **saturated fat,** while also staying within daily calorie limits.

Key Guideline 4: Limit Foods and Beverages Higher in Added Sugars, Saturated Fat, and Sodium, and Limit Alcoholic Beverages

Choose nutrient-dense foods and beverages across and within all food groups in place of less healthy choices. Consider cultural and personal preferences to make these shifts easier to accomplish and maintain.

While the *Dietary Guidelines* advocate an overall healthy and balanced dietary pattern that is low in added sugars, saturated fat, and sodium, the reality is that most Americans eat nothing like the eating patterns recommended by the *Dietary Guidelines*. By making shifts in dietary patterns, Americans can achieve and maintain a healthy body weight, meet nutrient needs, and decrease the risk of chronic disease by making healthy choices one day at a time.

FOOD COMPONENTS AND FOODS TO REDUCE

- *Sodium:* Limit to <2,300 mg per day.
- *Saturated fatty acids:* <10% of calories per day. Replace saturated fats with **monounsaturated fat** and **polyunsaturated fat,** such as those found in certain oils extracted from plants (e.g., olive, peanut, and soybean oils).
- *Trans fat:* Aim to keep intake as low as possible by limiting foods with **trans fats,** partially hydrogenated oil, and other saturated fats.
- *Added sugars:* Limit to <10% of total caloric intake.
- *Refined grains:* Limit consumption, especially from foods that contain solid fats, added sugars, and sodium.

- *Alcohol:* Drinking less is better for health than drinking more. If consumed, limit to one drink or less per day for women and two drinks or less per day for men.

FOOD COMPONENTS AND NUTRIENTS TO INCREASE

- *Vegetables and fruits:* Vegetables and fruits are high in vitamins, minerals, and fiber while being low in calories. People should eat a variety of whole fruits, as well as a variety of vegetables from all subgroups: dark green; red and orange; beans, peas, and lentils; starchy; and other.
- *Whole grains:* Whole grains are naturally rich in nutrients, including iron, magnesium, selenium, B vitamins, and dietary fiber. At least half of grains consumed should be whole grains.
- *Dairy and fortified soy alternatives:* While not necessary to meet nutrient needs, dairy and fortified soy alternatives contain many nutrients, including calcium, vitamin D, and potassium. People should choose fat-free or low-fat dairy products.
- *Seafood, nuts, and seeds:* These foods are high in protein, B vitamins, vitamin E, iron, zinc, magnesium, and healthy oils. Seafood is particularly high in **omega-3 fatty acids.** People should eat a variety of protein foods, including seafood, lean meats and poultry, eggs, legumes, nuts, seeds, and soy products.
- *Dietary fiber:* Dietary fiber increases feelings of fullness, promotes normal bowel function, and may help decrease the risk of cardiovascular disease, obesity, and type 2 diabetes.
- *Vitamins and minerals:*
  - Potassium
  - Calcium
  - Vitamin D
  - Iron
  - Folate
  - Vitamin B12

The GFI could target any or all of these areas as opportunities for positive nutrition changes when working with participants.

MYPLATE

One tool that the federal government employs in an effort to translate recommendations into action is an icon representing a healthy eating plan (Figure 3-33).

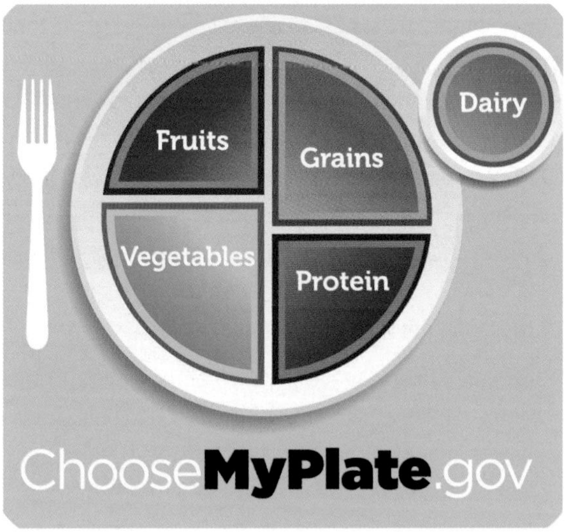

FIGURE 3-33
MyPlate graphic

Based on the *Dietary Guidelines*, MyPlate is an interactive online tool (www.myplate.gov). MyPlate simplifies the government's nutrition messages into an easily understood and implemented graphic—a dinner plate divided into four sections: fruits, vegetables, protein, and grains accompanied by a glass of 1% (low-fat) or non-fat milk. The goal is to influence Americans to eat a more balanced dietary pattern by encouraging people to make their plate 50% fruits and vegetables. Furthermore, a GFI can search the MyPlate website to find free downloadable materials to help facilitate the nutrition education process with their participants. Overall, MyPlate encourages people to do the following:

- Balance calories from an energy intake vs. energy output perspective.
- Enjoy food, but eat fewer calories.
- Eat more vegetables, fruits, whole grains, and fat-free or 1% milk dairy products for adequate potassium, calcium, vitamin D, and fiber.
- Make half their plate fruits and vegetables.
- Switch to fat-free or low-fat (1%) milk.
- Make at least half their grains whole grains.
- Eat fewer foods high in solid (typically saturated and trans) fat, added sugars, and salt.
- Compare sodium in foods and then choose the lower-sodium versions.
- Drink water instead of sugary drinks to help cut sugar and unnecessary calories.

LEGAL CONSIDERATIONS

Nutrition, Language, and Scope of Practice

Mark S. Nagel, EdD, Professor, Sport and Entertainment Management Department, University of South Carolina

One of the most important considerations for any health coach or exercise professional is to know their professional qualifications and how they impact their interactions with participants. To become certified, a GFI must understand and demonstrate the ability to convey proper exercise techniques, for example. However, though GFIs have knowledge and experience in a variety of areas, they may be limited in their understanding of many elements of health, particularly nutrition and advanced medicine. Because of these limitations, GFIs must be mindful of the language they utilize when advising participants in areas where they are not professionally certified or licensed. For example, many states permit only a licensed doctor to provide exercise "prescriptions," so GFIs should never use that word when discussing potential exercise "programs." Further, physical therapists help patients improve movement and manage pain through "rehabilitation" and "treatment." GFIs could potentially overstep their scope of practice if they utilized those terms when helping participants pursue their exercise goals.

Nutrition is an area of particular concern, as the proliferation of "new diets" continues unabated in modern society. Given the potentially close relationship between nutrition and health, it is common for participants to ask GFIs for their opinions about specific foods and supplements. Unless the GFI retains a degree or certification in nutrition, answering those questions opens areas of potential concern. Specific nutrition advice beyond that presented in accepted guidelines like the *Dietary Guidelines* and MyPlate can be given only by registered dietitians and/or doctors who have full access to a person's medical history. A GFI does not have expertise regarding the impact of certain foods or supplements upon a person's body. For this reason, questions about products to ingest should be answered with a statement that the GFI is not qualified to answer those questions and the participant should seek the assistance of a qualified professional to design an optimal dietary plan. Informing a participant that proper diet is a key to good health is a wise idea, but providing specific details beyond the scope of practice of a GFI presents not only health dangers, but also financial dangers in the form of lawsuits for unlicensed advice.

GFIs should resist the urge to even speculate about the benefits of certain foods, vitamins, minerals, or supplements, as the participant may take the GFI literally. For example, a simple comment such as, "consuming bananas is a good idea because they are high in potassium," could be misconstrued by a participant as meaning that they should be eating an extreme number of bananas a day, which could cause harm for a variety of reasons. GFIs might also tell a participant about their own food or supplement intake to the detriment of the participant. Just because a GFI is taking a supplement does not mean that every participant, or even any participant, should ingest that same substance. The discussion of supplements can become particularly concerning when a GFI works at a location that sells exercise-enhancing products, as the ingredients in each supplement can have a wide range of effects on an individual, given their underlying health conditions. A prominent lawsuit was settled for $4 million after a personal trainer advised a client to take a supplement that contained a substance that mixed badly with another medication that the client was taking for hypertension. The client unfortunately died as a direct result of the supplement (Capati v. Crunch Fitness, 2002).

Staying within scope of practice is vital for GFIs, which is why understanding the proper terminology when speaking with participants is essential. The difference between "designing classes" and "prescribing exercise" or between providing "nutrition advice" and "meal planning" may seem trivial, but that difference in terminology can help GFIs stay within their defined scope of practice and help protect them from legal liability.

ACE MOVER™ METHOD

What Should I Be Eating after Class?

One day after a **high-intensity interval training (HIIT)** class, a participant who just finished the workout approaches you to see if you have a few minutes to talk. You regularly build time for communicating with class participants both before and after classes into your schedule and you let the participant know that you would be glad to speak with them. After you find a quiet place to talk, they let you know that they are curious to learn more about what they should be eating after completing an intense workout. This participant has been attending your classes twice per week for the past two months and is interested in ensuring that they are eating properly to support their goal of becoming more physically active.

Speaking with class participants about nutrition-related topics can sometimes feel intimidating when considering how to have a meaningful conversation while also staying within your defined scope of practice. However, conversations such as this one can be mutually fulfilling for both the participant and GFI, as they are opportunities to build **rapport** through effective communication. Here is an example of how the ACE ABC Approach™ may be applied in this scenario.

ACE ABC APPROACH™

Ask: Asking powerful **open-ended questions** to start this conversation will help you find out more about what the participant is wanting to achieve by becoming more physically active. This also creates an opportunity to find out what additional information may be needed by the participant to achieve their goals.

GFI: Thank you for attending my class today and for taking the time to stay afterward to meet with me. You mentioned wanting to discuss what you should be eating after class. What are you hoping to achieve by eating more healthfully?

Participant: I'm enjoying the classes that you offer and find the duration and intensity of the class to be just right. Over the years, I have become less and less active and even reached a point where I would go weeks at a time without doing any physical activity. One morning, about three months ago, I woke up and was feeling like something had to change. I began moving more and sitting less and, for the past two months, have attended your classes twice per week. Today, I wanted to talk to you about what I should be eating after class. On most days after class, I don't eat or drink anything until I have my next meal at dinnertime. Because this is a lunch-time exercise class, this means I'm going many hours without food, and I often feel a lack of energy for the rest of the day. I also am trying to make better food choices, so I'm hoping we can discuss some ideas for post-workout nutrition.

GFI: Becoming more active, having more energy after exercise, and being mindful of the foods you eat are priorities for you. What is your current understanding of the role nutrition plays in leading an active lifestyle that includes regular exercise and physical activity?

Participant: I would say that I have a general understanding of the role nutrition plays. I understand that the food choices I make impact my weight, my energy levels, my performance, and my attitude. I know that my body uses energy from food to fuel my activities and that it is important to eat a balanced diet and to refuel after being active. I'm used to eating only when I'm hungry, and I don't often feel hungry immediately following a workout. I'm not sure where to begin.

GFI: Your understanding of the role of nutrition in leading a healthy lifestyle is accurate and you explained what you know clearly. There are some additional details that you may be interested to learn. Is it OK to go over that information in more detail?

Participant: Yes, please.

GFI: One key to understanding post-exercise nutrition is to think in terms of refueling and rebuilding. **Glycogen** is your primary energy source, and it is important to replenish this energy source through **carbohydrate** consumption after exercise. It is also important to consume protein to help rebuild the muscles that were fatigued with exercise. The best post-workout meals contain mostly carbohydrate accompanied by some protein. Ideal carbohydrate consumption is about 1.5 grams/kilogram of body weight and a protein intake of about 0.25 to 0.3 grams/kilogram, or about 15 to 25 grams of protein. Calculating the exact amount is something we can work on together if you are interested, but what is most important is that you consume a combination of protein and carbohydrate as soon as you can after completing your workout. An ideal ratio is approximately 3:1—that is 3 grams of carbohydrate for every 1 gram of protein. Does all of this make sense to you?

Participant: Yes, it does. I understand that I need to consume a snack after exercise that is made up of mostly carbohydrate and some protein. I don't think I am ready or need to calculate an exact amount to consume, but I like the idea of aiming for a 3:1 ratio of carbs to protein as a target. This is helpful.

Break down barriers: Group fitness instructors can empower participants to overcome potential barriers by asking open-ended questions to learn more about previous challenges and potential obstacles that may get in the way.

GFI: You have put a lot of thought into leading a healthy lifestyle and are ready to focus on your post-workout nutrition. What obstacles do you think may get in the way of eating more healthfully?

Participant: That's a good question. This is not my first time trying to improve my diet and it has always been a challenge. Currently, I think deciding on the foods to bring with me to the gym ahead of time will be important and, of course, budgeting for healthier foods will also be important. I guess planning ahead and money are two potential obstacles.

GFI: Deciding on what to eat, planning, and finding budget-friendly food options are important to you. What do you think could help you to achieve this goal of eating a healthy snack after your workout?

Participant: I think having some examples of nutritious snacks would be helpful, and perhaps a few resources I could use to find meal ideas for my budget would help me to be successful.

GFI: Having some examples of foods and resources will be helpful. Is it OK with you if I provide a few sample meal and snack options and a helpful resource?

Participant: Of course.

The GFI provides a handout with the following information:

Sample meals and snacks:

Snack 1: In the first several minutes after exercise, consume 16 oz of Gatorade or other sports drink, a power gel such as a Clif Shot or GU, and a medium banana. This quickly begins to replenish muscle carbohydrate stores. Carbohydrates: 73 g; Protein: 1 g; Calories: 290

Snack 2: After cooling down and showering, grab another quick snack such as 12 oz of orange juice and ¼ cup of raisins. Carbohydrates: 70 g; Protein 3 g; Calories: 295

Small meal appetizer: Enjoy a spinach salad with tomatoes, chickpeas, green beans, and tuna and a whole-grain baguette. Carbohydrates: 70 g; Protein: 37 g; Calories: 489

Small meal main course: Replenish with whole-grain pasta with diced tomatoes. Carbohydrates: 67 g; Protein: 2 g; Calories: 292

Dessert: After allowing ample time for the day's snacks and meals to digest, finish your refueling program with one cup of frozen yogurt and berries. Carbohydrates: 61 g; Protein: 8 g; Calories: 280

GFI: When it comes to helpful resources, you may enjoy using myplate.gov. This resource contains a variety of easy-to-understand information that you can begin applying right away. One section you may be especially interested in can be found in the Eat Healthy section. It is called Healthy Eating on a Budget. Does this information make sense to you?

Participant: This is great information and I appreciate the ideas you have shared with me!

Collaborate: Working together with the participant on goals and solutions is the next step and allows the participant to decide how they would like to move forward.

GFI: Based on your experience, you understand that making nutrition changes can be challenging and we have discussed a lot of information. Being as specific as possible, what will you do to move forward?

Participant: This week, I will visit myplate.gov and choose a snack to try and then buy the necessary ingredients. Starting next week, I will bring one snack with me to eat following the HIIT class. This seems reasonable to me and like something I can do.

GFI: Great! I look forward to seeing you in class next week and hearing about how things are going with your exercise and nutrition.

This interaction is an example of how a GFI can use the ACE ABC Approach to connect with class participants in a meaningful way that builds rapport, encourages **self-efficacy,** and empowers individuals to use their own expertise to set realistic goals. In this scenario, the GFI asked for permission before sharing relevant information, and then followed up by making sure the participant understood what was shared. This strategy is known as **elicit-provide-elicit,** and it is a participant-centered approach to sharing information. Ultimately, the participant arrives at a realistic goal and the ACE ABC Approach allows them to decide on their next steps.

ACE UNIVERSITY

If your study program includes ACE University, visit www.ACEfitness.org/MyACE and log in to your My ACE Account to take full advantage of the ACE Group Fitness Instructor Study Program and online guided study experience.

A variety of media to support and expand on the material in this text is provided to facilitate learning and best prepare you for the ACE Group Fitness Instructor Certification exam and a career as a group fitness instructor.

SUMMARY

Understanding human movement, the kinetic chain, planes of motion, and the *Dietary Guidelines* provides one of the most practical approaches to exercise instruction and healthy eating available to the GFI. This chapter has provided a brief region-by-region summary of the basic anatomy and movements of the body, along with information on joint stability and mobility, posture, muscle imbalances and postural deviations, alignment, examples of how to use anatomical cues when leading group exercise, and a brief description of the key components of *the 2020-2025 Dietary Guidelines for Americans.* A GFI can draw on this information to design and implement specific exercises and make general recommendations for a healthy dietary pattern that will safely and efficiently meet the objectives of the class and accomplish the goals of their group fitness participants.

REFERENCES

Capati v. Crunch Fitness International, Inc. et al. (N.Y. App. 2002). 295 A.D.2d 181.

Carini, F. et al. (2017). Posture and posturology, anatomical and physiological profiles: Overview and current state of art. *Acta Biomedica*, 88, 1, 11–16

U.S. Department of Agriculture (2020). *2020-2025 Dietary Guidelines for Americans* (9th ed.) www.dietaryguidelines.gov

SUGGESTED READINGS

American Council on Exercise (2020). *The Exercise Professional's Guide to Personal Training.* San Diego: American Council on Exercise.

Marieb, E.L. & Keller, S.M. (2022). *Essentials of Human Anatomy & Physiology* (13th ed.). New York: Pearson.

Porcari, J.P., Bryant, C.X., & Comana, F. (2015). *Exercise Physiology.* Philadelphia: F.A. Davis Company.

U.S. Department of Agriculture (2020). *2020-2025 Dietary Guidelines for Americans* (9th ed.) www.dietaryguidelines.gov

CHAPTER 4

Exercise Principles and Preparticipation Screening

CHRISTOPHER S. GAGLIARDI, MS | Scientific Education Content Manager, American Council on Exercise; ACE Certified Group Fitness Instructor, Personal Trainer, Health Coach, and Medical Exercise Specialist

IN THIS CHAPTER

LEARNING OBJECTIVES

Upon completion of this chapter, the reader will be able to:

- Describe the health- and skill-related components of physical fitness
- Explain the current cardiorespiratory, resistance, and flexibility exercise recommendations
- List and briefly explain the principles of training
- Differentiate between the components and phases of the ACE Integrated Fitness Training® Model
- Implement various methods for monitoring cardiorespiratory intensity
- Recognize warning signs of overexertion among class participants

ACE UNIVERSITY

If your study program includes ACE University, visit **www.ACEfitness.org/MyACE** and log in to your My ACE Account to take full advantage of the ACE Group Fitness Instructor Study Program and online guided study experience.

A variety of media to support and expand on the material in this text is provided to facilitate learning and best prepare you for the ACE Group Fitness Instructor Certification exam and a career as a group fitness instructor.

Physical fitness is defined as a set of measurable attributes that a person has achieved. A person who is physically fit has achieved a physiological state of well-being that allows them to successfully meet the demands of daily living and that provides the basis for sport performance. The most frequently cited components of physical fitness are divided into two groups: health-related attributes and skill-related attributes. The five health-related components of physical fitness are presented in Table 4-1. These attributes are important to overall health, as individuals with favorable measures of these components tend to enjoy an enhanced quality of life.

The skill-related components of physical fitness are presented in Table 4-2. Individuals who perform exercises to enhance these components typically have already achieved a certain level of conditioning through activities focused on improving the health-related components of physical fitness. Because these proficiencies are required for the performance of most sport activities, skill-related physical-fitness components are commonly pursued by athletes who want to maintain or improve their abilities in their chosen sport. As such, the health-related components of physical fitness are considered more important to general health than are the skill-related components, which is why research on physical fitness and health primarily focuses on the health-related components. However, focusing on the skill-related components of physical fitness is not

TABLE 4-1
Health-related Components of Physical Fitness

Component	Definition
Cardiorespiratory endurance	The ability of the circulatory and respiratory systems to supply oxygen to working muscles during sustained physical activity
Muscular endurance	The ability of a muscle to resist fatigue
Muscular strength	The ability of a muscle to exert maximal force
Flexibility	The range of motion at a joint
Body composition	The relative amounts of fat mass and fat-free mass in the body

Note: Fat mass = The actual amount of essential and non-essential fat in the body; Fat-free mass = That part of the body composition that represents everything but fat— including blood, bones, connective tissue, organs, and muscle; also called lean body mass

TABLE 4-2
Skill-related Components of Physical Fitness

Component	Definition
Agility	The ability to rapidly and accurately change the position of the body in space
Coordination	The ability to smoothly and accurately perform complex movements
Balance	The ability to maintain equilibrium while stationary or moving
Power	The rate of performing work; the product of force and velocity
Reaction time	The amount of time elapsed between the stimulus for movement and the beginning of the movement
Speed	The ability to perform a movement within a short period of time

a goal suited only for athletic populations. ACE Certified Group Fitness Instructors (GFIs) will design exercise classes for a variety of populations, and many classes will combine elements of both the health- and skill-related components of physical fitness. Some class objectives may be entirely focused on a skill such as **balance** or **reaction time** even though athletes are not the intended participants. For example, consider a class designed for individuals at risk for falls. This type of class may target both muscular conditioning and balance training, combining both health- and skill-related components of fitness.

The content in Tables 4-3 through 4-5 is based on the 11th edition of *ACSM's Guidelines for Exercise Testing and Prescription*. Please visit www.ACEfitness.org/Industry-Guidelines to confirm that this is the latest edition. If a newer set of guidelines is available, exam candidates should study that version to ensure they are up to date with the latest industry guidelines.

As the fitness industry is often driven by trends, programs are continuously being created by passionate and motivated health and exercise professionals wanting to share their knowledge and excitement with others. It is important for these programs to be created and evaluated with safety and efficacy in mind. The American College of Sports Medicine (ACSM, 2022) guidelines on exercise programming for healthy adults can serve as a template for class design (Tables 4-3 through 4-5). The guidelines include cardiorespiratory (also called aerobic or cardiovascular), resistance, and **flexibility** exercise recommendations.

Although evidence-based recommendations for cardiorespiratory, resistance, and flexibility exercise are presented separately, it is a combination of all three types of training (i.e., multicomponent training) that can best help GFIs plan for specific class goals. Beginning with a class goal or objective in mind, GFIs can adjust the amount of time focused on each component during a class to best guide participants toward achieving the desired outcome.

For example, if a GFI is designing a class intended to increase **muscular endurance,** the warm-up may include light-to-moderate intensity activities that target the specific muscle groups to be focused on during the conditioning segment, as well as an aerobic component to prepare the body for the changing physiologic demands. The conditioning

TABLE 4-3
Aerobic (Cardiovascular Endurance) Exercise Recommendations

FITT	Recommendation
Frequency	At least 3 days/week For most adults, spreading the exercise sessions across 3–5 days/week may be the most conducive strategy to reach the recommended amounts of physical activity.
Intensity	Moderate (40–59% HRR) and/or vigorous (60–89% HRR) intensity is recommended for most adults.
Time	Most adults should accumulate 30–60 minutes/day (≥150 minutes/week) of moderate-intensity exercise, 20–60 minutes/day (≥75 minutes/week) of vigorous-intensity exercise, or a combination of moderate- and vigorous-intensity exercise daily to attain the recommended targeted volumes of exercise.
Type	Aerobic exercise performed in a continuous or intermittent manner that involves major muscle groups is recommended for most adults.

Note: HRR = Heart-rate reserve

Reprinted with permission from American College of Sports Medicine (2022). *ACSM's Guidelines for Exercise Testing and Prescription* (11th ed.). Philadelphia: Wolters Kluwer.

TABLE 4-4

Resistance Training Exercise Recommendations

FITT	Recommendation
Frequency	For novices, each major muscle group should be trained at least 2 days/week.
	For experienced exercisers, frequency is secondary to training volume, thus individuals can choose a weekly frequency per muscle group based on personal preference.
Intensity	For novices, 60–70% 1-RM, performed for 8–12 repetitions are recommended to improve muscular fitness.
	For experienced exercisers, a wide range of intensities and repetitions are effective dependent on the specific muscular-fitness goals.
Type	Multijoint exercises affecting more than one muscle group and targeting agonist and antagonist muscle groups are recommended for all adults.
	Single-joint and core exercises may also be included in a resistance-training program, typically after performing multijoint exercise(s) for that particular muscle group.
	A variety of exercise equipment and/or body weight can be used to perform these exercises.

Note: 1-RM = One-repetition maximum

Reprinted with permission from American College of Sports Medicine (2022). *ACSM's Guidelines for Exercise Testing and Prescription* (11th ed.). Philadelphia: Wolters Kluwer.

TABLE 4-5

Flexibility Exercise Recommendations

FITT	Recommendation
Frequency	≥2–3 days/week with daily being most effective
Intensity	Stretch to the point of feeling tightness or slight discomfort.
Time	Holding a static stretch for 10–30 seconds is recommended for most adults.
	In older individuals, holding a stretch for 30–60 seconds may confer greater benefit.
	For proprioceptive neuromuscular facilitation (PNF) stretching, a 3–6 second light-to-moderate contraction (e.g., 20–75% of maximum voluntary contraction) followed by a 10- to 30-second assisted stretch is desirable.
Type	A series of flexibility exercises for each of the major muscle-tendon units is recommended.
	Static flexibility (i.e., active or passive), dynamic flexibility, ballistic flexibility, and PNF are each effective.

Adapted from Garber, C.E. et al. (2011). American College of Sports Medicine position stand. Quantity and quality of exercise for developing and maintaining cardiorespiratory, musculoskeletal, and neuromotor fitness in apparently healthy adults: Guidance for prescribing exercise. *Medicine & Science in Sports & Exercise*, 43, 7, 1334–1359.

Reprinted with permission from American College of Sports Medicine (2022). *ACSM's Guidelines for Exercise Testing and Prescription* (11th ed.). Philadelphia: Wolters Kluwer.

segment will emphasize muscular endurance by applying a specific number of exercises, repetitions, and sets and the cool-down may include flexibility exercises to bring about a more relaxed physiological state at the end of the class.

It is also appropriate to follow each recommendation individually. For example, a class participant may focus on cardiorespiratory exercise each morning Monday through Friday, attend a yoga class twice per week for flexibility training, and attend a strength and conditioning class three times per week. Whether combined or performed individually, it is the accumulated volume that brings about health benefits.

This content is based on recommendations from the World Health Organization and U.S. Department of Health & Human Services. Please visit www.ACEfitness.org/Industry-Guidelines to confirm that this is the latest edition of each. If a newer set of guidelines is available, exam candidates should study that version to ensure they are up to date with the latest industry guidelines.

Both the *Physical Activity Guidelines for Americans* and the *WHO Guidelines on Physical Activity and Sedentary Behavior* provide evidence-based multicomponent recommendations that include adults performing 150 to 300 minutes of moderate-intensity cardiorespiratory activity spread throughout the week and muscle-strengthening activities of at least a moderate intensity for each major muscle group on two or more days per week (World Health Organization, 2020; U.S. Department of Health & Human Services, 2018).

Another element of multicomponent exercise that is often considered when designing classes is neuromotor exercise, which combines elements of balance, proprioceptive, and **agility** training. The addition of balance training to cardiorespiratory and muscular training may improve physical function and decrease the risk of or injury from falls (ACSM, 2022; World Health Organization, 2020; U.S. Department of Health & Human Services, 2018).

GFIs can help participants reach daily and weekly physical-activity guidelines by applying the evidence-based recommendations for cardiorespiratory, muscular, and flexibility training in a variety of settings and through a wide array of class offerings.

ACE MOVER™ METHOD

Helping Participants Set Goals beyond Attending Class

Recently, a participant from your group exercise class asked if they could arrive 20 minutes early next week to discuss their current level of physical activity. This participant has been attending your dance-based class three days per week for the past six months. They were happy with the progress they were making initially but have noticed that they are no longer getting the same results. This participant is wondering if they should be doing more, what they could be doing differently, and how they might fit more activity into their daily life by decreasing sitting time.

ACE ABC APPROACH™

The following is an example of how the ACE Mover Method™ and ACE ABC Approach™ can be used to help participants explore the *Physical Activity Guidelines* and their current physical-activity levels, while empowering them to move forward with actionable steps for being more active and decreasing sitting time.

Ask: Asking powerful **open-ended questions** during this exploratory conversation can help to confirm what the participant already knows about the *Physical Activity Guidelines*, their physical-activity levels outside of class, and what they are hoping to accomplish.

GFI: Thank you for taking the time to show up early for class so that we could have some time to talk. I understand that you are wanting to talk about your current level of physical activity, if there is anything you could be doing differently, and what being more active might look like in your daily life. In your perfect vision of your future self, what would you like to see when it comes to physical activity?

Participant: What a good question! I appreciate you being open to meeting with me. When I think about the future, I want to be healthy enough to do all the things that are important to me, like travel and spend time with family. I also don't want my physical health to limit me. I've spent most of my adult life not exercising and could feel that my body was changing over the years. Once I decided to start exercising and began adhering to a consistent schedule, I started to have more energy, feel more fit, and even started to lose weight. Recently, the progress I was making has slowed down and I want to make sure I'm doing everything I can to keep my momentum moving in the right direction. In the future, I'd like to be more active but am concerned about how I might fit more activity into my daily life. In my vision for the future, I am exercising more and not spending so much time sitting around.

GFI: Thank you for sharing all this information with me. I'm curious to know more about your exercise and physical-activity levels outside of class. Also, do you already know about physical-activity recommendations?

Participant: Currently, the only exercise I'm doing is what you see when I'm in your class three days per week. Before and after class, not much physical activity is taking place. I work a job where I am seated at a desk and using a computer for eight hours a day. The days I attend class are the days when I feel best. When it comes to physical-activity recommendations, I know that exercise is recommended but I'm not familiar with any specifics. All I know is that I enjoy being active and think I should be doing more.

GFI: Is it OK with you if I share some more information about the *Physical Activity Guidelines*?

Participant: Yes, please.

GFI: You are off to a good start by exercising three days per week. And, feeling like you want to do more throughout your day aligns with a key focus of the *Physical Activity Guidelines*, which is to move more and sit less. More specifically, the guidelines include 150 to 300 minutes of moderate-intensity cardiorespiratory exercise per week and muscle-strengthening activities on at least two days per week. The main objective is spending less time engaged in **sedentary** behaviors. Does this make sense?

Participant: This makes sense and I don't have any questions about the guidelines, but I am wondering about what to do next.

Break down barriers: Ask more open-ended questions to find out what obstacles might get in the way of the participant decreasing sitting time.

GFI: You feel your best on the days you exercise, enjoy being active, and think you should be doing more. What is currently preventing you from adding more movement to your daily routine?

Participant: What's stopping me from doing more is that I'm busy with work and all the things that need my attention at home. I don't know that I can make it to the gym more than three times per week and I'm not sure I have the time to add more movement into my day.

Collaborate: Working together with the participant on goals and solutions is the next step now that they have expressed a desire to reduce sedentary behavior and overcome a barrier (lack of time).

GFI: I'm sure there was a time when it seemed like you were too busy to add one hour of exercise to your schedule three times per week and now you have maintained that goal for six months. How have you been successful with maintaining this goal?

Participant: That's a good point. There was a period where I wanted to exercise but continually talked myself out of doing it because I did not think I had the time. I think I was just not prioritizing my health. My health is a priority and once I decided to exercise on three days per week I came up with a plan and made up my mind to stick with it, no matter what.

GFI: Your health is a priority and having a plan helps you to be successful, but you can't make it to the gym more than three times per week. Time is a barrier to reaching your goal of being more active. Without going to the gym, what options do you have for moving more throughout your day?

Participant: I don't have time to take an entire hour, but I wonder if I can add small chunks of exercise into my day. If it's less than an hour, does it even count or make a difference?

GFI: Great question! Any amount of physical activity leads to health benefits, no matter the duration. Some activity is better than none and the total amount of accumulated activity during the day contributes to the health benefits of the total volume. Thinking in terms of activity "snacks" can be a helpful way to frame adding activity into your daily life. Instead of thinking about fitting in an hour for exercise, it may be helpful to think about taking activity breaks or snacks.

Participant: Activity snacks. I like that idea. Perhaps I can replace some of my food snacking throughout the day with a physical-activity snack.

GFI: Being as specific as possible, how will you move forward?

Participant: I currently have breaks built into my schedule, which I usually use for eating and checking my phone. I think I'll change the name on two of these breaks to "activity snacks" so it will serve as a reminder to be active. I think I'll take a walk for one of the breaks. You mentioned muscle-strengthening activities as being part of the *Physical*

Activity Guidelines, so I think for the second break I will do some body-weight exercises. I'd like to start doing push-ups, lunges, squats, and planks. I will have to do some research to learn more exercises, but I think I can add this to my routine twice per day.

GFI: Those are excellent ideas! I look forward to checking in with you throughout the week at class to see how you are doing with your activity snacks.

In this scenario, the participant is already making positive health-related changes by attending your class three days per week but has noticed that their fitness progress is slowing down. The participant has a desire to be more active but is challenged with overcoming the barrier of a perceived lack of time. The ACE ABC Approach can be used to identify expectations for the future, share information such as the *Physical Activity Guidelines*, and to guide participants toward any change they are wanting to make as they pursue better health.

Principles of Training

The basic training principles presented in this section apply to all forms of physical training. Successful exercise programs are the result of following established training principles from exercise science research. **Specificity, overload,** and **reversibility** are general training principles of which GFIs should have a good understanding in order to provide safe and effective fitness classes.

SPECIFICITY

The physiological changes caused by training are highly specific to the types of activities performed. This principle of training is called specificity and is also referred to as the SAID principle: specific adaptations to imposed demands. In other words, exercise is a form of stress that the body must overcome and to which it must adapt. Each mode of exercise places its own type of stress on the body. For example, traditional muscular training increases strength but has little effect on **cardiorespiratory endurance.** Furthermore, training at a specific intensity will cause a specific conditioning outcome. For example, lifting lighter loads and performing a higher number of repetitions (low-intensity muscular training) provides a training stimulus that favors muscular endurance, but not **muscular strength.** Conversely, lifting heavier loads and performing fewer repetitions (high-intensity muscular training) will result in an increase in muscular strength, but not necessarily endurance.

These low- and high-intensity weight-training examples illustrate that there is a clear relationship between intensity of exercise and duration. Namely, high-intensity exercise will be shorter in duration, whereas low-intensity exercise allows for a longer duration. The training protocol incorporated into classes also affects the energy system that is primarily used during the exercise set. For example, performing high-intensity stationary drills such as mountain climbers for 10 seconds predominantly uses the **phosphagen system** for energy, while performing ice skaters for 60 seconds relies mainly on **glycolysis** for energy (see Chapter 7).

Perhaps the most obvious aspect of training specificity involves exercising the appropriate muscles or movements to improve or prepare for a specific event or activity. Consider, for example, a class designed for new moms. For the GFI designing the class, it would be important to select exercises that target the specific challenges often encountered during the postpartum period and to prepare participants for the physical demands that go along with caring for a young child. This type of class may include exercises that focus on establishing good **posture,** low-back health, strengthening the abdominal muscles, carrying a load, and bend-and-lift movement patterns.

OVERLOAD

Another important principle of exercise is overload, which states that to improve physical fitness, the exerciser must regularly increase the demands or stress placed on the body in a timely and appropriate manner for physiological adaptations and improvement to occur. The amount of overload necessary to elicit a safe and effective training response depends on the individual's current level of conditioning, tolerance for increased training loads and volume, and program goals. A person accustomed to a sedentary lifestyle needs very little overload stimulus to bring about a training effect. For example, a person who has been ill or bedridden for an extended period of time may notice a sufficient training stimulus after walking 100 feet.

Similarly, a deconditioned individual with **overweight** may notice strength improvements after performing muscular training using only their own body weight. However, an experienced weightlifter may need to lift relatively large amounts of weight to produce an overload and stimulate a training effect. Since everyone presents with a different state of physical fitness, an individualized approach to overload must be applied for intensity, frequency, and duration. Overload that is progressed properly will allow enough time for the body to adapt, thereby improving performance. An exercise stimulus must be gradually increased over time to safely elicit continued improvements.

For muscular endurance, overload occurs when the number of repetitions is increased with a given resistance, such as by increasing from eight to 12 repetitions when doing body-weight squats. When this principle is applied to muscular strength, overload occurs when the individual is subjected to progressively heavier training loads. Even though a personalized approach is ideal for determining appropriate changes in load, GFIs can recommend a 5% increase as a general guideline for adding resistance. For example, assuming class participants are performing a particular exercise to the point of muscular fatigue with a goal of completing eight to 12 repetitions, once 12 repetitions are achieved it is advisable to add about 5% more resistance to provide a progressive overload. GFIs are often limited by equipment availability in a class setting. In such cases, participants should select the next resistance available.

APPLY WHAT YOU KNOW

Introducing the Overload Principle in a Group Setting

To guide participants to get the most out of their muscular training, it is important to be able to cue the group as a whole to introduce overload to their programs. Here is an example of how a GFI might address this during a class: "For the next portion of class, we will be completing a series of alternating lower- and upper-body exercises. For each exercise, work to complete eight to 12 repetitions while using good form. If you're stopping at 12 repetitions even though you can do more, it's time to increase your load. Try selecting the next available dumbbell size and see if you reach a point of fatigue within the eight to 12 repetition range."

REVERSIBILITY

The positive physiological effects of exercise training are reversible. The body adapts to decreases in training stimulus when exercise programs are discontinued and when inadequate training volumes and intensities are achieved. This is called the principle of reversibility. Exercise capacity diminishes relatively rapidly, and the fitness and performance improvements gained through training are lost within a few weeks to months of reduced physical-activity levels. Furthermore, complete lack of activity, such as periods of immobility due to bed rest during sickness, causes dramatic losses in strength and bone mass. The reversibility principle reinforces the importance of physical activity as a lifestyle component, rather than as a short-term process for attaining a temporary objective—in essence, "use it or lose it." Being fit as an adolescent or young adult does not provide continued benefits throughout the lifespan unless the exercise is maintained. Additionally, an exercise participant who suffers a setback and discontinues their fitness program for several months will have to start slowly and progress gradually if the exercise regimen is started again.

ACE-SPONSORED RESEARCH

Detraining

An ACE-sponsored study showed that muscular strength decreased significantly with the cessation of a 13-week muscular-training program following the ACE Integrated Fitness Training (ACE IFT®) Model (Nolan et al., 2018). In fact, after four weeks of detraining, two-thirds of the favorable muscular-strength gains achieved over the 13-week training period were lost. Detraining may not lead to a complete return to preparticipation fitness and performance levels, as some positive training adaptations, such as improved muscular strength and **power,** may be retained (Blocquiaux et al., 2020). However, the impact of detraining may be influenced by the overall duration and level of reductions to physical activity.

ACE Integrated Fitness Training Model

Fitness facilities face the mounting challenges associated with an aging and increasingly overweight population, as well as an overburdened healthcare system that is often unable to meet the need for preventive care. Health and exercise professionals, including GFIs, are seeing an influx of participants with an increasingly long list of special considerations (see Chapter 12), creating confusion as they attempt to develop group fitness classes that safely and effectively address individual needs.

To address these complex concerns, ACE created the ACE IFT Model, which provides a systematic and comprehensive approach to exercise programming to facilitate behavior change (see Chapter 2), while also improving posture, movement, flexibility, balance, core function, and cardiorespiratory and muscular fitness. While the ACE IFT Model was originally developed as a tool for personal trainers, its core concepts can be applied in the group fitness environment, as well.

The ACE IFT Model consists of two components, each of which is then divided into three phases that are named to accurately reflect the training focus of each phase (Figure 4-1). Behavior change and building and maintaining **rapport** form the foundation for success during all phases, whether the exerciser is highly motivated and enthusiastic about fitness or currently living a physically inactive lifestyle and looking to adopt more healthful habits. The primary focus of each phase of the ACE IFT Model is as follows:

- Muscular Training
  - *Functional Training:* This phase is focused on establishing, or reestablishing, postural **stability** and kinetic chain **mobility.**
  - *Movement Training:* This phase focuses on developing good movement patterns without compromising postural or joint stability.
  - *Load/Speed Training:* This phase focuses on applying external loads to movements that create a need for increased force production that results in muscular adaptations.
- Cardiorespiratory Training
  - *Base Training:* This phase focuses on developing an initial aerobic base, through positive exercise experiences, in individuals who have been insufficiently active.
  - *Fitness Training:* This phase focuses on enhancing the individual's aerobic efficiency by progressing the program through increased duration of sessions, increased frequency of sessions when possible, and the integration of more intense exercise.

FIGURE 4-1
ACE Integrated Fitness Training Model

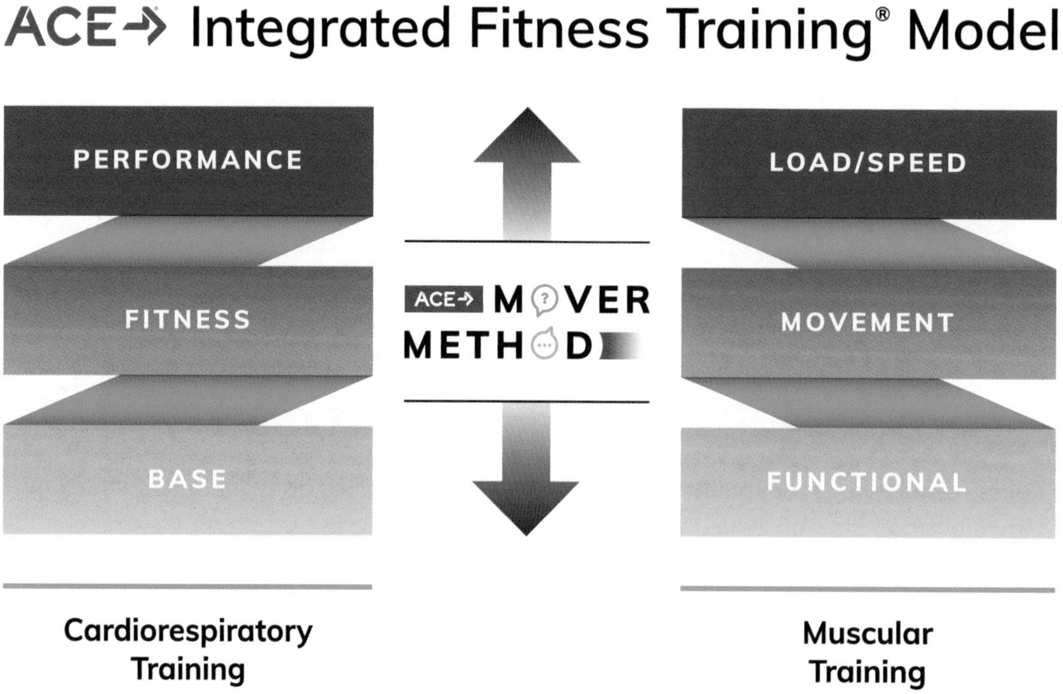

- *Performance Training:* This phase is for individuals who have goals that are focused on success in endurance sports and events and on outcomes such as increased **speed,** power, and endurance.

It is important that GFIs look at their classes and individual participants from multiple perspectives in order to keep people excited to continue exercising. Unlike personal trainers, who design a personalized exercise program for a given client, GFIs must first program for the group before offering **progressions** or **regressions** for individual participants who may be performing movements or exercises in various phases of the ACE IFT Model. The core challenge for many GFIs—whether they are novice or more experienced instructors—commonly involves finding a balance between instructing the entire group and making sure individual class participants progress appropriately and safely. For this reason, GFIs should always communicate to participants that it is their responsibility to manage their movements and work within their personal fitness levels.

One situation in which the ACE IFT Model may be applied more directly in a group setting involves the development of longer-term group programming for participants who begin a program together and progress as a group. For example, a GFI may lead a six-week bootcamp program or guide a group of new mothers through the postpartum return to exercise. In these cases, preparticipation screening can be used to classify each individual's health and fitness level, both as a baseline against which to measure future success and as a tool to support **motivation** and **adherence.**

APPLY WHAT YOU KNOW

Segmenting a Group Fitness Class to Include the ACE IFT Model

One example of how the ACE IFT Model can be applied in a group environment is to incorporate the phases that make up each component into the different segments of a group class. For instance, imagine a scenario where you are leading an exercise class for a group of athletes. These participants are already performing exercise in the Load/Speed Training phase but would benefit from a continued focus on Functional and Movement Training. As a result, you could design a circuit group strength training class incorporating exercises from each phase. The warm-up may include exercises that focus on postural stability and **kinetic chain** mobility and developing good movement patterns, followed by a conditioning portion of the class that includes three rounds of training. All round one movements would target Functional Training, round two would emphasize Movement Training, and Load/Speed Training exercises would be utilized in round three. This would all be followed by a cool-down that includes more Functional Training exercises. In this scenario, the ACE IFT Model can be used to create a unique group experience that caters to the needs of a specific population. This same application of the ACE IFT Model can be applied to cardiorespiratory training, as intervals can be used to reach intensities needed for Base, Fitness, and Performance Training.

Monitoring Intensity

Monitoring intensity is important when using the ACE IFT Model, and all group fitness formats have movements that can vary in impact and/or intensity. For example, in an indoor cycling class, a hill climb out of the saddle at a high resistance that lasts longer than three minutes is considered a higher-intensity option. This might be followed by a lower-resistance seated movement. It is the GFI's job to make sure that the intensity is balanced and appropriate for the participants. It is important to take this into consideration when choosing or choreographing movement combinations and segments.

Ultimately, it is up to the GFI to recommend an intensity-monitoring method that is most suitable for their skills and abilities, as well as one that is most practical for the class setting. Whether using **target heart rate (THR),** the **talk test** and the three-zone intensity model, **rating of perceived exertion (RPE),** or the **dyspnea scale,** all of which are commonly used in the group fitness setting and are discussed in this chapter, a GFI must feel comfortable with the method so that its application is simple and easy for the participants to understand.

PROMOTING SELF-RESPONSIBILITY

Whether teaching a Pilates, indoor rowing, or boot-camp class, it is impossible to be everywhere or help everyone simultaneously. Each participant is working at a different fitness level toward achieving their own set of goals. To help promote independence and self-responsibility, GFIs should encourage participants to work at their own pace; use the talk test, HR monitoring, or RPE check-ins; and inform participants how they should be feeling throughout the class. For example, during the peak portion of the cardiorespiratory segment, let them know that they should have an increased rate of respiration. During the cool-down, remind them that they should feel their **heart rate** and breathing rate slowing down. Be as descriptive as possible about perceived exertion throughout the workout. Also, it is important to demonstrate high-, medium-, and low-intensity options to teach multilevel classes. Help participants achieve the level of effort they want to reach and continually remind them to select an intensity based on their needs, goals, and fitness levels—the instructor cannot be solely responsible for participants' exercise intensity levels. Also, participants who are given **autonomy** often report a more positive exercise experience (Teixeira et al., 2012). One approach to help participants self-select their own appropriate effort levels is to maintain a moderate intensity most of the time, but also present other options and intensities as the need arises. Mastering this concept is the true "art" of group fitness instruction.

THINK IT THROUGH

Cueing Intensity

What specific cues could you provide participants to help them gauge their intensity level during the recovery segment of a **high-intensity interval training (HIIT)** class?

METHODS OF MONITORING CARDIORESPIRATORY INTENSITY

The appropriate intensity for aerobic exercise depends on several factors, including the exerciser's current level of health, fitness, exercise participation, individual preferences, and fitness goals. Beginners who are not participating in regular exercise (i.e., performing planned, structured physical activity for at least 30 minutes at a moderate intensity on at least three days/week for at least the past three months) should proceed with an exercise program that is of light-to-moderate intensity for longer durations and gradually progress to vigorous intensity following the ACE IFT Model. Those who are more fit and currently participating in regular exercise and are interested in maintaining or increasing their fitness levels can perform higher levels of intense cardiorespiratory exercise for shorter periods of time during each session.

Monitoring exercise intensity within the cardiorespiratory segment is important. Participants need to be given information regarding the purpose of monitoring exercise intensity and instruction on how to monitor heart rate, use the talk test, and rate their perceived exertion levels. Proper instruction on how to monitor intensity effectively is an important step for safe and effective exercise participation. Learning how to find and measure the pulse may be the first step in monitoring intensity.

The following are a few recommended sites for finding the pulse and monitoring heart rate:

- *Carotid pulse:* This pulse is taken from the carotid artery just to the side of the larynx using light pressure from the fingertips of the first two fingers. Remind participants never to palpate both carotid arteries at the same time and always press lightly to prevent a drop in HR and/or decreased blood flow to the brain (Figure 4-2).
- *Radial pulse:* This pulse is taken from the radial artery at the wrist, in line with the thumb, using the fingertips of the first two fingers (Figure 4-3).
- *Temporal pulse:* This pulse can sometimes be obtained from the left or right temple with light pressure from the fingertips of the first two fingers (Figure 4-4).

FIGURE 4-2
Carotid heart-rate monitoring

FIGURE 4-3
Radial heart-rate monitoring

FIGURE 4-4
Temporal heart-rate monitoring

Understanding the effective use of HR, RPE, the dyspnea scale, and the talk test is the next step in effectively monitoring exercise intensity. There are many different exercise intensity markers that can be used to delineate moderate- from vigorous-intensity exercise, or vigorous from maximal or near-maximal (anaerobic) exercise. However, HR at the **first ventilatory threshold (VT1)** and **second ventilatory threshold (VT2),** the talk test, and RPE using the 6 to 20 scale or the 0 to 10 category ratio scale are the recommended methods, as they are more accurate and enable more effective intensity monitoring among individual participants.

Some methods are preferred depending on the format. In a treadmill class or an indoor cycling class, use of HR monitors can be effective. However, in a kickboxing class, where the arms and legs are moving in many different directions and against gravity, RPE might be a better choice.

Safety

GFIs should keep in mind that there is no one preferred intensity-monitoring method for all group fitness class formats or participants. While some instructors have stopped using manual HR monitoring because it disrupts the flow of the class, others use HR monitors to gauge intensity. There are no hard-and-fast rules for monitoring intensity other than that it is an important responsibility of the participant and the GFI. Not monitoring intensity or failing to give constant intensity-monitoring gauges reflects an inadequate level of participant supervision and may compromise safety.

Target Heart Rate

Cardiorespiratory training has traditionally involved **steady-state exercise** with progressions based primarily on increased duration and intensity. While programs following these guidelines have shown positive results for decades, they are subject to substantial errors in training intensities, as the THRs are calculated as percentages of predicted **maximal heart rate (MHR),** which have been shown to have standard deviations of approximately 12 bpm using the long-standing equation of MHR = 220 – Age (Fox, Naughton, & Haskell, 1971), or closer to 7 bpm using newer formulas from Gellish et al. (2007) and Tanaka, Monahan, and Seals (2001). This means that when using the 220 – Age equation to determine an age-predicted MHR, the true MHR of the individual may actually be 12 beats per minute lower or higher than what the equation provides. For example, if a person is 20 years old, their age-predicted MHR is 200 beats per minute (bpm), which means that their true MHR could actually be anywhere from 188 to 212 bpm. This implies that for 68% of the population, their actual MHR will be plus or minus 12 bpm from the predicted value. The remaining 32% of the population will fall even further out of this range at plus or minus two standard deviations, or 24 bpm (Figure 4-5).

FIGURE 4-5
The standard deviation (i.e., 12 beats per minute) for the 220 – Age maximal heart rate prediction equation for 20 year olds

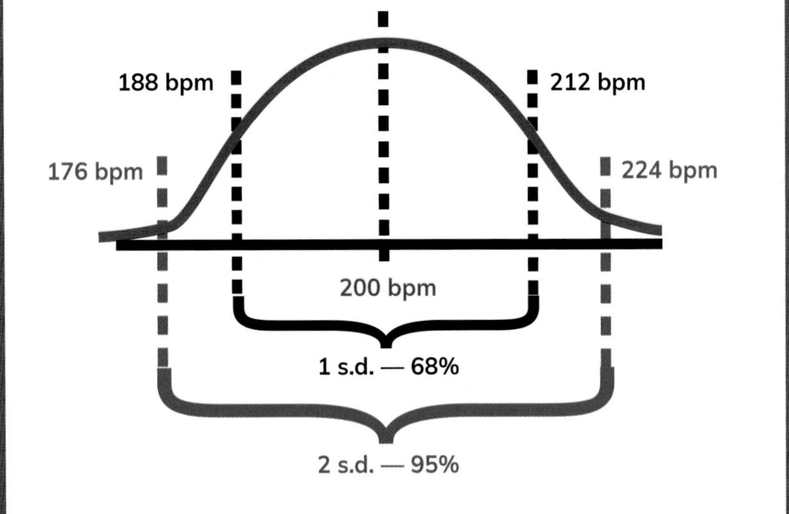

Note: bpm = Beats per minute; s.d. = Standard deviation

Gellish et al. formula:
Maximal heart rate = 206.9 – (0.67 x Age)

Tanaka, Monahan, and Seals formula:
Maximal heart rate = 208 – (0.7 x Age)

EXPAND YOUR KNOWLEDGE

Maximal Heart Rate: How Useful Is the Traditional Prediction Equation?

Two methods exist for determining MHR. The most accurate way is to directly measure the MHR with an **electrocardiogram (ECG)** monitoring device during a graded exercise test. The other way is to estimate MHR by using a simple prediction equation or formula. In 1971, the formula "220 – Age" was introduced and was widely accepted by the health and fitness community (Fox, Naughton, & Haskell, 1971). However, the validity of the formula has come under attack for several reasons. The subjects used in the study to determine the formula were not representative of the general population. In addition, even if the prediction equation did represent a reasonable average MHR, a significant percentage of individuals will deviate substantially from the average value for any given age. In fact, standard deviations of plus or minus 12 bpm have been observed. Consequently, basing a participant's exercise intensity (i.e., THR) on a potentially inaccurate estimation of MHR can be problematic. When the THR is based on an estimated MHR, it should be used in conjunction with RPE. GFIs should instruct participants to decrease the intensity of the exercise experience if they report a high level of perceived exertion, even if their THR has not been achieved.

This error in predicted MHR becomes amplified when this value is used to calculate THR ranges for cardiorespiratory exercise as either a direct percentage of MHR (as is represented on HR training zone charts commonly seen in fitness facilities) or using the Karvonen formula, which uses MHR and **resting heart rate** to first calculate **heart-rate reserve (HRR),** then calculate THR as a percentage of HRR.

Karvonen formula:
Heart-rate reserve = Maximal heart rate – Resting heart rate
Target heart rate = (Heart-rate reserve x % intensity) + Resting heart rate

Another option to assist in determining exercise intensity is called HR **telemetry.** In this method, the exerciser wears an electronic HR monitor strapped to their chest during the workout that transmits HR to a wristwatch. HR telemetry is especially convenient in group fitness classes that rely heavily on the individual participant's HR as a measure of intensity and progression throughout the class. The use of HR monitors is common in indoor cycling and treadmill-based classes, but the devices can be used in most other cardiorespiratory-based group fitness classes, as well. It is important to keep in mind, however, that HR-monitoring devices can produce erratic readings in addition to the standard deviations in determining MHR, as noted previously. It is advisable to use RPE and physical observation along with electronic HR-monitoring technology to ensure the exerciser's intensity stays within an acceptable range.

APPLY WHAT YOU KNOW

Incorporating Self-monitoring Intensity Cues During Class

In classes where participants are encouraged to track their exercise HR to monitor intensity, it is important to consistently give them opportunities to check their pulse or look at their HR monitors. At the very least, three different HR checks are appropriate—at the beginning of the conditioning segment, at the highest intensity point of the conditioning segment, and during the cool-down.

Here is an example of how this may be introduced during a class: "As we are working today, be mindful of your heart rate and make sure to stay within your target heart-rate range. We will be working within 64 to 95% of your maximal heart rate, as shown on the wall chart based on your age. I'll give you several opportunities to check your heart rate during class and then I'll let you know how hard you should be working at each point. Keep in mind, however, that if it feels too easy or too hard, adjust your intensity so that it matches the intended conditioning level of the workout."

It is a good idea to teach participants about RPE along with THR, so that their subjective experiences can be taken into account.

Talk Test and the Three-zone Intensity Model

Approaches that use a relative percent of predicted MHR, HRR, or even predicted **maximal oxygen uptake ($\dot{V}O_2max$)** or **$\dot{V}O_2$reserve ($\dot{V}O_2R$)**, are essentially flawed, as they do not take into account the individual's metabolic responses to exercise. Instead, exercise experiences can be tailored to each participant's unique metabolic markers by identifying and using the participant's HR at VT1 and VT2.

The talk test works on the assertion that at about the intensity of VT1, increased ventilation is accomplished by an increase in breathing frequency. This test takes into account an exerciser's ability to breathe and talk comfortably during a workout through the ability to control breathing frequency. If a person can recite something familiar such as the alphabet and then answer the question, "Can you speak comfortably?" with an unequivocal "yes" during exercise while still feeling like they are getting a good workout, it is likely that the activity being performed is appropriate for cardiorespiratory conditioning and the intensity is below the talk-test threshold. At the moment the response to this question becomes anything less than an unequivocal "yes," the participant is most likely right at the intensity of VTI, and if the answer is "no," they are likely above VT1. When a participant can no longer recite a few words between two breaths, they are most likely at or above VT2. The talk test is especially useful for beginners who are learning to pace themselves by monitoring their bodily responses to exercise. For those with higher fitness levels, the use of the talk test may not be as effective.

A GFI can facilitate the talk test by simply having the group recite something familiar and then asking the group if they can speak comfortably, or by asking questions to the group that require multiple-word responses. Individuals should be instructed to listen to their responses during each segment of a class, for a definitive yes, unsure, or a definitive no response. Ideally, when asking questions, the responses of the participants should be in the form of sentences, rather than one-word statements, such as "fine" or "okay." For example, a GFI could ask a participant to describe how they are feeling, and the participant could respond by saying, "I feel like I'm working pretty hard." If the exerciser can string those words together in a sentence without stopping and gasping for air, they are probably working at an appropriate intensity. In other words, if a person can talk comfortably, they are at a moderate intensity, if they are not sure if talking is comfortable, they are at a vigorous intensity, and if they definitely cannot talk comfortably, they are working at maximal or near-maximal effort.

Another, more simplified way for participants to use the talk test to determine if they are exercising at a moderate or vigorous intensity is to give the cue "if you can talk but not sing, you are at the right intensity for this drill." The expectation is not that the participants will start singing aloud, but with practice they will be able to determine an answer based on their breathing rate.

The concept behind the talk test can be explained by stating that this method takes into account an exerciser's ability to breathe and talk during a workout. Here is an example of how this may be introduced during a class: "If you can comfortably answer a question during our conditioning today while still feeling like you're getting a good workout, you're probably working at an appropriate intensity. However, if you feel like you can't speak, give yourself permission to take the intensity down. If you feel like you can sing a song and want to challenge yourself, go ahead and increase your intensity."

As mentioned earlier, the ability to talk during exertion is a reliable intensity marker, especially for beginning exercisers. For simplicity, exercisers can use a three-zone intensity model (Figure 4-6) in conjunction with the talk test to gauge appropriate exertion during cardiorespiratory activity, where:

- Zone 1 is light-to-moderate intensity exercise, during which the exerciser can talk comfortably.
- Zone 2 is vigorous-intensity aerobic exercise, during which the exerciser is not sure if talking is comfortable.
- Zone 3 is near-maximal to maximal exercise, during which the exerciser definitely cannot talk comfortably.

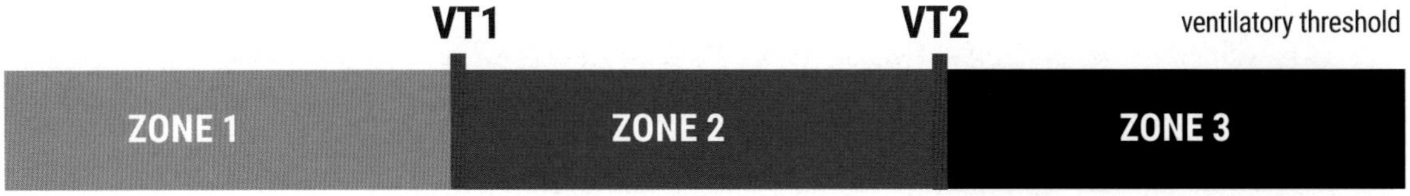

FIGURE 4-6
Three-zone intensity model

Note: VT1 = First ventilatory threshold; VT2 = Second ventilatory threshold

The three zones are separated by each participant's unique metabolic markers, known as VT1, where talking first becomes a little challenging, and VT2, where talking becomes very difficult and is reduced to one or two words at a time without pausing for a breath.

TABLE 4-6
Rating of Perceived Exertion (RPE)

RPE	Category Ratio Scale
6	0 Nothing at all
7 Very, very light	0.5 Very, very weak
8	1 Very weak
9 Very light	2 Weak
10	3 Moderate
11 Fairly light	4 Somewhat strong
12	5 Strong
13 Somewhat hard	6
14	7 Very strong
15 Hard	8
16	9
17 Very hard	10 Very, very strong
18	* Maximal
19 Very, very hard	
20	

Source: Borg, G. (1998). *Borg's Perceived Exertion and Pain Scales*. Champaign, Ill.: Human Kinetics.

This simple model can be useful for GFIs in class settings as they seek to gauge the intensity at which participants are working. A GFI can simply ask participants questions and listen for responses during the conditioning portion of class. It is important to educate participants on the concept of the three-zone intensity model and how it relates to talking, as doing so may elicit more responses from participants if they know the GFI is relying on their vocal cues as a way to monitor intensity. As participants become familiar with this model, they will be able to adjust their intensity during class based on cues such as "move from zone 1 to zone 2" and "for the next 10 seconds, push to zone 3 and then recover for 30 seconds in zone 1."

Rating of Perceived Exertion

Another method for measuring exercise intensity is by assigning a numerical value to subjective feelings of exercise exertion. Known as the RPE scale, this method, developed by Gunnar Borg, takes into account all that the exerciser is perceiving in terms of fatigue, including psychological, musculoskeletal, and environmental factors. RPE correlates well with physiological factors associated with exercise, such as HR, breathing rate, oxygen use, and overall fatigue. Table 4-6 lists two commonly used rating scales. For the RPE method of monitoring exercise intensity, the participant uses a scale to assign a rating to their physical effort.

When using the Borg 6 to 20 scale, an RPE of 12 to 13 (somewhat hard) corresponds to approximately 64 to 76% of MHR, whereas a rating of 14 to 17 (hard to very hard) corresponds to about 77 to 95% of MHR.

In the group fitness class setting, explaining the Borg 6 to 20 RPE scale to participants is usually difficult. A GFI who uses the 0 to 10 category ratio scale, rather than the 6 to 20 scale, as a means to incorporate RPE into the class setting will probably fare better in educating the participants about the use of RPE. An appropriate range of intensity for increasing cardiorespiratory fitness within the 0 to 10 scale is from 3 (moderate) to 6 (strong).

APPLY WHAT YOU KNOW

Introducing RPE as a Method for Self-monitoring During a Group Fitness Class

A practical way to use RPE in a group fitness class is to simply instruct the participants to use words, instead of numbers, to evaluate how hard they are working. For example, a GFI could explain prior to the conditioning segment of class that participants should gauge their intensities by feelings that correspond to the words "weak," "moderate," "strong," and "maximal." An appropriate perception of intensity, using these words as indicators, would range somewhere between *weak* and *strong*, whereas *nothing at all* and *maximal* are (depending on the class) intensities to avoid.

A simple explanation for RPE focuses on taking an inventory of things that the exerciser perceives in terms of fatigue and rating it on a scale of 0 to 10 or by descriptive words.

Here is an example of how this may be introduced during a class: "During class today, think about how hard you're working in terms of rating it on a scale of 0 to 10, with 0 being resting and 10 being the most maximal intensity you could imagine. To get the most out of our conditioning today, we want to work at a steady pace between 3 (moderate) and 4 (somewhat strong). However, if numbers aren't your cup of tea, you can gauge your intensity by feelings that correspond to the words "weak," "moderate," "strong," and "very strong." Using these words as indicators, you want to work somewhere between moderate and strong today, whereas just noticeable and maximal are to be avoided."

At several points throughout the conditioning segment of class, ask participants to do a quick RPE inventory of how they are feeling based on the numbered scale or descriptive words. Next, coach the class on how hard they should be working based on RPE to bring about the desired performance outcome.

Dyspnea Scale

When a deconditioned person attempts to exercise vigorously, they can experience **dyspnea** (difficult and labored breathing). Individuals who have pulmonary conditions, such as **asthma** and **emphysema,** also can experience problems with breathing during exercise. GFIs should observe their class participants for **signs** of difficulty with breathing so that the participants can be coached to reduce their exercise intensities if dyspnea occurs.

Participants can be taught the dyspnea scale to gauge the appropriateness of breathing performance during class. It is normal for participants engaging in cardiorespiratory exercise to experience mild and even moderate difficulty breathing, but those suffering from severe difficulty should be instructed to stop exercising and breathe deeply to recover from intense exercise.

The dyspnea scale is a subjective score that reflects the relative difficulty of breathing as perceived by the participant during physical activity (Table 4-7).

TABLE 4-7

Dyspnea Rating Scale

Rating	Description
0	No shortness of breath
1	Light, barely noticeable
2	Moderate, bothersome
3	Moderately severe, very uncomfortable
4	Most severe or intense dyspnea ever experienced

APPLY WHAT YOU KNOW

Introducing the Dyspnea Rating Scale as a Method for Self-monitoring During a Group Fitness Class

Here is an example of how a GFI may discuss using the dyspnea scale during class: "At certain times throughout class today, I'll be asking you to pay attention to how easy or how difficult it is for you to breathe, based on a scale of 0 to 4, with 0 being very easy with no shortness of breath and 4 being the most intense and severe breathlessness you have ever felt. Working at intensities that cause you to breathe at a rating of 1 (light, barely noticeable) and 2 (moderate, bothersome) is appropriate. However, avoid reaching a level of 4, which would indicate that you need to stop or drastically reduce your intensity so that you can catch your breath."

Similar to the RPE advice given previously, ask participants to do a quick dyspnea inventory based on the 0 to 4 scale. Then, coach the class on how hard they should be working based on their perception of breathing to bring about the desired performance outcome.

Refer to Table 4-8 for more information on some of the common methods for monitoring exercise intensity.

TABLE 4-8

Three-zone Intensity Model Using Various Intensity Markers

Intensity Markers		Zone 1	Zone 2	Zone 3	Advantages/Limitations
Category terminology for exercise programming	Light	Moderate	Vigorous	Near maximal/ maximal	
Metabolic markers: VT1 and VT2* (HR relative to VT1 and VT2)*		Below VT1 (HR <VT1)	VT1 to just below VT2 (HR ≥VT1 to <VT2)	VT2 and above (HR ≥VT2)	▸ Based on measured VT1 and VT2 ▸ Ideally, VT1 and VT2 are measured in a lab with a metabolic cart and blood lactate. ▸ Field assessments are relatively easy to administer, require minimal equipment, and provide accurate corresponding HRs at VT1 and VT2. ▸ Programming with metabolic markers allows for personalized programming.
Talk test*		Can talk comfortably Can talk but not sing	Not sure if talking is comfortable Cannot say more than a few words without pausing for a breath	Definitely cannot talk comfortably	▸ Based on actual changes in ventilation due to physiological adaptations to increasing exercise intensities ▸ Very easy for practical measurement ▸ No equipment required ▸ Can easily be taught to participants ▸ Allows for personalized programming

TABLE 4-8 *(continued)*

Intensity Markers		Zone 1	Zone 2	Zone 3	Advantages/Limitations
RPE (terminology)*	Very, very weak to light	"Moderate" to "somewhat hard/strong"	"Hard/strong" to "very hard"	"Very strong to very, very hard/strong to maximal"	▸ Good subjective intensity marker ▸ Correlates well with talk test, metabolic markers, and measured %$\dot{V}O_2$max ▸ Easy to teach to participants
RPE (0 to 10 scale)*	0.5 to 2	3 to 4	5 to 6	7 to 10	▸ Good subjective intensity marker ▸ Correlates well with talk test, metabolic markers, and measured %$\dot{V}O_2$max ▸ 0 to 10 scale is easy to teach to participants
RPE (6 to 20 scale)	9 to 11	12 to 13	14 to 17	≥18	▸ Good subjective intensity marker ▸ Correlates well with talk test, metabolic markers, and measured %$\dot{V}O_2$max ▸ 6 to 20 scale is not as easy to teach to participants as the 0 to 10 scale ▸ Note: An RPE of 20 represents maximal effort and cannot be sustained as a training intensity.
%$\dot{V}O_2$R	30 to 39%	40 to 59%	60 to 89%	≥90%	▸ Requires *measured* $\dot{V}O_2$max for most accurate programming ▸ Impractical due to expensive equipment needed for assessment ▸ Increased error with use of *predicted* $\dot{V}O_2$max or *predicted* MHR ▸ Relative percentages for programming are population-based and not individually specific.
%HRR	30 to 39%	40 to 59%	60 to 89%	≥90%	▸ Requires *measured* MHR and RHR for most accurate programming. ▸ Measured MHR is impractical for the vast majority of exercise professionals and clients/participants. ▸ Use of RHR increases individuality of programming vs. strict %MHR. ▸ Use of *predicted* MHR introduces potentially large error; the magnitude of the error is dependent on the specific equation used. ▸ Relative percentages for programming are population-based and not individually specific.
%MHR	57 to 63%	64 to 76%	77 to 95%	≥96%	▸ Requires *measured* MHR for accuracy in programming ▸ Measured MHR is impractical for the vast majority of exercise professionals and clients/participants. ▸ Use of *predicted* MHR introduces potentially large error; the magnitude of the error is dependent on the specific equation used.

Continued on the next page

TABLE 4-8 (*continued*)

Intensity Markers		Zone 1	Zone 2	Zone 3	Advantages/Limitations
					▸ Does not include RHR, as is used in %HRR. ▸ Relative percentages for programming are population-based and not individually specific.
METs	2 to 2.9	3 to 5.9	6 to 8.7	≥8.8	▸ Requires measured $\dot{V}O_2$max for most accurate programming
					▸ Can use in programming more easily than other intensity markers based off $\dot{V}O_2$max ▸ Limited in programming by knowledge of METs for given activities and/or equipment that gives MET estimates ▸ Relative MET ranges for programming are population-based and not individually specific (e.g., a 5-MET activity might initially be perceived as vigorous by a previously sedentary participant).
%$\dot{V}O_2$max	37 to 45%	46 to 63%	64 to 90%	≥91%	▸ Refer to %$\dot{V}O_2$R ▸ Actual measurement is individualized and not based on a prediction.

Note: VT1 = First ventilatory threshold; VT2 = Second ventilatory threshold; HR = Heart rate; RPE = Rating of perceived exertion; $\dot{V}O_2$max = Maximal oxygen uptake; $\dot{V}O_2$R = Oxygen uptake reserve; HRR = Heart-rate reserve; MHR = Maximal heart rate; RHR = Resting heart rate; METs = Metabolic equivalents

*These are the preferred intensity markers to use with the three-zone model when designing, implementing, and progressing cardiorespiratory training programs in the group fitness environment using the ACE Integrated Fitness Training Model.

APPLY WHAT YOU KNOW

Teaching Participants to Monitor Their Intensity

Monitoring exercise intensity during group fitness classes is a skill that GFIs must be able to teach to their participants, as the responsibility for exercising within an appropriate range of intensity ultimately rests with the participant. This concept should be explained by the GFI at the beginning of each class. It is important for the class to understand that while the GFI will do their best to provide a safe and effective exercise experience, each individual participant must gauge the intensity of their true effort and adjust their performance accordingly.

It is helpful to explain to the participants at the beginning of class the physical sensations that are normal with various intensities of exercise and how to adjust performance, if necessary. For example, a GFI could announce, "At different points during class, we will check the intensity of our effort. I will ask you to think about how hard you are working. You should reflect on how fast you are breathing and how fatigued you feel at the moment the question is asked. Those of you who are wearing HR monitors and who are aware of your THR range can check your monitor while simultaneously taking an inventory of how you feel. If you feel like you're working too hard (at a level that cannot be sustained), I will show you how to reduce the intensity of what we are doing at that time. If you feel as if you're not working hard enough, I'll show you how to increase the challenge."

It is advisable to perform intensity-monitoring checks several times during the workout. An intensity check can be as simple as taking 10 seconds to ask the participants how they feel. At the very least, an intensity check should be performed during a relatively high-intensity point of the cardiorespiratory conditioning portion of the class, and again after the cardiorespiratory cool-down portion of class. It is important for the GFI and each participant to acknowledge that the intensity of effort was elevated at the appropriate times during class and that it was decreased prior to the conclusion of class.

AWARENESS OF WARNING SIGNS

Sometimes, even while using intensity-monitoring strategies, participants can overexert themselves during a group fitness class. A competent GFI will be able to recognize cues or warning signs that necessitate the lowering of intensities for individual participants or the class as a whole.

Safety

The first, and perhaps most obvious, warning sign that a GFI is likely to observe when a participant is working too vigorously is a breakdown in proper form and exercise execution. For example, an individual who is beginning to fatigue during a step aerobics class might not be able to set their foot completely on top of the bench, resulting in the heel hanging off the platform. This increases the risk of tripping and poses a hazard to the participant and the individuals around them. Another situation that would illustrate compromised form due to overexertion is a participant getting fatigued while performing a bench press exercise in a muscle-conditioning class. Excessive arching of the back, shoulder elevation, and locking the elbows at the top of the repetition to rest would indicate that the exerciser has reached muscular fatique of the chest, shoulders, and triceps.

In either of these examples, it would be appropriate for the GFI to recommend a reduction in the intensity of the exercise. In most cases, it is adequate for a GFI to make a general statement to the entire class about proper execution of the exercise and how to reduce the intensity through modifications if the participants find themselves exhibiting poor form. Sometimes, however, it might be necessary for the GFI to approach a participant and use specific, corrective **feedback** if the exerciser continues to risk injury by performing movements incorrectly.

Other warning signs that could indicate a need for reducing exercise intensity include labored breathing, excessive sweating, and dizziness. A GFI should recommend to participants who are experiencing these signs and **symptoms** to stop exercising and lightly march in place until the signs and symptoms subside. As the HR lowers and the breathing becomes more normal, the participant can attempt to continue at a new lower intensity. However, it might be necessary to discontinue the exercise session if the signs and symptoms do not improve. More severe symptoms, such as chest pain or discomfort, heart **palpitations,** or severe musculoskeletal pain, indicate the need for immediate cessation of exercise and possibly the activation of emergency medical services (EMS). Refer to Chapter 12 for more information.

Preparticipation Screening

Safety

Preparticipation screening forms are health-history documents that are typically collected at the initiation of enrollment to a fitness facility or a defined group fitness program, along with **informed consent** and a release of liability **waiver** (see Chapter 14). It is the responsibility of the facility/business operator to determine if medical clearance is warranted prior to an individual participating in physical activity based on the health-related information provided on their preparticipation forms.

While most GFIs do not have access to participant health-history information, instructors should assume that some participants may have known or unknown medical conditions that could impact their exercise experience. In 2020, six in 10 adults in the U.S. had a chronic disease and four in 10 adults in the U.S. had two or more (Centers for Disease Control and Prevention, 2021).

Looking for on-the-spot indicators before the start of class, such as age, posture, and first-time participation, can provide insight into what modifications or teaching methods may be needed during class. GFIs should be sensitive toward participants and not make obvious judgments, but rather use the power of observation during class to provide appropriate progressions, regressions, and additional coaching cues to ensure the safety and effectiveness of the exercise experience. Health and exercise professionals, including GFIs, are important members of the healthcare continuum, as regularly physically active individuals are less likely to develop high-risk diseases such as heart disease and **type 2 diabetes** (Zhang et al., 2020; Hamasaki, 2016).

APPLY WHAT YOU KNOW

Getting to Know Your Participants

Establishing rapport with individuals before class time by welcoming new and returning participants is a GFI's first opportunity to make a great impression. This period can be used to investigate what participants like most and least about particular classes, as well as offer an opportunity for the GFI to learn about any specific limitations or considerations individual participants may have. Aside from the standard welcome greeting, GFIs can learn quite of bit of information by asking a few different participants at the beginning of each class some key questions, such as:

- "What brings you here today?"
- "Do you have any limitations that may affect your exercise performance?"
- "Have you ever participated in a Pilates class before?"
- "Thank you for regularly coming to my yoga class. What motivates you to be here every Monday morning?"
- "Remember when you first started class, you performed push-ups on your knees and now you can complete 15 push-ups on your toes? May I share your progress with the class?"
- "Would you like to see new exercises for a particular muscle group today? If so, which areas?"

Asking different participants a few questions each week will give GFIs information about participants' readiness to learn, prior experience, and level of motivation—all factors that affect the way adults learn and how a GFI modifies their teaching methods.

Acquainting participants at the beginning of class with one another is the first step toward creating a community. "Class cliques" may develop as a consequence of regular participants who form relationships, but GFIs can mitigate this by introducing new participants to regular class goers and identifying a commonality between them. One tactic that helps break the ice at the beginning of class is to ask everyone to introduce themselves to the person on their right and left and share what brings them to class. Overall, getting to know the participants and building community embodies excellent customer service.

In addition to social interaction, with experience GFIs can become proficient at using on-the-spot indicators to assess class needs prior to each session. There are three on-the-spot indicators that can be used to gauge participants' potential limitations and alert the instructor to the type of exercise progressions and regressions they may need to provide during the class. These indicators are:

- *Age:* While not always the case, some participants may have age-associated limitations that require the GFI to offer appropriate regression options for the movements and exercises included in the class.
- *Posture:* Poor posture is associated with some muscles being shortened, or overactive and others being lengthened or inhibited. This imbalance makes proper movement execution increasingly difficult and increases the importance of providing regression options to accommodate limited **range of motion.**
- *New participation:* New participants require increased attention and should be watched closely during class to ensure safety and success. The more frequently an individual attends classes, the less instruction they will need over time to understand how to modify movements and execute them with proper form.

Safety

APPLY WHAT YOU KNOW

Making Participant Privacy a Priority

Some class participants may share confidential information, such as medical conditions or health concerns, with a GFI through conversation before or after class. In addition, some GFIs may directly collect health-history information prior to the start of specific programs, such as a six-week boot-camp program. GFIs should maintain a level of security for each participant's personal information. Failure to do so could prove detrimental for the participant and the participant–instructor relationship and is in violation of the ACE Code of Ethics (see the Appendix), as well as state and federal privacy laws.

To help prevent violations of participant privacy, ACE GFIs should become familiar with, and adhere to, the **Health Insurance Portability and Accountability Act (HIPAA),** which addresses the use and disclosure of individuals' protected health information. By following HIPAA regulations, GFIs can maintain the confidentiality of each participant's protected health information according to the same rules that govern most healthcare professions. More details about participant privacy and keeping participants' protected health information secure can be found in Chapter 14.

ACE UNIVERSITY

If your study program includes ACE University, visit www.ACEfitness.org/MyACE and log in to your My ACE Account to take full advantage of the ACE Group Fitness Instructor Study Program and online guided study experience.

A variety of media to support and expand on the material in this text is provided to facilitate learning and best prepare you for the ACE Group Fitness Instructor Certification exam and a career as a group fitness instructor.

SUMMARY

Group fitness instructors have many roles and responsibilities to consider that extend above and beyond the time spent in class instructing. It is important that GFIs understand how to use the ACE IFT Model to design safe and effective exercise programs that support the promotion of both health- and skill-related components of physical fitness and incorporate ACSM's guidelines on exercise programming for healthy adults. The GFI must also understand basic training principles such as specificity, overload, and reversibility and promote self-responsibility of class participants by providing education about monitoring exercise intensity, opportunities to regularly assess intensity throughout class, and options for modifying exercises to adjust intensity. As part of a well-rounded group exercise experience, it is imperative that preparticipation health screening take place and that the GFI has knowledge of, and skill in, recognizing warning signs that indicate a participant should reduce exercise intensity.

REFERENCES

American College of Sports Medicine (2022). *ACSM's Guidelines for Exercise Testing and Prescription* (11th ed.). Philadelphia: Wolters Kluwer.

Blocquiaux, S. et al. (2020). The effect of resistance training, detraining, and retraining on muscle strength and power, myofibre size, satellite cells and myonuclei in older men. *Experimental Gerontology*, 133, 110860.

Borg, G. (1998). *Borg's Perceived Exertion and Pain Scales*. Champaign, Ill.: Human Kinetics.

Centers for Disease Control and Prevention (2021). *About Chronic Disease*. https://www.cdc.gov/chronicdisease/about/index.htm

Fox III, S.M., Naughton, J.P., & Haskell, W.L. (1971). Physical activity and the prevention of coronary heart disease. *Annals of Clinical Research*, 3, 404–432.

Garber, C.E. et al. (2011). American College of Sports Medicine position stand. Quantity and quality of exercise for developing and maintaining cardiorespiratory, musculoskeletal, and neuromotor fitness in apparently healthy adults: Guidance for prescribing exercise. *Medicine & Science in Sports & Exercise*, 43, 7, 1334–1359.

Gellish, R.L. et al. (2007). Longitudinal modeling of the relationship between age and maximal heart rate. *Medicine & Science in Sports & Exercise*, 39, 5, 822–829.

Hamasaki, H. (2016). Daily physical activity and type 2 diabetes: A review. *World Journal of Diabetes*, 7, 12, 243–251.

Nolan, P. et al. (2018). The effect of detraining after a period of training on cardiometabolic health in previously sedentary individuals. *International Journal of Environmental Research and Public Health*, 15, 10.

ACE-sponsored Research

Tanaka, H., Monahan, K.D., & Seals, D.R. (2001). Age-predicted maximal heart revisited. *Journal of the American College of Cardiology*, 37, 153–156.

Teixiera, P.J. et al. (2012). Exercise, physical activity, and self-determination theory: A systematic review. *International Journal of Behavioral Nutrition and Physical Activity*, 9, 78.

U.S. Department of Health & Human Services (2018). *Physical Activity Guidelines for Americans* (2nd ed.). www.health.gov/paguidelines

World Health Organization (2020). *WHO Guidelines on Physical Activity and Sedentary Behavior*. https://www.who.int/publications/i/item/9789240015128

Zhang, X. et al. (2020). Physical activity and risk of cardiovascular disease by weight status among U.S. adults. *PlosONE*, DOI: 10.1371/journal.pone.0132893

SUGGESTED READING

American College of Sports Medicine (2022). *ACSM's Guidelines for Exercise Testing and Prescription* (11th ed.). Philadelphia: Wolters Kluwer.

SECTION II

Preparation and Design for Group Fitness Classes

CHAPTER 5
Getting to the Core of Class Offerings

CHAPTER 6
Key Considerations for Group Fitness Classes

CHAPTER 7
Group Fitness Class Program Design

CHAPTER 8
Group Fitness Facility and Equipment Considerations

CHAPTER 5

Getting to the Core of Class Offerings

JAN SCHROEDER, PhD | Professor, Department of Kinesiology, California State University, Long Beach; ACE Certified Group Fitness Instructor

IN THIS CHAPTER

LEARNING OBJECTIVES

Upon completion of this chapter, the reader will be able to:

- Identify group fitness class formats
- Explain the difference between freestyle, pre-choreographed, and pre-planned methods of group fitness instruction
- Differentiate between the warm-up, conditioning, and cool-down segments of a group fitness class
- Explain the controversy surrounding performing static stretching during the warm-up

ACE UNIVERSITY

If your study program includes ACE University, visit www.ACEfitness.org/MyACE and log in to your My ACE Account to take full advantage of the ACE Group Fitness Instructor Study Program and online guided study experience.

A variety of media to support and expand on the material in this text is provided to facilitate learning and best prepare you for the ACE Group Fitness Instructor Certification exam and a career as a group

Group fitness classes use movement to enhance participants' health-related components of fitness, such as **cardiorespiratory endurance, muscular strength**, **muscular endurance, flexibility,** and **body composition,** as well as skill-related components of fitness, such as **balance, agility, coordination, reaction time, speed,** and **power.** Health and fitness improvement, plus social engagement with others during class, are powerful factors that empower people to improve their quality of life. Although no single class structure is appropriate for every type of group fitness class, there are general formatting practices that can help to ensure a safe and effective experience for participants.

Group Fitness Class Formats

Group exercise classes come in a variety of formats that are designed to improve the health-related and/or skill-related components of fitness. Some class formats incorporate just one component, such as cardiorespiratory fitness, while other classes may incorporate two or three components, such as a strength and balance class. The first step in designing a class is determining the objective or the goal of the class (Table 5-1).

TABLE 5-1
Group Fitness Class Formats

Format	Class Objective	Examples
Cardiorespiratory Training	The focus of the class is to improve cardiorespiratory fitness. Formats may be choreographed (movement to the beat of the music) or non-choreographed (with music in the background).	*Choreographed:* Dance-based, step, and sometimes boxing/kickboxing *Non-choreographed:* High-intensity interval training (HIIT), indoor cycling, and cardio-based circuit training
Muscular Training	The focus of the class is to improve muscular fitness and/or power. Formats may be considered traditional (focusing on one muscle group at a time) or functional (focused on body movements that mimic activities of daily living, such as a squat press) and can make use of body weight and/or various types of equipment.	Full-, upper-, or lower-body focus Core training classes Barbell-based sessions Circuit-training classes
Mobility/Flexibility	The focus of the class is to increase range of motion and mobility, either passively or actively. Some facilities may combine this category with mind-body formats, while others will provide separate classes designed to attract a different audience than mind/body formats.	Stretching Self–myofascial release
Mind-Body	The focus of the class is to promote muscular fitness, flexibility, and mindful breathing.	Yoga Pilates Barre Tai chi

Continued on the next page

TABLE 5-1 (*continued*)

Format	Class Objective	Examples
Aquatic Exercise	The focus of the class is to improve cardiorespiratory and muscular fitness while in the pool. While cardiorespiratory training, muscular training, fusion, mobility/flexibility, and mind-body classes can all be taught in the water, facilities usually separate these offerings.	Water jogging/running Interval classes Mobility classes Shallow- and deep-water options
Skill-related	The focus of the class is to improve skill-related components of fitness. These formats can be included in other formats such as cardiorespiratory or muscular training classes or be taught separately.	Balance classes Speed, agility, and quickness classes Plyometrics

Source: American Council on Exercise (2020). *Where to Start: Choosing Your Preferred Format for Group Fitness Classes.* https://www.acefitness.org/education-and-resources/professional/expert-articles/7735/where-to-start-choosing-your-preferred-format-for-group-fitness-classes/

Exercise selection, volume, order, intensity, and recovery periods are then chosen to meet that objective. For example, if the class objective is to improve cardiorespiratory fitness, exercises targeting the major muscle groups could be selected and organized with an aim to increase **heart rate (HR)** and breathing rate through continuous or intermittent movement.

In general, most group fitness classes are appropriate for individuals with various fitness skills and abilities, as long as the ACE Certified Group Fitness Instructor (GFI) is capable of student-centered instruction wherein exercise modifications are offered frequently throughout the class experience. However, some class formats may also be categorized as beginner or advanced. Classes designated as beginner classes should use basic moves, introduce terminology, and provide constructive feedback to the participants, while advanced classes assume the participants have a base level of fitness, an understanding of exercise terminology, and can grasp more complex exercises or choreography. In either case, GFIs should always be prepared to teach inclusive, multilevel classes in which appropriate **progressions** and **regressions** of exercises are provided, regardless of how the class is titled or described on the group fitness schedule.

Choreographic Methods

GFIs must be prepared to teach movements and exercises that together create a well-designed class experience. Choreography for any cardiorespiratory-, muscular training–, flexibility-, or skill-focused class can take many forms, from freestyle choreography in which the class content can vary dramatically from one class to another, to different types of pre-choreographed classes, where the class content is relatively consistent from one class to the next. There are three different choreographic methods from which instructors can choose.

FREESTYLE

The freestyle, or instructor-set, method of developing and delivering choreography occurs when the GFI chooses their own music, class design, and specific choreography. A freestyle class is unique to each individual instructor, as they are responsible for developing the class from start to finish.

PRE-CHOREOGRAPHED

Pre-choreographed, or pre-set, classes are offered in "scripted" form, in which instructors follow a written script with music, cues, and moves all outlined from start to finish. The class format is designed by fitness companies and provided to instructors through training workshops and typically quarterly releases of new class choreography. The intent is a "performance-like" consistency of delivery and class experience, discouraging variation among instructors.

PRE-PLANNED

In pre-planned or pre-styled, class formats, instructors receive guidelines and suggestions of what a class should include. As long as instructors follow these guidelines, they can make their own individual choices from a longer list of options on such things as song selection and sequence of moves as they plan for their classes, or they can choose to implement a completely pre-choreographed class plan. Again, a group exercise fitness company will develop new class choreography for instructors, usually on a monthly or quarterly basis, but the instructor has more freedom to manipulate class variables.

COMPARISON OF CHOREOGRAPHIC METHODS

Each of these types of choreographic methods has its own set of advantages and disadvantages for both the instructor and the participants (Table 5-2). Determining which choreographic method to use when teaching classes is really up to the GFI (and in some cases the facilities in which they teach). Many instructors teach multiple formats and will use all three methods, while other instructors will use just one format to teach their classes. If a GFI wishes to use pre-choreographed or pre-planned formats, they must be trained by the company in order to be able to use the choreography and class name.

TABLE 5-2
Advantages and Disadvantages of Choreographic Methods

Choreographic Method	Advantages for Instructor	Disadvantages for Instructor	Advantages for Participant	Disadvantages for Participant
Freestyle (Instructor-set)	Freedom to be creative in design, exercises, cues, transitions, etc., in order to offer a unique experience to participants as well as showcase the GFI's personality or style Potential to add variety to classes on a daily, weekly, or monthly basis Autonomy to offer progressions, regressions, and alternate exercises to class participants Ability to create unique music playlists Can teach the class anywhere	Time demand and knowledge required to develop choreography May take more time for participants to learn the choreography, as they do not have previous experience with it May be more challenging to find class coverage when the GFI cannot teach GFI is responsible for licensing music May need to rely on personal branding to promote the class	An always-changing environment that may reduce boredom	Participants are often unaware of what to expect from class to class, making it more challenging to improve proficiency over time because the sequence of movements constantly changes.
Pre-choreographed	Choreography is done for the GFI, who needs only to memorize the choreography. May be easier to find class coverage Music is provided, which allows the GFI to spend more time perfecting the format. Ongoing education and instructor support provided Brand recognition	Less freedom to be creative Can become repetitive, leading to boredom Less of an ability to tailor exercises to class participants' needs Can be expensive with license, training, and fees for new choreography May not be able to teach the format at all facilities	The consistency of these programs may allow for a better experience for class participants, as they know what to expect regardless of the instructor teaching the format. Participants are able to gauge their intensity more effectively, since they know the general format and can measure their own improvements over time.	As instructors must follow a script, there is often little room for customizing specific progressions and regressions as appropriate for the individuals in each class. Can become repetitive, leading to boredom
Pre-planned	The GFI has the choice of using pre-choreographed routines or developing their own based on guidelines provided.	Knowledge and time are required to organize a class plan from the options provided.	Ability to provide variety may reduce boredom	Inconsistency of choreography across instructors may lead to frustration among class participants.

TABLE 5-2 ***(continued)***

Choreographic Method	Advantages for Instructor	Disadvantages for Instructor	Advantages for Participant	Disadvantages for Participant
	Ability to suggest progressions, regressions, and alternate exercises to class participants Choice of music provided or a unique playlist Ongoing education and instructor support provided Brand recognition	Can be expensive with license, training, and fees for new choreography May not be able to teach the format at all facilities	Modifications may allow for a greater mix of abilities within class.	

THINK IT THROUGH

Considering Choreographic Methods

After reviewing the advantages and disadvantages of each of the different choreographic methods, which method appeals to you most and why?

Basic Components of a Class

Once the class format has been decided, the GFI can begin to outline their plan for the class. Group fitness classes tend to follow the exercise sequence of a warm-up, conditioning segment, and cool-down. This ordered system helps to increase the success and safety of each class by ensuring that there is a logical sequence and progression of exercises.

WARM-UP

The purpose of the warm-up is to prepare the body for the more rigorous demands of the class by raising the internal temperature and enhancing **neuromuscular efficiency,** which is the ability of the **neuromuscular system** to efficiently recruit and use the appropriate muscles to produce movement. At higher body temperatures, blood flow is shunted away from most internal organs and redirected to the working muscles, and the release of oxygen to the muscles begins to increase. Because these effects allow more efficient energy production to fuel muscle contraction, one goal of the warm-up should be to elevate internal temperatures so that sweating begins to occur. Another potential outcome of a good warm-up is to enhance neuromuscular efficiency such that joint-position sense improves, joint **stability** is enhanced, and protective joint reflexes are developed.

Increasing body temperature has other effects that are beneficial for exercisers, as well. The potential physiological benefits of the warm-up include:

- Increased blood flow to the exercising muscles
- Increased blood flow to the heart to reduce potential exercise-induced cardiac arrythmias

- Increased body temperature
- Increased metabolic rate
- An earlier onset of sweating to help with heat dissipation
- Enhanced speed of transmission of nerve impulses
- Increased speed and force of muscle contraction
- Decreased muscle-relaxation time following contraction
- Mental preparation for upcoming activity

Many of these physiological effects have the potential to reduce the risk of injury because they may increase neuromuscular coordination, delay **fatigue,** and make the tissues less susceptible to damage (Herman et al., 2012).

There are a few common principles guiding the warm-up for any group fitness class:

- The beginning segment includes an appropriate amount of dynamic movement.
- All major muscle groups (if appropriate) are addressed through dynamic **range of motion (ROM)** movements.
- The warm-up focuses largely on **rehearsal moves.**
- Verbal directions are clear and the volume, tempo, and mood created by the music, if used, are appropriate.

Appropriate Dynamic Movement

The warm-up should include specific movements to prepare for the conditioning segment, or main portion, of the class. These dynamic movements are performed at a low-to-moderate speed and reduced ROM. These movements gradually increase speed, ROM, or complexity as the warm-up progresses. For example, slow, small arm circles would progress to large arm circles, or alternating side lunges would progress to alternating side lunges with an overhead reach. These activities are designed to specifically raise internal body temperature in preparation for the activity to follow and to increase blood flow to the muscles.

Rehearsal Moves

Rehearsal moves are defined as movements that are similar to, but less intense than, the movements that participants will execute during the conditioning segment of class. Rehearsal moves prepare the participants mentally and physically for the conditioning segment of the class (See Chapter 7). Examples of rehearsal moves include a body-weight squat to prepare for a weighted squat during the conditioning segment or a march to prepare for high knees or a jog.

Other Considerations when Matching Choreography to the Needs of the Class

The warm-up segment of the class is also a time to assess the stage of learning and preferred learning style of the participants, allowing the GFI to adjust cueing and the choreography to meet the needs of the class. A successful GFI has prepared ahead of time for possible regressions and progressions that may be needed for the participants in the class. Music should also be assessed for the appropriate tempo, volume, and desired experience during the warm-up. The ambient environment needs to be considered, as cold weather may increase the amount of time needed to warm up. Finally, some populations may require additional warm-up time, such as older adults and those with arthritis, asthma, or other chronic conditions (see Chapter 12).

EXPAND YOUR KNOWLEDGE

Should Participants Stretch during the Warm-up?

To stretch or not to stretch during the warm-up to promote injury prevention and performance is a much-debated issue, and there is no clear consensus in the scientific literature (Lewis, 2014; Herman et al., 2012). Research shows that while it is safe to incorporate short-duration static stretches into a full dynamic warm-up, the benefits are negligible (Reid et al., 2018). It has also been found that prolonged static stretching prior to more vigorous exercise may have a detrimental effect on performance (Behm et al., 2016). The American College of Sports Medicine (ACSM, 2022) suggests that static stretching exercises be performed on their own as part of a program to increase ROM and not prior to any exercise activity, while dynamic stretches, such as walking knee hugs, leg swings, or arm circles, are encouraged before an exercise bout and may also be used to improve performance.

CONDITIONING SEGMENT

After the warm-up, the conditioning segment generally begins based on the goals and content of the class (e.g., cardiorespiratory exercise aimed at improving cardiorespiratory endurance or muscular training aimed at working the major muscle groups). There are a few common principles behind the conditioning segment of most group fitness classes. For a successful class experience, a GFI should:

- Promote independence/self-responsibility for participant exercise intensity (see Chapter 4). Teaching participants to identify and monitor their exercise intensity will encourage them to be an active member in their exercise journey and will help them to be accountable for their needs and goals.
- Gradually increase intensity. Intensity continues to build until it reaches the desired level to meet the class objectives, such as cardiorespiratory, muscular, or range-of-motion development.
- Monitor intensity using the **talk test,** HR, and/or **rating of perceived exertion** (see Chapter 4). The GFI needs to select an intensity-monitoring method that is most suitable for their skills and abilities, as well as one that is most practical for the class setting. Assessing intensity will allow the GFI and participants to identify if the class goals are being met and if modifications may be needed.
- Build sequences logically and progressively. The GFI should be able to systematically create movement patterns that progress from easy to more complex or from less intense to more intense while meeting the needs of varying learning styles and skill levels of the participants.
- Give progression and regression options. To meet the diverse skill levels of class participants, the GFI should provide modifications (progressions and regressions) to exercises. Adjusting intensity, impact level, speed/tempo, stability, and **lever length**

are just a few ways to progress or regress an exercise to suit the individual needs of participants.

While fusion classes can take on many different forms, they often involve blending two or more modalities, such as yoga and Pilates, into one intertwined class experience. These hybrid classes can also pair class formats with different goals, such as 30 minutes of indoor cycling to improve cardiorespiratory endurance followed by 30 minutes of resistance training to improve muscular endurance. These classes may be combined into one 60-minute class offering with two distinct portions or may be offered individually as back-to-back "express" classes that are each 30 minutes in length.

POST-CONDITIONING COOL-DOWN

Following the conditioning segment, a gradual cool-down slowly lowers the HR to near pre-exercise levels. A class typically ends with a flexibility-based component that includes stretching and relaxation exercises designed to further lower HR and enhance overall flexibility. The final portion of any group fitness session that contains moderate- to vigorous-intensity work should be less intense to allow the **cardiorespiratory system** to recover. During this final segment, GFIs should encourage participants to slow down, keep the arms below the level of the heart, and put less effort into the movements. Using less driving music, changing tone of voice, and verbalizing the transition to the participants can create this setting. Performing some static stretches at the end of this segment also works well. Participants often run off to their next commitment immediately after class, so they may risk missing important flexibility training if stretching is not included in this portion of the class format. The benefits of the post-conditioning cool-down are as follows:

- Allows the HR, breathing rate, **blood pressure,** and body temperature to return toward pre-exercise levels
- Helps to prevent blood from pooling in the extremities, which could lead to dizziness or fainting
- Offers time to self-reflect on a sense of accomplishment
- Provides stress relief
- Provides time for stretching to improve flexibility

Stretching

It is important that GFIs lead the class through the stretching of the major muscle groups in a safe and effective manner during the cool-down. Relaxation, visualization, and specific breathing techniques may be included at the end of the flexibility segment to enhance the participant experience.

GFIs should consider stretching both the muscle groups that have been the focus of the group fitness class format, as well as those muscles that are commonly tight from everyday activities. For example, after an indoor cycling class, stretching the hip flexors, quadriceps, hamstrings, calves, hips, and gluteals makes sense because they are major muscles used for cycling. The major muscle groups surrounding the joints people typically use during **activities of daily living (ADL)** (e.g., ankles, hips, spine, and shoulders) can also be targeted with stretching. Table 5-3 details different techniques for stretching.

TABLE 5-3
Stretching Techniques

Technique	Definition
Static Stretching	This is the most common method used to improve flexibility. Static stretching consists of slowly moving a muscle group to a point of minor discomfort and then holding that stretch for 10–30 seconds. This type of stretching is most often used during the cool-down segment of the group exercise class. Static stretching can be classified as passive stretching or active stretching. Passive stretching involves moving into a position and then either holding it with some other part of the body (e.g., arm), or with the assistance of a partner or some other apparatus (e.g., stretching strap). The goal is to slowly move the body part into the stretch to prevent a forceful action and possible injury. In active stretching, the individual holds the stretched position using the strength of the agonist muscle. This type of stretching is common during many forms of yoga.
Dynamic Stretching	Dynamic stretching involves moving parts of the body through a full ROM several times while gradually increasing the reach and/or speed of movement in a controlled manner. These exercises are very rhythmic in nature. Dynamic stretches are often incorporated in the group exercise warm-up due to their similarity to the movements or patterns that will be used during the conditioning period (that is, dynamic stretching can be used as rehearsal movements).
Ballistic Stretching	This approach involves a bouncing or jerky movement to use the momentum of the body to reach the muscle's ROM limits. This bouncing motion may produce a powerful stretch reflex that counteracts the muscle lengthening and could possibly lead to tissue injury. While ballistic stretching is not common practice for the general population, its use in training and rehabilitation of athletes where explosive movements are critical may be justified.
Proprioceptive Neuromuscular Facilitation (PNF)	PNF stretching involves both the stretching and contraction of the targeted muscle group. While there are several ways to employ PNF, a common technique is termed contract-relax. Following a passive 10-second pre-stretch, the muscle is concentrically activated through its full ROM against resistance from a partner. After the concentric muscle action, a passive stretch is held for 30 seconds. This method is not typically performed in group exercise classes, as it is most effective when a partner assists with the stretch, and it requires specific training on the part of the GFI, as well as the partner.

Note: ROM = Range of motion

APPLY WHAT YOU KNOW

Cueing a Stretch

It is important for stretching to be comfortable for participants. Encourage proper form by using cues such as "find a comfortable position where you feel gentle tension and hold; if you are shaking or if your muscles feel like rubber bands ready to snap, scale back the intensity of the stretch." Also, it is important for GFIs to model average flexibility so that participants do not imitate form they cannot comfortably or safely match. As with any other activity, it is important to progress participants appropriately. Yoga is a good example of a modality that has many advanced stretches that could be high-risk for some participants. If they are taught progressively, as is commonly done in dedicated yoga classes, the body adapts to the stretches and movements over time. However, putting advanced yoga poses into a traditional group fitness class does not allow for proper progression. Therefore, it is important that the GFI incorporate only moves that are appropriate for class participants.

Reminding participants of proper **posture** while stretching helps to promote overall body stability and balance and enhances the effectiveness of the stretching experience. Two to three concise verbal cues may be needed during each stretch to make sure body positioning is optimal for an effective stretch. For example, when teaching a standing hamstrings stretch, it is important to cue to tilt the pelvis anteriorly to lengthen the hamstring muscles and to extend the knee as much as is safely possible.

ACE MOVER METHOD™

Why Do I Need to Warm Up and Cool Down?

One day after class, a former participant stops by to say hello. They tell you that they had stopped exercising for a few months because of an increasingly hectic work schedule but are starting to exercise again sporadically. They plan to make it to the gym a few times per week but do not plan to attend group exercise classes because they don't have time to warm up and cool down. They only have enough time to work out for a short, but intense, period before heading home for the evening, so they thought working out on their own might make that easier.

ACE ABC APPROACH™

The following is an example of how the ACE ABC Approach™ can be used to share information about the importance of the different segments of an effective exercise class and guide participants toward getting back on track with their health-related physical-activity goals.

Ask: Asking powerful **open-ended questions** during this impromptu meeting will allow the GFI to help the former class participant revisit their "why" for wanting to become more active and keep the conversation moving in a positive direction.

GFI: It's great to see you! Thank you for making a point to see me and for sharing your plan to exercise at the gym a few times each week. It sounds like you recognize the value of exercise and are ready to get back to it. What are you hoping to achieve by becoming more physically active and why is that important to you?

Participant: It's great to see you, too! When I was exercising regularly, I was feeling better both physically and mentally. I also had more energy and, strangely, felt more productive even though I was taking time out of my day to exercise. Even though I stopped exercising for a few months, I still know that it's good for me and important for my health and fitness. I'm hoping to improve my fitness and get back to feeling better about myself and feel more comfortable in my body. Mentally, feeling better is important because it helps me focus more on work and to contribute more to life at home. Having a body that does not feel out of shape is also important because I like to be active when I can, and I recognize that there are some days when I barely move at all.

GFI: Exercising is important to your mental and physical health and you recognize the value of moving more in your daily life. How were you able to be successful when you were exercising regularly in the past?

Participant: Prior to the past few months, I was making it to the gym three days per week and was attending your classes on two of those days. I was able to be successful with my consistency by prioritizing my health and making my gym time a regular part of my schedule. I also liked attending classes because of the structure and the fact that I did not have to plan my own workouts. I also liked the built-in accountability and was even starting to become friends with a few of the other participants. I think all these factors made it enjoyable for me and added a social element that always made me feel welcomed and wanted.

Break down barriers: In this step, it is time to further investigate the participant's concerns to discover what obstacles may prevent them from exercising regularly.

GFI: Not having to plan your own workouts, accountability, and building friendships have helped you to stay on track and find success in the past. What can you start doing now to move closer to your goals?

Participant: For starters, I have added exercise to my schedule again on two days per week and plan to commit to taking care of my health on these days. I did really enjoy attending group classes but there just seems to be a lot of wasted time where we are not actually exercising at the beginning and end of class. This is why I would typically leave class early. I like the structure of group classes, but I feel like only the part where I was working hard was helping me reach my goals.

GFI: Having structure is important to you and, because you have a limited amount of time for exercise, you want to make sure you are getting the most out of your time at the gym. What you don't like is the beginning of the class and the end of class, or the warm-up and cool-down segments. What do you already know about why these elements are added to the class?

Participant: That's a good question. I assume there is a reason they are added to the classes, and I'm guessing the warm-up gets your body ready for the harder part of the class, but I'm not sure why I need to cool down if the whole point of exercising is to get my heart rate up.

GFI: Would you mind if I share a bit more information about the importance of a proper warm-up and cool-down?

Participant: That would be great. Thank you!

GFI: You are correct about the warm-up period being a time to get your body ready for the more challenging portion of the workout. This is accomplished by circulating more blood to the exercising muscles, getting you mentally prepared, and increasing your body temperature. In contrast, the cool-down is important because it gives your body a chance to return to its pre-activity state. This is accomplished by gradually decreasing your exercise intensity to lower your heart rate, breathing rate, and body temperature. Another feature of a cool-down that may be appealing is that it serves as a time to improve flexibility and for stress relief. The cool-down is also a time to reflect on what you just accomplished. Even if you are exercising on your own, warming up and cooling down are crucial elements of an effective exercise program. Does that make sense?

Participant: That does make sense. I didn't realize how important warming up and cooling down are for exercising effectively. Improving my flexibility is important to me and I could benefit from some stress relief.

Collaborate: Now that barriers to being successful have been discussed, working together with the participant on goals and solutions is the next step.

GFI: What steps could you see yourself taking toward your initial goal of exercising two days per week?

Participant: I absolutely want to set myself up for success and am excited to start exercising again. I'm committed to getting to the gym twice per week. I think initially I'll come to the gym one day per week to exercise on my own and dedicate a portion of my workout to warming up and cooling down. I'll also attend one group class per week and plan to stay for the entire duration of the class while remembering to view the cool-down as a chance to focus on flexibility and managing my stress levels. I think this is a good place to start. I also think I could really benefit from the accountability, structure, and friendship from exercising as part of a group. I really like knowing there are people in class who look forward to seeing me. My immediate next step will be to check the group exercise schedule and find a class day and time that works with my schedule.

GFI: It sounds like you have a thoughtful plan for exercising two days per week and that once you find a class day and time that works, you will be on your way to finding consistency by utilizing some strategies that helped you to be successful in the past. I look forward to seeing you at the gym more often and perhaps even seeing you in class!

The ACE ABC Approach provides GFIs with strategies that can be used in a variety of settings and in a variety of timeframes to ensure participants understand what barriers may get in the way and have a clear picture of how to move forward with health behavior change. In this example, the GFI takes a participant-centered approach to sharing information, uses **active listening,** and empowers the participant to set their own goals. During this interaction, the intent of the GFI was not to convince the participant that they should attend group classes, but rather to treat them as the expert on themselves and as being resourceful and capable of change. While the GFI did provide information about the importance of warming up and cooling down, it was up to the participant to see the connection between how group exercise was a part of their initial success and how it may be helpful now.

ACE UNIVERSITY

If your study program includes ACE University, visit www.ACEfitness.org/MyACE and log in to your My ACE Account to take full advantage of the ACE Group Fitness Instructor Study Program and online guided study experience.

A variety of media to support and expand on the material in this text is provided to facilitate learning and best prepare you for the ACE Group Fitness Instructor Certification exam and a career as a group fitness instructor.

SUMMARY

Most group fitness classes should integrate some form of a warm-up, conditioning segment, and cool-down. Cardiorespiratory, muscular, and/or flexibility exercise can be included in the conditioning portion, or main body, of the workout to meet the participants' goals and the objectives of the class format. Understanding and being able to apply the variables of frequency, intensity, duration, and exercise mode as they pertain to each type of modality and/or class format will help a GFI guide participants appropriately to their goals.

REFERENCES

American College of Sports Medicine (2022). *ACSM's Guidelines for Exercise Testing and Prescription* (11th ed.). Philadelphia: Wolters Kluwer.

American Council on Exercise (2020). *Where to Start: Choosing Your Preferred Format for Group Fitness Classes.* https://www.acefitness.org/education-and-resources/professional/expert-articles/7735/where-to-start-choosing-your-preferred-format-for-group-fitness-classes/

Behm, D.G. et al. (2016). Acute effects of muscle stretching on physical performance, range of motion, and injury incidence in healthy active individuals: A systematic review. *Applied Physiology, Nutrition, and Metabolism*, 41, 1, 1–11.

Herman, K. et al. (2012). The effectiveness of neuromuscular warm-up strategies that require no additional equipment, for preventing lower limb injuries during sports participation: A systematic review. *BMC Medicine*, 10, 75.

Lewis, J. (2014). A systematic literature review of the relationship between stretching and athletic injury prevention. *Orthopaedic Nursing*, 33, 6, 312–320.

Reid, J.C., et al. (2018). The effects of different durations of static stretching within a comprehensive warm-up on voluntary and evoked contractile properties. *European Journal of Applied Physiology*, 118, 7, 1427–1445.

SUGGESTED READING

American College of Sports Medicine (2022). *ACSM's Guidelines for Exercise Testing and Prescription* (11th ed.). Philadelphia: Wolters Kluwer.

CHAPTER 6

Key Considerations for Group Fitness Classes

JAN SCHROEDER, PhD | Professor, Department of Kinesiology, California State University Long Beach; ACE Certified Group Fitness Instructor

IN THIS CHAPTER

LEARNING OBJECTIVES

Upon completion of this chapter, readers will be able to:

- Promote positive class experiences through themed classes and powerful opening and closing statements
- Foster community among group exercise participants
- Identify ideal room characteristics, including flooring and exercise surface qualities, for group fitness classes
- Describe exercise apparel considerations, including the use of appropriate footwear in the group fitness setting
- Describe key equipment considerations for group fitness classes
- Demonstrate a basic understanding of music, including music selection, foreground and background music, tempo, and volume for group fitness classes

ACE UNIVERSITY

If your study program includes ACE University, visit www.ACEfitness.org/MyACE and log in to your My ACE Account to take full advantage of the ACE Group Fitness Instructor Study Program and online guided study experience.

A variety of media to support and expand on the material in this text is provided to facilitate learning

While all ACE Certified Group Fitness Instructors (GFIs) teach classes, outstanding instructors take the planning and instructional process one step further in order to create experiences. From establishing specific themes and incorporating elements such as visualization, to developing opening and closing statements constructed using positive and inclusive language, GFIs have the ability to create meaningful and memorable classes for participants by considering a few additional components even before building out the content or choreography of a class.

Considerations for Class Experiences

CREATING A THEME

One way to create an engaging group fitness experience is to establish a central theme for the day's class. The theme should emphasize a specific aspect of the experience that the GFI would like to make the focal point for participants. Themes not only offer the opportunity for participants to learn something new, but also provide a more cohesive class experience by weaving a common thread consistently from start to finish. Themes can focus on increasing **kinesthetic awareness** (e.g., utilizing a theme of posture in an aquatic fitness class); targeting a specific area of the body (e.g., a core-themed suspension training class); introducing a philosophical concept (e.g., a gratitude-themed yoga class); emphasizing a specific event or time of year (e.g., a Halloween-themed cycling class); or even highlighting a particular time period or musical genre [e.g., an 80s-themed **high-intensity interval training (HIIT)** class], just to name a few.

While there are countless themes from which to choose, GFIs should consider selecting a theme that fits the specific class format they are teaching, while also resonating with the needs, expectations, and preferences of class participants, as well as with the GFI themself. For example, a heart chakra theme might be a feasible option for a yoga class in which back-bending postures are appropriate for participants and the instructor is well-versed in the seven chakras. However, this particular theme would likely not resonate well with participants in a **muscular fitness** class in which the instructor is unfamiliar with the seven chakras and the purpose of the class is to increase **muscular strength** and **muscular endurance.**

GFIs should take time to brainstorm a list of themes for the classes they currently teach, and then choose one specific theme they feel most comfortable presenting that will resonate well with participants. From there, instructors can identify ways in which the theme will be emphasized throughout the class. In order for a theme to be most impactful, it should be clearly stated at the start of the class as well as evident throughout the entire experience, which includes being reiterated at the end of the class. Importantly, while creating a themed class is a great way to add a fun component, it is not necessary for every class to have a theme.

To ensure a well-developed theme that is of value to participants, GFIs should take time to carefully consider a variety of elements that will be used to convey the theme during the class experience. These elements may include the particular music used, the exact orientation of participants in the room, or the inclusion of specific keywords within verbal cues. When selecting music, GFIs should be mindful of the specific content of each song, including lyrics, if applicable. Instructors should also consider crafting a list of keywords that help bring the theme to life.

Another way in which GFIs can emphasize a theme is to incorporate quiet or silent relaxation segments, guided imagery, creative visualization, or storytelling, especially during times within the class when participants are most receptive (e.g., the last few minutes of class). The exact structure of these components should be determined based on what best supports the specific theme as well as the class format and participants.

THINK IT THROUGH

Developing a Theme

Spend some time considering potential themes that you might incorporate into your group fitness classes. Choose one and brainstorm ways in which to use that theme to engage all five senses over the course of the class experience, either in reality or through visualization.

OPENING AND CLOSING STATEMENTS

The beginning and ending of a class are crucial for success and for creating a noteworthy experience. It is recommended to utilize formal, memorized, and well-rehearsed opening and closing statements to define the purpose of a class, set a professional tone, and bring the class to an inspirational conclusion.

Opening statements generally include the following:

- A salutation and personal introduction
- An expression of gratitude to participants for attending
- Acknowledgment of new and familiar faces
- A statement regarding the class purpose and learning objectives
- Reference to equipment and specific exercises that will be explored
- Ways to monitor intensity and tailor movements
- An introduction of the day's theme to inspire individuals to stay for the entire experience (if a theme is planned)

GFIs may also choose to incorporate some form of an ice-breaker activity to better acquaint participants with one another. Refer to Chapter 10 for ideas for adding the "fun factor" to group fitness classes.

Closing statements generally include the following:

- A reiteration of the class purpose
- A reference to the theme of the experience
- Insight as to how what was covered in class applies in a meaningful way outside of the group fitness environment

- A heartfelt thank you to participants for attending
- A compelling reason why they should return to a future class (e.g., divulging an exciting theme for an upcoming dance-based fitness class or the introduction of new movements that expand on ones that were previously learned)

Positive and Inclusive Language

In both the opening and closing statements, as well as throughout the class experience, GFIs should make it a point to use positive and inclusive language that supports participants and appropriately conveys the theme. GFIs should also provide participants with ample and ongoing positive reinforcement and individual praise. Feedback that is specific and relevant to the participant may be a powerful reinforcement (see Chapter 9).

EQUITY, DIVERSITY, AND INCLUSION

Inclusive Language

Alex McLean, international fitness presenter, 25+ year fitness professional, ACE Certified since 2008

Language is powerful and can have a huge impact on individuals. More precisely, when language is used with a mindfulness for the perspectives and feelings of others, it can show respect and understanding, while careless or inappropriate language demonstrates a lack thereof.

Inclusive language avoids the use of certain expressions or words that might be considered to exclude particular groups of people. Inclusive language helps to avoid offending or demeaning people based on stereotypes or personal perceptions, which supports a safe and open environment where individuals are not judged or looked down upon for being who they are or for characteristics they cannot control.

Inclusive language helps usher in the next evolution of fitness by creating an experience and community where all members feel seen, appreciated, and respected. Small tweaks in language can deliver a lasting positive impression for the members, but it takes ongoing effort and commitment.

The first step to create community is to build connection by learning the individual's first name and correct pronouns. A simple addition to your standard introduction may sound like this: "Hi, my name is Alex and my pronouns are he/him. What's your name?" This opens the door for the other person to do the same. It eases a person's fears and dispels any assumptions.

Another tactic is to use gender-neutral words. In classes, replace "hey guys" and "hi ladies" with "hey everyone" or "hi friends." What words can be added to facilitate camaraderie among the participants? Some alternative choices include "team" and "folks." GFIs can also build their language around the name of the class, facility, or brand (e.g., "steppers, are you ready?").

Remember, not everyone in the room wants a bikini body or to do "curls for the girls." Instead, highlight the outcome of the movement as opposed to the aesthetics. For example, say "use your breath to power your legs for the last set of squats" instead of "summer is coming, who's ready for the beach and bikinis?"

Using inclusive language is a simple but powerful way to create a group exercise setting in which everyone feels respected and safe (Table 6-1).

TABLE 6-1

Examples of Inclusive Language

Instead of...	Try....
Hi guys!	Hi everyone!
Do you see how she is rotating her hip?	Do you see how Maria is rotating the hip?
Let's burn off those weekend drinks.	Let's start the week with some powerful and healthy movement.
Let's get bikini ready.	Let's move in a way that honors what our body needs right now.
Curls for the girls.	I love how strong I feel when I do biceps curls.

APPLY WHAT YOU KNOW

Managing Participant Expectations

As noted in Chapter 7, establishing a class purpose is essential when designing a group fitness class. As part of the class experience, it is important that GFIs communicate the purpose so that participants are well aware of what to expect during the class. For example, if a GFI is teaching a class titled "Boot Camp," it is valuable for the instructor to address at the start of class what the specific purpose and objectives are and how they will personally be approaching the class format, from the specific equipment used to the types of exercises and movements featured. Doing this will help better manage expectations, especially among those participants who may have preconceived notions about what the class will or will not entail based on their past experiences in classes of a similar nature.

Cultivating Community

It is particularly important for class members to feel a sense of cohesiveness. Research shows that individuals who have strong beliefs about the cohesiveness of their class attend more fitness classes, are less likely to drop out, are more likely to enjoy physical activity, and have high **self-efficacy** toward physical activity (Maher et al., 2015; Estabrooks, 2000). Group cohesion starts when participants gather around a shared task. Learning a new routine as a group or working to meet class objectives will enhance this type of group cohesion. As participants become satisfied with their accomplishments, social cohesion increases. The **social support** and reinforcement for exercise developed through group interactions is powerful and can be incorporated into every class.

TEAM COHESIVENESS

Community is created through connections, and when participants feel connected to fellow participants, they attend classes more frequently. This sense of community, which is a selling point of the facility, is due in large part to the teamwork among the group fitness staff.

A staff that communicates and works together produces a great environment and sense of community. When instructors take one another's classes and/or suggest that participants check out another instructor's class, individuals take note. A facility truly becomes a place of connection when participants feel like the focus is placed on them having positive experiences and becoming more active by attending a wide variety of class offerings within the facility, rather than GFIs competing for class numbers. When participants feel that they are valued and supported, they become more vested in the facility, and in turn become more loyal members and class participants.

THINK IT THROUGH

Building Cohesiveness

What steps will you take to help create a great group fitness environment that fosters a sense of community and builds cohesiveness among the team of exercise professionals in your fitness facility? How might you ensure that participants feel like part of a supporting, welcoming community when they step through your doors?

RECRUITING AND RETAINING PARTICIPANTS

In addition to creating dynamic and memorable class experiences and positively collaborating with fellow instructors, GFIs can utilize technology to further recruit and retain participants. Through the use of well-branded social media channels and websites, participants can choose to connect with GFIs outside of the group fitness environment. From encouraging individuals to opt in to email lists, follow the facility on social media platforms, and review monthly e-newsletters, there are many ways in which GFIs can leverage additional "touch points" through which to engage participants and further develop **rapport.**

Exercise Apparel Considerations

CLOTHING

The GFI should have a good understanding of the appropriate attire to wear when instructing and participating in the specific modalities they will be teaching. Class participants often look to the GFI as a role model with regard to determining appropriate attire for the class format. Instructors should wear clothing that allows participants to clearly view the key movements of the body performed during the class. For example, many Pilates and yoga exercises involve subtle joint movement. Clothing that has excess material could block the participant's view of the instructor's form, thus limiting the effectiveness of the instruction. However, care should also be taken to avoid wearing too little, as doing so could result in the GFI appearing unprofessional.

In addition to wearing appropriate, properly fitted apparel, the type of material from which the clothing is constructed should also be considered for both the GFI and participants. For example, cotton tends to sop up and retain moisture, whereas newer synthetic materials (e.g., polypropylene) wick away moisture. While cotton can be a good choice for exercising in the heat due to the fact that it readily soaks up sweat, for those same reasons cotton is a poor choice for exercising in the cold. Synthetic materials and synthetic blends tend to be a good choice because they allow for evaporation and keep skin dry, cool, and comfortable.

The equipment and apparel needed varies among formats, instructors, and types of exercise programming. Table 6-2 provides some basic recommendations to consider. Most classes do not require specific apparel to participate, as instructors can typically adjust their programming as necessary. However, for some classes, having specific equipment and apparel can allow for a more complete level of participation, may make exercise more comfortable, and, in some cases, may be required for safety reasons (e.g., wearing wrist wraps or gloves with wrist support during a class that involves striking a bag).

TABLE 6-2

Equipment and Apparel Needs for Various Class Types

Class Type	Equipment/Apparel Needs
Cycling	Cycling shoes, socks, shorts, jersey (moisture-wicking materials), and towel
Combat sport–inspired	Boxing or mixed martial arts gloves, wrist wraps, and padded shin guards
Aquatic exercise	Aquatic gloves, foam dumbbells, kickboards, aquatic ankle weights, and aquatic exercise belts (avoid swim caps that prevent heat dissipation)
Barre	Grip socks (to prevent slipping)
Dance-based	Dance shoes or athletic shoes with a pivot point (a circular patch of rubber on the shoe's sole)
Mind/body	Yoga mat (which is typically thin with a nonslip surface) or Pilates mat (which is usually thick and compliant)

EQUITY, DIVERSITY, AND INCLUSION

EDI and Apparel Considerations

Alex McLean, international fitness presenter, 25+ year fitness professional, ACE Certified since 2008

Fitness is a visual industry. It sells aesthetics, as images of chiseled legs, sculpted arms, and six-pack abs bombard society at every turn. This imagery promotes the external benefits of exercise, the results that people can "see," and an "ideal"—and largely unattainable—body type for most. If fitness is for everybody and every "body," fitness apparel becomes an increasingly important discussion. Inherent in this conversation is body image, which is a person's perception of their physical self, and the positive and negative feelings that accompany that perception.

There are several considerations related to **equity, diversity,** and **inclusion** that should be part of any discussion about exercise apparel and what is or is not appropriate in a fitness setting. Some fitness modalities may typically call for the wearing of more form-fitting clothing that assists the instructor in observing proper form and movement, but GFIs should be mindful that not all participants will be comfortable in that type of clothing.

Religion can also be a factor in exercise apparel selection, as it may prescribe specific guidelines. For example, Islam promotes a more holistic approach to a healthy lifestyle, incorporating good habits for the mind and body through physical activity, fasting, and prayer. However, Muslim women encounter distinct challenges in a fitness setting because they practice modesty and tend to keep certain body parts covered. As a result, many Muslim women wear skirts over their workout attire.

There are countless EDI-related reasons why a particular participant may not be wearing apparel that is typically seen in a group fitness setting. In addition to gender identity and religion, these may include body size, ethnicity, and disability status. For this reason, a GFI should always be considerate and accepting of all participants, regardless of what they choose to wear and their reasons for doing so unless there is a concern for safety. It is certainly not the role of the GFI to question or call attention to anyone's choices. Instead, understand that every individual brings their own personal values and experiences with them when they walk into the fitness facility, and make everyone feel welcomed, accepted, and empowered.

FOOTWEAR

Proper footwear provides good cushioning, support, and flexibility. Many group fitness formats, including step and kickboxing classes, require that the balls of the feet absorb repetitive impact during the landing and pushing-off of dynamic movements. Footwear must provide cushioning under the forefoot in addition to heel cushioning to reduce the possibility of injury to the foot from repeated impact. Lateral movement, such as shuffling or traveling side-to-side, demands support on the lateral aspect of the shoe to prevent the foot from rolling over the **base of support** and causing an ankle sprain. Running shoes are designed for forward-movement efficiency and are not appropriate for classes with excessive lateral or pivoting movements, such as dance-based fitness classes.

Various sole designs allow for good forefoot flexibility without sacrificing traction. They provide freedom of movement without slipping during cutting, stopping, or rapid changes of direction, such as in sports-conditioning classes. Forefoot flexibility is also necessary for many flexibility-based classes in which full **range of motion (ROM)** is desired.

For indoor cycling, participants should wear stiff-soled or cycling shoes because soft-soled shoes flex over the pedal, which can lead to numbness, bruising, or other soft-tissue injuries such as Achilles tendinitis or calf muscle **strains.** Cycling shoes also help improve cycling-specific muscle recruitment patterns and pedaling efficiency, which may reduce **overuse injuries.**

Surface, equipment, intensity, and quality of movement determine the requirements of appropriate footwear. GFIs should be sure to evaluate the class content and adhere to any footwear guidelines indicated for different formats.

APPLY WHAT YOU KNOW

Educating Participants on Proper Footwear

GFIs can offer some basic guidelines to help participants make more informed decisions when purchasing appropriate footwear for physical activity. If a participant engages in a specific activity two or three times each week, such as running, walking, tennis, basketball, or a specific group fitness class format like kickboxing, they will want a shoe designed specifically for that sport or activity. Multipurpose shoes such as cross trainers may be a good alternative for individuals who participate in several sports or activities, such as cardiorespiratory exercise and resistance training, in a single workout. Ideally, participants should look for an athletic shoe store with a good reputation in the community. Their sales staff are likely to be knowledgeable about selecting appropriate shoes for the individual, considering their activity level and specific foot type. Some stores even offer a free **gait** analysis to better understand the individual's unique needs. General recommendations when purchasing footwear include the following:

- Get fitted for footwear toward the end of the day. It is not unusual for an individual's foot to increase by half a shoe size during the course of a single day. However, if an individual plans to exercise consistently at a specific time, they should consider getting fitted at that time.
- Allow a space up to the width of the index finger between the end of the longest toe and the end of the shoe. This space will accommodate foot size increases, a variety of socks, and foot movement within the shoe without hurting the toes.
- The heel of the foot should not slip out of the shoe during **plantar flexion,** as in walking or stepping.
- The ball of the foot should match the widest part of the shoe, and the participant should have plenty of room for the toes to wiggle without experiencing slippage in the heel.
- Shoes should not rub or pinch any area of the foot or ankle. The individual should rotate the ankles when trying on shoes and pay attention to the sides of the feet and the top of the toes, both of which are common areas for blisters.
- The participant should wear the same weight of socks that they intend to use during activity. Participants should look for socks that are made with synthetic fibers such as acrylic or polyester for better blister prevention.

It is also important that participants understand factors that determine when shoes need to be replaced. If shoes are no longer absorbing the pounding and jarring action, the individual is more likely to sustain ankle, shin, and knee injuries. Athletic shoes will lose their cushioning after three to six months of regular use [or 350 to 500 miles (~560 to 800 km) of running]. However, participants should look at the wear patterns as a good indicator for replacement. Any time the shoe appears to be wearing down unevenly, especially at the heel, it is time to replace the shoes. Additionally, if the traction on the soles of the shoes is worn flat, it is time for new shoes. Also, if your feet feel tired or your shins, knees, or hips hurt after activity, these may be signs that it is time to replace your shoes (National Institute on Aging, 2020).

Equipment Considerations and Options

The use of equipment is prevalent in group exercise classes. From steps and elastic resistance tubing to bikes and agility ladders, each piece of equipment has specific set-up, use, and/or fit requirements. To minimize the risk of injury among participants, GFIs must check equipment regularly for wear and tear and replace items when necessary. Additionally, if equipment is manufactured in various sizes, ideally all size options should be made available to accommodate participants. A GFI should also possess knowledge of specific equipment or accessories that can make a class more effective and enjoyable for participants. Even if a particular fitness facility does not currently own the equipment, the GFI can be an advocate by educating facility staff about the benefits of incorporating such items into classes. For example, yoga class participants can greatly benefit from having props such as yoga blocks, blankets, bolsters, and straps available to enable them to achieve positions that may otherwise not be possible. Additionally, specific types of mats are better for certain modalities than others, such as yoga mats that are thin and "sticky," allowing for a better grip during standing movements compared to traditional exercise mats.

APPLY WHAT YOU KNOW

New and Varied Equipment Options

Introducing new equipment options is an easy way to add variety to a class format. For example, if a GFI has always used hand weights and weighted bars in a muscular fitness class, incorporating elastic resistance bands could reinvigorate the exercise experience for participants. As with new choreography and exercise ideas, equipment should not be added solely to make exercises more complex or difficult, as the training tools used should match the overall goal of the class and be suitable for the intended participants. GFIs should keep in mind that some equipment requires more in-depth training and experience prior to teaching with it (e.g., kettlebells and suspension training systems), which necessitates specific continuing education on the training tool before introducing it as an equipment option in class. Misuse of equipment can lead to injury, so it is especially important to learn the intended use, limitations, and safety precautions for all equipment.

Another consideration when deciding to incorporate equipment is the number of pieces to use in one class. It is important that each participant have appropriate space around them while exercising. Having too much equipment cluttered around the room poses a tripping hazard. Limiting classes to one or two pieces of resistance equipment and one prop (such as a step that serves as a bench) is generally recommended. Keep in mind that fitness equipment is not always as exciting for new members as it is for experienced participants and the GFI. For some, equipment can be intimidating, and new participants may become overwhelmed at the sight of too many training tools scattered about the room.

Music

Music serves multiple purposes in group fitness classes, such as motivation, pacing for certain movements, and overall positive experience. It provides motivation through its changing keys, lyrics, and instruments. The use of music can be a way to motivate participants and create more overall enjoyment in the class experience. Several research studies have validated the idea that music is beneficial from a motivational standpoint (Alter et al., 2015; van der Vlist et al., 2011). It can set the pace for a particular activity, such as pedaling in an indoor cycling class or moving around the room in a dance-based fitness class. Research has also shown that caloric expenditure is greater and duration is longer in classes with music as compared to classes without music (Guerrero et al., 2020; Thakare, Mehrotra, & Singh, 2017).

Ultimately, all music chosen should contribute to, rather than detract from, the overall desired experience. Asking participants about their preference for music is one option to increase enjoyment of the class, though GFIs should strive to incorporate various music styles and genres to appeal to a wide variety of participants. Instructors often make the mistake of choosing music they find motivating for their own workouts but, while it is important that the music selected motivates the instructor, it is imperative that it motivate the participants. A participant-centered instructor will make every effort to provide an enjoyable and memorable movement experience.

LEGAL CONSIDERATIONS

Understanding Music and Copyright Law

Mark S. Nagel, EdD, Professor, Sport and Entertainment Management Department, University of South Carolina

The choice of music not only needs to provide the appropriate rhythm and motivation level, but also must be legal to use. Unlike playing music in one's residence for personal enjoyment, playing music as part of a group-led exercise activity is typically considered an integral component of group fitness instruction and is therefore subject to **copyright** law. It may appear that publicly playing music while instructing participants is a harmless activity, but the owners of copyrights will often investigate gyms, educational settings, and online class activities to determine if copyrighted music is being utilized in an exercise setting without a license. Initial violations will usually elicit a stern warning through a cease-and-desist letter, with additional violations resulting in potential fines and other negative repercussions.

Fortunately, GFIs do not have to secure a license for the use of each individual song they may wish to play in a class setting. There are ways to secure a **performance license** that covers an extensive list of artists through several companies that enforce copyrights in this area. In some cases, a facility may secure a license that covers all activities in all areas of the gym (e.g., general exercise area, group fitness room, and pool area), but in other cases group fitness classes may not be covered by the facility and the GFI must have the necessary licenses for using copyrighted music while teaching. The usual cost of securing a license is affordable and the potential fines for violations can be steep, so GFIs should not hesitate to secure permission to utilize music in their classes. They should also consider the following:

- The cost of a license is typically determined by the number of participants who will be taught, so if an initial license is secured assuming one level of participation but future classes expand greatly, the GFI may need to secure a license that matches the increased class size.
- Because there are multiple license holders, GFIs need to make sure the songs they have chosen to play are covered by the appropriate license holder. In many cases, GFIs and fitness facilities secure licenses with all the major license holders to create greater music choice flexibility.
- If working at one location that has a musical license covering all classes, GFIs will be protected, but should never assume—especially if working at multiple locations—that each facility has secured a license for all class sizes. GFIs should verify they are covered before teaching classes (if the GFI does not have individual licenses secured).
- If the GFI is unsure if a musical composition is covered under a secured license, they should not play it in a class setting.

Refer to Chapter 14 for more information on the legal use of music in group fitness settings.

FOREGROUND AND BACKGROUND MUSIC

When choosing music for a particular class, the GFI needs to determine whether the music's role will be in the foreground or background. When music is in the foreground, instructors will incorporate its **tempo** (and sometimes its lyrics or general feeling) into the class (Table 6-3). Examples of using music in the foreground include stepping to the **downbeat** of a musical compilation, doing dance-based movements, and performing choreographed formats. When music is in the background, instructors do not incorporate the tempo or volume as an integrated aspect of the experience. In classes such as boot camp, aquatic exercise, and yoga, music is often used in the background to help motivate or set a mood in classes. Not all classes delineate these two roles of music clearly. Classes like aquatic exercise and group indoor cycling, for example, generally include both foreground and background music. For example, during some songs, instructors ask participants to move at the rate of the music, while during others, the music is part of the background ambience.

TABLE 6-3

Basic Music Terminology

Term	Definition
Beat	Regular pulsations that usually have an even rhythm and occur in a continuous pattern of strong and weak pulsations
Downbeat	Strong pulsations
Phrase	32 counts of music, composed of four segments of eight beats each
Tempo	The rate or speed of the music, expressed as beats per minute (bpm)

MUSIC TEMPO

Deciding what tempo of music to use in the exercise class is another consideration of utmost importance for the GFI. Music tempo can determine the pace as well as the intensity of exercise. The tempo assists GFIs in determining a piece of music's appropriateness for a particular class. For example, choosing the proper tempo [as measured in **beats** per minute (bpm)] for a resistance-training class will allow participants to move the weight through a full ROM with control and provide the needed stimulus for strength development. Choosing a tempo that is faster than is recommended could lead to injury and/or insufficient stimulus for muscular development.

Legal Considerations

To ensure the most professional experience, GFIs should purchase legally licensed music specifically prepared for group fitness classes, because its **phrases** and beats are consistently developed according to industry-standardized bpm guidelines without the fluctuations and bridges, or sections of a song specifically designed to contrast the rest of the composition, that occur in music that one hears on the radio. Table 6-4 presents the industry guidelines for music tempo when instructors use the music in the foreground and have their participants execute all movements on the downbeat, while Table 6-5 presents appropriate music tempos for aquatic exercise classes.

TABLE 6-4

Music Tempo for Common Group Fitness Modalities

Tempo (beats per minute)	Modalities
<100	Most often used for background music or slower, mind-body classes like Pilates, yoga, or stretching classes
100–122	Beginner step classes, low end of low-impact aerobics, and hip-hop classes If cycling on the beat and using pedal stroke as a measure of beats per minute, this range represents the upper limit of music tempo.
122–129	Group strength classes, advanced step classes, low-to-mid impact aerobics, some dance-based fitness classes, and aquatic fitness classes
130–160	Faster-paced movement classes, mid-to-high impact classes, some dance-based fitness classes, trampoline-based classes, and some martial arts–based classes

MUSIC SELECTION

The two main considerations when selecting music are purpose and participants. Understanding the music's purpose helps GFIs understand what types of music would be most appropriate for the objectives chosen. For example, if the purpose is steady-state training, such as in step or aquatic exercise classes, choosing music with a consistent tempo would be prudent. Alternatively, if the purpose is to introduce mindfulness and introspection, such as in a stretching or mind-body class, perhaps softer music with no beat would be appropriate. An awareness of the participants also helps provide a successful musical experience for everyone, as different populations and demographics will have preferences about both music type and volume.

TABLE 6-5

Music Tempo for Common Aquatic Exercise Classes

Modality	Tempo (beats per minute)
Shallow-water cardiorespiratory exercise	125–150
Deep-water cardiorespiratory exercise	100–135
Aquatic kickboxing	125–132 (basic techniques/skills and drills) 128–140 (advanced combinations)
Muscular conditioning	115–130
Shallow-water interval training	125–150 (interspersed with faster or slower tempos)
Deep-water interval training	100–130 (interspersed with faster or slower tempos)
Circuit training	125–150 (aerobic segments) 115–130 (resistance-training segments)

Reprinted with permission from Aquatic Exercise Association (2020). *Aquatic Fitness Programming: Standards and Guidelines.* https://aeawave.org/Portals/0/AEA_Cert_Docs/AEA_Standards_Guidlines_2020.pdf?ver=2019-12-18-131623-417&timestamp=1576696862726

MUSIC VOLUME

Music volume in a group exercise class may vary due to the class format. However, it is generally recommended that GFIs keep their music volume under 85 decibels (dB) (Figure 6-1). Instructors who use loud music are not only at risk of damaging their own hearing and that of their participants, but they are also much more likely to suffer from voice injury, as they find themselves having to shout over loud music, even when using a microphone (see Chapter 10). Research has shown that if music volume in group exercise classes remains dangerously high, participants report ringing in the ears or muffled hearing following classes and prefer a lower volume (Lee et al., 2021).

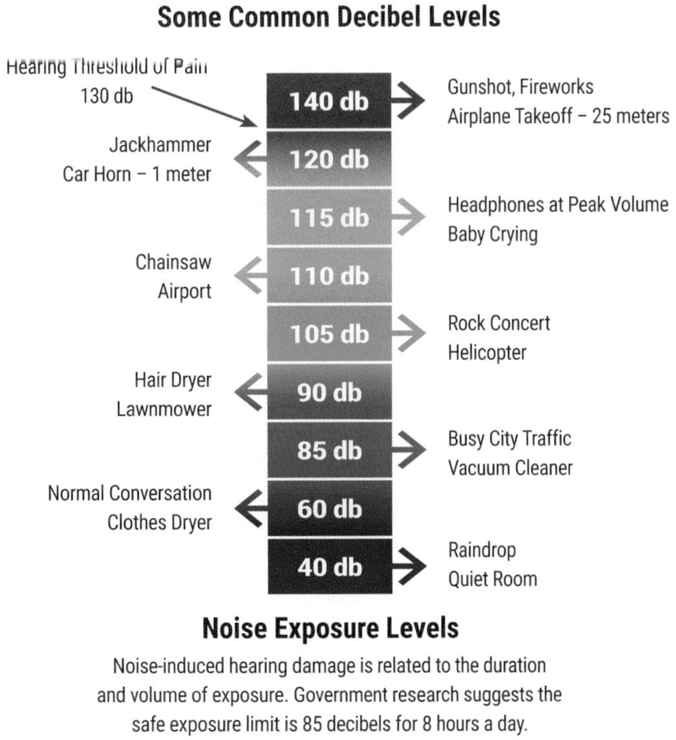

FIGURE 6-1
Common decibel (db) levels

ACE UNIVERSITY

If your study program includes ACE University, visit www.ACEfitness.org/MyACE and log in to your My ACE Account to take full advantage of the ACE Group Fitness Instructor Study Program and online guided study experience.

A variety of media to support and expand on the material in this text is provided to facilitate learning and best prepare you for the ACE Group Fitness Instructor Certification exam and a career as a group fitness instructor.

SUMMARY

GFIs have the ability to foster a community within the group exercise class by creating a positive, inclusive, and extraordinary group exercise experience for participants. This community goal can be accomplished by scripting opening and closing statements, choosing appropriate clothing and footwear, as well as selecting suitable equipment and music. Time spent enhancing the class design will take the class experience from good to outstanding.

REFERENCES

Alter, D.A. et al. (2015). Synchronized personalized music audio-playlists to improve adherence to physical activity among patients participating in a structured exercise program: A proof-of-principle feasibility study. *Sports Medicine – Open*, 1, 1, 23.

Aquatic Exercise Association (2020). *Aquatic Fitness Programming: Standards and Guidelines.* https://aeawave.org/Portals/0/AEA_Cert_Docs/AEA_Standards_Guidlines_2020.pdf?ver=2019-12-18-131623-417&timestamp=1576696862726

Estabrooks, P.A. (2000). Sustaining exercise participation through group cohesion. *Exercise and Sport Sciences Reviews*, 28, 63–67.

Guerrero, C. et al. (2020). Metabolic costs of a 58-minute multi-intensity exercise session with and without music and cueing. *International Journal of Exercise Science*, 13, 2, 358–365.

Lee, L. et al. (2021). Music level preference and perceived exercise intensity in group spin classes. *Noise and Health*, 23, 108, 42–49.

Maher J.P. et al. (2015). Perceptions of the activity, the social climate, and the self during group exercise classes regulate intrinsic satisfaction. *Frontiers in Psychology*, 6, 1236.

National Institute on Aging (2020). *Finding the Right Fitness Shoes and Clothes.* https://www.nia.nih.gov/health/finding-right-fitness-shoes-and-clothes

Thakare, A. E., Mehrotra, R., & Singh, A. (2017). Effect of music tempo on exercise performance and heart rate among young adults. *International Journal of Physiology, Pathophysiology and Pharmacology*, 9, 2, 35–39.

van der Vlist, B. et al. (2011). Using interactive music to guide and motivate users during aerobic exercising. *Applied Psychophysiology Biofeedback*, 36, 2, 135–145.

SUGGESTED READING

Biscontini, L. (2011). *Cream Rises: Excellence in Private and Group Fitness Education.* New York: FG2000.

CHAPTER 7

Group Fitness Class Program Design

JAN SCHROEDER, PhD | Professor, Department of Kinesiology, California State University Long Beach; ACE Certified Group Fitness Instructor

IN THIS CHAPTER

LEARNING OBJECTIVES

Upon completion of this chapter, the reader will be able to:

- Define class purpose and objectives
- Apply knowledge of exercise science to the three core components of a group fitness class
- Design intelligently structured and sequenced classes through the use of proper exercise order, work-to-recovery ratios, and balanced movement patterns
- Evaluate movements and exercises to determine safety and effectiveness

ACE UNIVERSITY

If your study program includes ACE University, visit www.ACEfitness.org/MyACE and log in to your My ACE Account to take full advantage of the ACE Group Fitness Instructor Study Program and online guided study experience.

A variety of media to support and expand on the material in this text is provided to facilitate learning and best prepare you for the ACE Group Fitness Instructor Certification exam and a career as a group fitness instructor.

The safest and most effective group fitness experiences are well-planned, applying the most up-to-date exercise science–related principles in a practical and thoughtful way. From identifying the purpose and objectives of a class to evaluating specific movements and exercises, an ACE Certified Group Fitness Instructor (GFI) must be well-versed in constructing classes in which the success and safety of the participant is always a top priority. This chapter discusses key considerations for designing a comprehensive, logically structured group fitness class plan.

Systematic Class Design

The difference between truly amazing classes and mediocre ones boils down to proper planning. While some aspects of an experience cannot always be controlled, such as mishaps with audio equipment, the GFI should make it a point to plan as many aspects of the class experience as possible, including devising back-up plans should unexpected issues arise. The newer the instructor, the more important it is that the class design be planned out and thoroughly practiced. Effective GFIs begin this systematic planning process by first identifying the overall goal of the class and the intended outcomes for participants. Considering this important information first will allow for more informed decisions regarding specific movements, exercises, and instructional techniques that will be needed to accomplish the established class objectives.

CLASS PURPOSE

To best serve class participants, the GFI should have a strong understanding of the goal of the specific class they intend to teach, as well as an idea of the types of participants who will most likely attend. Beginning the planning process by identifying the broader focus of what the class intends to accomplish will prove instrumental in designing a well-organized class blueprint. For example, the primary goal of an indoor cycling class may be to improve participants' **cardiorespiratory endurance,** whereas the intent of a restorative yoga class may be to reduce stress and promote relaxation. Regardless of the format the GFI is teaching, identifying the overall emphasis of the class will provide a framework for determining specific objectives.

APPLY WHAT YOU KNOW

Class Titles

Properly naming a class not only proves helpful in attracting individuals for whom the class format would be most appropriate, but it can also aid in managing participant expectations by providing insight into what they can anticipate during the class experience. Many GFIs will teach classes in gyms and studios that already have set class titles and descriptions, and/or will lead pre-choreographed classes with specifically branded names. However, some GFIs will be asked to craft their own class titles, especially if being hired for the primary purpose of bringing a new class format to a facility. Care and consideration should be taken when deciding how to most appropriately title a new class offering. For example, while an all-encompassing class name like "Senior Fitness" aptly states who the class is for, what exactly is being offered to participants is less clear. A class title such as "Chairobics for Active Agers" may be a more suitable option, as it (1) clearly and concisely denotes for whom the class is primarily intended and (2) it creatively, yet descriptively, expresses what participants can expect during the class, which is to perform chair-based exercises to improve **cardiorespiratory fitness.**

ESTABLISHING OBJECTIVES

With the general purpose for the class established, a GFI should construct specific learning objectives that appropriately capture the knowledge and skills that participants should be able to exhibit following instruction. The class objectives can encompass all three domains of learning, as discussed in Chapter 9. Examples of common class objectives include:

- *Indoor cycling class:* Participants will be able to demonstrate the three hand positions and identify the foundational movements that correspond with each.
- *Dance-based fitness class:* Participants will be able to perform a basic salsa step.
- *Yoga class:* Participants will be able to adopt two different ways to use a yoga block to perform crow pose (bakasana).

One option for creating an even more compelling and focused class experience is to establish a specific theme. The theme can be thought of as a central focus that the GFI would like participants to see as a common thread weaving through the entire class. While setting a theme is not an essential component of the class blueprint, it can assist in ensuring that class objectives are successfully met while creating a more memorable movement experience for participants.

WARM-UP CONSIDERATIONS

As discussed in Chapter 5, the warm-up is a period of lighter exercise intensity preceding the conditioning phase of the exercise bout. A more efficient, effective, and engaging class experience starts with a dynamic warm-up that properly prepares the body for the activity to come. While there are many options for warming up, there are some general guidelines and key considerations that GFIs should keep in mind when planning this important component of the group fitness class experience.

Ideally, the warm-up should last at least five to 10 minutes, beginning with low-to-moderate intensity exercise or activity that gradually increases in intensity. Depending on what is planned during the conditioning phase, the warm-up should be adjusted accordingly. For example, if the GFI is teaching a **high-intensity interval training (HIIT)** class, the latter portion of the warm-up could include some brief higher-intensity exercises to prepare participants for the intense elements they will experience later on in the class. As a general principle, the harder the conditioning phase, the more extensive the warm-up should be. However, the warm-up should not be so demanding that it creates **fatigue** that would reduce performance.

An extended warm-up may also be needed when leading classes such as dance-based and aquatic exercise classes geared toward specific demographics of participants, such as older adults and/or deconditioned individuals. Refer to Chapter 12 for detailed information on developing inclusive class experiences that serve various populations of participants.

Exercises to Enhance Stability and Mobility

A well-rounded warm-up routine can help decrease the risk of developing overuse injuries by addressing underlying muscle imbalances and enhancing quality of movements to be performed during the main portion of class, whether the focus is cardiorespiratory, muscular fitness, or a combination of the two. When it comes to preventing injury, ensuring adequate joint **mobility** is a must. As discussed in Chapter 3, the body is a **kinetic chain** comprised of certain joints that tend to favor **stability**—such as the scapulothoracic region, lumbar spine, knee, and foot—as well as joints that favor mobility—such as the ankles, hips, thoracic spine, and glenohumeral region. To help participants develop more effective movement patterns, the GFI should develop a dynamic warm-up that focuses on establishing adequate mobility and stability throughout the entire kinetic chain.

APPLY WHAT YOU KNOW

Warm-up Ideas to Enhance Stability and Mobility

While there are many movement and exercise options, a dynamic warm-up should be designed in a way that best serves the needs of the class participants while supporting the overall purpose and objectives of the class format. The following are sample exercise ideas that focus on enhancing joint stability and mobility as outlined in the Functional Training phase of the Muscular Training component of the ACE Integrated Fitness Training® (ACE IFT®) Model (see Chapter 4):

- *Cat-cow:* To promote thoracic spine mobility (Figure 7-1)
- *Bird dog:* To enhance stability of the core (Figure 7-2)
- *I, Y, W, O formations:* To improve shoulder stability and mobility (Figure 7-3)
- *Glute bridge:* To enhance hip mobility and core stability (Figure 7-4)
- *Kneeling thoracic rotation:* To improve thoracic spine mobility (Figure 7-5)
- *Standing ankle mobilization:* To promote ankle mobility (Figure 7-6)
- *Arm circles and standing diagonals:* To improve shoulder mobility (Figures 7-7 and 7-8)

FIGURE 7-1
Cat-cow

FIGURE 7-2
Bird dog

FIGURE 7-3
I, Y, W, O formations

I formation

Y formation

W formation

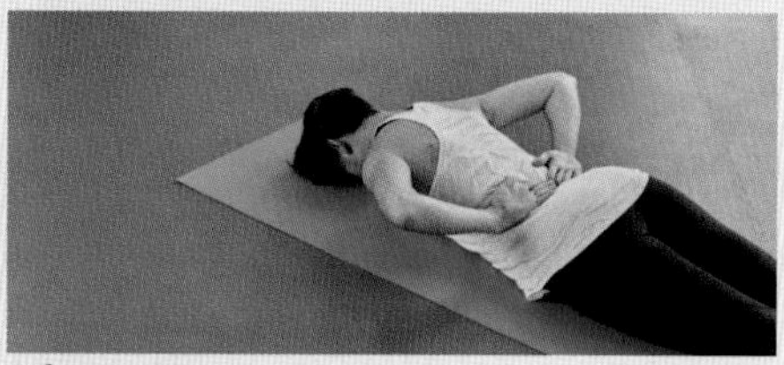

O formation

FIGURE 7-4
Glute bridge

FIGURE 7-5
Kneeling thoracic rotation

FIGURE 7-6
Standing ankle mobilization

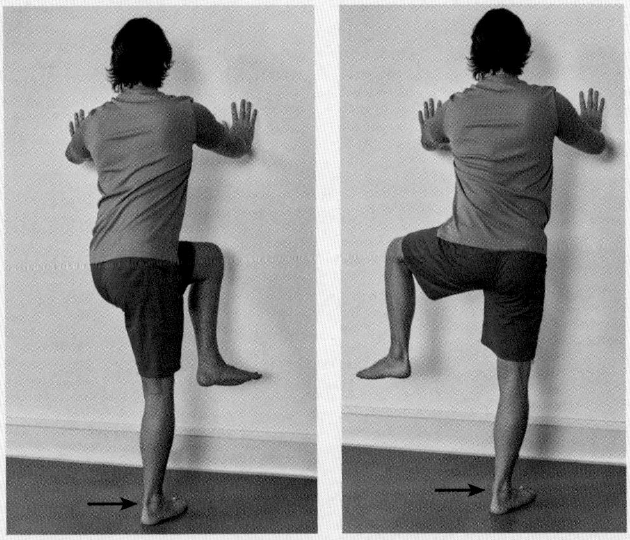

FIGURE 7-7
Arm circles

FIGURE 7-8
Standing diagonals

Rehearsal Moves

Participants may become frustrated in a group fitness class when they find themselves unable to perform the movements and exercises effectively. For this reason, it is important that **rehearsal moves** be incorporated throughout the warm-up, preparing participants mentally and physically for the challenges of the workout ahead. Rehearsal moves are defined as movements that are similar to, but less intense than, the movements that participants will execute during the conditioning segment of the class. The concept of rehearsal moves relates to the principle of **specificity** (see Chapter 4), which states that the body adapts specifically to whatever demands are placed on it. Rehearsal moves make up a large part of the warm-up, as their purpose is to prepare the body from a neuromuscular standpoint, as introducing new movement patterns in the warm-up will assist with activating associated **motor units.**

Examples of rehearsal moves include teaching participants how to adjust hand positioning and rise slowly out of the saddle for a brief hill climb in an indoor cycling class, incorporating basic body-weight exercises at a low-to-moderate intensity to prepare for loaded movements later on in a muscular fitness class, or practicing a side kick slowly at half-tempo with music during a kickboxing class warm-up before performing the move as part of the conditioning segment at a higher intensity level.

To successfully perform movements, participants must be provided with the opportunity to practice. These rehearsal opportunities will promote movement safety, as well as provide a greater sense of success and accomplishment, which in turn can enhance overall exercise **adherence.**

CONDITIONING CONSIDERATIONS

Functional movements, such as squats and lunges, are not only staple exercises in many group fitness class formats, but also movements that participants use in everyday life, from rising out of a chair to walking and stairclimbing. Incorporating exercises that mimic the five primary movement patterns, as outlined in the Movement Training phase of the Muscular Training component of the ACE IFT Model (see Chapter 4), can help create a class experience that enhances participants' overall function, both inside and outside of the group fitness environment.

With this integrated approach to exercise, GFIs should incorporate multijoint movements that train the body to function as one continuous unit, which better mimics participants' **activities of daily living (ADL).** Multijoint movements also add intensity, given that more muscle groups are working simultaneously, and more oxygen is required compared to when performing isolated, single-joint exercises. This movement-based approach should also include multiplanar training, in which exercises and movement patterns are performed in all three **planes of motion** (see Chapter 3).

A GFI should consider the primary audience of their class and make exercise decisions accordingly. For example, if leading a class primarily designed for participants who are not currently physically active, it may be most appropriate to incorporate movements performed in a supported position using a bench or chair, focusing on one joint moving in one plane of motion. In time, the movements can be progressed to more unsupported, free standing, multijoint exercises moving in multiple planes of motion in order to more closely mimic ADL.

APPLY WHAT YOU KNOW

Exercise Evaluation

Learning how to choose the appropriate exercises is among the most important tasks performed by GFIs. Having both an understanding of exercise science and a specific framework in which to initially judge all exercises will prove valuable in the class-planning process. GFIs should consider physiological, biomechanical, and psychological factors for any exercise or movement pattern. To this end, an **exercise evaluation** can be done for each movement in class to determine its effectiveness and safety.

Exercise-evaluation Criteria

1. What is the objective of this exercise?
    - Is the goal to improve cardiorespiratory fitness, muscular strength, balance, or flexibility, or a combination of two or more health- or skill-related components of physical fitness?
    - Am I trying to teach an isolated or integrated movement?
    - How does this movement or skill enhance the participants' ability to perform ADL and improve overall functionality?
2. What muscle(s) are being worked during the exercise or skill?
    - Which joint actions (and other movements) must be performed to achieve the objective safely?
    - When using equipment, is the appropriate muscle(s) being sufficiently and safely challenged?
    - When using body weight as resistance, is the body positioned appropriately against gravity?
3. Do the benefits of the exercise outweigh the potential risks?
    - Does the exercise commence from a point of stability and add mobility as appropriate within a safe **range of motion (ROM)**?
4. Can this movement or skill be scaled to various ability levels?
    - Who are my participants?
    - Am I prepared to offer **progressions** and **regressions** to ensure the success of all individuals?

The ability to evaluate the effectiveness and safety of exercises will improve as a GFI learns more about functional anatomy and the many factors that can affect efficient human movement. Using the exercise-evaluation criteria helps instructors get into the habit of exploring their understanding of exercise specificity, joint actions and **biomechanics,** safety, and progressions and regressions. Working through the analysis requires thought, time, and practice at the onset, but with continued use this work will eventually become second nature.

Scaling Exercise Intensity and Complexity

To ensure the safety, success, enjoyment, and effectiveness of the fitness experience for participants, GFIs must be prepared to offer scaled variations of the exercises and movements included in the class. In order to accommodate individuals at different ability levels, GFIs must understand how to decrease the intensity or complexity of a skill (known as a regression) as well as how to increase the intensity or complexity of a skill (known as a progression). A regression of an exercise may include decreasing **lever length** by lowering the hands to the hips, as opposed to reaching the arms overhead. A progression of an exercise may include transitioning from a tandem, or heel-to-toe, stance to a single-leg stance to more effectively challenge balance. Appropriate progression and regression options should be included within the class blueprint in order to ensure the GFI is adequately prepared to lead inclusive movement experiences.

THINK IT THROUGH

Scaling Intensity

When designing a muscular fitness class, you decide to include dumbbell front squats. In what ways could you scale the exercise intensity to ensure the safety and success of all participants by offering both less and more challenging exercise options?

COOL-DOWN CONSIDERATIONS

Just as it is important to gradually increase core body temperature and **heart rate (HR)** during the warm-up portion of a class, it is critical to gradually decrease the intensity of exercise during the cool-down, or conclusion of class. The cool-down should be of approximately the same duration and intensity as the warm-up (i.e., five to 10 minutes of low-to-moderate intensity activity). This will provide ample time within the class to allow participants' HRs to gradually lower and their bodies to comfortably and safely transition to a diminished level of work. An active cool-down also helps remove metabolic waste from the muscles so that it can be metabolized by other tissues. Walking at a reduced speed and incline during the final phase of a treadmill-based class is an example of an effective strategy used to gradually decrease the intensity of the class experience. GFIs should take care to avoid abruptly stopping intense exercise, which can cause blood to pool in the lower extremities and lead to dizziness and even fainting post-workout, especially in individuals who may have compromised cardiovascular health.

Stretching and Myofascial Release

In addition to generally decreasing the overall intensity of the class experience, GFIs should include stretching. To be most effective, joint-specific, prolonged static stretching should be performed when the muscles are warm. The exact stretches incorporated into the cool-down can vary depending on a number of factors, including the class format, intensity of the movements, and exercises included in the conditioning phase. Figures 7-9 through 7-13 present examples of targeted stretches that can be incorporated at the end of an indoor cycling class as part of an effective cool-down.

FIGURE 7-9
Hip flexor stretch

FIGURE 7-10
Quadriceps stretch

FIGURE 7-11
Hamstrings stretch

FIGURE 7-12
Calf stretch

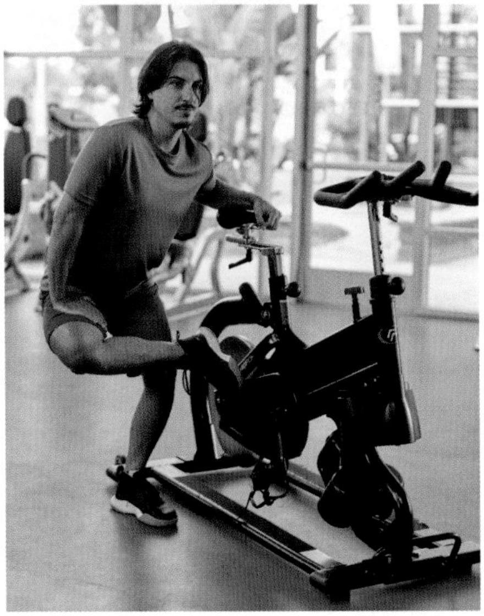

FIGURE 7-13
Hip/glute stretch

GFIs may also wish to consider incorporating **self–myofascial release (SMR)** as part of the cool-down if equipment such as foam rollers are available. Myofascial release is a technique that applies pressure to tight, restricted areas of fascia and underlying muscle tissue in an attempt to relieve tension and improve flexibility. Tender areas of soft tissues can be diminished by applying pressure (myofascial release) to relieve tension, increase blood flow, and improve tissue density, followed by static stretching of the tight areas to address tissue length and enhance joint ROM.

APPLY WHAT YOU KNOW

Incorporating Foam Rolling into Group Fitness Classes

If choosing to incorporate myofascial release as part of the class cool-down, GFIs may choose to use foam rollers, where participants control their own intensity and duration or pressure. A common technique is to instruct participants to perform small, continuous, back-and-forth movements on a foam roller, covering an area of 2 to 6 inches (5 to 15 cm). Once a tender spot is located, participants should be instructed to maintain back-and-forth pressure over the region for 20 to 30 seconds. The GFI should advise participants to ease into foam rolling gradually, given the discomfort that comes with exerting pressure on an already tender area of the body. At the conclusion of class, SMR should focus on addressing all major muscles worked during the movement experience. Figure 7-14 depicts several examples of SMR techniques for targeting major muscles of the lower body, including the gluteals, quadriceps, and iliotibial band.

FIGURE 7-14
Self–myofascial release using a foam roller

Gluteals

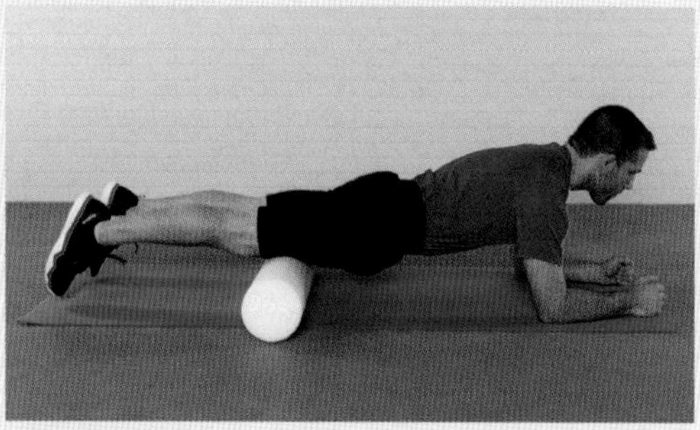

Quadriceps

Iliotibial band

Intelligently Structured and Sequenced Classes

A GFI must take great care in designing intelligently structured and sequenced group fitness class experiences. In addition to selecting exercises and movements that complement and balance each other, they must be able to apply principles of exercise science to make smart decisions regarding how to order exercises, structure work-to-recovery ratios, and seamlessly transition from one movement to the next to minimize risk of injury among participants and ensure that class objectives are successfully met.

DETERMINING EXERCISE SELECTION AND ORDER

Determining exercise selection and order is a complex process for which there is not a one-size-fits-all approach. As noted earlier, it is important that the GFI incorporate rehearsal moves within the warm-up to prepare for exercises and skills later in the class, as well as utilize the exercise-evaluation criteria when determining which specific movements best serve participants and meet the overall purpose and objectives of the class. Within the conditioning segment of a muscular fitness, boot camp, or HIIT class, GFIs may choose to have participants perform foundational movements first, such as multijoint linear exercises like squats, lunges, and shoulder presses. These movements can then be followed by accessory exercises involving more isolated movements and targeting smaller muscle groups, such as lateral raises, biceps curls, and chest flys. The multijoint to single-joint approach may enhance safety by ensuring that the larger muscle groups that are executing complex movements are minimally fatigued earlier in the workout compared to at the end of a workout (Simao et al., 2012).

If power-type, explosive exercises—such as **plyometrics**—and heavy muscular-training exercises are incorporated into a class, these should be performed at the beginning of the conditioning segment of the workout after an appropriate warm-up, when energy and concentration levels are highest and fatigue level is lowest. Performing these exercises later in a workout when higher levels of fatigue are present may increase the risk of injury.

Based on a review of the available research, the chief determining factors for exercise ordering should be the goal and intended outcomes of the class, as well as the movement-pattern needs of the participants (Simao et al., 2012).

EXPAND YOUR KNOWLEDGE

Research Highlights on Exercise Ordering

While the American College of Sports Medicine (2022) recommends resistance exercise–based programs focus on performing multijoint exercises before performing single-joint exercises, some studies have shown that this is not always an absolute rule. Simao et al. (2012) summarized various training studies investigating the chronic effect on exercise order and concluded that exercise order does not always have to proceed according to the conventional large-muscle-group to small-muscle-group sequence. The most important determinant of exercise order should be the movement patterns most in need of improvement.

Gentil et al. (2007) investigated the effects of the pre-exhaustion technique, which involves performing a single-joint exercise immediately before a multijoint exercise for the same muscle group (e.g., performing a set of chest flys immediately before performing a set of bench presses). This was compared to the reverse order, in which the multijoint exercise was performed immediately before the single-joint exercise. The study found that the number of exercise repetitions performed was always greater for the exercise performed first, regardless of whether it was a multijoint or single-joint movement. The researchers concluded that the exercise that is of most importance to the overall goals or objectives should be placed at the beginning of the conditioning portion of the class, regardless of whether the exercise is a multijoint or single-joint exercise.

ACE-sponsored Research

An ACE-sponsored study had subjects perform 24 exercise sessions, which was the minimum number of workouts needed to allow for every possible combination of workout order to include cardiorespiratory, muscular, flexibility, and neuromotor exercise (Dalleck, 2014). According to this study, to maximize the benefit of an individual workout, the exerciser should first perform cardiorespiratory exercise, then complete the resistance-training component. The flexibility and neuromotor exercises should be performed third and fourth in the sequence, in either order. Performing the exercises in this order maximized the effect of the overall workout.

Mindful Transitions

Safety

In order to create a cohesive class experience, GFIs should not only consider the ordering of exercises, but also the transitions between the movements. While transitioning techniques can vary, GFIs should be mindful to avoid quick changes in body positioning when sequencing exercises and transitioning between movements in order to maximize safety and enhance the overall class flow. Abrupt changes to **posture,** especially during intense exercise, can produce significant changes in **blood pressure.** **Orthostatic hypotension**—also known as **postural hypotension**—is defined as a sharp drop in blood pressure often caused by transitioning from a **supine** or seated position to standing, resulting in dizziness or even loss of consciousness. GFIs should carefully sequence movements and transitions to avoid extreme and rapid changes in body position.

CONSIDERING ENERGY PATHWAYS IN CLASS DESIGN

The energy that powers movement comes from the foods people eat and drink. **Carbohydrates** are easy for the body to break down and provide quick energy, while **fats** provide a seemingly endless supply of stored energy. **Proteins** are the building blocks of human structure and are not a primary source of energy. The body stores carbohydrates and fats in their most basic forms—**glucose** and **triglycerides,** respectively. When the body needs energy, it breaks down the chemical bonds in the stored energy, releasing **adenosine triphosphate (ATP),** the basic substance that the body uses for energy.

When people work at extreme intensities for just seconds, they use up the small amount of **creatine phosphate** they have in the body, via the **creatine phosphate system,** or **phosphagen system,** to produce ATP. An example is sprinting as fast as possible, which people can generally sustain for only a few seconds.

When people work at hard intensities for a few minutes, they use up carbohydrate stores, via the **glycolytic anaerobic system,** which can produce ATP without oxygen. An example is doing a one-minute high-intensity interval, and then having to recover while breathing in oxygen to replenish the muscles before continuing.

When people work at moderate and low intensities for longer than a few minutes, they use a combination of carbohydrates and fats to produce ATP for energy to move. This is accomplished via the **aerobic system,** or **oxidative system,** as sufficient oxygen is present for the production of ATP. Examples of this include swimming, most movements in cardiorespiratory classes, and step classes.

Exercise intensity and duration determine the fuel sources used. Generally, there is an inverse relationship between exercise intensity and duration, as the more intense the workout, the less time participants are able to maintain the intensity (Table 7-1).

It is important to note that these systems do not work independently of each other. That is, one energy system serves as the dominate pathway during an activity but all three are utilized to provide the body with the fuel required to complete the task and contribute to the total energy needs of the body during physical activity (Table 7-2).

TABLE 7-1

Contributions from Energy Pathways to Total Energy Needs at Different Intensities and Durations

Activity/Task Duration	Oxygen Necessary?	Intensity	Primary Energy System	Group Exercise Examples
0–5 seconds	No	Maximal effort	Predominantly phosphagen system	Squat jump
6–30 seconds	No	Near-maximal effort	After approximately 10 seconds, phosphagen becomes depleted and anaerobic glycolysis begins to assume the primary role.	All-out 20-second sprints within an indoor cycle class, followed by a recovery period 30-second plyometric drill
30–120 seconds	No	Moderate to vigorous	Predominantly glycolysis	HIIT cardiorespiratory class (40 seconds of exercise, followed by 20 seconds of recovery) One-minute muscular-conditioning drill
2–3 minutes	Yes	Moderate	Glycolysis becomes depleted and the oxidative system begins to assume the primary role.	Hill climb on a stationary cycle Muscle-conditioning circuit in an aquatic exercise class
>3 minutes	Yes	Light to moderate	Almost exclusively the oxidative system	Steady-state low-impact dance Yoga or Pilates classes

Note: HIIT = High-intensity interval training

TABLE 7-2

Percent Energy Contribution from Anaerobic and Aerobic Pathways at Different Activity Durations

Time	1–3 seconds	10 seconds	30 seconds	60 seconds	2 minutes	4 minutes	10 minutes	30 minutes	60 minutes	120 minutes
Anaerobic %	100	90	80	70	50	35	15	5	2	1
Aerobic %	0	10	20	30	50	65	85	95	98	99

Source: Porcari, J., Bryant, C., & Comana, F. (2015). *Exercise Physiology.* Philadelphia: FA Davis.

ACE→ MOVER™ METHOD

The Fat-burning Zone

After class, one of your regular participants asks if they can ask you a few questions and you arrange to meet in a more quiet and private location. The participant lets you know that they enjoy your class and have been attending regularly for six months, but they are feeling like they should be working harder during class and trying some of the more advanced exercise options but are hesitant to increase their exercise intensity.

Following is an example of how the ACE Mover Method™ philosophy and ACE ABC Approach™ can be used to discover more about a person's concerns for increasing exercise intensity, uncover any barriers preventing a new behavior, and collaborate to set a new goal or decide on next steps.

ACE→ ABC APPROACH™

Ask: Use powerful **open-ended questions** during the conversation to find out what the participant is hoping to accomplish with their exercise-related goals.

GFI: It has been so nice to see you regularly attending class three days per week. You mentioned that you have some concerns about increasing your exercise intensity and I wonder if you could tell me more about your health-related goals and what you'd like to achieve during our conversation?

Participant: I'm glad that you had some time to meet with me today. For the past six months, I've been attending your class on a regular basis and I've also been increasing my physical-activity level throughout the day to spend less time being **sedentary.** I have also been trying to eat healthier and reduce my stress levels. My main goals are to become more physically fit and, ultimately, I would like to continue to lose weight. This is part of why I wanted to talk with you today. When I first started becoming more active, I could feel a change in my body. I felt healthier, stronger, and more fit, and the extra weight was coming off. However, for the past 10 days I noticed I was not losing any weight and, while I am happy that I have not gained any weight, I would like to keep the scale moving toward weight loss. I'm hopeful that we can discuss ways for me to maintain my current exercise intensity and continue to become healthier and lose more weight.

GFI: Thank you for sharing so much information with me. Let me make sure I understand what you have shared so far. For the past six months, you have made changes in your life to become more physically active throughout your day and have added regular exercise to your daily routine three days per week. Your goals are to increase your fitness levels and to lose weight. Initially, you were reaching your goals, but lately it seems like you are not making as much progress. You would also like to discuss maintaining your exercise intensity. Have I captured what you said so far correctly?

Participant: Yes. I know I shared a lot of information with you, but I think we are on the same page.

Break down barriers: At this point, you may ask more open-ended questions to find out more about the participant's hesitancy to change their exercise intensity.

GFI: You mentioned feeling like you could be working harder in class, and you've also made it clear that you don't want to increase your exercise intensity. What is preventing you from working at an exercise intensity where you feel you are working hard enough?

Participant: Good question. Physically, there is nothing stopping me from exercising more intensely. In fact, I'm feeling like I could work harder and that is letting me know I'm reaching my goal of becoming more fit. The challenge I'm having is that I also want to lose weight. More specifically, I really want to lose fat, so it is important to me that I stay within my fat-burning zone and not work too hard.

GFI: Will you please tell me more about what you already know regarding intensity and the fat-burning zone?

Participant: Sure. It is my understanding that when exercising, I must keep my intensity low to optimize weight loss and burn more fat. Is that true?

GFI: Great question! I can tell that your health-related goals are important you and that you are not only increasing your physical-activity levels, but you are also striving to gain a deeper understanding of how to get the most out of the work you are doing. When it comes to exercise intensity and the idea of a specific fat-burning zone, I can offer you some more information. While it is true that exercise at a lower intensity uses a greater percentage of calories from fat, the overall number of calories being burned is less than when doing the same exercise at a higher intensity. Does that make sense?

Participant: I think so. Let me see if I am understanding you correctly. When exercising at a lower intensity, a greater percentage of calories used is coming from fat, but I am not burning as many calories as I would be when exercising at a higher intensity. The intensity of exercise seems to be more important to burning calories overall, and that is important for weight loss. Does that sound right?

GFI: You got it!

Collaborate: After you have worked together to discuss the participant's goals and to clarify the concept of a fat-burning zone, it is time to reinforce that the participant has ownership of their goals by letting them to decide what to do next.

GFI: Now that we've discussed your goals and talked through the connection between exercise intensity and using fat as a fuel, how do you plan to move forward?

Participant: At this point, I would like to gradually increase my exercise intensity. The clarification you provided, plus my gut instinct pushing me to do more, has helped me to see a path forward. I would like to start by trying some of the more intense exercise options you provide and will be more mindful of how hard I'm working using the methods you teach us in class. I'm excited to turn things up a notch.

GFI: Great. It sounds like gradually increasing your intensity is a good next step for you and that you are motivated to use the different intensity-monitoring methods to make sure you are working at a level that is appropriate for you. I look forward to seeing you in class later this week and please keep me posted on how things are going with your new goals.

In this example, the class participant is already making several lifestyle changes and is purposely not exercising too hard to stay within the "fat-burning zone." The GFI uses the ACE Mover Method and ACE ABC Approach to understand the participant's goals, identify barriers (which in this case was a lack of information), and empower the participant to decide how they would like to move forward. This process can be used when working with participant's in a variety of settings and is a great way to build **rapport** and to authentically show that you believe each person in your classes is resourceful and capable of change.

WORK-TO-RECOVERY RATIOS

Interval-based classes continue to grow in popularity in the group fitness environment. From aquatic exercise classes to outdoor boot camps, many GFIs are utilizing this approach to exercise in structuring their class experiences. Interval training generally involves bouts of higher-intensity exercise followed by a return to lower-intensity exercise for the recovery portion of the interval. It is important that when designing an interval-based class plan, GFIs ensure an adequate work-to-recovery ratio. Intervals often utilize work-to-recovery ratios between 1:2 and 1:1. An example of a 1:1 work-to-recovery ratio involves performing a one minute bout of zone 2 exercise [HR at and above the **first ventilatory threshold (VT1)** but below the **second ventilatory threshold (VT2)**] followed by a one-minute recovery period at a lower intensity (HR below VT1), while a 1:2 ratio involves performing a recovery interval that is twice as long as the exercise interval time.

When first introducing intervals to a class, or to participants who are new to this type of training, it may be best to keep the intervals relatively brief (e.g., about 30 seconds) with an approximate work-to-recovery ratio of 1:3. For example, an interval in a spin class may include a 30-second sprint followed by a 90-second recovery period at a lower exercise intensity. Depending on the class objectives, the number of intervals and the duration of the work and recovery periods can be adjusted in regular increments. When progressing zone 2 intervals, it is best to first increase the time of each interval (e.g., 30, 60, or 90 seconds of work followed by 90, 180, or 270 seconds of recovery) before adjusting the ratio to 1:2 and 1:1. In other words, initially the ratio stays the same but time increases. Eventually, the ratio changes to accommodate a higher intensity of training (work) followed by a shorter recovery period.

With a desire among many participants to "exercise smarter, not longer," express classes (i.e., shortened versions of traditional hour-long classes, typically 20 or 30 minutes in length) have been added to many group fitness class schedules. Due to the condensed timeframe of these classes, GFIs may opt to include higher-intensity intervals, in which the duration of the work interval will often range between 15 and 60 seconds. The recovery interval in these higher-intensity classes should still be equal to, or longer than, the work interval.

APPLY WHAT YOU KNOW

Designing an Interval-based Treadmill Class Using the ACE IFT Model

Using the ACE IFT Model as a guide, GFIs can plan safe, effective, and enjoyable interval-based treadmill classes. As noted in Chapter 4, the Fitness Training phase of the Cardiorespiratory Training component of the ACE IFT Model focuses on improving participants' aerobic efficiency by incorporating intervals performed at and above VT1 to just below VT2 into the class design and using **rating of perceived exertion (RPE)** to assess intensity level. One way in which this could be done within the conditioning segment of class is to include aerobic intervals in a 1:2 work-to-recovery ratio, in which participants perform a "work" interval at a RPE of 5 to 6 on the 0 to 10 scale for 60 seconds at an increased speed, followed by a recovery interval of 120 seconds at an RPE of 3 to 4 at a decreased speed. The duration of the class will then dictate how many interval bouts can be performed, while still ensuring ample time is allocated for an appropriate warm-up and cool-down.

A COMPREHENSIVE APPROACH TO CLASS DESIGN

A well-rounded exercise routine includes both the health- and skill-related components of physical activity. It is up to the GFI to determine which training elements will be included in each class based on the specific goals and objectives to be achieved. For example, if the goal of a class is to increase **muscular endurance** and cardiorespiratory fitness, both of these components will be addressed within the same class format. GFIs may choose to focus on one component before the other or elect to alternate between the two in a circuit-style format. If the goal of a class is to increase flexibility, this can either become a class in itself (such as a dedicated stretching or yoga class) or specific flexibility exercises can be performed at the end of a muscular fitness, cardiorespiratory fitness, or fusion class, as it is most effective to stretch muscles that are properly warmed and therefore more pliable.

As an instructor, it is important to understand that all participants should engage in cardiorespiratory, muscular, neuromotor, and flexibility training. A well-rounded exercise program that incorporates these four elements reflects the concept of balance.

Overall, the principle of balance applies to group exercise in two ways:

- Neuromuscular:
  - Being able to stand on one leg
  - Being able to stand equally supported on both feet
  - Raising one arm or leg (or one arm *and* one leg) in the quadruped position

- Maintaining neutral pelvic position and spinal posture
- Performing exercises on an unstable surface, as appropriate
- Raising one knee or foot off the floor in a plank position

- Programming:
  - Both sides of the body (if split into right and left halves) need to be trained equally because together they connect and create a whole. This type of approach is called **bilateral training.** Instructors who train with a unilateral approach during cardiorespiratory moves (such as only doing mambos with the left leg, leaping only to the right, and stepping only with the right lead leg) or strength moves (such as only doing lunges with the right foot stepping forward) fail to integrate this principle of balance into their classes.
  - When GFIs teach movement patterns that utilize both sides of a given movement pattern (such as performing lunges to the right and left), it is called "transitional" and "reversible" because the movement is repeated on both sides and/or in both directions to ensure this type of balance.
  - It is also important to consider the body as being divided into top and bottom segments that need to be trained equally. This can be achieved by participating in a variety of classes with specific training objectives and by alternating upper- and lower-extremity exercises within a single muscular-training class, for example. Yet another way to think of the body being divided is in front and back portions, as it is important to train opposing muscles on the front and back of the body equally. For example, you would want to perform exercises for both the front and back of the torso to target the abdominal muscles and back musculature.
  - Instructors should consider opposing muscles (**agonists,** or **prime movers,** and the **antagonist** muscles on the opposite side of the joint), as well as varying planes of motion when choosing exercises and movements for their participants. This type of functional pairing of muscles is found throughout the body. For example, the quadriceps muscle group in the front of the thigh produces knee **extension,** whereas on the opposite side of the joint the hamstrings—the antagonist

muscles—produce knee **flexion.** In order to ensure proper postural alignment, when functioning normally, opposing muscle groups maintain an adequate degree of pull on either side of a joint and share essential information from the nervous system. This enables the joint to move freely and with equal efficiency in all directions. However, when imbalances in this relationship occur, deviations to posture and faulty movement patterns can result, placing abnormal loading and excessive stress on various structures and joints within the body.

- As a cardiorespiratory example, always doing movement in the **frontal plane** with exercises like side-to-side step touches instead of sometimes incorporating marching forward and backward (**sagittal plane**) or rotation with exercises like hopping and twisting (**transverse plane**) could not only be repetitive but could also limit the participants from experiencing exercises in all three planes of motion.
- As a muscular fitness example, performing biceps curls in a group strength training class without an exercise for the triceps (the opposing, or antagonist, muscle group) would not be well-balanced for the muscles of the upper arm. Other strategies include alternating pushing and pulling movements, using different exercises to address each major muscle group within a circuit class, and utilizing supersets (alternating exercise for opposing muscle groups with little rest between sets) and compound sets (performing two or more exercises for the same muscle group in rapid succession) to appropriately fatigue a specific muscle group before resting or transitioning to the opposing muscle group.
- Balance in training also means that an individual should strive to be equally balanced among the four key components of training—cardiorespiratory, muscular, neuromotor, and flexibility training. For example, if a participant only attends indoor cycling classes, they should seek out additional modes of exercise that focus on muscular fitness as well, such as a group strength training class that includes resistance exercises, especially for the upper body. Similarly, a yoga enthusiast should seek out modes of cardiorespiratory training to complement their yoga practice, such as dance-based fitness classes.

THINK IT THROUGH

Creating Balance between Muscle Groups

When teaching a dance-based fitness class, what movements could you incorporate into the class sequence to create balance between opposing muscle groups in the body? When evaluating exercises, be sure to consider the joint actions that are taking place, as well as the muscles that are producing the movements (see Chapter 3).

Sample Class Blueprint

Figure 7-15 maps out a sample blueprint for a beginner-level HIIT class designed to improve muscular fitness for the performance of ADL. Notice in this sample blueprint that the five primary movement patterns are incorporated, each exercise has a clearly defined purpose and can be connected to a phase of the Muscular Training component of the ACE IFT Model, and progressions and regressions are listed.

FIGURE 7-15
Sample class blueprint: High-intensity interval training (HIIT) to develop muscular fitness

Class title: Beginning HIIT for Muscular Fitness

Class purpose: To develop muscular fitness

Objective(s): To relate exercise to daily movement patterns

Primary audience: General population

Class duration: 30 minutes

Class theme: Exercises for activities of daily living

General format: HIIT

Equipment: Dumbbells and mat

Music: In the background and upbeat (e.g., 128 bpm)

Warm-up (6 minutes)

Duration/ Repetitions	Movement (with Progressions/Regressions)	Intensity/ Zone	Primary Purpose	ACE IFT Model Phase
60 seconds	March in place	Moderate/ Zone 1	Increase heart rate and core body temperature without compromising postural and joint stability	Movement Training
60 seconds	Hamstrings curl	Moderate/ Zone 1	Increase heart rate and core body temperature without compromising postural and joint stability	Movement Training
60 seconds	Body-weight squat with overhead reach Regression: Body-weight squat with biceps curl Progression: Body-weight squat with overhead reach and balance on one foot	Moderate/ Zone 1	Dynamic ROM in both the lower and upper body without compromising postural and joint stability	Movement Training
60 seconds	Alternating lunge with side arm raise Regression: Split squat Progression: Alternating lunge with hands on hips	Moderate/ Zone 1	Dynamic ROM in the lower body without compromising postural and joint stability	Movement Training

FIGURE 7-15
(continued)

Duration/ Repetitions	Movement (with Progressions/Regressions)	Intensity/ Zone	Primary Purpose	ACE IFT Model Phase
60 seconds	March in place	Moderate/ Zone 1	Increase heart rate and core body temperature without compromising postural and joint stability	Movement Training
60 seconds	Alternating lunge with rotation, arms at 90 degrees Regression: Split squat with rotation Progression: Alternating lunge with rotation; arms extended to front	Moderate/ Zone 1	Dynamic ROM in both the lower and upper body without compromising postural and joint stability	Movement Training

Conditioning (18 minutes)

Duration/ Repetitions	Movement (with Progressions/Regressions)	Intensity/ Zone	Primary Purpose	ACE IFT Model Phase
Perform 3 rounds of the exercises listed For reach round, perform each exercise for 1 set at a 1:1 (30 seconds:30 seconds) work-to-recovery ratio 6 minutes/ round	**Squat** Regression: Body-weight squat Progression: Increase load **Push-up** Regression: Knee push-up Progression: Increase ROM **Alternating side lunge** Regression: Body weight Progression: Increase load **Bent-over row** Regression: Single-arm row Progression: Increase load **Crunch with rotation** Regression: Remove rotation Progression: Increase ROM **Bird dog** Regression: Lift one limb at a time Progression: Bring elbow to knee	20–70% 1-RM Use a weight that allows for 8–15 repetitions to be completed for each exercise	Focus on maintaining postural stability and kinetic chain mobility while training the five primary movement patterns. Add load to the primary movement patterns. Emphasize controlled motion.	Functional, Movement, and Load/ Speed Training

Continued on the next page

FIGURE 7-15
(continued)

Cool-down (6 minutes)

Duration/ Repetitions	Movement (with Progressions/ Regressions)	Intensity/Zone	Purpose	ACE IFT Model Phase
30 seconds each side	Child's pose with shoulder stretch	Stretch to a point of tightness or slight discomfort.	Improve joint function through improved ROM of the back and shoulders.	Functional Training
30 seconds each side	Alternating quadriceps stretch	Stretch to a point of tightness or slight discomfort.	Improve joint function through improved ROM of the quadriceps.	Functional Training
30 seconds each side	Alternating hamstring stretch	Stretch to a point of tightness or slight discomfort.	Improve joint function through improved ROM of the hamstrings.	Functional Training
30 seconds each side	Alternating hip flexor stretch with triceps stretch	Stretch to a point of tightness or slight discomfort.	Improve joint function through improved ROM of the hip flexors and triceps.	Functional Training
30 seconds each side	Alternating calf stretch	Stretch to a point of tightness or slight discomfort.	Improve joint function through improved ROM of the calves.	Functional Training
30 seconds	Chest stretch	Stretch to a point of tightness or slight discomfort.	Improve joint function through improved ROM of the chest.	Functional Training
30 seconds	Cat-cow	Emphasize motion over pushing at the end ranges of flexion and extension.	Improve flexibility of the spine with rhythmic motion.	Functional Training
	Closing remarks		Thank you Reminder of purpose and objective: To develop muscular fitness and apply it to activities of daily living Invitation to return to class next week	

Note: ROM = Range of motion; 1-RM = One-repetition maximum

Completing a class blueprint is an important step in creating and delivering a well-rounded group exercise session. While the blueprint will look different according to the format, purpose, audience, and duration of each class, utilizing an outline will help to ensure that the class objectives are being met and the flow of the class is well organized.

GFIs should be prepared to offer exercise progressions and regressions during class based on the specific needs of the participants. The following are a few examples of regressions that might be made to the class presented in Figure 7-15.

- Participant with balance issues
  - Place a chair nearby for balance recovery
- Participant with difficulty getting down to and up from the ground
  - Push-ups can be performed against a wall
  - Crunch with rotation can be replaced with lateral flexion
  - Bird dog can be substituted with hip extension – overhead reach
- Participant who is pregnant
  - Crunch with rotation can be replaced with standing transverse abdominis bracing
  - Standing child's pose against a wall can replace child's pose on the floor
- Participant with **hypertension**
  - Cue to breathe regularly throughout each lift

ACE UNIVERSITY

If your study program includes ACE University, visit www.ACEfitness.org/MyACE and log in to your My ACE Account to take full advantage of the ACE Group Fitness Instructor Study Program and online guided study experience.

A variety of media to support and expand on the material in this text is provided to facilitate learning and best prepare you for the ACE Group Fitness Instructor Certification exam and a career as a group fitness instructor.

SUMMARY

Designing an effective group fitness class blueprint requires an application of exercise science–related principles in an intelligently structured manner. From selecting appropriate exercises to determining how to appropriately order movements within each of the three core components of the class plan, a successful GFI dedicates time to appropriately planning and thoroughly practicing the class plan they design. In addition, a GFI should map out the class purpose and objectives to ensure that participants' expectations are met. Finally, it is essential to be prepared to modify the class blueprint and offer progressions and regressions throughout class to accommodate the needs of individual participants.

REFERENCES

American College of Sports Medicine (2022). *ACSM's Guidelines for Exercise Testing and Prescription* (11th ed.). Philadelphia: Wolters Kluwer.

ACE-sponsored Research

Dalleck, L. (2014). Developing a comprehensive exercise prescription: The optimal order for cardiorespiratory, resistance, flexibility, and neuromotor exercise. *Journal of Fitness Research*, 3, 13–25.

Gentil, P. et al. (2007). Effects of exercise order on upper-body muscle activation and exercise performance. *Journal of Strength and Conditioning Research*, 21, 4, 1082–1086.

Porcari, J., Bryant, C., & Comana, F. (2015). *Exercise Physiology*. Philadelphia: FA Davis.

Simao, R. et al. (2012). Exercise order in resistance training. *Sports Medicine*, 42, 3, 251–265.

SUGGESTED READINGS

Biscontini, L. (2011). *Cream Rises: Excellence in Private and Group Fitness Education*. New York: FG2000.

Mad Dogg Athletics (2015). *Spinning Instructor Manual* (2nd ed.). Venice, Calif.: Mad Dogg Athletics.

CHAPTER 8

Group Fitness Facility and Equipment Considerations

JAN SCHROEDER, PhD | Professor, Department of Kinesiology, California State University Long Beach; ACE Certified Group Fitness Instructor

IN THIS CHAPTER

LEARNING OBJECTIVES

Upon completion of this chapter, the reader will be able to:

- Assess a group room/exercise area for potential hazards and appropriate fitness flooring to ensure a successful group exercise experience for participants
- Understand the difference between cleaning and disinfecting equipment
- Recognize common music and equipment issues
- Determine the best arrangement of participants based on space, class format, and supervision requirements
- Adapt to unexpected equipment issues and technical difficulties

ACE UNIVERSITY

If your study program includes ACE University, visit www.ACEfitness.org/MyACE and log in to your My ACE Account to take full advantage of the ACE Group Fitness Instructor Study Program and online guided study experience.

A variety of media to support and expand on the material in this text is provided to facilitate learning and best prepare you for the ACE Group Fitness

From orienting new participants to teaching class without a properly functioning audio system, an ACE Certified Group Fitness Instructor (GFI) must demonstrate professionalism by diffusing unpredictable situations and devising creative ways to adjust to conditions that are less than ideal. This chapter discusses day-of-class considerations and offers suggestions for immediate onsite solutions to potential setbacks.

Initial Onsite Procedures and Responsibilities

Arrival time is very important. GFIs should arrive early to class to complete pre-class responsibilities, communicate with participants, and set the atmosphere for the experience to follow. Turning on music and adjusting the lighting and temperature (if possible) to complement the format sets the tone for the class. In the event a GFI does arrive late to class, they should turn on the music and get the class warming up while assessing the room and equipment for any safety hazards, adjusting participants' set-up as needed. A GFI should strive to employ the following best practices at the beginning of each class to create a safe, enjoyable, and successful experience for participants.

ROOM/EXERCISE AREA ASSESSMENT

Upon arrival, the GFI should let the front desk/facility operator know they are present on site. If there are no standard facility practices in place pertaining to instructor arrival, a simple wave or hello is sufficient. This verifies the GFI has arrived, which is helpful in case there are facility-related issues that the staff needs to notify the instructor about, and it also gives everyone peace of mind that the class will start on time.

Next, unless there is a class currently taking place in the group fitness room/space, the GFI should enter the room to check the temperature and lighting and identify any immediate hazards such as leaks or electrical problems, notifying staff immediately if any are observed. If it is not possible to enter the room, the GFI should wait outside the room to ensure they are the first person to enter the room once access is possible. If the class is outdoors, the GFI should be mindful of any hazards in the proximity of the movement area, especially objects that cannot be moved. Marking holes, large tree roots, or wet areas with cones is highly recommended (see Chapter 11).

Although GFIs often have minimal input in terms of the space in which they teach, instructors should strive for the following characteristics when teaching in a room or area dedicated to group fitness:

- An air temperature between 68 and 72° F (20.0 and 22.2° C) for most class formats where participants are engaging in moderate to vigorous physical activity
- Relative humidity levels below 60%, with 50% or lower being the desired goal
- An adequate mix of recirculated internal air and external fresh air moving through the facility
- Flooring with a protective function should be utilized to reduce the risk of **chronic** and **acute** impact injuries. This flooring should provide adequate shock absorption, minimal vertical deformation, or "give," and an appropriate level of friction.
- Sufficient space for each participant to move comfortably as appropriate to meet the needs of the specific class format

- Mirrors should be positioned across both the front and sides of the room for participants to be able to observe their own exercise movements and postures. Ideally, mirrors can be covered by drapes at the instructor's discretion when they prove inappropriate or a distraction.
- A raised platform for the instructor, particularly in large, "fish-bowl" style studios
- Controls for lighting, temperature, and sound connections (e.g., wireless microphone receivers and transmitters, CD player, and digital music player connection), all within easy access of the GFI's primary place of instruction
- Easy access to drinking water
- Easy and safe access to necessary cardiorespiratory and muscular-training equipment for instructors and participants to use in classes, as appropriate
- In aquatic exercise classes, water temperature must be appropriate for the specific type of class based on the intensity level and participant needs. The Aquatic Exercise Association (2020) suggests that a water temperature varying from 83 to 86°F (28.3 to 30.0° C) is the most comfortable for typical aquatic exercise classes (AEA, 2020).

FLOORING/EXERCISE SURFACE

Some activities that take place in a group exercise room can more than double the amount of force that is normally applied to a participant's body [American College of Sports Medicine (ACSM), 2019]. For this reason, it is important that appropriate flooring is selected and installed so that many of the additional forces can be absorbed by the floor surface instead of the individual's **musculoskeletal system.** Appropriate group fitness flooring serves a protective function and absorbs shock to reduce the negative effects on the joints and the risk of acute and chronic impact injuries. Repeated jarring can result in stress fractures and **tendinitis.** Appropriate flooring should not only absorb shock but should also have a minimal level of deformation while also providing an appropriate amount of friction. This type of flooring typically is made up of three layers—a bottom shock-absorbing section (rubber pads, shock pads, or neoprene), a middle section combining multiple layers of plywood, and a top level consisting of a rubber or wood surface (ACSM, 2019). Concrete is not recommended as a surface for group fitness classes, as it absorbs little shock and can be quite dangerous in the event of a fall.

Carpeting is typically a poor choice for group fitness rooms, as well, as it can catch the edge of shoes during dynamic lateral movements or pivoting, resulting in ankle **sprains** or knee injuries. In addition, carpeting is difficult to maintain hygienically and can trap bacteria and odors from the perspiration and body oils of the participants.

CLEANING/DISINFECTING

Facility cleanliness is an important factor that influences a person's decision to join a fitness facility and proper cleaning and disinfecting can help to prevent the spread of germs that cause illness (ACSM, 2019). Facilities should develop, implement, and adhere to a formal schedule for cleaning all areas and equipment (and disinfecting when and where appropriate). Importantly, cleaning and disinfecting are not the same thing. Cleaning can be accomplished using soap and detergent and will physically remove dirt, most germs, and organic matter and should be done before disinfection if the disinfectant being used is not indicated for both cleaning and disinfecting (check the product label). Disinfection will kill any remaining germs (Environmental Protection Agency, 2021; Centers for Disease Control and Prevention, 2021). Be sure to follow the manufacturer recommendations for safe and effective disinfectant use. Consider the following cleaning and disinfecting schedule for a group fitness studio (ACSM, 2019):

- Daily
  - Dust all horizontal surfaces.
  - Spot-clean mirrors and glass surfaces.
  - Clean mirrors thoroughly.
  - Remove trash.
  - Dry-mop wood floors.
  - Wet-mop wood floors.
  - Clean and disinfect exercise tools (e.g., mats, steps, and exercise balls).
  - Clean control panels of all equipment, including treadmills, bikes, and elliptical trainers.
  - Clean the handles and seats of all equipment with antibacterial soap and a damp cloth.
  - Clean dumbbells and all bar handles (plus any free-weight attachment handles) with an antimicrobial solution on a damp cloth or an antibacterial wipe.
  - Clean frames and upholstery with mild soap and water.
- Monthly
  - Clean light fixtures.
  - Clean HVAC ducts.
  - Clean audio equipment.
  - Wash solid walls.
- Annually
  - Refinish wood floor surfaces.

FIGURE 8-1
Staggered arrangement

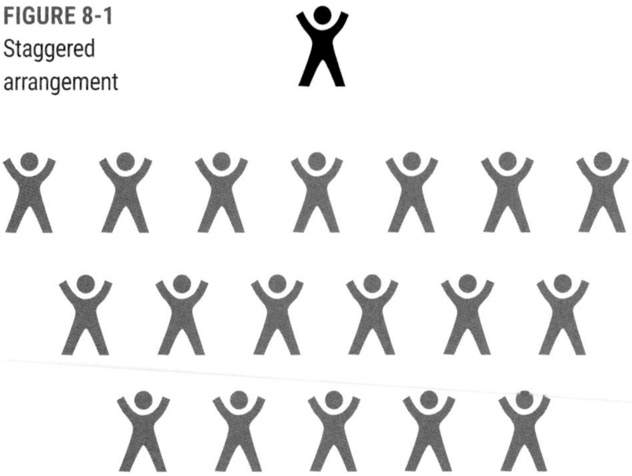

ARRANGEMENT AND POSITIONING OF PARTICIPANTS

The arrangement and positioning of participants are important for a couple of reasons, depending on the class format. First, regardless of the arrangement used, consider the spacing needs for the class and ensure the arrangement is appropriate and safe for the class. In formats that rely on instructor demonstration, participants' positions need to be arranged so that everyone can see the front of the room and the instructor. A staggered arrangement is suggested for these formats, especially when teaching larger groups (Figure 8-1). A staggered arrangement can take on a curved shape as well, such as in aquatic exercise, indoor cycling, dance-based, and yoga classes.

FIGURE 8-2
Parallel lines

Instructor often walking around

For circuit classes with stations, large Pilates reformer classes, mat/floor-based classes, or partner classes, two parallel rows work well (Figure 8-2). The distance between the two rows depends on the personal space needed for each participant. This arrangement allows the GFI to walk up and down the rows to supervise the class.

Some instructors like a circle arrangement for groups such as older adults and youth, as well as for formats like circuit training, and boot-camp classes (Figure 8-3). It makes supervision simple and encourages a sense of community.

Some GFIs prefer everyone in a horizontal line, provided the class size allows, so they can see everyone's movement and coordination pattern in a synchronized fashion from all angles (Figure 8-4). Kettlebell, suspension training, barre, and small- to moderate-sized reformer classes are a few examples of when this arrangement may be useful.

FIGURE 8-3
Circle arrangement

FIGURE 8-4
Horizontal line

MUSIC AND EQUIPMENT SETUP

After the room/space assessment, if using music, the GFI should check the pitch position (which can be adjusted to control music tempo), volume, treble, and bass controls of both the sound system and microphone to guarantee the most appropriate experience for all. Chapter 6 provides additional information on appropriate music volume.

Any exercise equipment that does not appear to be functioning properly or that has obvious signs of deterioration should be removed from the group fitness space or locked in a secure location that is not accessible by participants. If removing the equipment is not an option because it is too large (e.g., indoor cycling bike, Pilates reformer, or rebounder), the item should first be completely disabled (so movable parts are fixed in place) and a clearly visible sign should alert participants that the equipment is out of order and could result in injury if used in its present condition. The policies of each fitness facility typically dictate the responsibilities of the staff regarding placing signage on faulty equipment. The GFI must fully understand those policies and notify the appropriate staff member, if necessary, to place the signage on the equipment prior to the start of class. Failure to remove broken, defective, or malfunctioning equipment increases a facility's **liability** exposure and places the establishment at risk for **negligence** claims and lawsuits (see Chapter 14). Allegations could arise from any of the following (Eickhoff-Shemek, Herbert, & Connaughton, 2009):

- Purchasing substandard or defective equipment
- Improper assembly
- Inadequate spacing between equipment units per the manufacturer's standards
- Failure to maintain equipment per the manufacturer's standards
- Failure to remove or replace defective equipment
- Failure to keep equipment clean
- Failure to provide appropriate instruction and adequate supervision

It is also the responsibility of the GFI to follow up with the appropriate staff member regarding the status of the malfunctioning equipment to find out if the piece will be repaired or replaced. Reporting equipment issues to staff ahead of class time can help prevent capacity issues such as having one fewer stability ball available for use.

Common equipment issues of which GFIs should be mindful include:

- Chipped dumbbells or barbells
- Torn or peeling rubber strip on step platforms
- Tears or small nicks in resistance tubes
- Broken pedal clips, stripped knobs, or saddle upholstery damage on indoor cycle bikes
- Deflated or damaged stability balls, or other inflatable equipment options
- Torn yoga mats
- Damaged flotation devices or aquatic dumbbells
- Torn or fraying suspension straps
- Broken springs on Pilates apparatus or rebounders

Lastly, any technical equipment required to effectively teach a class (e.g., microphone or sound system) should be checked for proper functioning prior to starting each class. Often, facilities will have backup equipment and batteries for situations when technical problems arise. The GFI should know if these backup items exist, as well as how to access and use them when necessary.

LEGAL CONSIDERATIONS

Selecting, Inspecting, and Maintaining Equipment

Mark S. Nagel, EdD, Professor, Sport and Entertainment Management Department, University of South Carolina

The choice of exercise equipment is important. Anything that is available for use by a participant must be properly designed and maintained. In most cases, purchasing equipment from reputable companies will meet the safety and fitness needs of participants. However, GFIs who have input in equipment purchase decisions must fully evaluate the price and short- and long-term quality of offerings. Often, though not always, the least expensive equipment choices last for the shortest time and frequently experience maintenance and/or replacement needs before more expensive equipment.

Though it may be possible for a GFI to design and build equipment capable of fulfilling the needs of participants, this is a potentially dangerous and legally precarious decision to make. Individually designed and produced equipment poses a legal risk for the designer and user, as there are no established testing standards or maintenance protocols. If an injury were to occur while using such equipment, it would be difficult to establish the product as being of sound design if it is not part of a larger product line that has an established track record of safety and effectiveness.

The purchase of equipment from established and reputable suppliers transfers some of the potential liability to the manufacturer. For this reason, GFI-designed equipment should be avoided. In some cases, participants may desire to utilize their own equipment for various classes and other fitness activities. In situations where a GFI is instructing in a gym, participants should be discouraged or even prevented from utilizing homemade exercise equipment due to the potential problems such equipment poses. In cases where a GFI may instruct a participant in the participant's home, the use of homemade equipment may be unavoidable, but the GFI should require the participant to acknowledge their own responsibility for using potentially substandard equipment that could cause unnecessary injury.

All equipment, whether used in a gym or a participant's home, should be inspected by the GFI before use. Most exercise equipment will have established maintenance schedules and protocols that should be followed explicitly. However, in some cases, a piece of equipment that may not be "scheduled" for maintenance may require upkeep and/or replacement before its expected time. The GFI must not assume that because a timeframe has not been met that the equipment is still capable of being utilized safely. Inspections ensure that "surprises" do not occur that could cause significant injury. As part of a sound inspection and maintenance strategy, a log containing dates and specific actions taken should be maintained. This log may become critically important in the case of an injury caused by a participant's misuse of equipment, as resulting legal action may center on the GFI being able to confirm that regular maintenance was performed and all equipment was inspected prior to its use.

THINK IT THROUGH

No Access to Equipment

Upon entering the group exercise room, you find that the dumbbell storage rack has a new lock on it and the previous combination no longer works. What steps would you take to start your group strength training class on time?

For classes that require a dedicated space for each participant (e.g., step or group strength training classes), instructors should orient their equipment prior to class to provide a visual example for how everyone should position their equipment. As a safety practice, the GFI may suggest that participants keep their equipment to the right side of their personal space so that they and neighboring participants always know where the equipment is—"right is right!" For circuit classes that rely on stations, the GFI should set out the equipment, or at least supervise the set-up to ensure equipment is positioned safety.

Proper equipment set-up is important to ensure each participant is comfortable on the equipment. Discomfort could affect the participants' **self-efficacy** and overall experience (Hu et al., 2007). Common set-up hazards include:

- Improper bike fit
- Incorrectly stacking step platforms atop risers
- Unfastened barbell clips
- Unstable suspension strap anchor
- Placing equipment on unleveled surfaces
- Incorrect foot bar, headrest, carriage, and tower set-up on reformers (and other Pilates apparatus such as Cadillacs and chairs)
- Bench pop-pins not fastened or secured

Safety

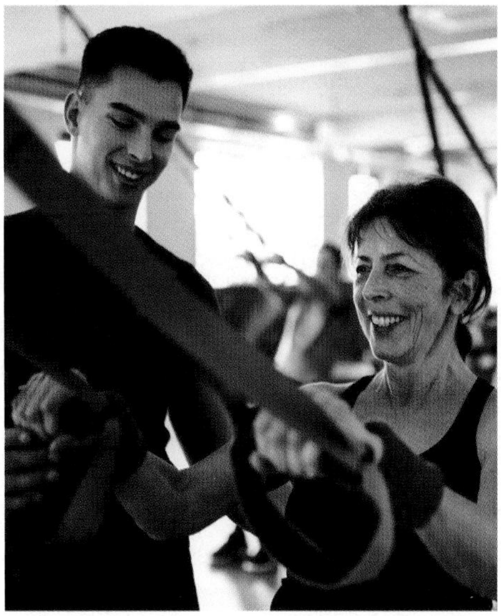

The GFI should set up suspension trainers to ensure straps are adjusted properly and that the anchor point is sturdy and stable. Pilates instructors who teach classes using apparatus should be formally trained to do so, and should personally check all springs, straps, and moving parts prior to class. Adjusting bike fit for every participant in an indoor cycling class is rarely necessary, but new riders should be oriented and educated about proper bike fit. While it is highly recommended that GFIs obtain instructor training through organizations that specialize in indoor cycling, basic knowledge of bike set-up is helpful.

APPLY WHAT YOU KNOW

FIGURE 8-5
Proper bike fit

Indoor Cycling Bike Fit

GFIs should know the critical steps to ensure comfort, proper **biomechanics,** and efficient pedaling (Figure 8-5). The standard steps for proper bike fit are:

- Adjust the resistance knob so there is a small amount of resistance on the flywheel.
- For saddle height, ask the rider to stand beside the bike facing the handlebars and lift their leg to bring the hip and knee to 90 degrees. Position the saddle to match the height of the thigh/lap. Adjust the saddle accordingly and fasten the pop-pins and knobs.
- Ask the rider to mount the bike by placing their hands on the handlebars, stepping over the frame to straddle the bike, and then placing the foot into the pedal basket or clips and lifting up onto the saddle. They are ready for the next step once the second foot is positioned on the pedal.
- To ensure saddle height is appropriate, the knee should be at 25 to 35 degrees of flexion when the foot is at the bottom of the pedal stroke (6 o'clock position). If the rider is rocking side to side while pedaling (because it is too high), or if the knee is over-flexed (because it is too low), make adjustments to the saddle height.
- For the seat fore and aft adjustment, ask the rider to position the pedals at the 3 and 9 o'clock positions. The saddle position is correct when the rider's knee cap is directly above and in line with the pedal spindle (the bolt that is screwed through the pedal) and they can hold a slight bend in the elbow with the hands on the handlebars (when seated, riders should not reach out toward the tips of the handlebars because that section of the handlebars is for standing movements only).
- Ask the rider to pedal to check the saddle height one more time.
- For the handlebar adjustment, a beginner's handlebars should be adjusted to the same height as the saddle or higher. Experienced riders may prefer a handlebar height that is lower than the saddle.
- If the bike has a handlebar fore and aft adjustment, a rider can make even finer adjustments for their arm reach. Simply slide the handlebars fore or aft to find a comfortable position. The elbows should not be locked.

Make sure all pop-pins, knobs, and sliders are fastened and that the rider understands how to stop the flywheel and safely dismount the bike. Again, GFIs are strongly encouraged to seek modality-specific continuing education before teaching formats such as indoor cycling to learn proper technique, safety protocols, teaching methods, and discipline-specific knowledge.

Adapting to Unexpected Situations

Adapting to and overcoming unexpected situations comes with the territory of leading a class. It is not uncommon for a GFI to arrive with a well-planned class only to find factors outside of their control hamper the class plan. A GFI's ability to utilize their training and devise solutions with minimal resources is the mark of a professional.

LACK OF EQUIPMENT

Broken or out-of-order equipment can affect a participant's ability to participate in a class. Damaged equipment in an indoor cycling, Pilates reformer, suspension training, rebounder, or other class format that requires one dedicated unit per participant may leave participants feeling like they are not being accommodated. When lack of equipment is an issue, either the participants will have to share equipment and/or the GFI will have to adjust the class plan to best serve all individuals.

If possible, a GFI should consider these solutions:

- Teach without equipment in order to make equipment available to another participant.
- Pair participants for partner-based exercises when equipment is limited and must be shared. For example, if there is a bike shortage during an indoor cycling class, alternate drills. For instance, as one participant performs a drill on the bike, their partner performs body-weight exercises, after which they switch roles. Splitting the class into two groups helps to keep instruction manageable for the GFI while ensuring every participant experiences an effective workout.
- Change the set-up in a group strength class to a circuit-style format, arranging stations around the room using specific equipment.
- When teaching outdoor classes, always have a backup plan ready in case the class has to be moved indoors due to inclement weather.
- Design a "no equipment needed" class in case room or equipment availability changes without notice.

TECHNICAL DIFFICULTIES

Technical difficulties can transpire at any time during class, but in most situations the GFI will know if the stereo, lighting, or other audio/visual aids are not working before a class begins. During class, instructors may be faced with abrupt technical difficulties that may interrupt instruction. In any case, GFIs must be resourceful and ready to deal with worst-case scenarios related to technical malfunctions.

Consider these troubleshooting solutions:

- Always have a back-up music option. In the event a facility's sound system may not be updated for portable electronic devices (e.g., MP3 player or smartphone), it may be helpful to also have music saved on a CD. Alternatively, because of advances in technology, many facilities may now only have the option to play music from a portable electronic device, so GFIs should plan on having music also available digitally. Additionally, to avoid having portable electronic devices lose battery power during class, ensure that any device being used is fully charged or that an external battery charger is available. If using a mobile phone to access the class playlist, switch the device into airplane mode to avoid disruptions to the music in the event of an incoming call or text message.

- If playing music is not an option, shift the focus to mental training. Keep participants' minds engaged with shorter intervals and purpose-driven drills (e.g., "for 60 seconds, do as many push-ups as possible," or "for 90 seconds, bring your intensity to a 7 on a scale of 0 to 10"), using imagery or corrective cueing along the way.
- For GFIs who teach classes that are dependent on music, invest in a back-up portable speaker that connects to portable electronic devices.
- Bring extra batteries for the microphone.
- If the lights are not dimming for classes meant for darker settings (e.g., yoga), ask participants to close their eyes at times and incorporate more imagery and mindfulness cues. Of course, safety must always be a top priority, so use common sense before asking participants to close their eyes.

Safety

- If the lights do not turn on, do not teach movement-based classes in a dim room. If possible, move outdoors or offer to teach a different format that limits movement (e.g., mat Pilates, core conditioning, and restorative yoga).
- When visual aids (e.g., smart devices, virtual backgrounds, **rating of perceived exertion** signage, and heart-rate monitoring systems) are not functioning properly in indoor cycling or circuit-based classes, focus on motivational cueing and emphasize technique.

APPLY WHAT YOU KNOW

What's in Your Duffle Bag?

Every GFI has essential items and tricks of the trade that they stow in their duffle bags for every class they teach. In many cases, GFIs bring extra gear to ensure participants are comfortable, while also being prepared for unexpected situations that might arise. Below is a list of "must haves" from seasoned GFIs:

- ☐ First-aid kit (critical for outdoor classes)
- ☐ Extra batteries for microphone
- ☐ Sports drink (in case someone experiences low blood sugar or dehydration)
- ☐ Extra bottle of water
- ☐ Hair ties, bobby pins, and safety pins
- ☐ Headbands (to hold loose headsets in place)

- ☐ Extra CDs and a back-up portable electronic device in case the one you plan on using is not operable
- ☐ A/V cords to connect portable devices (e.g., HDMI, auxiliary cable, and charger)
- ☐ Microphone windscreens
- ☐ Snacks (e.g., protein bar and nuts)
- ☐ Towels (one small hand towel and one larger bath towel)
- ☐ Dry change of clothes, including an extra pair of socks
- ☐ Deodorant
- ☐ Wet wipes and/or hand sanitizer

THINK IT THROUGH

Coping with Technical Difficulties

The microphone suddenly stops working during class. What steps will you take to remedy the situation?

ACE UNIVERSITY

If your study program includes ACE University, visit www.ACEfitness.org/MyACE and log in to your My ACE Account to take full advantage of the ACE Group Fitness Instructor Study Program and online guided study experience.

A variety of media to support and expand on the material in this text is provided to facilitate learning and best prepare you for the ACE Group Fitness Instructor Certification exam and a career as a group fitness instructor.

SUMMARY

Teaching successful group fitness classes requires knowing how to adapt and overcome potentially stressful situations while maintaining composure and a positive attitude. Coming prepared and ready to adjust the plan at a moment's notice is an important part of demonstrating professionalism as a GFI. When participants see a GFI who can troubleshoot, problem-solve, assist, place others before themselves, and make a potentially unpleasant situation pleasant, it sets a good example for the types of people the fitness industry develops and employs.

REFERENCES

American College of Sports Medicine (2019). *ACSM's Health/Fitness Facility Standards and Guidelines* (5th ed.). Champaign, Ill.: Human Kinetics.

Aquatic Exercise Association (2020). *Aquatic Fitness Programming: Standards and Guidelines.* https://aeawave.org/Portals/0/AEA_Cert_Docs/AEA_Standards_Guidlines_2020.pdf?ver=2019-12-18-131623-417&timestamp=1576696862726

Centers for Disease Control and Prevention (2021). *Cleaning and Disinfecting Your Facility.* https://www.cdc.gov/coronavirus/2019-ncov/community/disinfecting-building-facility.html

Eickhoff-Shemek, J.M, Herbert, D.L, & Connaughton, D.P. (2009). *Risk Management for Health/Fitness Professionals: Legal Issues and Strategies.* Philadelphia: Wolters Kluwer/Lippincott Williams & Wilkins.

Environmental Protection Agency (2021). About List N: *Disinfectants for Coronavirus (COVID-19).* https://www.epa.gov/coronavirus/about-list-n-disinfectants-coronavirus-covid-19-0

Hu, L. et al. (2007). Effects of self-efficacy on physical activity enjoyment in college-aged women. *International Journal of Behavioral Medicine*, 14, 2, 92–96.

SUGGESTED READINGS

American College of Sports Medicine (2019). *ACSM's Health/Fitness Facility Standards and Guidelines* (5th ed.). Champaign, Ill.: Human Kinetics.

Biscontini, L. (2011). *Cream Rises: Excellence in Private and Group Fitness Education.* New York: FG2000.

Eickhoff-Shemek, J.M, Herbert, D.L, & Connaughton, D.P. (2009). *Risk Management for Health/Fitness Professionals: Legal Issues and Strategies.* Philadelphia: Wolters Kluwer/Lippincott Williams & Wilkins.

IDEA Health and Fitness Association (2011). IDEA code of ethics: Group fitness instructors. *IDEA Fitness Journal*, 9, 6.

Mad Dogg Athletics (2015). *Spinning Instructor Manual* (2nd ed.). Venice, Calif.: Mad Dogg Athletics.

SECTION

III

Elements of Leading Group Fitness Classes

CHAPTER 9
Participant-centered Instruction

CHAPTER 10
Leading Group Fitness Classes

CHAPTER 11
Offering Group Fitness Classes in Diverse Settings

CHAPTER 12
Working with Participants with Health Considerations

CHAPTER 9

Participant-centered Instruction

AMBER LONG, MEd | Executive Director of Wellness & Recreation Services, University of Colorado, Denver; ACE Certified Group Fitness Instructor, Personal Trainer, Health Coach, and Medical Exercise Specialist

IN THIS CHAPTER

LEARNING OBJECTIVES

Upon completion of this chapter, the reader will be able to:

- Understand the domains of learning
- Explain the three stages of learning
- Describe the three participant learning styles
- Apply effective teaching strategies to address the three participant learning styles
- Apply appropriate progressions and regressions of movements
- Provide feedback to participants based on exercise performance
- Understand the importance of disseminating meaningful education to participants

ACE UNIVERSITY

If your study program includes ACE University, visit www.ACEfitness.org/MyACE and log in to your My ACE Account to take full advantage of the ACE Group Fitness Instructor Study Program and online guided study experience.

A variety of media to support and expand on the material in this text is provided to facilitate learning and best prepare you for the ACE Group Fitness Instructor Certification exam and a career as a group

This chapter is dedicated to participant learning and outlines methods that ACE Certified Group Fitness Instructors (GFIs) can use to help participants learn most effectively. GFIs lead groups of people. Within each group, each individual is on a unique learning, health, and wellness journey. Each person is at a different place in terms of competency, fitness level, and **motivation.** The GFI is tasked with teaching group fitness classes in a way that resonates with each individual person, as well as with the group as a whole.

GFIs have control over the environment they create in physical-activity settings, which can positively or negatively impact participants' experiences. Participants' motivation will most likely be optimized when they perceive a task-involving climate where an emphasis is placed on individual effort and improvement as well as camaraderie among peers. This focus reduces feelings of competition and intimidation and is the foundation of the ACE RRAMP Approach™ (see Chapter 10). Task-involving climates build **intrinsic motivation.** In contrast, if the climate is perceived to place importance on ego, outcome, performance, and comparisons, new participants especially may feel intimidated. Outcome-focused coaching fosters **extrinsic motivation,** which is associated with avoidance of challenging tasks and exertion of less effort when perceived ability is low (Brown & Fry, 2014).

GFIs can also enhance the motivational climate by establishing a caring climate. Caring climates have been defined as places where individuals treat one another with mutual respect and kindness and individuals feel a sense of belonging and are considered an important component of the motivational climate (Magyar et al., 2007).

The following strategies can be implemented to enhance the motivational climate and experience of any group fitness class:

- Encourage and praise effort rather than focus on results.
- Create a welcoming and inclusive environment.
- Learn and remember participants' names and facilitate participant introductions.
- Recognize individual efforts and use participants' names when coaching and cueing.
- Engage with participants and make them feel seen, heard, and valued.
- Encourage group feedback and motivational support.
- Encourage participants to connect and support each other.
- Facilitate engagement by asking for participant input on music and their favorite movements.
- Build camaraderie by utilizing words like "we," "let's," and "us" and team-based cues, which are group-based descriptions.
- Make physical connections (when applicable) by offering high fives and fist bumps.

The motivational climate that a GFI creates can assist participants in developing a positive relationship with physical activity, the fitness center setting, the instructor, and fellow participants. A positive motivational climate can also help the instructor prevent class-related conflicts.

EXPAND YOUR KNOWLEDGE

Fun Factor

GFIs have the opportunity to create a memorable experience every time they teach. Class design and teaching strategy are always foundational. The fun factor often has little to do with *what* is instructed, but with *how* the class is taught. GFIs can incorporate ice breakers and engagement-based exercises to help participants get to know one another. Games and other elements of fun, like novelty props or themes (see Chapter 6), create excitement and make classes stimulating and memorable. Opportunities to laugh, smile, and connect can foster team camaraderie and positive regard for the instructor. Little efforts can make a big impact in helping participants intrinsically enjoy exercise.

Here are a few examples of how a GFI can add the fun factor to their classes:

- Make the possibility of mistakes fun by preemptively celebrating the potential loss of balance out of a yoga pose, for example. This can make hard movements seem playful. For example, a GFI might say, "Welcome the wobbles during class today! They're a part of the learning process, so don't be afraid to smile as you regain your balance."
- Use positive language and say things like, "Let's have some fun!"
- Dance around the room when moving around to observe participants' form.
- Add some humor, while making sure any jokes are appropriate.
- Be sure to smile and laugh before, during, and after class.
- Introduce participants to each other and have them share something playful about themselves, like their favorite ice cream or TV show.
- Introduce fun themes, such as a Halloween-themed class with a superhero versus villain theme.
- Choose music from a specific decade and feature fun dance moves from that era.
- Introduce fun partner movements, like push-ups with a high five or one partner performing movements while the other holds a plank.
- Add relay races or other ways to engage as a group in a fun, non-competitive way.
- Incorporate games that focus on teamwork and bonding, as opposed to winning and losing (though some groups may enjoy a bit of friendly competition).

Domains of Learning

During every class, a GFI must be able to quickly ascertain the group's abilities, strengths, and limitations. By the end of the warm-up, the instructor must decide which types of cues and what exercise intensity level will prove most appropriate and effective for the participants present. By understanding the learning process and being familiar with strategies that facilitate the teaching of **motor skills,** the GFI will be better able to educate participants.

Motor learning is a relatively permanent change in the ability to execute a motor skill as a result of practice or experience. This is in contrast to performance, or the act of executing a motor skill that results in a temporary, nonpermanent change (Haibach-Beach, Reid, & Collier, 2018).

It is important that GFIs understand the difference between performing and teaching. When performing, a GFI engages participants in a follow-the-leader type approach. Participants perform the movement, almost on auto pilot, without actually processing and learning to complete movements autonomously. In true teaching, however, the GFI imparts knowledge to the participants, and they in turn demonstrate an "internal change" toward "permanent improvement" as they begin to learn, practice, and remember new behaviors and movement patterns. Over time, participants are able to reproduce these new skills independently in class and in their daily lives.

Learning takes place in three levels or categories of human behavior—cognitive, affective, and psychomotor (Figure 9-1). People develop new skills or knowledge in all three domains of learning at the same time. Each domain has a direct application for a GFI in leading a group fitness class.

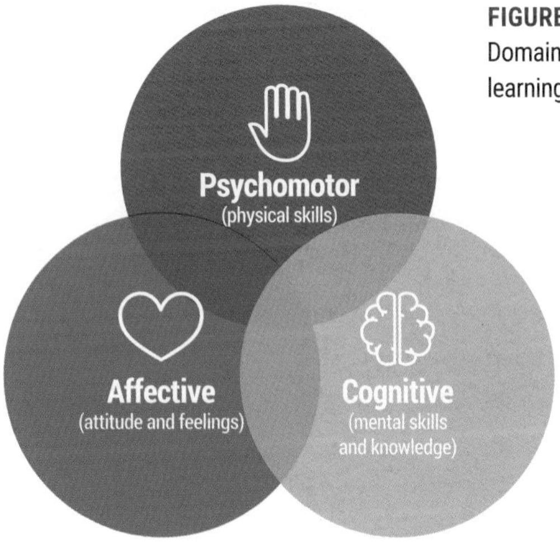

FIGURE 9-1
Domains of learning

COGNITIVE DOMAIN

The **cognitive domain** (acquisition, comprehension, application, analysis, synthesis, and evaluation) describes the brain's ability to gather, retain, apply, and evaluate information and knowledge. This includes skills such as counting out movements, remembering patterns of **choreography,** or applying what was learned about muscle recruitment during an exercise in a new situation. When participants understand and apply knowledge, motivation and exercise compliance are positively affected. Therefore, GFIs should incorporate some elements of education into their classes (Casey, Benson, & MacDonald, 2004). To positively affect learning in the cognitive domain, GFIs should present educational opportunities such as helping participants understand the benefits of performing a specific exercise, or imparting knowledge on proper footwear, for example.

AFFECTIVE DOMAIN

The **affective domain** (emotion) describes emotional behaviors, beliefs, values, and attitudes. Overall motivational attitude and personal feelings regarding health will shape a person's feelings about exercise. This domain is closely linked to exercise enjoyment

and, therefore, **adherence.** GFIs hold the potential to help participants develop positive attitudes about physical activity by enhancing how they receive, respond to, value, organize, and characterize their emotions related to the physical movements produced both in class and in everyday life (Hoque, 2017). GFIs can positively influence the affective learning domain by serving as role models with a positive attitude toward healthy behaviors. It is also important that GFIs create a welcoming and inclusive class environment to help others begin to enjoy the class experience.

PSYCHOMOTOR DOMAIN

Finally, the **psychomotor domain** (physical) refers to those activities requiring the utilization and coordination of motor skills (Hoque, 2017). Learning new motor skills forms the basic foundation of most group fitness classes. GFIs can positively influence the psychomotor domain of learning through purposeful class design to include fundamental movements, movements demonstrating progressive or increased skills, and options for all physical abilities. While most instructors pay careful attention to the psychomotor domain as they design classes, it is important to include teaching strategies for all three domains of learning to provide a more comprehensive approach to instruction and learning.

APPLY WHAT YOU KNOW

Psychomotor Development: Heightening Participants' Kinesthetic Awareness

The goal of a GFI as an educator should be to teach in a way that empowers participants to independently execute moves with proper form. GFIs can incorporate alignment and movement cues into each segment of a group fitness class to help participants gain **kinesthetic awareness** and improve how they perform. Safe and proper technique in class will encourage proper movement in everyday life, when performing **activities of daily living (ADL).**

For example, if a participant demonstrates good alignment when performing a hip hinge in class, the participant is not only moving safely, but they will also move more effectively when transitioning to other hip-dominant exercises, such as squats or lunges, during class. However, if this participant hinges with incorrect form at home, such as with a rounded spine when bending down to pick up their child, then the participant is not reaping the benefits of the quality of movement practiced in class, as they have not changed their behavior and body mechanics in everyday life. It is impactful for GFIs to educate participants about the transfer of movement technique from class to ADL.

To assist participants in learning to move with proper mechanics, GFIs can provide cues that make them more aware of how they position their bodies in space, which is known as **spatial awareness.** When instructing new movements, the GFI may opt to reference body parts in relation to other body parts or surroundings in the room. For example, when standing, the GFI may begin by establishing stability in the body using a "ground up" approach, bringing heightened attention to the position of the feet, and then move up the body using the metaphor of building a house with a firm foundation. In other positions, it can be beneficial to focus on aligning body parts. For example, in the quadruped position, a GFI may begin cueing by saying "come to hands and knees to find a position where the torso is parallel to the floor with wrists aligned below the shoulders and knees aligned below the hips."

Stages of Learning

Understanding the stages of learning helps GFIs understand how to teach participants with a wide variety of competencies. The traditional Fitts and Posner model (1967) explains the three stages of learning for motor skills: cognitive, associative, and autonomous. This model can be applied to new exercises, job tasks, or any new experience or skill.

GFIs must take into consideration the learning stages of participants in order help each person feel successful. The more successful an individual feels, the more motivated they become. Refer to Chapter 2 for detailed information on improving both motivation and adherence.

While the use of the term "cognitive" in both the domains of learning and stages of learning models can cause some confusion, it is important to note that all three domains of learning (cognitive, affective, and psychomotor) are utilized *within* the stages of learning (cognitive, associative, and autonomous). The *domains* of learning are simply categories in which learning takes place (see Figure 9-1). The *stages* of learning (as seen in Figure 9-2) refer to the progressive process that individuals experience as they become more competent at a skill or task.

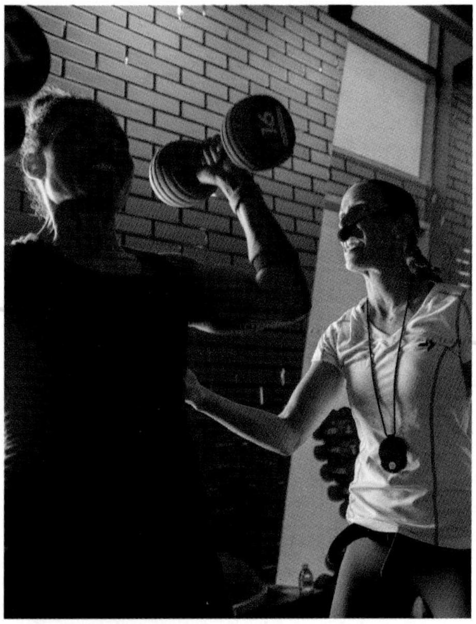

COGNITIVE STAGE OF LEARNING

During the first stage, the **cognitive stage of learning,** movements are slow, inconsistent, and inefficient. When a person learns a new skill for the first time, they are experiencing the cognitive stage of learning. When a new exercise is introduced, large parts of the movement are controlled consciously, requiring a lot of focus. Errors and imperfect form may be the norm. An example of this occurs the first time a group performs a grapevine together at a particular music speed. Many participants struggle with the skill itself, the direction, and the coordination of timing the movement with the music. Individuals in the cognitive stage of learning will benefit from being offered **regressions,** or options for decreasing intensity and complexity, in order to become more proficient at the basics of a movement. Participants in the cognitive stage will also benefit from cues that focus on the most important aspects of the movement. Cues should be concise and direct, so they don't overwhelm new participants with too much information.

ASSOCIATIVE STAGE OF LEARNING

The second stage, the **associative stage of learning,** is reached after the individual has practiced a skill and become more proficient. Movements become more fluid, reliable, and comfortable. Improvements are found in the basic fundamentals of the skill. In this stage, for example, the majority of participants are able to grapevine back and forth in time with the music and can concentrate on occasional cues from the instructor to improve performance. Individuals in the associative stage of learning benefit from individual, specific, and positive feedback in order to continue to refine their skills and abilities.

AUTONOMOUS STAGE OF LEARNING

During the **autonomous stage of learning,** the skill becomes automatic or habitual. Movements are accurate, consistent, and efficient. Learners can perform without following an instructor and can detect their own errors. In a group fitness setting, participants in this stage of learning react automatically with music, direction, and movement upon hearing the instructor's cue: "grapevine left." Individuals in the autonomous stage of learning benefit from being offered **progressions,** or options to increase intensity or complexity, in order to continue to improve their physical abilities and experience success. Individuals in the autonomous stage may appreciate additional motivational cues to encourage them to accomplish personal progress.

COGNITIVE

Movements are slow and inconsistent.

Considerable cognitive activity is required.

Errors are common.

Frequent instructional and corrective feedback is necessary.

ASSOCIATIVE

Movements are more fluid and efficient.

Less cognitive activity is required.

Errors are less common.

People are able to make corrections with feedback.

AUTONOMOUS

Movements are accurate and consistent.

Little or no cognitive activity is required.

Few errors are made.

Minimal feedback is required, primarily to enhance performance.

FIGURE 9-2
Stages of learning

THINK IT THROUGH

Stages of Learning

When performing lunges, what movement errors might be observed in a participant who is in the cognitive stage of learning? How might those errors change as they move through the associative and autonomous stages of learning?

APPLY WHAT YOU KNOW

Mindful Instruction

Instructors must be aware of all participants in a group fitness class at all times. Though there are exceptions, often the most experienced and proficient participants (those in the autonomous stage of learning) tend to congregate toward the front of the room. Such participants are usually able to perform all skills that the GFI cues, often opting for ways in which to increase the intensity of exercises throughout the class experience.

Participants with average skill levels (i.e., those in the associative stage of learning) often congregate toward the center of the room and are able to do most skills the GFI cues, often seeking ways in which to refine their form to enhance movement execution.

Newer and less skilled students (i.e., those in the cognitive stage of learning) will often congregate toward the rear of the room, particularly if they are timid or nervous about attending the class. These participants may feel intimidated and will often benefit from exploring ways in which to make exercises less intense while learning the fundamental skills of the class.

Ultimately, when leading group fitness classes, instructors must teach so that all class participants experience success. To do this, GFIs should consider providing multiple options for exercises, and leading classes with the following saying in mind:

Have an ear for the front row, an eye for the middle row, and a heart for the back row.

Participant Learning Styles

People learn in three major ways: visual (see), auditory (hear), and kinesthetic (feel/touch/do) (Table 9-1). GFIs are tasked with providing cues for all three types of learners at the same time. While most participants can use all three techniques to varying degrees, most learners tend to favor one particular instructional method as their preferred way to obtain information.

TABLE 9-1
Participant Learning Styles

	Visual	Auditory	Kinesthetic
Preferred Learning Methods	See, watch, observe	Listen, hear	Physically perform, do
Instructor Considerations	Model proper execution of movement, to include body positioning, range of motion, and overall technique.	Project clear, direct, specific, and concise verbal cues.	Encourage movement performance and point out sensations experienced during movement—how does it feel?

VISUAL LEARNERS

A visual learner needs to see or watch in order to understand. Visual learners may position themselves to ensure that they can see clearly. To create the most successful experience for this type of learner, GFIs should focus on incorporating appropriate body language and gestures that allow participants to see and understand the desired movement. For example, when targeting a specific muscle group, such as the quadriceps, a GFI may choose to visibly refer to the area on their own body (in this case, the front of the thigh), in addition to providing appropriate technique-related cues to convey to participants what part of the body is being worked during the exercise.

AUDITORY LEARNERS

Auditory learners need to hear specific cues. Auditory learners may position themselves near a speaker to ensure they can hear clearly. To create the most successful experience for this type of learner, GFIs should ensure that verbal cues are specific and succinct. In addition, GFIs should perform sound system checks prior to the start of class to ensure microphone and music levels are appropriate for verbal instruction and cues to be heard by all participants.

KINESTHETIC LEARNERS

Kinesthetic learning takes place when a person physically completes a task or exercise. Kinesthetic learners prefer to "do" the movement in order to understand. These individuals may engage in movement with the instructor, even if the instructor asks the class to stop and watch, as they are eager to see how it feels. To create the most successful experience for this type of learner, GFIs should get in the habit of utilizing cues that offer participants an element of sensation. This can be done by using words such as "feel," "imagine," and "pretend," through which the GFI strives to convey where and how a sensation should be felt and/or when a mental component of visualization may be appropriate.

Instructional Strategies to Enhance Learning

In understanding that participants have various learning styles, GFIs should strive to effectively integrate visual, auditory, and kinesthetic cues to coach participants through the execution of exercises. The following sections outline considerations for cueing to relate to the preferred learning style of all types of learners.

CUEING FOR VISUAL LEARNERS

Visual learners understand by watching. To improve the experience and performance of visual learners, GFIs must execute movements with proper form and technique. GFIs can utilize their body to point, gesture, or signal information to participants who are watching intently. For example, if giving the verbal cue "lateral lunge right," the instructor may simultaneously outstretch their arm and point to the participant's right, giving a visual cue to move in that direction. GFIs should perform visual cues with confidence to improve the clarity of instruction.

Visual cueing also assists with creating an inclusive class experience. Participants whose primary language may be different from that of the GFI may be able to understand visual cues more easily. In addition, purposeful visual cueing can enhance the class experience for persons who are hearing impaired.

Some common visual cues are shown in Figure 9-3. In addition, GFIs should consider the class format and determine additional visual cues that are specifically appropriate for the mode of exercise and instructional need of participants.

FIGURE 9-3
Examples of visual cues

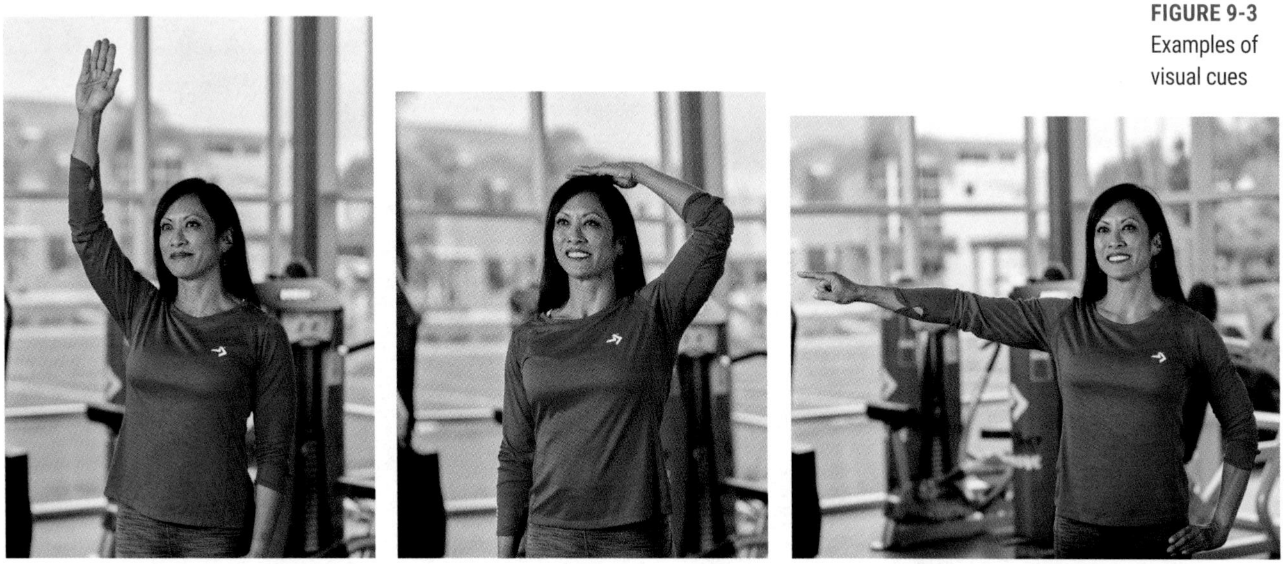

Hold/stay | From the top | Direction (arm fully outstretched right/left)

Continued on the next page

FIGURE 9-3
(continued)

Direction (forward and back – bent elbow, index point, or thumb)

Lead leg

Breathe through the nose

Breathe through the mouth

Hands at hip – hip hinge

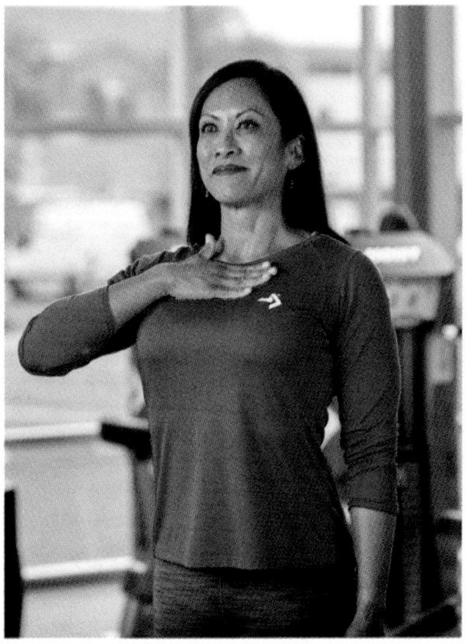

Chest up – tall spine, hand at heart

Chin tucked in – hand on chin, neck retracted

APPLY WHAT YOU KNOW

Effectively Demonstrating Movements in Class

The majority of people are primarily visual leaners (Knowles et al. 2021), so it is important that GFIs model optimal movement technique and alignment. GFIs should demonstrate each movement and provide a variety of options or modifications from which participants can choose. GFIs can further enhance visual learning outcomes by moving in a slightly exaggerated manner, as if performing on stage. This can be particularly helpful for participants positioned near the back of class. The execution of strong movements will make the pattern of movement clear and motivate the participants to complete the exercise with effort. Instructors can enhance their form, technique, and performance of movement through practice. Practicing in front of a mirror, video recording one's performance, or requesting feedback and evaluation from colleagues and supervisors can be particularly beneficial when learning new exercises, formats, or techniques.

CUEING FOR AUDITORY LEARNERS

Auditory learners understand by listening. GFIs convey information to auditory learners through verbal cues. Verbal cues should be specific and concise, such as "feet are hip-width apart, sit back into a squat, bending knees just over toes." The most important aspects of a movement should be provided first. In addition, as the class is taking place, it is important for the instructor to observe the skills and abilities of participants and provide verbal feedback such as "slide the shoulders away from the ears" or "push the hips back farther." GFIs might occasionally feel as though they have already effectively cued a movement, but perhaps it was not understood by some participants. In such cases, a cue like "shoulders back" might need to be restated as "lift the chest." It is important to continue to try to connect with participants by saying things in different ways in order to help them learn proper movement techniques. Additional information on the delivery of verbal cues is provided in Chapter 10.

APPLY WHAT YOU KNOW

Verbal Cueing Practice

To become more efficient at providing verbal cues, GFIs can utilize the following tips:

- Prepare the class plan, including sample cues that correlate with each section.
- Practice verbal cues while listening to music (especially helpful if teaching a beat-based class).
- Film a class and analyze your cueing performance.
- Take classes from a variety of instructors to observe others' verbal cueing strategies.

FIGURE 9-4
Triangle pose

CUEING FOR KINESTHETIC LEARNERS

A kinesthetic learner needs to feel or do in order to understand. To create the most successful experience for this type of learner, GFIs should get in the habit of utilizing cues that offer participants an element of sensation. This can be done by using words such as "feel," "imagine," and "pretend," through which the GFI strives to convey where and how a sensation should be felt and/or when a mental component of visualization may be appropriate. For example, when a GFI is cueing the triangle pose during a yoga class (Figure 9-4), they might say to participants "imagine your body is between two sheets of glass" to help create an appropriate mental image of proper body positioning in the posture.

Kinesthetic learners may also find value in being provided with a subtle physical touch by the GFI that helps them better experience the movement or exercise. However, it is imperative that GFIs always ask for and receive permission from participants before offering any type of physical touch or assist. Instead of physically touching a participant to assist with form and alignment, a GFI may opt to cue participants to the solution, placing an open hand near the participant and instructing the participant to move their body toward it. In this way, instructors avoid the issue of having to touch the participants directly because, in teaching kinesthetic awareness, participants take responsibility for positioning their bodies in space and learn to move away from misalignment and toward correct form.

APPLY WHAT YOU KNOW

Asking for Permission to Provide Hands-on Assists

One way in which a GFI can broach the subject of providing cues and feedback through hands-on assists is to ask for permission from the group as a whole at the beginning of a group fitness class. For example, during a yoga class, the subject of physical touch can be addressed at the start of the practice when participants have privacy in an eyes-closed posture, such as extended child's pose. The GFI may offer a blanket statement to the group, such as, "Today I will be offering gentle hands-on assists to help further explore alignment and sensation with each pose. If you prefer that I offer feedback in a way that does not involve physical touch, simply flip both palms to the sky to let me know, and I will certainly honor your personal space throughout the class."

It is also important that the GFI be familiar with the facility's policy regarding hands-on assists, as many gyms do not allow instructors to provide any physical touch whatsoever for fear of legal action (McCarthy, 2012).

Effective GFIs are able to provide cues in a three-dimensional manner for all three learning styles (i.e., visual, auditory, and kinesthetic) at the same time.

For example, during a push-up, a GFI can visually demonstrate the exercise along with the class, while providing a few verbal execution cues during the movement ("bend the elbows, allowing them to flare out slightly; your upper and lower body move as one") and a quick kinesthetic cue ("brace your core, slightly stiffening your abdominals"). Adding brief learning opportunities, such as identifying target muscle groups and benefits ("working the muscles of our shoulders, chest, and core in one functional movement"), improves the overall experience and the GFI's credibility.

APPLY WHAT YOU KNOW

Three-dimensional Cueing

Biscontini (2011) recommends utilizing the following types of **three-dimensional cueing** (i.e., delivering multiple pieces of information simultaneously, while addressing all three learning styles):

- *Alignment:* Cues that include exercise set-up, general posture, and kinesthetic awareness of body dynamics before and during a movement
- *Anatomical:* Cues that reference the body to enhance kinesthetic awareness and inform participants which muscles are active during an exercise or movement pattern
- *Breathing:* Cues that indicate the best breathing technique to match the discipline, exercise, or movement series, and can indicate both *when* (e.g., on which phase of a movement to inhale or exhale) and *how* to breathe (e.g., in through the nose and out through the mouth)
- *Directional:* Cues that tell participants where a movement will be taking place in relation to the classroom space and their own bodies
- *Humorous:* Cues that are designed to create an enjoyable, entertaining, yet educational experience in which participants feel comfortable
- *Motivational:* Cues that are directed toward the group or individual exercisers to encourage positive reinforcement
- *Numerical:* Cues that tell participants how many repetitions of an exercise or movement series will be performed in total or how many remain and allow participants to gauge their intensity accordingly. This may include rhythm cueing.
- *Rhythm*: Cues that indicate the pace at which the movements or exercise will occur
- *Safety:* Cues that emphasize proper execution of the movement or exercise to minimize the risk of injury
- *Spatial:* Cues that reference areas of the body, equipment set-up around the body, and/or the body's orientation to the equipment and/or the group fitness space

Teaching Multilevel Classes

While it would be easier to instruct a group of participants who all possess the same fitness and skill levels, almost every group fitness class brings an assortment of participants with a variety of competencies. Effective GFIs, therefore, must be keen observers and provide options for all skill levels via exercise modifications in order for participants to explore any movement within the class and experience success. Modifications refer to changes to an exercise that increase the intensity (progression) or decrease the intensity (regression). A modification could also involve an adaptation or change to the exercise to suit the individual needs of a participant. For example, a person who is unable to get on the ground because of an injury or disability might need a core exercise adapted to an option performed in a standing or seated position.

GFIs must understand how to progress, regress, or adapt any given exercise in order to fully serve the individual needs of each participant. Thus, when planning a class, it is important that a GFI selects exercises that they understand how to modify. Instructors should aim to provide multiple variations of each exercise and encourage participants to choose the version that suits them best. Table 9-2 provides common principles used to progress or regress a movement. In addition to what is presented in Table 9-2, GFIs can modify movements by adjusting their speed, tempo, or rhythm. Depending on the exercise being performed, increasing or decreasing movement speed can provide either a regression or progression. Also, allowing participants to choose their own speed and rhythm can enable them to work at the appropriate intensity.

TABLE 9-2
Principles of Progression and Regression

Regression	Primary Principle	Progression
	Stability	
Increase stability/base of support ▸ Wider base of support/stance ▸ More points of contact ▸ Hold on to external support (wall, bar, or suspension trainer) (Figure 9-5)	Exercise example: Body-weight squat (Figure 9-6)	Reduce stability/base of support ▸ Narrower base of support ▸ Fewer points of contact (alternating arms/legs, single leg) (Figure 9-7) ▸ Unstable surface (half foam roller, BOSU)
 **FIGURE 9-5** Body-weight squat: Supported by a suspension trainer	 **FIGURE 9-6** Body-weight squat	 **FIGURE 9-7** Body-weight squat: Single-leg variation

TABLE 9-2 (*continued*)

Regression	Primary Principle	Progression
	Load	
Decrease load ▸ Remove or decrease resistance (Figure 9-8)  **FIGURE 9-8** Stationary lunge: Supported by a suspension trainer	Exercise example: Stationary lunge (Figure 9-9)  **FIGURE 9-9** Stationary lunge	Increase load ▸ Increase resistance (Figure 9-10)  **FIGURE 9-10** Stationary lunge with dumbbells
	Range of Motion	
Decrease range of motion ▸ Decrease lever length (bend elbows or knees) (Figure 9-11)  **FIGURE 9-11** Bicycle crunch: Decreased lever length	Exercise example: Bicycle crunch (Figure 9-12)  **FIGURE 9-12** Bicycle crunch	Increase range of motion ▸ Increase lever length (extend elbows or knees) (Figure 9-13)  **FIGURE 9-13** Bicycle crunch: Increased lever length
	Movement Complexity	
Decrease complexity ▸ Static (holding a movement) (Figure 9-14)  **FIGURE 9-14** Bear crawl: Crouch hold (knees off ground)	Exercise example: Bear crawl (Figure 9-15)  **FIGURE 9-15** Bear crawl	Increase complexity ▸ Dynamic (movement or traveling) (Figure 9-16)  **FIGURE 9-16** Bear crawl: Sideways

Continued on the next page

TABLE 9-2 *(continued)*

Regression	Primary Principle	Progression
	Plane of Motion/Movement	
Reduced movement ▸ Sagittal plane (feet fixed in place) (Figure 9-17)	Exercise example: Forward lunge (Figure 9-18)	Multiplanar ▸ Frontal plane (lateral movement) ▸ Transverse plane (rotational movement) (Figure 9-19)
 **FIGURE 9-17** Stationary lunge: Feet stay in place as the body moves up and down	 **FIGURE 9-18** Forward lunge	 **FIGURE 9-19** Lunge: Curtsy lunge in transverse plane

In addition to understanding the various ways that exercises can be progressed and regressed, GFIs can consider offering movements along a continuum. Thinking of each exercise in this way provides GFIs with a method to consider progression options to fit the needs of participants during class. This allows participants to try each variation, challenging themselves to progress. GFIs should encourage participants to choose a movement option based on the goal of the exercise. For example, in a balance-training segment, a GFI might say, "You should feel that your balance is slightly challenged while remaining in control of your body without fear of falling." Figure 9-20 outlines the continuum for stabilization, lower-body movements, and upper-body movements.

FIGURE 9-20
Exercise progression continuum

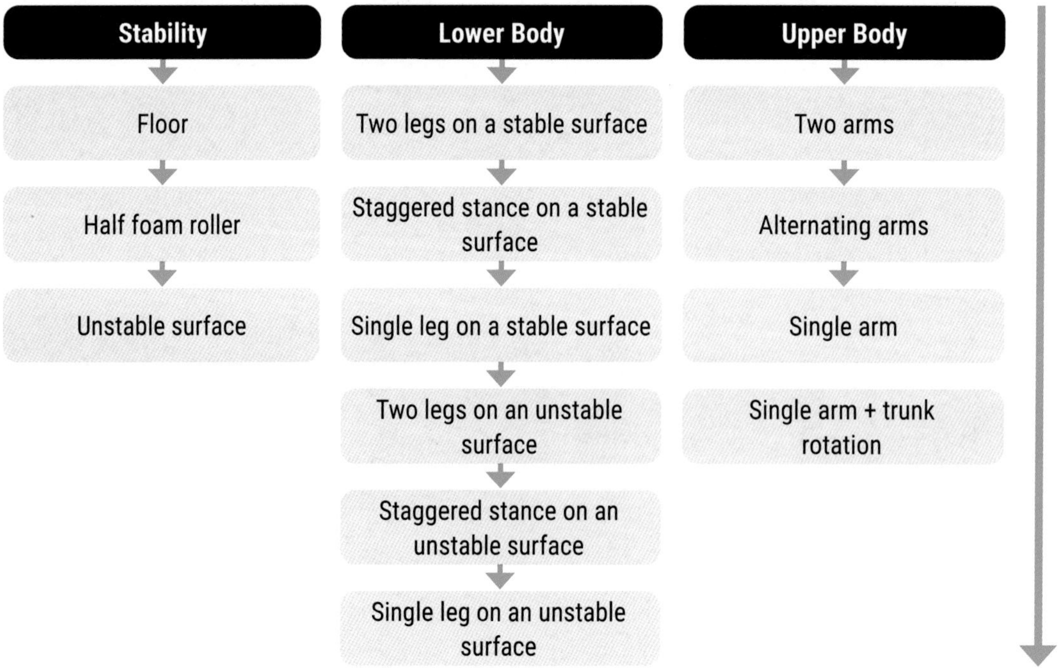

THINK IT THROUGH

Progressions and Regressions

How might an instructor provide a base level, regression, and progression of the following exercises?

- Push-up
- Knee strike
- Burpee
- Jumping jack
- Mountain climber

When increasing (progressing) or decreasing (regressing) the difficulty, complexity, or intensity of a movement, GFIs should be sure to label the skill, as opposed to the individual. This creates a more supportive and accepting environment in which participants can learn and thrive. One way to create this supportive environment is to cue options for how to perform an exercise, as opposed to using labels like "harder" and "easier" or "beginner" and "advanced." The GFI might simply offer "options" rather than labeling the versions of movements in any way. This begins with explaining the goal of the exercise and then providing options to make that goal a reality. The idea is to empower the participants to find their own way.

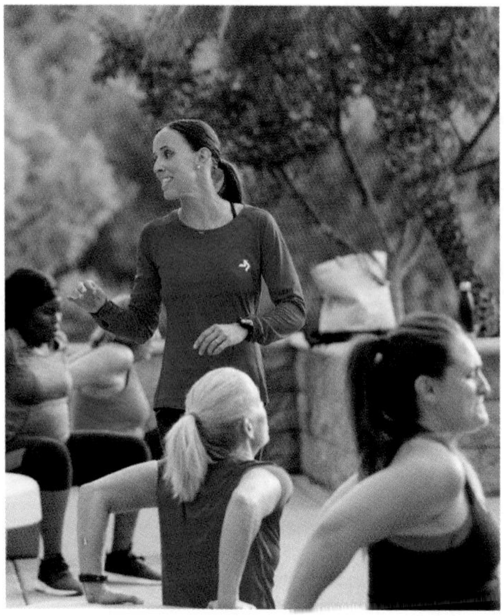

OBSERVING PARTICIPANTS AND PROVIDING FEEDBACK

One of the most powerful instructional strategies that can be used by a GFI is to observe participants while they are performing a movement and then provide specific feedback based on those observations. Each participant's posture, exercise form and technique, and tolerance to fatigue should be monitored by the GFI throughout the class.

Posture and Movement

A GFI should be able to recognize the important characteristics associated with proper spinal alignment and good overall posture. The following points represent what to look for when assessing a participant's standing posture.

Frontal views (anterior and posterior) (Figures 9-21a and 9-21b):

- The feet should be shoulder-width apart with the weight evenly distributed. Excessive foot **pronation** or **supination** could lead to musculoskeletal injuries if a participant performs high volumes of exercise with poor foot mechanics. Any individual who complains of joint pain in the ankles, knees, hips, or back should consult their healthcare provider, especially if they exhibit high arches (excessive supination) or flat feet (excessive pronation).

- There should be overall symmetry between the right and left sides of the body with no visible lateral shifting or leaning to one side.
- The arms should hang with equal space between each arm and the torso and the hands should hang such that only the thumbs and index fingers are visible (i.e., no knuckles should be visible from the frontal plane anterior view). Hands that hang with the knuckles facing forward indicate an imbalance of the muscles of the shoulder and/or forearm.
- The kneecaps (patellae) should be oriented forward without deviation inward or outward (internal or external rotation, respectively). A patella that appears rotated inward or outward is an indication of a potential muscular imbalance or structural deviation of the hips and/or foot/ankle complex.

Sagittal view (Figure 9-21c):

- The head should be suspended (not pushed back or dropped forward) with the ears in line with the shoulders, shoulders over hips, hips over knees, and knees over ankles.
- Participants must maintain the three natural curves of the spine. A decrease or increase in the spinal curvature changes the amount of compression the spine can withstand. The hips can be tucked slightly, particularly for individuals with exaggerated lumbar **lordosis,** women who are pregnant, and participants with large, protruding abdominal areas.
- The knees should be unlocked or soft. Hyperextended knees shift the pelvis, contributing to an increased low-back curve and back strain, along with decreased blood flow to and from the legs.

FIGURE 9-21
Postural assessment example (frontal and sagittal plane views)

Note that the participant's knuckles are facing forward in the anterior view. This is an example of a potential muscular imbalance to look for during a postural assessment.

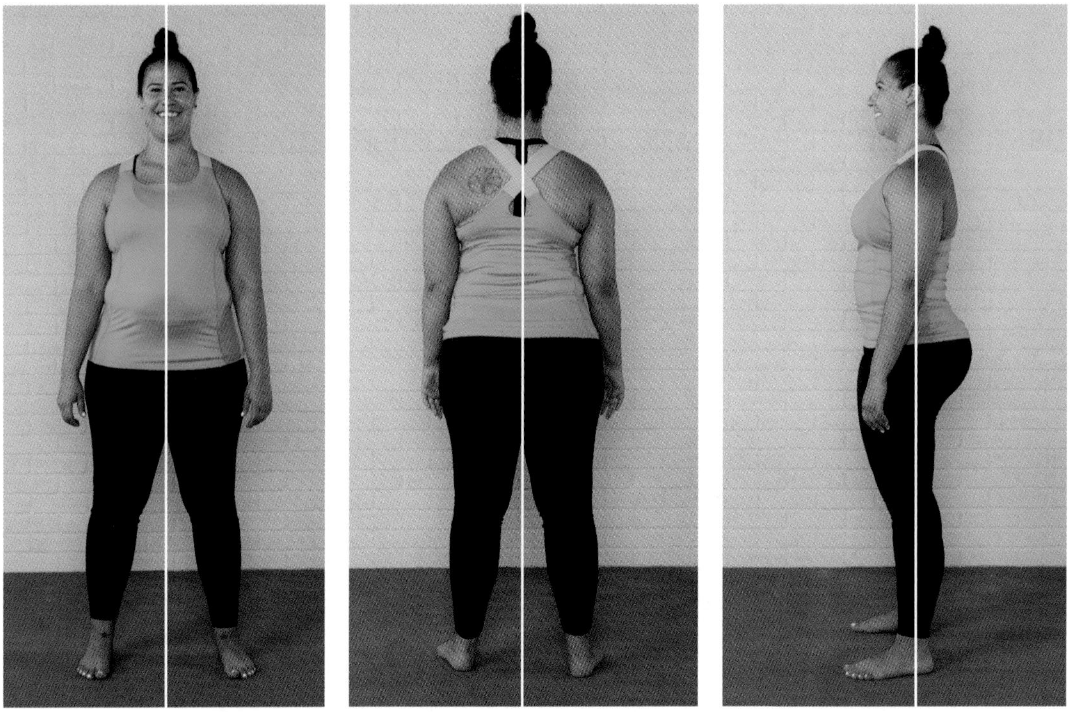

a. Frontal plane view (anterior) b. Frontal plane view (posterior) c. Sagittal plane view

Form and Technique

While it certainly is not the responsibility of the GFI to conduct individual postural assessments and design personalized exercise programs for participants, knowledge of ideal postural alignment is crucial for understanding proper exercise technique. A GFI can cue participants to maintain correct posture throughout the exercise class with statements such as, "Keep your shoulders down and your knees slightly bent while we do this exercise."

Muscular imbalances are often found around the hips, trunk, and shoulder girdle due to prolonged sitting throughout the day. Giving participants in group fitness classes an opportunity to work those joints through their intended ROMs while simultaneously promoting adequate strength and flexibility of the joints' associated structures, is one way to help all participants improve posture.

Generally, a participant's exercise technique should adhere to a few basic guidelines:

- Controlled, purposeful movements require more muscle involvement, and thus protect the joints better than quick, uncontrolled movements.
- The availability of specific amounts of weight in group strength classes is often limited, resulting in some participants lifting loads that are too light for advancing muscular fitness. In these situations, it is important to cue the participant to focus even more on the muscular contraction being performed to move the weight rather than increasing the velocity of the lift. In classes that promote momentum training, such as in kettlebell classes, it is essential for a GFI to have the proper knowledge and training to correctly instruct technique.
- In load-bearing cardiorespiratory classes, such as traditional aerobics and step classes, participants should be cued to control the descent of the lower extremity as it makes contact with the ground (or step) surface by making as little noise as possible with the feet. This practice will ensure a thoughtful impact with the ground and result in muscular deceleration forces that attenuate much of the **ground reaction forces** that could affect the body's joints. Coaching a participant to "land quietly" or to "be light on your feet" are helpful cues.
- Regardless of the exercise being performed, participants should be coached to always demonstrate good posture. This typically means that the spine and pelvis should maintain their neutral, or ideal, positions through a mild contraction or bracing of the core musculature, and the knees should remain slightly bent.

CONSIDERATIONS FOR PROVIDING FEEDBACK

GFIs who give individual feedback show that they care for the true progress of their participants. Corrective and supportive feedback, while important across all stages of learning, is of the utmost importance during the associative stage of learning, in which participants are working toward skill mastery and are able to process efficient and effective cues offered to help improve performance. Feedback can be broad such that the instructor might be addressing the performance challenges or necessary correction of multiple people in the class, or feedback can be specifically addressed to one individual.

Regardless of format, there are some standard guidelines for corrective cueing:

- Provide no more than one corrective action at a time and choose the most critical. For example, during a deadlift, if one participant is rounding their back and another is holding the bar too wide (a non-critical issue), cue the participants to maintain an extended, neutral spine—"draw your shoulders back, imagining you're balancing a glass of water on your upper back." GFIs should strive to ensure gross movement errors are addressed first before refining other aspects of form and technique.
- Form and corrective cues should be sequential, often starting from the trunk/core (**proximal** stability) then moving to the extremities (**distal** mobility), unless the gross errors are critically apparent in a specific area of the body. For many exercises, setting up and later evaluating movements may be done from "the ground up."
- Cues should be positive and solution-based. GFIs should refrain from words such as "don't" and "no," as this language feels punitive. Instead, instructors should build vocabulary to cue what to do, as opposed to what *not* to do. Filler words such as "the next exercise is" or "next we're going to..." should be removed as well, allowing for more direct cues.

In addition, the manner in which corrective feedback is offered to participants can play a role in building or diminishing **rapport** with participants. It is important to deliver corrective feedback in a supportive and non-threatening manner. When offering individual feedback, GFIs can use the following system outlined:

- Deliver feedback to the whole group. It is likely that more than one person may benefit from the information.
- If individual feedback is necessary, aim to connect with the participant by making eye contact. Once connection is established, it is important to point out something positive the individual is doing. This helps establish trust and focus.
- Cue the needed correction and the rationale, known as the performance standard of the movement or exercise.
- Offer positive reinforcement on the immediate correction.

For example, consider a situation in which a GFI notices that a participant's shoulders are elevated when performing standing biceps curls. A sample script could be, "Let's relax our shoulders away from our ears" (group feedback). Then, the GFI could direct attention while making eye contact with a specific participant who might need additional feedback. "Great job keeping your spine extended and chest lifted" (positive point). "To better challenge the muscles we're working, keep the shoulders down away from the ears" (performance standard). "Yes, that's great, notice how much more you feel the muscles in the arms working" (positive reinforcement). Refer to Chapter 10 for additional strategies on providing feedback.

Offering specific and immediate feedback always takes a bit more thought and time but signifies a seasoned instructor who is able to spot good form and verbalize it. Instead of cueing "Good job, Rebecca," for example, an instructor may cue specifically what the participant is doing well. Stating both what is good and why it merits mention constitutes effective and appropriate feedback. For example, saying, "Great work hinging at the hips to initiate the squat (performance standard). You are protecting your lower back (rationale)," may take a moment more to verbalize, but incorporates all of the components of effective cueing.

THINK IT THROUGH

Effective Cueing

Imagine you are leading a group strength class and are teaching reverse lunges to participants. As you look around the room, you notice that many participants are performing the exercise with incorrect form. Script out how you would clearly and concisely provide feedback to participants in the form of positive cues that are free of filler words.

Educating Group Fitness Participants

As educators, GFIs impart knowledge to participants using a variety of research-supported teaching strategies and techniques rooted in a firm understanding of educational philosophies. The transfer of knowledge enhances **autonomy** and exercise adherence. Participants who take greater ownership in their own fitness experiences are more likely to continue regular exercise.

While personal trainers and other health and exercise professionals commonly work one-on-one with clients and provide individualized education based on their clients' unique abilities, needs, and goals, GFIs must educate groups of people all at once. As a result, education typically caters to the general population while being mindful of individual participants' needs, goals, and limitations.

While GFIs do not have the benefit of understanding each participant's background as thoroughly as a personal trainer might, it is important to stay abreast of a variety of exercise science subjects that will enable the GFI to educate participants in a meaningful way during each class.

To enhance the effectiveness of instruction, GFIs must deliver clear and concise information, using only a few moments to deliver the most important points, while also ensuring the content is not too technical. Remember, a good instructor does not show off what they know and what others do not. Instead, a good teacher inspires others. Keeping this in mind, there are three primary strategies for educating group fitness participants.

TRIPLE F: FORM, FUNCTION, AND FIT

This strategy educates participants on the benefits of performing the exercise with proper technique and form and goes into greater detail about how the movement fits within the overall plan to target muscles to produce the desired function. GFIs can help participants understand how an exercise performed properly in class enhances their abilities in daily life. The following example features a GFI teaching participants how to perform a body-weight squat:

- *Form:* "Stand with feet hip-width apart to create a solid base of support. Keeping the core engaged, initiate the movement by hinging at the hips."
- *Function:* "We perform squats frequently in our everyday lives inside and outside of the gym. For example, bracing the core in class helps to stabilize the lumbar spine, reducing the potential for developing low-back issues in other activities of life."
- *Fit (target muscles):* "This is a multijoint exercise involving multiple muscles. It primarily targets the quadriceps, hamstrings, and glutes."

PERFORMANCE

This strategy solely focuses on the performance benefits of an exercise or class. Consider these examples (Hall, 2014):

- *Hammer curl versus biceps curl:* "In hammer curls, your forearms are in a neutral position, so you're not using the biceps brachii to their full potential. In a traditional biceps curl, your forearms and palms face forward. This position activates the biceps brachii more effectively."
- *Body-weight lunge:* "Lunges are transferable to activities of daily living like climbing steps, getting up off the floor, or getting in and out of your car. Body-weight lunges help you master the lunge technique so you can perform these activities efficiently."

HEALTH BENEFITS

Educating participants on the behavioral and health aspects of exercise can help bridge the gap between fitness and wellness by building participants' awareness about their health and overall well-being. Consider these examples:

- *Exercise intensity:* "Appropriate effort will help you get the most out of your exercise experience. So, if you're new to indoor cycling and you haven't been consistently exercising, keep your intensity between a 3 and 4 on the **rating of perceived exertion (RPE)** scale for today" (pointing to the RPE poster). This helps acquaint newer participants with what moderate-intensity exercise feels like, allowing them to monitor their own effort appropriately. (See Chapter 4 for more information on proper use of the RPE scale.)
- *Mood:* At the beginning of class, ask participants to acknowledge their current state of mind or mood. At the end of class, ask the question again. Encourage them to

make a mental note of their pre- and post-exercise mood and track how many times in 30 days they left a workout feeling better. Although the GFI is not providing explicit information or knowledge, they are teaching mindfulness and acknowledging some of the behavioral benefits of exercise, which can lead to greater intrinsic motivation and exercise adherence for participants.

- *Sedentary work environments:* "If you work behind a desk, these next four yoga poses can also be performed at your desk to help improve posture."

APPLY WHAT YOU KNOW

Providing Movement Education

In addition to naming the exercise and the starting positions, GFIs should educate participants about the differences between body positions and movement techniques during the set-up. For example, in preparing for a dumbbell lateral raise, the GFI may share that a straight-arm lateral raise is more challenging than a bent-arm lateral raise due to the fact that the lever is longer in the straight-arm variation. Additional information about progression and regression options empowers individuals to choose movements and exercises that they feel best serve them and their personal fitness experience.

ACE UNIVERSITY

If your study program includes ACE University, visit www.ACEfitness.org/MyACE and log in to your My ACE Account to take full advantage of the ACE Group Fitness Instructor Study Program and online guided study experience.

A variety of media to support and expand on the material in this text is provided to facilitate learning and best prepare you for the ACE Group Fitness Instructor Certification exam and a career as a group fitness instructor.

SUMMARY

A successful GFI has a firm understanding of the various ways in which participants learn and has the ability to utilize and adapt various instructional methods in order to ensure that the diverse needs of all participants are safely and effectively met. The knowledge, skills, and overall experience that GFIs impart enables participants to experience movement success both inside and outside of the group fitness environment, leading to a healthier lifestyle.

REFERENCES

Biscontini, L. (2011). Cueing in three dimensions. *IDEA Pilates Today*, 2, 1.

Brown, T.C. & Fry, M.D. (2014). Motivational climate, staff and members' behaviors, and members' psychological well-being at a national fitness franchise. *Research Quarterly for Exercise and Sport*, 85, 2, 208–217.

Casey, A., Benson, H., & MacDonald, A. (2004). *Mind Your Heart: A Mind/Body Approach to Stress Management Exercise and Nutrition for Heart Health*. New York: Free Press.

Fitts, P.M. & Posner, M.I. (1967). *Human Performance*. Belmont, Calif: Brooks/Cole.

Haibach-Beach, P.S., Reid, G., & Collier, D.H. (2018). *Motor Learning and Development*. Champaign, Ill.: Human Kinetics.

Hall, S. (2014). *Basic Biomechanics* (7th ed.). New York: McGraw-Hill.

Hoque, M.E. (2017). Three domains of learning: Cognitive, affective and psychomotor. *The Journal of EFL Education and Research*, 2, 2.

Knowles, M.S. et al. (2021). *The Adult Learner: The Definitive Classic in Adult Education and Human Resource Development* (9th ed.). Abingdon, UK: Routledge.

Magyar, T.M. et al. (2007). The influence of leader efficacy and emotional intelligence on personal caring in physical activity. *Journal of Teaching in Physical Education*, 26, 310–319.

McCarthy, S. (2012). *Transformation Teaching Through Yoga Adjustments: Adjustments and Strategies to Build a Thriving and Sustainable Yoga Career*. San Diego: Yoga Namastacy.

SUGGESTED READINGS

Ayers, S.F. & Sariscsany, M. (Eds.) (2011). *Physical Education for Lifelong Fitness* (3rd ed.). Champaign, Ill.: Human Kinetics.

Biscontini, L. (2011). *Cream Rises: Excellence in Private and Group Fitness Education*. New York: FG2000.

Kennedy-Armbruster, C. & Yoke, M.M. (2020). *Methods of Group Exercise Instruction* (4th ed.). Champaign, Ill.: Human Kinetics.

Magill, R.A. & Anderson, D. (2021). *Motor Learning and Control: Concepts and Application* (12th ed.). New York: McGraw-Hill.

McCall, P. (2017). *Effective Strategies for Exercise Cueing*. https://www.acefitness.org/education-and-resources/professional/prosource/september-2016/6043/effective-strategies-for-exercise-cueing/

Stull, K. (2021). *Exercise Progressions, Are You Asking the Right Questions?* https://blog.nasm.org/certified-personal-trainer/exercise-progressions-asking-right-questions

CHAPTER 10

Leading Group Fitness Classes

AMBER LONG, MEd | Executive Director of Wellness & Recreation Services, University of Colorado, Denver; ACE Certified Group Fitness Instructor, Personal Trainer, Health Coach, and Medical Exercise Specialist

IN THIS CHAPTER

LEARNING OBJECTIVES

Upon completion of this chapter, the reader will be able to:

- Differentiate between styles of teaching for group fitness classes
- Apply effective teaching strategies for group fitness classes
- Modify teaching styles, methods, and strategies to meet the needs of participants during group fitness classes
- Solicit meaningful feedback from a variety of sources and incorporate information to enhance the class experience or modify teaching strategies
- Understand leadership strategies that can be utilized to manage and enhance the group fitness class experience
- Implement strategies to avoid group fitness instructor burnout

ACE UNIVERSITY

If your study program includes ACE University, visit **www.ACEfitness.org/MyACE** and log in to your My ACE Account to take full advantage of the ACE Group Fitness Instructor Study Program and online guided study experience.

A variety of media to support and expand on the material in this text is provided to facilitate learning and best prepare you for the ACE Group Fitness Instructor Certification exam and a career as a group fitness instructor.

While previous chapters help ACE Certified Group Fitness Instructors (GFIs) decide *what* to teach (i.e., appropriate exercises and general sequencing of movements), this is only half of the challenge. GFIs must also explore *how* to teach each movement, which is one of the most exciting aspects of group fitness instruction.

Teaching **pedagogy** applies to all subject matter and forms the basis of learning and application. The way one learns to tie their shoes is the same way one learns to cut hair or perform a choreographed dance. Learning to teach human movement is complex because the learner must possess the motor skills necessary to execute the movements, be able to memorize the steps or sequence, understand how an exercise is supposed to look and feel, and have the body awareness to perform movements correctly and repeatedly. Additionally, GFIs must possess the ability to build **rapport** and provide effective instructions that are clear and concise. Teaching mastery evolves over time and with practice.

To accommodate the variety of formats and styles of modern group fitness classes, instructors must understand different strategies of teaching in the group fitness setting. Yoke and Armbruster (2020) identify two major styles of teaching: coaching-based teaching, which has become more popular in recent years, and the more traditional beat-based teaching styles. Table 10-1 outlines the major differences between coaching-based teaching and beat-based teaching styles and strategies. This chapter explores coaching-based teaching strategies, beat-based teaching strategies, and general leadership considerations for GFIs.

TABLE 10-1
Teaching Techniques

	Coaching-based Teaching	Beat-based Teaching
Music	The musical beat/tempo is not utilized, and participants move at their own pace.	The musical beat/tempo is utilized, and participants move together, in rhythm.
Instructor Demonstration/ Performance	The instructor acts as a coach and demonstrates the movement a few times before moving around the room to provide feedback to participants individually.	The instructor performs the majority or all movements, seeking replication and uniformity among participants.
Cueing	Cueing is flexible; precise anticipatory cueing is not necessary.	Timing of cues is important; anticipatory cues are essential.
Participant Performance	Individual performance and effort are encouraged.	Group uniformity and performance are encouraged.
Choreography	Not choreographed	Choreographed to music, often utilizing chorus and phrase segments of a song to determine how the chorography flows and maintain consistent movement
Formats/Class Types	High-intensity interval training (HIIT), boot camp, cycling, sports conditioning, kickboxing, and aquatic exercise	Dance, kickboxing, step aerobics, aquatic exercise, barre classes, and most pre-choreographed formats
Instructor Communication Style	Practice style or self-check style	Command-based style

ACE→ MOVER™ METHOD

An Introduction to the ACE RRAMP Approach™

Shannon Fable, owner of SF Resources; ACE Certified Group Fitness Instructor, Health Coach, and Personal Trainer

Learning to teach multilevel classes is essential for all GFIs. Doing so in a way that allows participants to progress through the stages of learning and experience the intended outcomes of class while having a positive experience is the ultimate goal. Creating a caring and task-involving climate using the ACE RRAMP Approach, which was introduced in Chapter 2, is the secret.

ACE→ RRAMP APPROACH™

The ACE RRAMP Approach helps the GFI create compelling class openings, successful programming, powerful cueing, and meaningful closings that all support a positive motivational climate.

RRAMP is an acronym for the five "ingredients" that allow GFIs to build an environment and experience that considers and serves everyone who participates in class.

R – Respect

R – Recognition

A – Alignment

M – Mistakes

P – Participant

Throughout this chapter, ACE Mover Method™ features will teach GFIs how to bring each element to life before, during, and after classes.

Coaching-based Teaching

Coaching-based teaching is driven by the class plan and often utilizes music in the background, meaning that this style of teaching does not use the musical beat to organize participant movement. In fact, it encourages participants to move freely at their own pace and intensity. The instructor performs the movement, offering visual, auditory, and kinesthetic cues, and then asks participants to join in, often using a timer to organize the class. The instructor is free to move around the room and act as more of a coach.

GFIs using a coaching style of teaching are tasked with providing a supportive environment that celebrates effort and participation rather than performance and perfection. Therefore, it is important that instructors using this method integrate a variety of movement options, including **progressions** and **regressions.** GFIs must ensure all participants are able to participate in a way that allows them to feel challenged and successful.

PRACTICE STYLE OF TEACHING

In a coaching-based class, participants may be performing movements together, such as in an indoor cycling class, or they may be performing movement at their own pace, such as in a time-based **high-intensity interval training (HIIT)** or boot-camp class. This **practice style of teaching** provides opportunities for individualization and one-on-one instructor **feedback** for participants within the group experience. Each workout is viewed as an opportunity to practice, rather than achieve a specific result determined by the instructor. For example, in a HIIT class, all participants are working on the same task, such as performing as many push-ups as possible during a one-minute round. The GFI encourages everyone to choose their own intensity level [e.g., speed, **range of motion (ROM), lever length,** and push-up variation] to promote individual success. The effect created is one of nurturing and support, as it provides participants the freedom to discover what works best for them via practice.

When utilizing the coaching style of teaching, it is important for GFIs to move around the room to effectively instruct all participants. Viewing and coaching participants from different places in the room allows the GFI to observe from different angles and to offer assistance and/or specific feedback on form. A GFI should consider demonstrating a movement for several repetitions, then, if possible, focus on observing and coaching. Instructors should keep in mind that when teaching group fitness classes, the focus is on providing the best experience possible for participants, rather than the performance of a personal workout.

SELF-CHECK STYLE OF TEACHING

When implementing coaching-based teaching, GFIs can also utilize the **self-check style of teaching** (Mosston, 2001). The self-check style relies on participants to provide their own feedback. Self-check is often used in equipment-based classes that utilize machines like rowers, treadmills, or indoor cycling bikes with electronic consoles. Participants may be striving to attain a certain distance in a given time or maintain a certain level of effort for a specific amount of time. Participants perform a given task and then view or record the results, comparing their performance against given criteria or past performances.

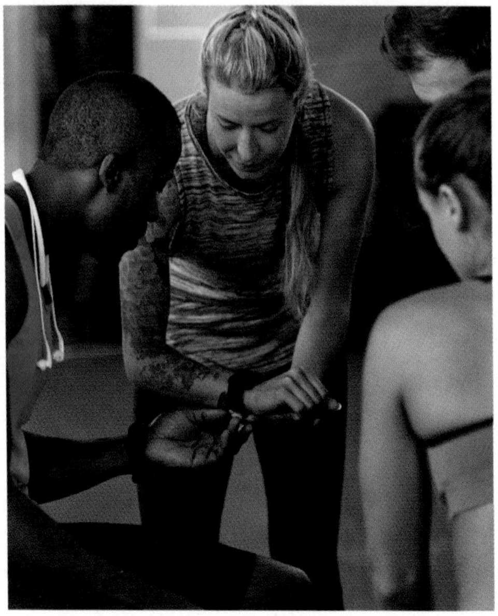

Instructors who emphasize **target heart rate** or **recovery heart rate** with their participants, or who opt to utilize other intensity-gauging measures such as **rating of perceived exertion (RPE)** or the **talk test,** may incorporate self-check into any group fitness format to encourage individuals to be active participants in the class experience.

ACE MOVER™ METHOD

R – Respect

Shannon Fable, owner of SF Resources; ACE Certified Group Fitness Instructor, Health Coach, and Personal Trainer

The first R in the ACE RRAMP Approach—Respect—reminds the GFI that *each* class participant should feel *valued*. Each participant in every class deserves, and should receive, the same amount of care. More importantly, the participants should, at all times, believe this is the case. Their experience should be as rich as that of the person in front of, behind, or next to them in class.

GFIs should keep this question in mind when creating, scripting, and delivering classes:

How can I create a kind and respectful environment?

ACE RRAMP APPROACH™

GFIs should consider the following ideas:

Arrive with enough time to get situated before participants begin to arrive. That way, the GFI will be ready to greet as many people as possible when participants start to arrive. Greetings should be made with open body language, a warm smile, and a genuine appreciation of their presence. If possible, the GFI should engage with one or two new or less-familiar faces. It is tempting to catch up with the regulars, but focusing on those who have not yet *become* regulars will go a long way toward helping them feel valued.

During the introduction to class, consider building in a request for each class member to acknowledge another. For example, it may be as simple as including, "Please turn to a person beside or behind you and introduce yourself," right before the warm-up commences.

Once class begins, intentionally focus on cueing toward all rows and all corners of the room. No matter where someone is in the room or on their journey, they should receive the instruction and encouragement needed to believe the GFI created the class with them in mind. The GFI should plan to teach in a way that allows them to maintain eye contact as often as possible and with as many participants as possible. To do so, the GFI should practice **mirroring** while teaching, walking the room (if appropriate), and avoiding looking at themself in the mirror.

When closing out the class, include sincere appreciation for all participants and, when possible, encourage class members to do so, as well. For example, the GFI may end class by saying, "I greatly appreciate you taking time out of your lives to attend class today. Turn to a person beside you and thank them for helping you have a great experience today!"

If possible, keep the music playing once the class is complete and hold off on clean-up. Instead, the GFI can position themself near the door or wherever participants will go to put away their equipment. The GFI should seek out two or three participants to whom they will express their gratitude individually. Consider using their names, express appreciation for them showing up, and, if possible, point out something specific they did during class that stood out, such as increasing the weight during a set, trying something new, or helping another class participant.

ADDITIONAL COACHING-BASED TEACHING CONSIDERATIONS

GFIs who use the coaching-based teaching method should consider utilizing cues that address visual, auditory, and kinesthetic learners. A successful GFI teaches in a way that will help all participants feel included and successful, regardless of their physical-fitness level or competency. GFIs should focus on providing appropriate movement progressions and regressions and consistently employ the tell-show-do method sometimes utilized in personal training:

Tell-Show-Do

- *Tell* participants what you want them to do.
  - "We are going to perform burpees next."
- *Show* them what to do.
  - Demonstrate the movement with proper form and provide **instructional cues.** Show two to three options, preferably a progression and a regression, to accommodate diverse needs. (Note that these should always be described as "options" when talking to participants, rather than as easier/harder, beginning/advanced, or levels 1, 2, and 3. This language encourages participants to choose the option that works best for them, rather than feeling the need to compete with others and labels the skill or intensity of the movement rather than the individual participant.)

    Option 1: Traditional burpee (squat, hands to floor, jump back to plank, jump up to squat, stand up)

    Option 2: Regression (squat, place hands on elevated surface or floor, step one foot and then the other back to plank, step up to squat, stand up)

    Option 3: Progression [squat, jump back to a plank with an option to lower the entire body to the floor (belly button touching the ground), jump forward to squat, jump squat].
- Let participants *Do* it.
  - Demonstrate and coach: "Let's try a few burpees together. First, step back to plank, step up to squat. Next, squat, jump to plank, squat, stand. Finally, if you want, try the belly-button-to-floor option, and add a jump! Choose the option that suits you today."
  - Observe and provide feedback (specific group and individual feedback): "Great tempo everyone! I see your efforts. Let's make sure to keep the spine straight and core engaged in the plank position." "Great job, Alex, make sure to use your exhale to stabilize your core."

The tell-show-do method is a simple way to ensure that participants clearly understand the task ahead. It clarifies what the exercise is and how it should be performed and addresses a variety of learning styles and participants in different stages of competency.

Beat-based Teaching

Music has the ability to affect human emotion and **motivation.** Baker, Garcia, and Belity (2019) found that participants experience a heightened level of motivation or inspiration while using music as an external stimulus during exercise. GFIs who use the beat-based style of teaching rely on music as a focal point, and use it to deliver **choreography,** maintain **rhythm,** and create uniform movement among class participants.

COMMAND STYLE OF TEACHING

In most beat-based classes, the instructor makes all decisions about **posture,** rhythm, and duration, seeking imitation by all participants. The GFI provides a specific way in which to perform an exercise or sequence, and participants follow along. This **command style of teaching** creates an effect of uniformity (Mosston, 2001). This style requires proper planning to ensure an inclusive class experience for participants of varying ability levels.

The command style of teaching is most commonly used in choreographed classes such as dance, kickboxing, or step classes. Effective leaders using the command style are able to follow the gist of a standardized script (such as those required in pre-choreographed classes), while still offering purposeful options, progressions, and regressions to create a successful experience for all.

ACE MOVER™ METHOD

R – Recognition

Shannon Fable, owner of SF Resources; ACE Certified Group Fitness Instructor, Health Coach, and Personal Trainer

The second R in the ACE RRAMP Approach—Recognition—reminds GFIs that effort and improvement should be prioritized and honored. Specific acknowledgment, instead of general statements such as "good job" or "well done," are essential. Aim to recognize individuals' achievements for all behaviors that contribute to positive outcomes of the class, such as showing up, trying something new, smiling, or helping another participant. While working hard, performing progressions, and improving are important, GFIs must look beyond achievements that focus solely on physical outcomes.

GFIs should keep this question in mind when creating, scripting, and delivering classes:

How can I create opportunities for recognition?

ACE RRAMP APPROACH™

GFIs should consider the following ideas:

Whenever possible, GFIs should make a note of class participants' milestones, such as birthdays, anniversaries, streaks (i.e., the number of classes or weeks in a row they have participated), weight selection in a strength class, mastery of a move, or other goals of which the GFI might be aware. Then, as participants are arriving, the GFI can seek out at least one person and acknowledge one of these milestones. GFIs can offer additional congratulations publicly during class or privately after class.

When creating the opening statement, the GFI should include genuine congratulations for attendance. Respect that participants have choices, and the act of showing up is a reason to celebrate. It is impactful to recognize the effort it took to get there and encourage participants to congratulate themselves for prioritizing this type of self-care.

Throughout the class, GFIs should point out any improvements they see, being careful to include recognition for all individuals rather than focusing on a select few "star" performers. Whether the progress is from set to set or from one week to the next, publicly commenting on participants' progress toward expressed goals, or task-oriented improvements such as completing all the repetitions in a challenging set of exercises, promotes a positive motivational climate. To help participants with self-recognition, consider ways to build in opportunities for participants to gauge their own progress. For example, in a cycling class, the GFI might ask participants to glance at the peak wattage they achieve during the all-out interval. Then, repeat the interval and ask them to meet or beat their personal high from the previous one.

Encourage participants to congratulate themselves and others. For example, the GFI might say, "Look at yourself in the mirror and give yourself a wink—you just completed the most challenging part of class!" Or, ask each participant to turn to someone beside them and give a thumbs up for finishing a set.

Finally, during the closing, the GFI can provide specific guidance that helps participants focus on what went well in class, which will help increase confidence and get them excited about returning. For example, the GFI could lead the class through a minute of reflection by asking participants to close their eyes and think of at least two things they accomplished in class. After a pause, the GFI can suggest they seal these positive thoughts in with a real or imagined self-hug. Then, the GFI should be sure to find at least one or two individuals to congratulate for specific achievements made during class as everyone is departing.

Beat-based Teaching Strategies

Beat-based classes most commonly utilize choreography or movement combinations paired with music to organize and facilitate a continual movement workout. Dance-based classes or traditional **high-low** classes are typically facilitated using the beat-based teaching strategy. Many instructors teach beat-based classes utilizing a 32-count musical phrase to create a combination.

Musical phrases are made up of multiple measures. Measures are like sentences, strung together to make a paragraph, or a phrase. It is typical for group fitness music to be created in a series of 32 counts, with each sentence (measure) containing eight counts and each paragraph or phrase containing four measures. When creating a class blueprint (see Chapter 7), it can be helpful to arrange beat-based choreography using A, B, C, and D to label each sentence, as in the example below.

- (A) 8 counts = 1 sentence
- (B) 8 counts = 1 sentence
- (C) 8 counts = 1 sentence
- (D) 8 counts = 1 sentence

32 counts (total) = 1 phrase

For example:

A	Shuffle right, shuffle left	Counts 1–8
B	Alternating high knees	Counts 9–16
C	Jumping jacks	Counts 17–24
D	Body-weight squats	Counts 25–32

This combination utilizes four different movements, labeled as A, B, C, and D. Each movement is performed for eight counts, which, when strung together, totals 32 counts, or one musical phrase. This phrase would be considered one block of choreography, which could be linked to other blocks of choreography to fill the class.

The more complicated the combinations are, the more important it is to intentionally plan, strategize, and rehearse methods that can be used to break down or progressively teach the movement patterns, so participants can feel successful. Participants will need to perform each movement repetitively to learn how to execute the movement and then learn how to put the movement in a pattern or combination.

There are five common strategies that GFIs can use to deliver beat-based choreography: slow-to-fast, part-to-whole, repetition-reduction, simple-to-complex, and **linear progression,** which are covered in the following sections. Each method is designed to help participants master each individual movement, as well as form a cognitive understanding of the choreography patterns.

SLOW-TO-FAST

When using the **slow-to-fast teaching strategy,** instructors introduce movement patterns so that participants are first performing the exercise at a reduced speed. This often includes a rhythmic variation, as instructors use the half-time of the music. As outlined in Table 10-2, when introducing a squat to participants for the first time, for example, a GFI may teach the move more slowly so participants can learn proper movement techniques. The squat would first be performed at quarter-time, or a 4x4 tempo, or lower/sit for four counts and stand for four counts. During this slow tempo, the instructor has more time to provide initial instructional cues, to help participants master the movement. Because the slow pace of this strategy may reduce exercise intensity, GFIs should minimize using this approach for extended periods of time during the peak of the conditioning segment of class.

After a few repetitions at the slow pace, a GFI can increase the tempo to half-time, or a 2x2 tempo, which is lower for two counts and stand for two counts. As the pace increases, the instructor might provide additional **follow-up cues** and corrective cues. Finally, the squat could be instructed at full tempo, or at a 1x1 tempo,

TABLE 10-2

Slow-to-Fast Teaching Strategy Example: Squat

Music Timing	Movement Speed	Repetitions
32 counts of music (1 phrase)	4x4 (quarter-time) 4 counts down, 4 counts up	4
32 counts of music (1 phrase)	2x2 (half-time) 2 counts down, 2 counts up	8
32 counts of music (1 phrase)	1x1 (single-time) 1 count down, 1 count up	16

which involves lowering for one count and standing for one count. This pace of movement is much faster and will require more physical control and effort. GFIs can focus primarily on **motivational cues** when participants move at this pace and should continue to observe participants in order to offer feedback, ensure safety, and promote positive outcomes.

PART-TO-WHOLE

A GFI using the **part-to-whole teaching strategy,** which is also called the **add-in strategy,** breaks down skills and teaches movement in isolation before integration. Starting with each part of the movement in its simplest form, the instructor teaches sections or parts of a move, followed by the performance of an isolated movement. For example, an instructor teaching a squat and biceps curl combination may begin by teaching a squat, and then move on to teaching a biceps curl, each in isolation. When the instructor observes mastery of each part or movement individually, they can then demonstrate the whole movement as a combination, or new integrated move. For example, the GFI might teach a concentric biceps curl while standing up from a squat.

REPETITION-REDUCTION

The **repetition-reduction teaching strategy** involves reducing the number of repetitions that make up a movement sequence. An instructor may have participants learn a knee strike and cross punch combination using the repetition-reduction method (Table 10-3). In this example, the number of repetitions is reduced by half. Eight, four, and two repetitions are used to align with 32 counts of music.

TABLE 10-3

Repetition-reduction Teaching Strategy Example: Knee Strike and Cross Punch Combination

Exercise	Repetitions
Knee strike	8
Cross punch	8
Knee strike	4
Cross punch	4
Knee strike	2
Cross punch	2
Combo: 1 knee strike + 1 cross punch	1 of each, repeated

SIMPLE-TO-COMPLEX

The **simple-to-complex teaching strategy** is an advanced teaching strategy that is sometimes called **layering.** Instead of separating movement patterns into sections, the instructor will perform one movement for a few repetitions and then add another movement to the sequence or combination. As the sequence progresses, the GFI adds layers of complexity.

For example, consider the performance of a grapevine in one direction for four counts, plus two knee lifts for a total of eight counts. Using this teaching strategy, the instructor engages all participants in this pattern from the start. While everyone is performing repetitions of the grapevine with alternating knee lifts, the instructor offers additional options, which could include two leaps instead of two knee lifts and a three-point turn (walking turn) rather than a grapevine. Participants are free to choose any of the following variations, and the GFI relies on a pattern to assist with repetition and skill development.

- Grapevine + two knee lifts (8 counts)
- Grapevine + two leaps side to side (8 counts)
- Three-point turn + two knee lifts (8 counts)

Generally, the available variables for layering additional complexity involve changes in direction, rhythm, and lever length.

Choreography: Elements of Variation

GFIs can update or vary choreography in small but meaningful ways to create the perception that new moves or sequences are being utilized. The primary elements of variation used with beat-based teaching styles are listed in Table 10-4. GFIs can change one or more of these elements to change any given exercise or movement.

TABLE 10-4
Elements of Variation

	Explanation	Example
Lever Length	Change the lever length from short to long or long to short.	▸ Knee lift progresses to kick ▸ Arms overhead with bent elbow to arms overhead with extended (straight) elbows
Direction	Add or change direction (performing a movement facing front or facing side/back). Travel forward, backward, sideways, or diagonally.	▸ Shuffles performed side to side changes to forward/backward ▸ Salsa performed front to back changes to side to side
Plane	Change the plane of motion.	▸ Front kick changes to side kick ▸ Front raise changes to side raise
Rhythm	Change the rhythm or speed of a move.	▸ Alternating jab, cross, jab, cross can be executed at various speeds: ▪ Half-time; 4-count move ▪ Single time: 2-count move

TABLE 10-4 (*continued*)

	Explanation	Example
		▪ Double-time: 1-count move ▪ Rhythm could also be changed: jab (2 counts), jab-cross (2 counts), indicating the use of half-time and single-time movement in one pattern ▸ Jumping jacks change from single-time to half-time and become more exaggerated
Intensity	Increase or decrease intensity.	▸ Step touch changes to side leaps ▸ ROM increases in dance movements ▸ Knee raises/strikes changes to a tuck jump
Style	Basic movements change to include a style.	▸ Athletic style ▸ Dance style (e.g., Latin, hip-hop, or tribal) ▸ Martial arts

Note: ROM = Range of motion

ACE→ MOVER™ METHOD

A – Alignment

Shannon Fable, owner of SF Resources; ACE Certified Group Fitness Instructor, Health Coach, and Personal Trainer

The A in the ACE RRAMP Approach stands for Alignment. This does not refer to physical alignment or including cues focused on proper exercise execution, though this is certainly an integral part of the GFI's job. Creating a caring and task-involving climate requires looking at alignment from a different perspective.

Alignment, in this instance, serves to remind GFIs that participants should feel like they are part of an *alliance* with their classmates. The GFI's job is to ensure that cooperation is fostered and valued in their classes.

GFIs should keep this question in mind when creating, scripting, and delivering classes:

How can I create the feeling that the entire group is in this together?

ACE→ RRAMP APPROACH™

GFIs should consider the following ideas:

Creating the feeling of camaraderie can begin before class. GFIs should attempt to introduce any new participants to one of the regulars and ask the veteran to help the new class member become acclimated by helping them set up (i.e., find and select the equipment) and giving them an "insider's perspective" on the experience. The new participant will immediately see that they have an ally in class.

The GFI can also provide a moment toward the end of the warm-up when they encourage all participants to keep in mind that the GFI's role is that of the group facilitator. The GFI will be leading the way, but the entire group is in this together.

Throughout the class, be sure to use inclusive cueing when appropriate. Try to cue using the pronoun "we" (versus "I") to reinforce the sense of teamwork. For example, while setting up a new section of class, the GFI might say, "We are heading into our second set of lunges. I think we can try to increase our range of motion. What do you say?" If it feels authentic, calling the class a team or squad can help, too.

While it may not work in every class, changing the group's orientation from time to time can enhance their alliance. The GFI can try to identify a point in class that works to turn the group toward one another and perform a drill, exercise, or set. For example, have the participants break out into two groups have them face the center of the room for the next set of jumping jacks. Encourage eye contact and suggest they send positive energy to someone across the room. If this will not work with the entire group, consider doing so with pairs or smaller groups.

Create cooperative games or interaction in class versus competitions. Instead of pitting one participant against another, the GFI can find ways to have the drills be team-oriented (e.g., relay races that will most likely end up being close with no clear winner) or cooperative (e.g., a game that requires everyone to work together to complete a goal).

Toward the end of class, the GFI can reflect on specific moments when the group came together and supported one another. Finally, as participants are putting away equipment and preparing to head out the door, the GFI might suggest they help one another with clean up and let someone else know how much their presence impacted them during class.

LINEAR PROGRESSION

The freestyle method of delivering choreography most often involves linear progression where one move flows into another without specific patterns or combinations. Newer instructors often find the linear-progression method easier because they have to change only one aspect of movement at a time and do not need to create repeating sequences or patterns. The method is simple: one skill at a time.

For example:

- *Base movement:* Four alternating knee lifts in place (eight counts of music)
- *Add arms:* Four overhead reaches (eight counts of music)
- *Add direction:* Travel forward (eight counts of music); travel backward (eight counts of music)

Ready to move on? Change the movements:

- *Change the legs:* Eight alternating hamstrings curls with same arm movements (16 counts of music)
- *Change the arms:* Clapping hands while moving front and back (16 counts of music)

ADDITIONAL BEAT-BASED TEACHING CONSIDERATIONS

Beat-based classes generally involve continual movement, as one movement flows into the next. Three common ways to transition movements are **matching, mending,** and **patching** (Table 10-5) (Khai-Cronin, Ganulin, & Metzo, 2013).

TABLE 10-5
Transition Techniques

	Description	Example
Matching	Complete one exercise in full and then perform the next exercise.	Strength: A barbell front squat *followed by* an overhead press High-low: Grapevine *followed by* single-leg hamstrings curls
Mending	String two exercises/ movements or combine multiple movements into one exercise.	High-intensity interval training: Thrusters (a squat and overhead press in unison); reverse lunges paired with biceps curls Strength: Reverse lunges and biceps curls (step back to lunge, perform elbow flexion/curl upon standing) Step: Basic right step paired in unison with a lateral arm raise
Patching	Perform an additional movement between two exercises or movements for a seamless transition	Mat Pilates: To transition from the 100 to the roll up, the participant pulls their knees into the chest to patch the two exercises together. Dance: Utilize a squat or shimmy, which are neutral, filler moves to patch two different dance-based moves together.

THINK IT THROUGH

Transitions

Squats are a neutral move, which means that the exercise does not contain a right or left lead. Neutral moves can be utilized to patch any two movements together or to change from a right to a left lead. For example, two knee strikes right (counts 1 through 4) can be paired with a squat (counts 5 through 8). The move can then repeat on the opposite lead—two knee strikes left, then squat. What other moves can be used as neutral moves when executing transitions?

EXPAND YOUR KNOWLEDGE

Utilizing Tempo

Tempo in choreographed classes depends on the music's beats per minute (bpm) or the instructor's cueing. In some strength-based classes, tempo can manipulate the cadence or movement speed, which can affect **overload.** For example, when performing a biceps curl, a GFI may choose a one-count concentric movement (flexing the elbows to lift the dumbbells) and a three-count eccentric movement (extending the elbows to lower the weights down to the starting position).

Tempo, however, is not exclusive to music. GFIs can verbalize the tempo of the movement or exercise to better meet the needs of those who prefer auditory learning who are trying to execute the movement but are having trouble mastering the timing and motor patterns of the skill. For example, an instructor might cue "down two, up two" in time with the speed of the music or pace at which the movement is being executed.

Ultimately, all methods and teaching strategies are available to instructors when developing choreography, and GFIs should consider instructing movement patterns using a combination of teaching strategies. Observant instructors continuously monitor their participants to see which techniques work best for which groups and teach using the methods that promote the highest rate of success. There may be times when a particular teaching strategy is not resonating with the class. An observant instructor can decide to alter the teaching strategy or plan to best suit the needs of participants. Understanding how to deliver and adjust teaching methods is key not only to meeting participant needs, but also to ensuring performance success and minimizing the risk of injury.

ACE MOVER METHOD™

M – Mistakes

Shannon Fable, owner of SF Resources; ACE Certified Group Fitness Instructor, Health Coach, and Personal Trainer

The M in the ACE RRAMP Approach stands for Mistakes, which are inevitable in the group fitness setting. The GFI will make them, veteran participants will make them, and new participants will make them. Mistakes should be considered a part of learning by both the GFI and the participants. GFIs can take their teaching to the next level by expecting mistakes, being supportive when they occur, and anticipating them in the class experience.

GFIs should keep this question in mind when creating, scripting, and delivering classes:

> *How can I ensure that mistakes are an acceptable part of the learning experience?*

ACE RRAMP APPROACH™

GFIs should consider the following ideas to increase the competence and self-confidence of their participants:

Before class begins, the GFI should ask participants about limitations or preferences they may have so the GFI can strategize before class gets started. For example, if the GFI sees a new participant, they can introduce themself and provide an overview of what is to come. The GFI can also ask if there are any concerns based on injuries, likes, dislikes, or preferences based on what they are looking for in the class experience.

Then, during the introduction, build in an acknowledgment of how mistakes will show improvement or effort throughout the class. For example, the GFI might set a goal for the number of times they want participants to push their limits and safely "fail," such as using a weight that makes finishing a set challenging. If the GFI can plan for the class to "mess up" together during the warm-up, that would be a bonus.

Throughout the class, the GFI can use cues to encourage trying something that might not be perfect. Then, celebrate as a group when it does not go quite right. The GFI should be sure to frequently remind participants that mistakes are a sign of growth, learning, or giving maximal effort. When the GFI makes a mistake, they should consider pointing it out and congratulating themself in the same way.

The GFI should program classes with everyone's success in mind by choosing exercises, choreography, or sequences that will be doable by a majority of participants, with opportunities for increasing or decreasing the challenge without judgment. If possible, repeat exercises and build in practice opportunities during the first set.

At the end of class, the GFI can ask participants to identify one thing they could strive to improve next time and remind everyone that doing everything perfectly is not the goal. Finally, the GFI can aim to provide a personal congratulations to one or two participants who showed courage and growth by taking on the challenge of learning from a mistake during class.

Cueing Strategies

Regardless of the teaching strategies a GFI employs, they must execute cues in an effective manner in order to ensure participants clearly understand what to do and how and when to do it. Mastering the art of cueing takes time and practice. GFIs can practice timing and vocal variety of cues by rehearsing class plans in front of a mirror or with family and friends.

TIMING OF CUES: STAGES OF CUEING

The timing of cue delivery is a crucial part of helping participants know what to do, how to do it, and when to do it. A late cue will cause participants to lag behind, while a cue delivered too early will cause participants to feel confused and disconnected. Cues can be organized in a flexible, but systematic manner. GFIs should consider offering cues in order of the stages of cueing, starting with **anticipatory cues** to indicate a change in movement, providing instructional cues to impart knowledge on exercise technique, offering follow-up cues to provide feedback for corrections or enhancements, and finally providing motivational cues to inspire greater participant effort and emotional connection to the group experience.

Anticipatory Cues

In cueing a new exercise, instructors might utilize anticipatory cues, which tell participants what the next move will be, and when to do it. Anticipatory cues could include a countdown of repetitions, while stating a new exercise or directional gesture. Anticipatory cues should be clear and concise to alert that change is coming. Anticipatory cues are most commonly used in beat-based formats, paired with music, such as "4, 3, step touch right." When using music, anticipatory cues must be delivered in time with the music and in a way that allows participants to understand the transition before it takes place.

APPLY WHAT YOU KNOW

Anticipatory Cues

Anticipatory cues are one of the more challenging skills for new instructors to master. GFIs who teach to music must have an understanding of music structure and choreography strategies in order to properly execute anticipatory cues. When cueing to music, GFIs should provide cues at least four counts before movement is initiated. When not using music, a few moments should be given to allow participants to process instructions before the movement begins. In most group fitness classes, counting down (e.g., "4-3-2"), as opposed to counting up, will help participants know how many movements remain before a change ensues. GFIs can practice their cueing skills by speaking cues out load in time with music. When practicing, count backward toward an upcoming move. For example, when the GFI counts "4, 3, step touch," the name of the move is inserted where "2 and 1" would typically be. This indicates to participants that the new move begins directly after 1. Moves that need more time such as "knee-kick right, arms up" would need to be delivered sooner, such as "5, 4, knee-kick right, arms up." Utilizing half-tempo to provide anticipatory cues can be very beneficial, as well. For example, the GFI would count "4, 3, knee kick," but start the cue at count 8, and utilize two counts to provide the cue, rather than one.

Practice anticipatory cues: Play music and cue on the fourth sentence of every 32-count phrase: "8, 7, 6, 5, now I start to cue." Once that cue becomes comfortable, replace "now I start to cue" with any exercise that you might teach. Continue changing the exercise on the fourth sentence of every phrase until the rhythm of anticipatory cues feels more comfortable when spoken with music. Then, progress to practicing the physical movement while cueing.

Instructional Cues

Once the anticipatory cue is delivered, instructional cues can be used to properly set up and execute the exercise. Instructional cues focus on the most important aspects of the exercise, such as posture/alignment, safety considerations, ROM, and speed of movement. Instructional cues might also include exercise variations or modification options.

Follow-up Cues

When the exercise has started, a GFI should observe participant performance, and utilize follow-up cues, which provide tangible and immediate feedback. Follow-up cues might be used to correct form or enhance the exercise. Follow-up cues are specific and help the participant improve performance, such as increasing ROM or improving alignment. Additional progression or regression options can also be offered as follow-up cues.

Motivational Cues

When participants have mastered the exercise and are able to perform the movement in a safe and effective manner, GFIs can offer motivational cues, which enhance the overall experience, foster enjoyment, and encourage participants to give stronger effort.

This systematic timing of cueing continuum, outlined in Figure 10-1, can be used each time a new exercise is introduced.

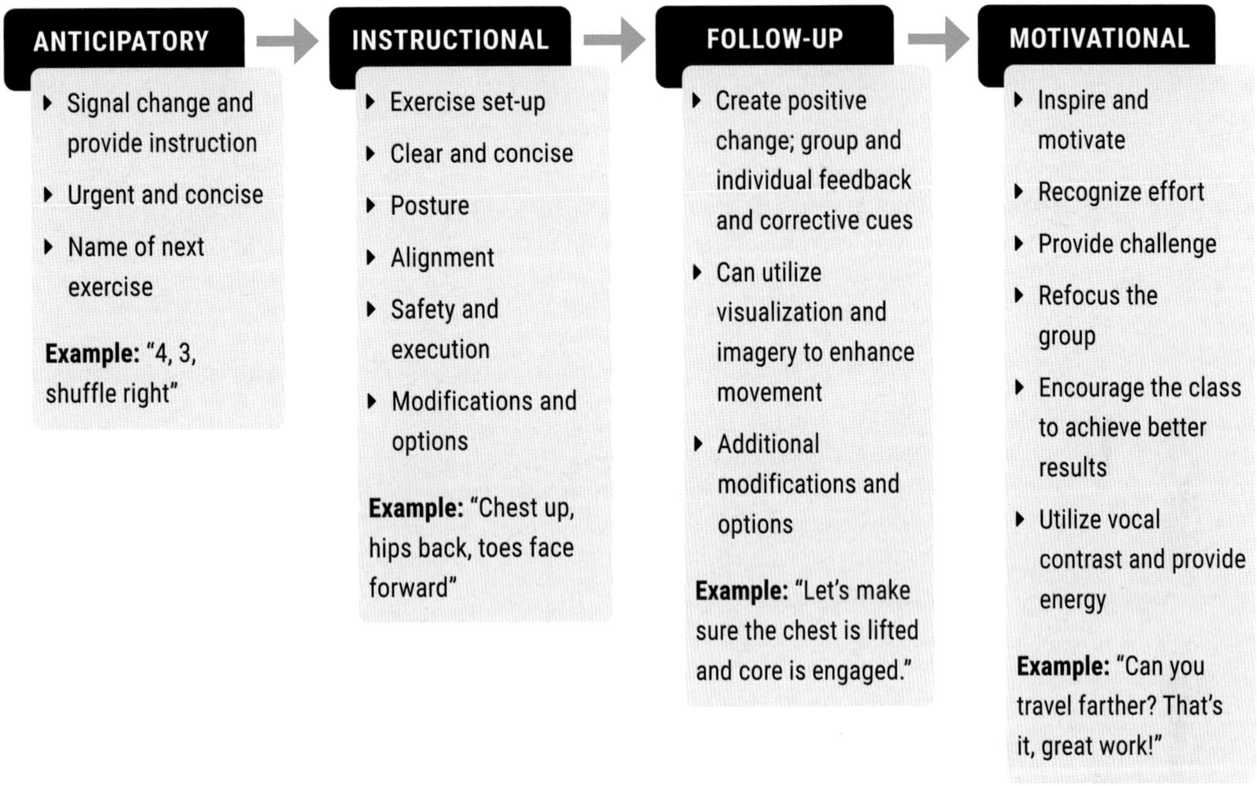

ANTICIPATORY
Signal change and provide instruction
Urgent and concise
Name of next exercise
Example: "4, 3, shuffle right"
INSTRUCTIONAL
Exercise set-up
Clear and concise
Posture
Alignment
Safety and execution
Modifications and options
Example: "Chest up, hips back, toes face forward"
FOLLOW-UP
Create positive change; group and individual feedback and corrective cues
Can utilize visualization and imagery to enhance movement
Additional modifications and options
Example: "Let's make sure the chest is lifted and core is engaged."
MOTIVATIONAL
Inspire and motivate
Recognize effort
Provide challenge
Refocus the group
Encourage the class to achieve better results
Utilize vocal contrast and provide energy
Example: "Can you travel farther? That's it, great work!"

FIGURE 10-1
Timing of cueing techniques

New GFIs may benefit from pre-planning or scripting verbal cues to match the class plan. However, as the class is taking place, it is important for the instructor to observe the skills and abilities of participants in order to tailor teaching strategies and ensure the safety and success of all individuals. Verbal cues may be necessary to assist participants with correcting their form, such as "slide the shoulders away from the ears" or "push the hips back farther." GFIs might occasionally feel as though they have already effectively cued a movement, but perhaps it was not understood by some participants. A cue like "shoulders back" might need to be restated as "lift the chest." It is important to continue to try to connect with participants in different ways in order to help them learn proper movement techniques.

Mastering the art of cueing takes practice and dedication. GFIs can enhance their cueing skills by rehearsing the class plan. This might entail practicing cues out loud while performing movement with music or scripting specific verbal and nonverbal cues for each segment or exercise. GFIs can practice teaching with friends, family, or fellow instructors to see if cues and teaching strategies are well received. Purposeful practice will enable the GFI to refine the class plan and associated cues in order to ensure a positive and successful experience for participants. As a GFI becomes more effective at delivering cues, less practice will be required.

CUEING CONSIDERATIONS

Instructor Orientation

In addition to mastering the timing and execution of verbal cues, GFIs must consider methods to enhance visual cues provided to participants. For example, GFIs should think about the orientation they will use when delivering information and evaluate the pros and cons associated with it. If teaching in a room with a mirror, a GFI may choose to face the mirror when cueing, observing participants' movements in the reflection. An advantage of teaching while facing the same direction as the participants is that this positioning gives the participants an easy understanding of movement orientations and directions, allowing participants to follow the GFI exactly as they move. A disadvantage to this approach is that the personal connection with each participant diminishes because instructors can only make indirect eye contact through the reflection in the mirror.

An advantage of the GFI facing the class with one's back to the mirror or front wall is that this position allows the GFI to build rapport with participants through direct eye contact. It also allows participants to see the front of the instructor's body more clearly with no reflection. A disadvantage of facing the class, however, is that participants often initially have difficulty understanding how to follow an instructor cueing "reach the right arm," if the GFI is reaching with their right arm (which would be to the participants' left).

One solution to reducing this confusion is to use a technique known as mirroring, where an instructor provides a mirror image of the movements that participants are performing. An example of mirroring is when the GFI, positioned facing toward the participants, moves their left arm while calling out to the participants to move their right arms. This enables the participants to see a mirror image of the move they are being cued to perform. However, mirroring can be difficult to learn. Therefore, the GFI must thoroughly practice this technique before using it in a class.

Vocal Quality

The vocal quality or intonation of the cues a GFI uses can impact the effectiveness of the cue, as well as the overall class experience for participants. To enhance the experience, GFIs can include different pitch tones or voice inflections to evoke excitement and urgency, enhance motivation and focus, or create calm and relaxation. The voice a GFI uses is a reflection of their personality, and also an effective way to set the tone of the class. For example, the warm-up might have a lighter, more conversational tone, while the peak intensity of a class would require a more urgent and effort-focused tone. Voice inflection makes the workout more relatable and enjoyable for the participant. GFIs can use any of the following tips to enhance verbal cueing:

- *Clarity:* Overemphasize enunciations or exaggerate delivery by using facial muscles.
- *Pitch:* Maintain a strong and lower tone by using purposeful breathing when cueing.
- *Speed:* Speak slowly enough for the class to understand, but fast enough to convey urgency and the feeling that things will continue moving. Increase the speed of speech without losing clarity.
- *Contrast:* Create the mood or tone of class with the voice (e.g., quiet, loud, celebratory, or creative).

APPLY WHAT YOU KNOW

Voice Care Tips

A GFI must take care to protect their voice to ensure that verbal cues can be delivered safely, properly, and consistently from class to class. Employing the following tips can help minimize the potential for vocal injuries and issues:

- Project from the diaphragm, regardless of whether a microphone is being used.
- Speak at a normal volume when using a microphone.
- Keep music at a decibel level that does not require shouting over the music (see Chapter 6).
- Avoid frequent coughing, which can stress the voice box (larynx).
- Avoid cueing at biomechanically inopportune times (e.g., in positions that constrict the vocal tract, such as when performing push-ups). It is preferable to give cues before the exercise is executed or to not perform the exercise yourself and instead walk around while providing verbal cueing.
- Take small, frequent sips of water to keep the larynx lubricated.

ACE MOVER METHOD™

P – Participant

Shannon Fable, owner of SF Resources; ACE Certified Group Fitness Instructor, Health Coach, and Personal Trainer

The last piece of the ACE RRAMP Approach puzzle is P, which stands for Participant. The P shines a light on how each person's uniqueness contributes to the overall class experience. More specifically, it reminds the GFI that the class they are teaching with this particular group can happen only once. The GFI will never have this opportunity again—it is not possible to replicate—so they should treat the event as the special, unique occasion it truly is.

GFIs should keep this question in mind when creating, scripting, and delivering classes:

How can I ensure that each individual understands their unique and important role in the class?

ACE RRAMP APPROACH™

GFIs should consider the following ideas:

As participants are arriving, the GFI can choose one or two people to greet privately. Focus on acknowledging each participant's presence, uniqueness, and contribution in previous classes or, if they are newcomers, greet them and tell them how exciting it is that they have joined the group for the class that is about to start.

Then, during the class opening, the GFI might remind participants that never again will they be in this class, at this moment, with these people, under these circumstances. Encourage each member to recognize the gifts they bring to the group and celebrate the contributions of others throughout the experience.

Personalized cueing reinforces the unique part each participant plays. The GFI should consider using the word "your" instead of this, that, and those. For example, the GFI could say, "Focus on moving *your* handweights in a slow and controlled manner."

Programming to honor each unique individual is more challenging. Rethinking the way to present progressions, regressions, or modifications will benefit everyone in attendance. GFIs allow participants to embrace their uniqueness when considering different versions of exercises as tools, resources, options, and choices. To make this work, the GFIs needs to explain the goal of the activity and provide the ways a participant might choose to get there. For example, if doing a set of push-ups, explain how many sets, repetitions, and rest periods there will be, then explain the intended outcome (e.g., "to feel as if you couldn't do one more at the end of the set"). The GFI should provide options and allow the participant to make the best choice for themself in the moment. For example, the GFI could say, "You can choose to do the push-ups on your toes, your knees, or anything in between. You do you! Just be sure you choose the version that will make you feel like you couldn't do one more when we're done."

At the end of class, the GFI should encourage participants to reflect on what they brought to the room that day. Or, they can thank everyone in the room for the unique experience the group created together. Also, the GFI should be sure to remind them it would not have been the same without every person present. If the instructor spotted someone who made an exercise their own or otherwise showed up uniquely, they should be sure to acknowledge them privately before they head out the door.

Leadership Considerations

Although group fitness classes are typically a positive environment, when a group of people convene, no matter the purpose or setting, conflicts can arise. From disruptive participants and lack of equipment to arguments over someone's favorite spot in the room, conflicts can arise when least expected. As leaders, GFIs must address concerns in a professional and timely manner. Prior to concerns arising, GFIs can take steps to create a positive and collaborative motivational environment.

RESOLVING CONFLICT

Despite an instructor's best intentions, it is possible that they may experience moments of conflict with participants, before, during, or after the class experience. GFIs must be prepared to de-escalate situations of conflict should a situation arise. Some common conflicts are as follows.

- *Lack of equipment:* If equipment availability is an issue, participants may need to share equipment or the GFI might have to change the format to a circuit or interval-based class so less equipment is needed. GFIs should also be prepared to lead the class without using any equipment, if necessary.
- *Location preferences in the room:* Regular attendees often enjoy standing in the same place for each class. If two participants are arguing over the same spot or piece of equipment (e.g., bike) in the room, the GFI should institute a first-come, first-served rule. Moving forward, politely make this announcement at the beginning of each class so that all participants are aware.
- *Music:* When participants voice concerns or ideas about music, GFIs can incorporate their ideas into the next class, if appropriate. Some branded formats, however, require instructors to use specific music. If this is the case and someone does not like the music, explain that it is a requirement to teach the format and that a new set of songs will be launched soon. Most branded formats have a customer service email or phone number that participants can use, which is something GFIs may choose to share with participants as well.
- *Partner exercises:* Some classes call for partner exercises. This can be uncomfortable for some participants, since there may be body contact with another person. Some participants may simply be shy. First, the class description on the schedule should clearly indicate it is a partner-based class. Before the start of class, the GFI should announce, "If you would like to partner with someone, please do so now. If you would like me to help you find a partner, please come to the front of the room."
- *Odors:* If body odor from another person is an issue, this can create conflict because participants may not wish to partner with, or set up near, that person. If a GFI is not comfortable addressing the issue with the participant, they should notify a supervisor. If the GFI does choose to resolve the conflict, it is a good idea to first try to indirectly address the issue to the entire class by saying, "Everyone, please be mindful of others around you and wash your gym clothes and bathe in between workouts. I know we're all busy, but personal hygiene can affect other participants' class experiences." If this approach does not resolve the issue, politely address the individual directly without other participants around or ask a supervisor to do so.
- *Interpersonal issues between participants:* Interpersonal issues can arise in class, especially if the class is held at a community-based, corporate, or school facility where participants know each other and may have issues outside of the group fitness class. If arguments arise due to interpersonal conflicts, the GFI should ask participants to refrain from talking or respectfully ask them to leave the room. If unforeseen conflicts arise, such as a participant becoming irate because the person in front of them keeps obstructing the view of the mirror, suggest the participant move to an alternative location in the room and return their attention back to class. If the conflict continues to elevate, or be repeated, notify a supervisor who can take further action.
- *Intercultural nuances:* Each of these conflicts can be further complicated by cultural and identity-based nuances. For example, some women, for cultural reasons, may

need to partner only with other women. A GFI should welcome these types of requests, respond with sensitivity and openness, and be sure to meet the needs of all participants. Hygiene concerns may sometimes result from socio-economic barriers that limit access to washing machines. In such situations, GFIs can find a community resource that can be shared with participants to support this need. Finally, cultural differences may escalate the interpersonal issues between participants. A GFI should be prepared to navigate these types of concerns with a person-first approach and **cultural competency.** Considering how differences in culture and identity might intensify conflicts in classes is a key consideration to advance **equity, diversity,** and **inclusion** in the fitness industry.

HARASSMENT OR THREATS

Any complaints about harassment or threats from other participants or facility members must be reported to management or the facility operator immediately. This is not just a conflict; it is a potential violation or criminal act. Overall, a GFI should act as the "quiet professional," resolving any issues as quickly as possible without becoming emotional or drawing too much attention to the conflict. Resuming class and maintaining a positive environment is the goal when faced with unforeseen challenges.

RECEIVING AND UTILIZING FEEDBACK

Personal and career development is important in any industry. A GFI's class is a reflection of their personality, breadth of knowledge, and passion. Accepting feedback is one of the best ways to develop one's craft. Along with education and experience, feedback from participants, supervisors, and colleagues can help shape one's personal "brand" and enhance marketability.

Feedback from Participants

Some participants will be brutally honest, while others may be more passive with their feedback. There will be feedback to which an instructor can immediately adjust, while other times the feedback may lead an instructor to solicit the advice of their supervisors. Common comments that a GFI can respond to may concern the following:

- Fan use
- Music or microphone volume
- Audibility of the instructor's cues
- Music selection
- Exercise variety
- The need for exercise progressions or regressions

Feedback a GFI may need to forward to supervisors includes the following:

- Temperature of the room
- Lack of equipment
- Equipment quality and cleanliness
- Crowdedness

- Odors (in the room or from other participants)
- Complaints about other instructors
- Class schedule (formats and times)

When possible, GFIs should make changes to respond to the feedback provided by participants. A successful GFI understands that the workout is for the participants, and that satisfied participants are more likely to adhere to a regular fitness routine, reducing attrition rate. If a participant has a question that a GFI cannot readily answer, the GFI should agree to have an answer for the next class or refer the participant to someone who can answer the specific question.

Some participants may not want to approach the GFI in class to provide feedback. Some ways GFIs can overcome this include offering an email address or communication channel through social media, suggesting that participants leave feedback with the front desk or facility supervisor at any time, and periodically handing out evaluation surveys to be completed anonymously.

Feedback from Supervisors

Most group fitness managers perform periodic evaluations of their instructors, which typically include verification of credentials and continuing education, as well as a practical in-class appraisal. Occasionally, supervisors may ask for participants' feedback as well. Following the evaluation, the GFI and supervisor meet to review the GFI's performance. Supervisors will offer constructive feedback and provide advice on implementing constructive feedback moving forward. Some GFIs may receive feedback about their professional conduct, attire, or failure to adhere to format or facility guidelines. This type of feedback should be corrected immediately. Performance evaluations are conducted in almost all fields of business, as they are a normal and valuable part of professional development. Group fitness instruction is a soft science, meaning there are very few absolutes and more than one way to successfully lead group fitness classes.

Feedback from Peers and Colleagues

Soliciting feedback from colleagues is a great way to receive constructive feedback outside of evaluation periods. Moreover, this is an opportunity to seek advice and industry guidance from other practicing professionals. Bear in mind that the need for constructive criticism is not exclusive to new instructors, as the fitness industry is always evolving and new techniques and standards emerge continuously. Attending other instructors' classes and even observing people speak, present, and teach outside of the fitness industry is beneficial in terms of enhancing one's instructional abilities.

APPLY WHAT YOU KNOW

Tips for a Positive Evaluation

- Maintain a positive attitude and coaching demeanor.
- Dress in a professional manner.
- Arrive to class early and prepared.
- Maintain an appropriate music and microphone volume.
- Avoid touching participants without permission.
- Utilize music from a variety of genres.
- Avoid using explicit language or making remarks regarding sensitive subjects (e.g., politics).
- Cool the room by using fans, if needed.
- Be a supportive team player.
- Maintain professional credentials and education.
- Confide in supervisors and veteran instructors or seek out additional resources to best accommodate participants.

AVOIDING INSTRUCTOR BURNOUT

Teaching fitness classes demands mental and physical energy, which can result in burnout and/or overtraining. **Signs** and **symptoms** of **overtraining syndrome** may include sleep loss, elevated **resting heart rate,** fatigue, and changes in weight. Burnout symptoms may include disinterest in exercise and teaching classes, lack of motivation, poor class preparation, and **depression.** Many health and exercise professionals will experience this phenomenon to some degree at some point in their careers. The following strategies are designed to help the GFI remain engaged and enthusiastic about their craft:

- Talk with other GFIs about how to prevent or address burnout.
- Take a vacation to relax and recharge, both physically and mentally.
- Learn a new class modality.
- If possible, hone other teaching skills such as imagery or the use of informative cueing to minimize the amount of time physically demonstrating with the class (e.g., instruct

off the bike during an indoor cycling class or lead a yoga class without physically performing all of the poses along with the group).

- Attend classes as a participant or engage in activities outside of the gym, such as hiking or road cycling (provided signs and symptoms of overtraining syndrome are not present).
- Explore other self-care strategies such as meditation, creative outlets, nourishment, rest, or sleep.
- Speak with a mental health professional.

ACE MOVER™ METHOD

ACE RRAMP Approach Conclusion

Shannon Fable, owner of SF Resources; ACE Certified Group Fitness Instructor, Health Coach, and Personal Trainer

While it is important to break down each letter in the ACE RRAMP Approach for understanding, GFIs should keep in mind that the lines between the five elements are blurry. When considering specific ways to integrate Respect, Recognition, Alignment, Mistakes, and Participant into classes, the GFI should avoid treating this like a bullet-pointed "to-do list."

ACE RRAMP APPROACH™

GFIs should consider the following plan to implement the ACE RRAMP Approach and realize the full benefits over time:

Step 1: Develop a deep understanding of the ACE RRAMP Approach as a whole, then each of the elements individually. The GFI should keep the five letters in the back of their mind while teaching.

Step 2: Next, commit to integrating one element at a time. Start by layering them in before class and during class openings. Then, try using one at the end and after class. Finally, incorporate a letter into cueing and programming.

Step 3: Set goals to use all five ACE RRAMP Approach elements in one class section (e.g., warm-up, conditioning segment, and cool-down).

Step 4: Attempt to weave the entire approach throughout the class. Then, over time, plan to expand, evaluate, and improve the use of the ACE RRAMP Approach.

ACE UNIVERSITY

If your study program includes ACE University, visit www.ACEfitness.org/MyACE and log in to your My ACE Account to take full advantage of the ACE Group Fitness Instructor Study Program and online guided study experience.

A variety of media to support and expand on the material in this text is provided to facilitate learning and best prepare you for the ACE Group Fitness Instructor Certification exam and a career as a group fitness instructor.

SUMMARY

Teaching group fitness classes extends beyond just leading exercises and emulating ideal form and technique; GFIs need to transfer knowledge. To do this effectively, GFIs must develop and adopt diverse teaching methods to meet the needs of participants. This is accomplished by incorporating various instructional styles and strategies and maintaining an aura of positive leadership.

REFERENCES

Baker, K.M., Garcia, J., & Belity, T. (2019). Emotional influence of music in relation to the effect of music on exercise performance. *Medicine & Science in Sports & Exercise*, 51(S), 394.

Khai-Cronin, A., Ganulin, D., & Metzo, V. (2003). *Level 1 Introduction to Kettlebell Lifting Instructor Course Manual*. New York: Kettlebell Concepts.

Mosston, M. (2001). *Teaching Physical Education* (5th ed.). San Francisco: Benjamin Cummings.

Yoke, M.M. & Armbruster, C. (2020). *Methods of Group Exercise Instruction* (4th ed.). Champaign, Ill.: Human Kinetics.

SUGGESTED READINGS

Long, J. et al. (1998). Voice problems and risk factors among aerobic instructors. *Journal of Voice*, 12, 2, 197–207.

Muth, N.D. (2016). *Coaching Behavior Change: Why Self-monitoring Is a Key Ingredient in Successful Behavior Change*. https://www.acefitness.org/education-and-resources/professional/prosource/june-2016/5920/coaching-behavior-change-why-self-monitoring-is-a-key-ingredient-in-successful-behavior-change/

Popowych, K. (2005). Cuing beyond counting. *IDEA Fitness Journal*, 2, 4.

Vogel, A. (2019). *Infuse Your Classes and Training Sessions with the Fun Factor*. https://www.acefitness.org/education-and-resources/professional/prosource/group-fitness-special-issue/5515/infuse-your-classes-and-training-sessions-with-the-fun-factor/

CHAPTER 11

Offering Group Fitness Classes in Diverse Settings

AMBER LONG, MEd | Executive Director of Wellness & Recreation Services, University of Colorado, Denver; ACE Certified Group Fitness Instructor, Personal Trainer, Health Coach, and Medical Exercise Specialist

IN THIS CHAPTER

LEARNING OBJECTIVES

Upon completion of this chapter, the reader will be able to:

- Explain the considerations for different types of online classes
- Understand music considerations for the online and outdoor environments
- Understand the legal and safety considerations for teaching in online and outdoor environments
- Create appropriate class blueprints for online and outdoor classes
- Apply effective teaching strategies in the online fitness environment as well as the outdoor environment
- Utilize leadership methods to build rapport and create community in the online and outdoor environments
- Recognize the environmental concerns in an outdoor fitness setting

ACE UNIVERSITY

If your study program includes ACE University, visit www.ACEfitness.org/MyACE and log in to your My ACE Account to take full advantage of the ACE Group Fitness Instructor Study Program and online guided study experience.

A variety of media to support and expand on the material in this text is provided to facilitate learning and best prepare you for the ACE Group Fitness Instructor Certification exam and a career as a group

The COVID-19 pandemic forever changed the physical-activity and exercise world, as many people began to exercise more frequently in online and outdoor settings. ACE Certified Group Fitness Instructors (GFIs) can increase their versatility by understanding how to adapt teaching strategies and leadership techniques to diverse class settings. This chapter outlines considerations, teaching strategies, and leadership techniques for online and outdoor class settings.

Online Group Fitness Classes

The American College of Sports Medicine's Worldwide Survey of Fitness Trends ranked online training as the top consumer trend in 2021 (Thompson, 2021). Online fitness classes allowed individuals to begin or maintain physical-activity habits during the COVID-19 pandemic and made it easier to access group fitness classes anywhere, anytime. The convenience factor of online group fitness classes can help participants maintain a more consistent habit, even when their schedules are tight. In addition, online fitness classes allow participants to experience a group activity in a private environment, which can remove the intimidation or pressure to perform that may be experienced in a studio environment. Finally, online classes encourage participants to be more aware of their bodies and take ownership of their experience by refining their movements and feeling their way into alignment and proper form.

Online fitness classes can be delivered in a live format, where the GFI livestreams to an audience in real time, as a prerecorded format, where the GFI records themself teaching a class and posts it for participants to access on-demand at any time, or in a hybrid format where the instructor is teaching a class with in-person participants and streaming the class at the same time.

Legal Considerations

It is important to remember that regardless of the delivery method employed, adhering to applicable laws and implementing proper risk-management strategies are critical. Whether the format is live, prerecorded, or hybrid, an introduction to each class should inform participants that their safety is of upmost importance. Participants should be reminded that if they experience any health concerns or **signs** of physical distress (e.g., difficulty breathing or an unusually rapid pulse rate), they should stop the exercise and seek medical assistance, if needed. Because the online environment presents challenges for GFIs to closely monitor participants in the same manner they would during an in-person class, instructors should inform participants that they need to be particularly aware of their own surroundings to make sure they are exercising in a safe area that is appropriate for fitness activities and their own body movements can be completed without obstruction. Given that participants will be monitoring the class through a computer, cell phone, or other electronic device, GFIs should slow down their explanations and extend the transition time between exercises so that participants can see and fully understand demonstrations of technique before beginning their own physical movements.

Prior to designing any online class, GFIs must ensure that they can legally utilize music as part of their sessions. Many music licenses that GFIs can obtain permit the GFI to pick songs from a collection of artists and use them during an in-person class. There may be additional permissions needed to utilize those same musical selections in an online format. Further, even after securing permission to utilize music in an online fitness class, there may be concerns that various online platforms may not permit the use of copyrighted music. In some cases, websites detect the use of "protected" copyrighted music and automatically mute that music regardless of the potential relationship the GFI has secured with the music licensing agency.

Given the emerging proliferation of online instruction of physical activity, there are several legal issues that are unresolved. For example, because GFIs may teach a class from one city or state to participants in another city or state, the use of **waivers** and other pre-exercise documentation may need to be properly formatted to match the jurisdiction of each participant. In addition, transmission of participants' images through an online webpage may require their specific permission.

LIVE ONLINE CLASSES

Live online classes happen in real time and allow the GFI to interact directly with participants through technological devices. Live classes can be offered online via Zoom, Instagram live, or a host of pay-for-service streaming platforms. Live online classes allow the instructor to interact with participants in real time, offering **feedback, motivation,** and time-sensitive information like instructional cues or corrections.

Live online fitness classes provide a platform for creating a community, as participants engage together in the shared experience. Live online classes, however, require the instructor to be prepared to navigate technical difficulties, participant needs, and unexpected changes in the class plan.

PRERECORDED ONLINE CLASSES

Prerecorded or on-demand classes enable the participant to access the class at any time, increasing the convenience factor. Prerecorded classes also allow the instructor to create a more polished product, as videos can be edited and refilmed as necessary. However, prerecorded classes offer no opportunity for the GFI to observe and provide feedback to participants, so the initial instructions provided regarding health and safety and the ongoing in-class instructions regarding proper technique must be particularly thorough. Prerecorded classes require digital access for participants to view the content, such as a website, or a platform like YouTube or another video streaming application. GFIs must be aware of potential permissions needed to utilize music, not only from the copyright holder but also the web platform. Because prerecorded classes may be accessed by participants in other countries, a potential future area of consideration involves protecting copyrighted products developed by the GFI and receiving proper renumeration for accessing and utilizing those materials.

Legal Considerations

HYBRID CLASSES

Hybrid group fitness classes require the instructor to deliver a class to a live, in-person audience, and at the same time address and teach online or video-based participants. This means the GFI must manage streaming technology and in-studio technology concurrently. As with live online classes and prerecorded classes, GFIs should ensure that they are able to be seen clearly in the camera frame. In addition, GFIs would need to adapt their class plan to ensure a positive experience for both in-person participants and online participants. For example, classes that require specialized equipment in-person might not be a good fit as a hybrid class because online participants may not have access to that equipment. Hybrid classes also require instructors to be attentive to cueing and coaching strategies for two different groups of people. Finally, hybrid classes require additional legal considerations, as in-person participants may appear on the livestream video. For example, local ordinances may indicate the maximum number of participants that can be supervised in a given facility or area of a facility. Additional online class participants may be deemed inappropriate if the maximum number of patrons for that in-person class is now exceeded with the addition of online participants. The hybrid class format requires the GFI to provide proper instruction and supervision to both groups of participants, but the online participants may require additional time to comprehend instruction of techniques and safely transition to new exercises.

Legal Considerations

APPLY WHAT YOU KNOW

Tips for Teaching Hybrid Group Fitness Classes

- Practice the technology setup prior to class time.
- Remind participants before and during activity about the importance of health and safety.
- Determine how music will be utilized and what permissions are needed from both the copyright holders and the online platform being utilized.
- Consider camera placement. The focus should primarily be on the instructor.
- If participants will be in the video frame, include a statement about being filmed in the preparticipation waiver.
- Create a class plan that is inclusive of online and in-person participants throughout the training session.
- Purposefully engage with both in-person and online participants.
- Create a class community by allowing in-person participants to engage with online participants, if possible.
- Acknowledge and respond to the feedback of participants to make adjustments over time.
- Dedicate a place for privacy for in-person participants who do not want to be seen on camera (Mcclelland, 2020).
- If working for a fitness facility, coordinate with the group fitness manager to ensure enough time for equipment setup between classes.
- Arrive earlier than normal to set up and check streaming equipment.

- Consider the arrangement of in-class participants and the level of supervision needed for each exercise.
- Keep in mind that watching, comprehending, and implementing an exercise technique takes longer online than in person. Therefore, GFIs must provide adequate time for online participants to properly react to their instructions.

ONLINE GROUP FITNESS CONSIDERATIONS

As the popularity of online group fitness increases, more instructors are moving their classes online. Before embarking on teaching online group fitness classes, GFIs should consider the technical and legal requirements to facilitate a safe and positive class experience. In addition, GFIs should understand and implement best practices for teaching in the online environment.

Technical Considerations

Online fitness classes should be safe and effective, with the same level of professionalism and expertise that participants expect with an in-person experience. In addition to class blueprinting and rehearsal, online fitness classes require planning and practice with various technology platforms.

Online fitness classes can be facilitated on a variety of technology applications or streaming platforms. Some of the most popular free apps include Zoom, Skype, WhatsApp, Instagram Live, and Facebook Live. Each application has its pros and cons. GFIs must consider the needs of participants and the accessibility of the streaming platform. In addition to free applications, there are many private video-hosting services that GFIs can consider.

Regardless of the platform or application chosen, it is important for GFIs to know the capabilities of the platform and feel comfortable using the technology. For example, some platforms will allow the GFI to enlarge each participant window to fill the screen and then scroll through the windows. This affords an opportunity to quickly offer feedback to participants as they perform an exercise sequence. Others might enable only small tiles for each participant, which makes it more difficult to provide feedback.

For the best results, GFIs should use a laptop or tablet, rather than a smartphone, when conducting online fitness classes. The larger screen enables a better view of participants. Visually, online classes should look as professional as possible, even when filmed in the GFI's home. GFIs should consider the following video-specific tips:

- Connect directly to an internet router via an ethernet cable, rather than relying on Wi-Fi for electronic devices. This will improve digital uploading and reduce the potential for lagging video displays. If a direct connection is not possible, be as close as possible to the internet router to receive the strongest Wi-Fi signal possible.
- Be visible. Ensure that your camera positioning and lighting provides a clear, full-body picture.

- Utilize a well-lit space. GFIs can experiment with different lighting methods, such as filming with their face toward a window for natural daylight, or utilize an additional external light.
- If using a virtual background, consider hanging a greenscreen backdrop to optimize the participants' visual experience. The greenscreen allows the camera to capture a crisper image of whatever is in front of it (such as a GFI's body while demonstrating movements), which could make it easier for participants to see important details during class.
- Film in a space that permits the demonstration of the full **range of motion** for all planned exercises.
- Clear visual clutter from the video frame and purposely include class-specific props for easy access and recognition for participants.
- Consider the class blueprint and ensure that both standing and ground-based exercises are clearly visible on camera without having to reposition the camera frequently.
- Simplify the class blueprint and choreography to ensure participants can clearly and successfully follow sequences and cues. Consider minimizing transitions from standing to ground-based exercises. Transitions may require the instructor or the participants to reposition their screens.
- Suggest that participants enable their video so that the GFI can provide feedback on exercise form and create a sense of community within the online class.
- Consider if and how music will be used in the class experience.

APPLY WHAT YOU KNOW

Technical Difficulties

Even with advanced preparation and practice, technical difficulties during online fitness classes are inevitable. GFIs can prevent some technical difficulties by practicing with technology in advance. The internet connection and computer streaming capabilities must all be tested to ensure a positive online class experience. As with in-person classes, regardless of preparation, there is always the possibility of general technology failure. For example, the camera or microphone on a computer may stop working, a power failure may occur, or any number of unanticipated issues may arise. When technology disruptions occur, it is important that GFIs act in a calm and professional manner. For example, GFIs can have a backup plan in the event that certain aspects of the class, like music, are disrupted. Chat functions can also be used, when necessary, to instruct the class. A follow-up email to participants after a class disruption to thank them for their patience during the technical difficulty can be a nice way to reconnect and invite them to the next class. Additionally, having a sense of humor and remaining professional and confident during a technical issue can help with building **rapport** with participants.

Music

Online fitness classes require additional planning and preparation for music use, given the permissions that are needed by both the copyright holder and, potentially, the online platforms. GFIs must consider if and how music will be used within live, prerecorded, or hybrid classes. Some video streaming platforms are better than others at allowing music to be played through the computer, while also capturing the verbal cues of the instructor. In some cases, it may be necessary for the GFI to advise participants to listen to a suggested playlist, use their own music, or exercise without music. Live online classes may experience music and video lag, so it is sometimes difficult to maintain accuracy when using the beat-based teaching strategies often used in choreographed classes. GFIs can improve the auditory learning experience by utilizing computer-compatible audio equipment like an external microphone and mixer.

Planning Ahead to Avoid Unexpected Disruptions

Even with proper planning, the unexpected will sometimes happen. Consider all the possible disruptions that may occur when leading online group fitness classes that are not concerns when teaching classes in a studio or gym setting. At any moment, an unexpected visitor may knock or ring the doorbell, a curious pet may join the class, a phone may ring, or a family member may unintentionally be visible on screen. Planning in advance to limit these types of situations is helpful, but it is also important to think about what to do when something like this occurs. GFIs must be prepared to handle these unexpected challenges with grace and confidence, while minimizing the disruption to the class.

LEGAL CONSIDERATIONS

Legal Considerations for Online Fitness Classes

Mark S. Nagel, EdD, Professor, Sport and Entertainment Management Department, University of South Carolina

Though the teaching of online fitness classes is largely an emerging and unsettled area of law, GFIs who choose to instruct online fitness classes should take into account additional risk-management considerations, such as the following:

- Be sure to use participant waivers or other appropriate pre-exercise documentation that specifically mentions online instruction and is appropriately worded for each participant's home state (and potentially city or county).
- Have an emergency response plan for how to prepare for (through pre-exercise reminders) and react to potential emergencies experienced by participants. Though the legal requirements in this area are evolving, suggestions for participants to stop exercising and seek help if experiencing any unusual physical outcomes are advised.
- Secure professional liability insurance that specifically mentions online instruction.
- Only utilize legally permitted music.
- Attain acknowledgment and agreement from each participant via a digital **informed consent** and waiver of liability.

To learn more about legal considerations for teaching online classes, see Chapter 14.

TEACHING ONLINE FITNESS CLASSES

Regardless of the platform, the preparation and set up of live online fitness classes is crucial in order to provide a positive participant experience. The following tips can help GFIs create a successful online class.

- Ensure the class experience reflects the class description. Participants initially choose to participate in an online fitness class based on the description.
- Be early. Log into the streaming platform at least 15 minutes prior to class to test audio and visual technology and make sure participants can hear and see clearly.
- Dress professionally. A GFI's clothing should be professional and provide visual contrast from the background. Bright clothing can stand out against a white wall or dark curtains and help participants see the GFI demonstrate movement.
- Provide critical pre-class safety information verbally, and post in the chat function if available on the streaming platform.
- Begin and end the class on time.
- Be aware that online participants will have various levels of experience in the delivery format, which may impact their ability to understand and implement technical instructions.
- Offer time at the end of class to engage with participants who may have questions or concerns.
- Invite participants to provide feedback and incorporate that feedback when applicable.

Program Design/Class Blueprint

Any fitness class can be adapted to the online setting with advanced planning. Each class blueprint should include a warm-up and cool-down that compliments the class format, as well as **progressions** and **regressions** for each exercise. During an in-person class, instructors can provide additional adjustments and provide feedback in response to participant **posture** and improper mechanics, as well as other signs of **fatigue** and overexertion. Because online classes have the potential to reach more participants, but therefore limit the visibility between the instructor and participants, a GFI's ability to provide specific feedback is reduced. GFIs must plan and teach the class in a way that strategically provides various options for individuals of different ability levels, learning styles, and preferences at all times.

Maintaining participant focus and motivation in the online setting can be more challenging than it is in-person. Individual participants may be logging on from a variety of spaces that contain various distractions. Classes may need to be simplified in order to enhance participant focus. For example, exercise sequences can be broken into smaller chunks to create short combinations or supersets rather than performing two or three consecutive sets of a particular exercise.

Choreographed classes, like dance-based or Latin-inspired classes, may also need to be simplified to ensure that participants can follow along, especially during live online classes, where music may lag due to internet connectivity. Choreographed classes can be broken into shorter combinations or segments to enhance focus and teachability.

TEACHING METHODS

GFIs who choose to lead online group fitness classes should ensure that their teaching methods address diverse participants with varying ability levels, competencies, and preferred learning methods (e.g., audio, visual, and kinesthetic). The principles of teaching outlined in Chapter 9 for in-person classes are also applicable to online classes, with additional considerations.

As mentioned earlier in this chapter, a beat-based style of teaching may present some challenges due to video or music lag, which is commonly experienced on online platforms. Beat-based formats may be best offered as a prerecorded or on-demand offering. This allows the video to be edited as necessary and ensures that the music aligns with the instructor's movement and cues. Beat-based classes offered via livestream will require instructors to be patient if confronted with technical difficulties and provide clear instruction.

Coaching-based teaching is the most common mode of instruction for online classes. Time-based **high-intensity interval training (HIIT),** boot-camp, muscular-fitness, and athletic conditioning–type classes can be led using the coaching strategy where the instructor employs the tell-show-do method (see Chapter 10). This can be advantageous because the participant can pause briefly to watch and listen while the instructor explains (tells) and demonstrates (shows) the move, before performing (doing) the exercise themselves. Participants may find it easier to focus with this stop-and-go method.

When leading coaching-based online classes, GFIs can also use the **practice style of teaching,** encouraging participants to practice exercises at their own pace and within the intensity range that suits them best. This is beneficial in the online environment because movement in unison, or with the music, is not required.

CUEING CONSIDERATIONS

Online instruction requires GFIs to master the art of cueing, as online class instruction should focus on creating a positive and successful experience for all participants. The clarity of communication and cueing greatly influences the overall class experience. GFIs should take into account cueing methods that address the stages of learning and preferred learning methods detailed in Chapter 9. In-person classes rely heavily on visual cues, whereas online classes may not provide as much clarity for participants by just watching the instructor. Instructors who can master the art of verbal cueing will find it easier to teach in the online setting.

Verbal cues for the online setting should be clear, crisp, concise, and specific, minimizing the use of transitional words like "now we are going to" or "moving on to," as filler words lessen the impact of the most important cues. The use of descriptive internal and external auditory cues can also be helpful in the online environment. **Internal cues** direct the exerciser's attention inwardly, toward their own body and the movement process. For example, telling participants to "keep the wrists directly below the shoulders" during a push-up is an internal cue. This type of cueing can enhance motor learning and kinesthetic performance, especially for beginners.

In contrast, **external cues** move the attention outward, toward the environment and the outcome of the movement. For example, telling participants to "explode off the ground" during a plyometric jump is an external cue. External cues are used to enhance performance and increase movement effectiveness. Visualization is also an important external cueing method. For example, when teaching a lateral leap, a GFI could cue participants to imagine or visualize that they were jumping over a puddle of water.

Vocal Quality

Vocal quality is an important consideration for online class settings. The voice a GFI uses is a reflection of their personality, and also an effective way to set the tone of the class. GFIs can use the following tips to enhance the vocal quality of verbal cues:

- *Clarity:* Overemphasize enunciations, make cues concise, and speak clearly. Avoid detailed instructional cues during movements that require strong physical exertion.
- *Pitch:* Maintain a strong and lower tone by using steady, purposeful breathing when cueing. Avoid high-pitched sounds, as this can be uncomfortable to hear in the online environment.
- *Speed:* Speak slowly enough to maintain clarity for everyone to understand.
- *Contrast:* Create the mood of class with voice (e.g., quiet, enthusiastic, celebratory, or creative). Make sure that all tones of voice are picked up by the streaming microphone.

LEADERSHIP STRATEGIES

The online environment presents new challenges, opportunities, and experiences for GFIs. Teaching any format in the online environment requires patience, dedication, and leadership skills. Learning to teach group fitness is a challenging process, and moving a class online only adds to the complexity. Some GFIs thrive in the online environment, while others prefer teaching in-person classes. It is not a requirement for all instructors to teach online. However, it is important for GFIs to know about, and refer participants to, online offerings when appropriate.

Becoming an effective online instructor requires time and commitment. GFIs must put time into learning and embracing the technology, as well as refining and practicing class plans, teaching methods, and strategies for the online environment. In addition, online instructors must be very comfortable and confident in front of the camera. They must execute movements and cues with dynamism. An online GFI must command the digital space with charisma, enthusiasm, and leadership skills, much like in-person instructors are in charge of the room. As leaders of the class experience, they must respond to technical concerns with professionalism, flexibility, and creative back-up plans.

APPLY WHAT YOU KNOW

Authenticity

It is important that instructors show up as the most authentic version of themselves. Although being authentic happens quite naturally in-person, it may require more conscious work when teaching classes online. Authenticity leads to rapport with participants. To build this rapport, GFIs can share information about themselves. It can be helpful to acknowledge common challenges or successes, life experiences, or professionally appropriate stories. This helps participants feel as though they know the instructor on a more relatable level.

In addition, GFIs can sometimes feel stressed or anxious in the moments before teaching a class. Culos-Reed et al. (2021) recommend completing a self-check before login to help GFIs regain focus and show up more authentically when teaching online classes:

- Is there anything you need to set aside or let go of before you begin leading the class?
- Take at least one minute to pause and get focused to teach.
- Take five slow breaths, breathing in for the count of three and breathing out for the count of three. Notice the sensations during the inhale and exhale.

APPLY WHAT YOU KNOW

Building a Sense of Community in Online Classes

The online environment can be a challenging space in which to create a community. Therefore, GFIs must be intentional in their efforts to help participants feel connected to the class experience. The following strategies can be used to enhance an online group fitness community:

- Provide time before and after class to engage with participants.
- Engage in a question or ice breaker as participants join.

- Utilize the chat function when it is available.
- Encourage participants to keep their cameras on to create a sense of camaraderie and allow for performance feedback.
- Make an effort to use participants' names in greetings and cueing.
- Provide health and fitness tips before or after class.
- Create in-class or out-of-class fitness or wellness challenges.
- Plan short fitness-based games on occasion.
- Create class themes (e.g., Olympics, music-based, and costume parties).
- Consider adding a moderator to welcome and check in participants.
- Use **open-ended questions** to foster dialogue.
- Seek and utilize feedback (e.g., song or exercise requests and class improvements).
- Intentionally invite participants to the next class. Provide previews to encourage participants to look forward to the next workout.

Outdoor Fitness Classes

The 2021 ACSM Worldwide Survey of Fitness Trends ranked outdoor activities as the fourth most popular fitness trend (Thompson, 2021). While outdoor activity has always held a place on the trend ranking, it has become more popular as a result of the COVID-19 pandemic. GFIs are holding classes more frequently in outdoor settings such as parks, stadiums, or fields rather than in controlled, indoor environments. Fitness classes of various modalities can be adapted to the outdoor environment with careful planning and consideration. By taking classes outdoors, GFIs have the opportunity to make group exercise more accessible and help groups of people realize the many positive benefits of outdoor exercise.

HEALTH BENEFITS OF OUTDOOR EXERCISE

Outdoor exercise, also known as **green exercise,** provides a plethora of health benefits. In addition to the physical benefits of movement, exposure to nature and outdoor elements has been linked to mental health improvements such as stress reduction, improved mood, and enhanced cognitive function. Mitchell (2013) found that people who regularly exercised outdoors in the natural environment (defined as at least once per week) had about half the risk of poor mental health compared to those who did not. Additionally, each extra weekly day of nature-based physical activity was shown to reduce the risk of poor mental health by an additional 6%. Finally, exposure to sunlight enhances natural vitamin D production, which may be partially responsible for the mood-enhancing effect (Kerr et al., 2015). Given the **sedentary** lifestyle and mental health challenges individuals are facing across the globe, offering group fitness classes in the great outdoors is a wonderful way to help groups of people realize the mental and physical health benefits of green exercise.

COMMUNITY BENEFITS OF OUTDOOR CLASSES

Group outdoor exercise removes significant barriers to physical activity that exist in communities, including:

- *Accessibility:* Outdoor exercise classes can be held in convenient neighborhood public spaces that are within walking distance for many community members.
- *Affordability:* Group exercise classes are an affordable alternative to one-on-one personal-training services, and participants still get the benefit of a live, professional instructor. Also, holding these classes in outdoor spaces eliminates the overhead costs associated with conducting classes in brick and mortar facilities.

OUTDOOR FITNESS CONSIDERATIONS

Legal Considerations

When considering a location in which to hold an outdoor group fitness class, instructors should first consider if the area to be utilized permits formal physical-fitness activities. Certainly, private landowners will likely balk at the use of their property for the financial benefit of others, especially if permission is not sought before beginning an activity. If a desirable privately owned area for an outdoor class is identified, there is a possibility to ask or negotiate the use of the space, potentially for a nominal fee that permits the class to remain financially viable for the GFI. In some cases where the private landowner sells products (e.g., food and beverages) that might complement the fitness class, a mutually beneficial relationship could be established.

In the case of public lands, the GFI should not assume that they can offer a class simply because the location is public property. Often, it is illegal to instruct participants on public beaches, parks, or trails, even if the class offered is donation-based or not-for-profit. In other cases, pre-planned classes are permitted to occur, but the class must be scheduled and approved by the appropriate government agency responsible for the public land. It is the GFI's responsibility to know the local laws prior to using these areas and to seek formal permission before beginning classes.

Regardless of the location, GFIs should plan outdoor classes with an eye for risk mitigation. Prior to hosting an outdoor class, GFIs should physically visit and assess the location to ensure safety and establish a class plan, both for what will happen under "normal" circumstances and for the potential of an emergency (e.g., a participant experiences a health issue requiring immediate attention or non–class participants interfere with class activities). It is easy to envision how the class will occur in "good times," but the GFI must also anticipate potential problems. For example, if a participant needs immediate medical attention, can emergency response vehicles quickly access the fitness area? Instructors should take care to blueprint each section of the class and be aware of environmental elements like stairs, hills, benches, playgrounds, trees, and bushes. GFIs should also carefully observe the space for potential hazards and make a point to avoid spaces that present risk. This is especially important when the ground is uneven due to tree roots or the presence of rocks that may be kicked into the instruction area. The GFI should consider the potential impact of weather upon the class, as extreme temperatures or precipitation could make a normally acceptable exercise area unacceptable. The next sections outline legal, environmental, equipment, and emergency response considerations for teaching outdoor group fitness classes.

LEGAL CONSIDERATIONS

Legal Considerations for Outdoor Classes

Mark S. Nagel, EdD, Professor, Sport and Entertainment Management Department, University of South Carolina

GFIs who choose to instruct outdoor fitness classes should think about additional legal and risk-management considerations, such as the following:

- Be sure to use participant waivers specifically for outdoor classes. Do not assume a "standard waiver" covers outdoor activities. GFIs may need to have a specific policy not only for a remote location, but also one for specific types of environments (e.g., beach or forest).
- Have an emergency response plan. What will you do if a situation arises that mandates the class be stopped, moved, or significantly altered? Class participants should be aware of important elements of the plan before the class begins. A critical element of any response time is ensuring cell phones are usable at the class location.
- GFIs should review their professional **liability insurance.** In many cases, specific language covering off-site, outdoor activities needs to be included in the insurance plan.
- Be mindful of local laws regarding the use of public, outdoor spaces, and never assume that a space can be utilized without first verifying (in writing) that the space is usable for a group fitness class.
- Be sure that all parties have agreed to the use of space through a **shared-use agreement.** Do not deviate from the agreed upon location (such as by moving "up the beach" past the identified and agreed upon location).
- Consider the legal use of music. Outdoor locations do not lessen the need for securing proper rights to utilize copyrighted music. In some cases, locations may require you to produce verification of appropriate music performance licenses before each class session.

To learn more about legal considerations for teaching outdoor classes, see Chapter 14.

APPLY WHAT YOU KNOW

Shared Environment Considerations

Most outdoor areas are public, shared-space environments. The fitness community must be good stewards of public lands and facilities and positive representatives of the profession by taking the following actions (American Council on Exercise, 2021):

- *Comply with all laws and ordinances that apply to the space:* Obtain and maintain all use permits and business licenses required by the municipality. Limit classes to established hours and avoid the use of amplified music or equipment that generates excessive noise.
- *Respect the rights of other users:* Provide education and leadership to your participants on best practices and etiquette for their interactions with other users of the space. Avoid crowding high traffic areas of the space, including walkways and trails. Maintain access to available resources and facilities for others.

- *Leave no trace:* Minimize the impact on infrastructure, by avoiding excessive wear and tear on the space, equipment, and habitat. Landscaping, furniture, lighting, and other fixtures should not be used as attachment points for equipment unless specifically designed for fitness activities. Instructor-provided equipment should be limited to portable options. Remove all garbage and debris from the area following every class.

EXPAND YOUR KNOWLEDGE

Moving Together Outside

The COVID-19 pandemic has forced many traditional fitness facilities, studios, and recreation centers to close their doors due to state and local restrictions prohibiting or limiting indoor exercise. As a result, thousands of exercise professionals and business owners have had to develop creative solutions to open safely and/or lead physical activity and exercise programs outdoors while following public health guidelines.

The ACE Moving Together Outside Campaign specifically calls for local and state governments to expand access and reduce restrictions to using green spaces, parks, schools, and other community spaces for safe, structured, physical-activity experiences led by well-qualified exercise and health professionals. To learn more about this campaign, visit https://general.acefitness.org/moving-together-outside.

Environmental Considerations

The outdoor environment is unpredictable. When selecting a space to host an outdoor class, GFIs should assess all parts of the environment for safety and class suitability. GFIs should consider the following elements and create a class plan that is appropriate for the space:

- Ground surface (smooth, rough, incline, decline, hard, or soft)
- Hazards or debris
- Sun exposure or shade
- Pedestrian and automotive traffic
- Access to drinking water
- Access to electricity (if needed for microphones, cell phones, or other technology)
- Access and locations of medical and public safety resources
- Weather forecasts and the need to cancel or move the class indoors

WEATHER AND TEMPERATURE

Outdoor exercisers will experience variable environmental temperatures. Extreme environmental conditions like very hot temperatures, high humidity, extreme cold, or wind can add significant stress to the cardiovascular and thermoregulatory systems. GFIs should take special precautions under these conditions and should be aware of the signs and **symptoms** of heat- and cold-related illnesses and emergencies (Table 11-1).

TABLE 11-1

Environmental Temperature-related Illnesses

Condition	Description	Signs and/or Symptoms	Active EMS?
Heat cramps	Muscle spasms in the arms, legs, and stomach due to loss of electrolytes and fluids	Painful cramps, loss of strength, thirst, and dehydration	No, but medical attention may be necessary if vomiting or nausea occur
Heat exhaustion	Heat-related illness attributed to hot, humid temperatures and the loss of electrolytes and fluids	Weak, rapid pulse; low blood pressure; fatigue; headache; dizziness; weakness; cold, clammy skin; profuse sweating; dehydration; elevated core temperature	Possibly, if symptoms progress and participant's temperature is not decreasing
Heat stroke	Medical emergency and the most serious heat-related illness resulting from overexposure to heat	Hot, dry skin; red skin color; rapid pulse; anxiety; irritability; dyspnea; dehydration; elevated core temperature (>104° F/40° C); syncope	Yes
Hypothermia	A drop in body temperature below 95° F/35°C.	Shivering, tingling, numbness in fingers and toes, and burning feeling in nose and ears. Extreme exposure can result in fatigue, lethargy, and possible cardiac arrest.	Possibly, if symptoms progress to extreme exposure symptoms, or if participant's temperature is not rising

HYDRATION

Table 11-2 presents recommendations about fluid intake before, during, and after exercising or working outdoors.

The content in Table 11-2 is based on the 11th edition of *ACSM's Guidelines for Exercise Testing and Prescription*. Please visit www.ACEfitness.org/Industry-Guidelines to confirm that this is the latest edition. If a newer set of guidelines is available, exam candidates should study that version to ensure they are up to date with the latest industry guidelines.

TABLE 11-2

Fluid Replacement Recommendations Before, During, and After Exercise

	Fluid	Comments
Before Exercise	▸ Drink 5–7 mL/kg (0.08–0.11 oz/lb) at least 4 hours before exercise (12–17 ounces for a 154-lb individual)	▸ If urine is not produced or is very dark, drink another 3–5 mL/kg (0.05–0.08 oz/lb) two hours before exercise. ▸ Sodium-containing beverages or salted snacks will help retain fluid.
During Exercise	▸ Monitor individual body-weight changes during exercise to estimate sweat loss. ▸ Composition of fluid should include 20–30 mEq/L of sodium, 2–5 mEq/L of potassium, and 5–10% of carbohydrate.	▸ Prevent a >2% loss in body weight. ▸ Amount and rate of fluid replacement depends on individual sweating rate, environment, and exercise duration.
After Exercise	▸ Consumption of normal meals and beverages will restore euhydration. ▸ If rapid recovery is needed, drink 1.5 L/kg (23 oz/lb) of body weight lost.	▸ Goal is to fully replace fluid and electrolyte deficits. ▸ Consuming sodium will help recovery by stimulating thirst and fluid retention.

Reprinted with permission from American College of Sports Medicine (2022). *ACSM's Guidelines for Exercise Testing and Prescription* (11th ed.). Philadelphia: Wolters Kluwer.

SUN PROTECTION

Outdoor exercise often occurs in warm weather and participants often wear minimal clothing, thus risking skin damage from sun exposure, which can be short term (sunburn) or long term (skin cancer and photo aging). GFIs who lead by example and educate participants about sun protection are more likely to foster a culture where the group practices healthy sun-safety habits such as:

- Prevent sun damage with broad-spectrum sunscreens with sun protection factor (SPF) greater than 30. Sunscreens should be applied a half hour before going outdoors and reapplied after prolonged exposure and/or sweating.
- Wear effective sun-protective clothing (e.g., long sleeve shirts), sunglasses, and wide-brimmed hats (with a four-inch brim) (American College of Sports Medicine, 2015).

Emergency Response

In an outdoor environment, a GFI may be teaching a class without the support of other individuals who are typically available in the fitness studio or gym setting. This means that the GFI is responsible to act in the event of an emergency. GFIs should be familiar with the locations of medical and public safety resources and develop an emergency response plan specific to the venue. In addition, instructors should keep a first-aid kit, extra water, and a cell phone available at all times.

TEACHING OUTDOOR CLASSES

Teaching outdoor classes can be a personally and professionally rewarding experience. Some GFIs thrive with the dynamic nature of the great outdoors, and some prefer the consistency of the indoor environment. Regardless, GFIs should understand the basic setup and execution of delivering outdoor classes, so they can consider if outdoor classes would be a good fit for their experience and personality. Outdoor classes require GFIs to prepare a class blueprint that includes plans for teaching, cueing, and leadership strategies that reflect the outdoor environment and the uniqueness of the outdoor experience.

Program Design/Class Blueprint

Regardless of the format, a class blueprint or plan is essential (see Chapter 7). The blueprint must be flexible enough to adjust to the dynamic outdoor environment, as needed. The blueprint should include a warm-up, which will help participants acclimate to the outdoor environment, the general objective and training plan for the day, and a cool-down. The warm-up and cool-down are often overlooked but are particularly important in the outdoor setting, given the need to help participants who likely spend most of their day indoors adjust to the outdoor environment. The class plan should include transitions, timing, and the intentional use of equipment, if needed.

One of the benefits of hosting group fitness classes outdoors is that the space often provides the opportunity to use the environment in the class plan. Hills or stairs, for example, provide an opportunity to incorporate incline training. GFIs who choose to utilize fitness equipment during outdoor classes should take into account the need to transport the equipment. Small, light, and portable equipment can enhance the outdoor fitness class

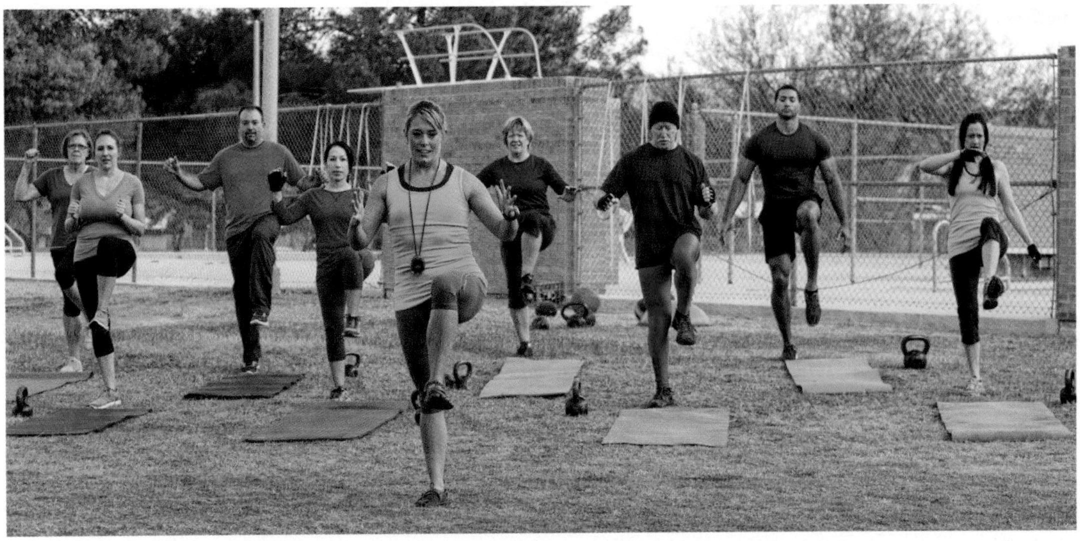

experience. Bands, medicine balls, suspension trainers, and mats for use on the ground are common equipment choices for outdoor classes. GFIs should inspect equipment before and after each class, as outdoor elements may provide more wear on equipment. Performing regular maintenance on equipment at the end of class to remove debris and chemicals (e.g., mud, dust, water, lotion, and sunscreen) may help to increase the lifespan of certain equipment. Also, exposing or storing equipment in direct sunlight or in a hot vehicle may cause materials to break down more quickly. GFIs should also be mindful of how different exercise surfaces might impact certain types of equipment, as contact with rough surfaces such as pavement can cause excessive wear and tear on some materials (e.g., rubber resistance bands or jump ropes). Equipment used on rough surfaces should be inspected regularly for cracks, holes, and fraying. In addition to equipment considerations, GFIs may need to strategize how they will lead and teach the group fitness class in the outdoor environment.

Cueing Considerations

Cueing and verbal communication is especially difficult outdoors because the acoustical quality of the outdoor environment is quite poor. Instructors should give special consideration to communication and cueing strategies. GFIs should avoid yelling and vocal straining and can protect their vocal cords by utilizing exaggerated nonverbal cueing strategies (see Chapter 9) and concise verbal cues, when necessary. A portable microphone system can also be helpful, especially for formats that require music. Printed signage can also be utilized for classes that feature exercise stations.

Teaching Methods

GFIs who choose to lead outdoor classes should ensure that teaching methods address participants in all stages of learning and utilize teaching methods to accommodate different learning preferences (i.e., auditory, visual, and kinesthetic). Just as with classes that are offered indoors or online, each outdoor fitness class will contain a diverse group of individual exercisers. Principles of teaching that are used indoors can easily be transferred outdoors. Outdoor fitness classes can be led using a coaching-based style of teaching or beat-based style of teaching.

The beat-based style of teaching may present some challenges due to the poor acoustical quality of the outdoor environment and the possible lack of availability of a microphone. Both of these issues could make it challenging to maintain group movement in time with music. Regardless, if the instructor has adequate audio equipment and is able to overcome these challenges, outdoor beat-based workouts can be a positive fitness experience for participants. In fact, beat-based formats are frequently offered in parks in order to make the class more accessible to community members.

Coaching-based teaching is the most common mode of instruction for outdoor group fitness classes. HIIT, boot-camp, and athletic conditioning–type classes can be led using the coaching strategy where the instructor employs the tell-show-do method and then walks around to observe participants and offer feedback. Class organization and training strategies like circuit training and time-based interval training [e.g., traditional work/recovery interval training, as many repetitions (or rounds) as possible (**AMRAPs**), Tabata, and every minute on the minute (**EMOM**)] can be led using coaching strategies.

Additionally, the practice style of teaching works well in the outdoor environment because it enables participants to exercise at their own pace and within the intensity range that suits them best. Participants may find that exercises or workouts that they have completed indoors may feel more challenging outside due to variable environmental factors like temperature and humidity. It is important that instructors advocate for participants to work at their own pace, monitor their own intensity, and take breaks when needed.

The **self-check style of teaching** can also be very useful in the outdoor environment because it encourages participants to take ownership of monitoring their own performance. GFIs can employ this method by instructing participants to complete a task and record their results. For example, a short "challenge course" could be created. Participants could complete the course and record their time and their **rating of perceived exertion (RPE).** Participants will be motivated to improve their results over time.

LEADERSHIP STRATEGIES

The outdoor environment provides a welcome change from the daily, sedentary, and indoor environment to which most people are accustomed. The ability to be outside can be exciting for participants, and GFIs have the opportunity to be intentional about creating a special and memorable group experience, rather than just a class. GFIs can focus on rapport building, group dynamics, and making fitness fun to take their outdoor class to the next level.

While group fitness classes are intended to be both positive and fun, feelings of apprehension or insecurity are common for those who are new to the experience or new to exercising in the outdoor environment. GFIs can ease the anxiety and uncertainty that may come along with trying something new by taking time and care to develop rapport with individual participants. It is also important to establish a group dynamic that ensures everyone knows they are valued and can trust that their safety, enjoyment, and success is a top priority.

APPLY WHAT YOU KNOW

Best Practices to Facilitate a Positive Group Dynamic in Outdoor Fitness Classes

- Set the outdoor stage by arriving early and having all equipment ready.
- Begin and end class on time.
- Provide clear opening statements that outline the plan for the day and summative closing statements that provide closure, inspiration, and an invitation to provide feedback.
- Be present before and after class for participants to ask questions and to get to know one another.
- Plan group or partner challenges and activities.
- Intentionally plan games and fun activities as part of the workout.
- Offer various exercise options to ensure the experience is inclusive for all.
- Create a closing ritual or cheer.

Small efforts can create big results when it comes to creating a group dynamic. GFIs who invest time and energy into planning and facilitating opportunities for connection, engagement, and interaction will find that their participants will likely have greater adherence and retention rates.

ACE UNIVERSITY

If your study program includes ACE University, visit **www.ACEfitness.org/MyACE** and log in to your My ACE Account to take full advantage of the ACE Group Fitness Instructor Study Program and online guided study experience.

A variety of media to support and expand on the material in this text is provided to facilitate learning and best prepare you for the ACE Group Fitness Instructor Certification exam and a career as a group fitness instructor.

SUMMARY

GFIs can increase their versatility by understanding how to adapt teaching strategies and leadership techniques to diverse class settings. Online and outdoor classes provide an opportunity for GFIs to expand their skill set and their audience. Each class setting requires consideration of setup, troubleshooting, teaching strategies, and leadership techniques. As the industry continues to progress, GFIs should stay informed about changing trends in digital and physical environments.

REFERENCES

American College of Sports Medicine (2022). *ACSM's Guidelines for Exercise Testing and Prescription* (11th ed.). Philadelphia: Wolters Kluwer.

American College of Sports Medicine (2015). *Sun Protection for Outdoor Sports*. https://www.acsm.org/docs/default-source/files-for-resource-library/sun-protection-for-outdoor-sports.pdf?sfvrsn=ad09204d_4#:~:text=Wear%20effective%20sun%20protective%20clothing,plan%20to%20stay%20out%20longer

American Council on Exercise (2021). *Maximizing the Impact of Shared-use Agreements*. https://acewebcontent.azureedge.net/advocacy/ACESharedUseParkEtiquetteAndSafety.pdf

Culos-Reed, N. et al. (2021). Moving online? How to effectively deliver virtual fitness. *ACSM's Health & Fitness Journal*, 25, 2, 16–20.

Kerr, D.C. et al. (2015). Associations between vitamin D levels and depressive symptoms in healthy young adult women. *Psychiatry Research*, 227, 1, 46–51.

Mcclelland, L. (2020). *Six Tips for Successful Hybrid Fitness Classes*. https://articles.fitgrid.com/six-tips-for-successful-hybrid-fitness-classes

Mitchell, R. (2013). Is physical activity in natural environments better for mental health than physical activity in other environments? *Social Science & Medicine*, 91, 130–134.

Thompson, W.R. (2021). Worldwide survey of fitness trends for 2021. *ACSM's Health & Fitness Journal*, 12, 1, 10–19.

SUGGESTED READINGS

American Council on Exercise (2020). *Expert Insights on How to Deliver an Online Exercise Session: One-on-One and Small Group*. https://www.acefitness.org/education-and-resources/professional/expert-articles/7511/expert-insights-on-how-to-deliver-an-online-exercise-session-one-on-one-and-group/

American Council on Exercise (2009). *Summer Skin*. https://www.acefitness.org/education-and-resources/lifestyle/blog/6715/summer-skin/

Cohen, D.A. et al. (2007). Contribution of public parks to physical activity. *American Journal of Public Health*, 97, 3, 509–514.

Core to Couer (2019). *Top 10 Tips for Teaching Live Online Movement*. https://medium.com/coretocoeur-com/10-tools-for-instructing-live-online-movement-pilates-yoga-fitness-f2f38787703b

Frey, R.J. & Atkins, W.A. (2019). Hydration. In: Hiam, D.S. (Ed.) *The Gale Encyclopedia of Diets* (3rd ed.). pp. 703–707. *Gale eBooks*.

Graham, K. (2017). *Get Out! 5 Benefits of Outdoor Exercise*. https://www.acefitness.org/education-and-resources/lifestyle/blog/6360/get-out-5-benefits-of-outdoor-exercise/

Green, D. (2020). *Cueing in a Virtual Setting*. https://www.acefitness.org/education-and-resources/professional/expert-articles/7517/cueing-in-a-virtual-setting/

Green, D. (2020). *Programming Considerations to Deliver a Great Virtual Experience*. https://www.acefitness.org/education-and-resources/professional/expert-articles/7516/programming-considerations-to-deliver-a-great-virtual-experience/

Green, D. (2020). *Technical Considerations for Virtual Coaching*. https://www.acefitness.org/education-and-resources/professional/expert-articles/7518/technical-considerations-for-virtual-coaching/

Matthews, J. (2016). *Creating Memorable Movement Experiences for Clients and Participants*. https://www.acefitness.org/education-and-resources/professional/prosource/april-2016/5864/creating-memorable-movement-experiences-for-clients-and-participants/

Myers, C. (2012). *Think Outside the (Gym) Box: Creative Techniques for Taking Your Favorite Classes and Workouts into the Great Outdoors*. https://www.acefitness.org/certifiednewsarticle/2581/think-outside-the-gym-box-creative-techniques-for-taking-your-favorite-classes-and-workouts-into-the-great-outdoors/

Nagel, M. (2020). *Legal and Insurance Issues in the Time of COVID-19*. https://www.acefitness.org/education-and-resources/professional/expert-articles/7512/legal-and-insurance-issues-in-the-time-of-covid-19/

Vogel, A. (2015). *Infuse Your Classes and Training with the Fun Factor*. https://www.acefitness.org/education-and-resources/professional/prosource/group-fitness-special-issue/5515/infuse-your-classes-and-training-sessions-with-the-fun-factor/

CHAPTER 12

Working with Participants with Health Considerations

JAN SCHROEDER, PhD | Professor, Department of Kinesiology, California State University Long Beach; ACE Certified Group Fitness Instructor

IN THIS CHAPTER

LEARNING OBJECTIVES

Upon completion of this chapter, the reader will be able to:

- Explain how common chronic conditions, such as coronary heart disease, asthma, arthritis, and diabetes, may influence participation in group fitness classes
- Identify and apply appropriate modifications and other exercise considerations to ensure a safe and effective class experience for all participants
- Demonstrate appropriate exercises to enhance low-back health
- Describe how common medications affect heart rate

ACE UNIVERSITY

If your study program includes ACE University, visit www.ACEfitness.org/MyACE and log in to your My ACE Account to take full advantage of the ACE Group Fitness Instructor Study Program and online guided study experience.

A variety of media to support and expand on the material in this text is provided to facilitate learning and best prepare you for the ACE Group Fitness Instructor Certification exam and a career as a group fitness instructor.

ACE Certified Group Fitness Instructors (GFIs) regularly encounter participants with specific needs and health considerations when leading various group fitness classes. While screening for health concerns is not typically the responsibility of a GFI, it is important to understand how these **chronic** conditions may influence a participant's ability to perform physical activity. GFIs should know what types of exercise to emphasize, modify, or avoid, as well as the recommended intensities and durations of exercise for those with health conditions.

Cardiac Conditions

Cardiovascular disease (CVD) refers to any disease that affects the **cardiovascular system,** principally cardiac disease, vascular diseases of the brain and kidney, and **peripheral arterial disease.** Risk factors for CVD include **hypertension** and blood **lipid** disorders. Specific mechanisms, treatments, considerations, and exercise programming for each condition are beyond the **scope of practice** for a GFI. It is important, however, for the GFI to learn general information about CVD to ensure safety and inclusiveness for all participants.

CORONARY HEART DISEASE

A common subset of CVD is **coronary heart disease (CHD)** (also called **coronary artery disease**). CHD results from the development of **atherosclerosis** in the coronary arteries, which involves the hardening and accumulation of lipid-rich plaques within the walls of the arteries that supply the **myocardium** (the muscle of the heart). Over time, the coronary arterial walls narrow, blocking the flow of blood and oxygen (**ischemia**), and, if left untreated, can lead to a **myocardial infarction (MI), stroke,** or peripheral arterial disease. CHD is the most common cause of sudden death, and the most common cause of death in people over 65 years old. Men are 10 times more likely to develop CHD than women (Benjamin et al., 2019).

HYPERTENSION

Hypertension, or high **blood pressure (BP),** is defined as a **systolic blood pressure (SBP)** ≥130 mmHg and/or a **diastolic blood pressure (DBP)** of ≥80 mmHg (Whelton et al., 2017). According to these criteria, 103 million Americans need treatment, though it is important to note that the majority of these individuals can be treated with lifestyle changes, including physical activity, instead of medications (Ioannidis, 2018). The incidence increases with age, with approximately 70% of Americans over the age of 75 having hypertension (Whelton et al., 2017).

The content in this section and in Table 12-1 is based on the 2017 blood pressure guidelines from the American College of Cardiology/American Heart Assocation Task Force. Please visit **www.ACEfitness.org/Industry-Guidelines** to confirm that this is the latest edition. If a newer set of guidelines is available, exam candidates should study that version to ensure they are up to date with the latest industry guidelines.

The nervous system acts like telephone lines between the brain and the sensory nerve endings, called **baroreceptors,** constantly forwarding signals to adjust and maintain a BP that is commensurate with the current demands on the body. When BP is too low, there is not enough force to push blood through the vessels quickly enough to reach the organs and tissues in need of oxygen and **nutrients.** When BP is chronically too high, that constant force pushing against the arterial walls can be damaging, not only to the arteries but to other organs as well. This constant stress on the arterial walls promotes chronic inflammatory responses that are involved in the plaque accumulation and narrowing of arteries. More pressure is required to shunt blood through narrow arteries, thereby creating a vicious cycle of wear and tear on numerous systems in the body, including the source of the force—the heart.

Hypertension is classified based on severity of the condition. Table 12-1 lists BP classifications for adults 18 and older.

TABLE 12-1

Categories of Blood Pressure in Adults*

Category	SBP		DBP
Normal	<120 mmHg	and	<80 mmHg
Elevated	120–129 mmHg	and	<80 mmHg
Hypertension			
Stage 1	130–139 mmHg	or	80–89 mmHg
Stage 2	≥140 mmHg	or	≥90 mmHg

Note: SBP = Systolic blood pressure; DBP = Diastolic blood pressure

*Individuals with SBP and DBP in two categories should be designated to the higher BP category. BP is based on an average of two or more careful readings obtained on two or more occasions.

Reprinted with permission from Whelton, P.K. et al. (2017). 2017 ACC/AHA/AAPA/ABC/ACPM/AGS/APhA/ASH/ASPC/NMA/PCNA guideline for the prevention, detection, evaluation, and management of high blood pressure in adults: A report of the American College of Cardiology/American Heart Association Task Force on Clinical Practice Guidelines. *Journal of the American College of Cardiology*, Nov 7. pii: S0735-1097 (17) 41519-1.

EXERCISE CONSIDERATIONS FOR PARTICIPANTS WITH CARDIAC CONDITIONS

GFIs should keep the general exercise guidelines presented in Table 12-2 in mind when instructing participants with known CVD or risk factors for CVD.

TABLE 12-2

General Exercise Guidelines for Participants with Cardiovascular Disease

Points of Emphasis	▸ Encourage self-monitoring of exercise intensity. ▸ Do not exceed the target HR and/or a "somewhat hard" RPE of 12 to 13 on the 6 to 20 scale or 4 to 5 on the 0 to 10 scale. ▸ Focus on proper breathing patterns.
Modifications	▸ Change exercise order to complete all standing, seated, or floorwork together, as abruptly changing from lying down or seated to standing may elicit **orthostatic hypotension** (i.e., a rapid drop in BP), causing dizziness. ▸ Extend the cool-down, as antihypertensive medication may lead to post-exercise hypotension.
Things to Avoid	▸ Avoid the **Valsalva maneuver.** ▸ Avoid exercises with significant **isometric** activation hold times, which may elicit a significant rise in BP.
Additional Precautions	▸ Exercise should not continue if any abnormal signs or symptoms are observed, such as **angina,** dyspnea, lightheadedness or dizziness, pallor, or rapid HR above established targets. ▸ Understand the effects of medication on the heart-rate response to exercise (see Table 12-17).

Note: HR = Heart rate; RPE = Rating of perceived exertion; BP = Blood pressure

Pulmonary Conditions

Pulmonary diseases and disorders can be debilitating for some exercisers because they can affect the ability to progress exercise intensity, and sometimes physical activity itself can instigate the onset of **symptoms. Asthma** and **chronic obstructive pulmonary disease (COPD)** are the most common pulmonary conditions, affecting more than 328 million and 262 million people worldwide, respectively [World Health Organization (WHO), 2021a; Quaderi & Hurst, 2018]. COPD is the third leading cause of death worldwide and asthma is the most common chronic disease among children (WHO, 2021a; WHO, 2021b). Exercise is strongly recommended for pulmonary rehabilitation and management because it helps individuals overcome the psychological and cognitive comorbidities that may accompany these conditions (Cai et al., 2017).

Regardless of the type of pulmonary disease, the goals of physical activity for people with pulmonary conditions include improved exercise tolerance and performance; alleviation of the magnitude of **dyspnea**; improved state of mind, emotional state, and quality of life; enhanced ability to perform **activities of daily living (ADL)**; improved gas exchange in the lungs and circulatory system; and improved mechanical efficiency of the anatomical structures involved in breathing (i.e., lungs, diaphragm, and inspiratory muscles).

ASTHMA

Asthma is a chronic inflammatory disorder of the airways that causes airflow obstruction characterized by varying degrees of difficulty breathing, wheezing, coughing, and chest tightness. Asthma symptoms can present at any time during the human lifecycle, although the onset typically begins in childhood. In some individuals, exercise and physical activity can induce an asthmatic response, which is referred to as **exercise-induced bronchoconstriction (EIB)** [American College of Sports Medicine (ACSM), 2022].

Because ventilatory rate increases during higher-intensity exercise, the risk for experiencing EIB grows during vigorous, near maximal, and maximal exercise [**rating of perceived exertion (RPE)** ≥14 on the 6 to 20 scale or ≥6 on the 0 to 10 scale]. However, low- to moderate-intensity aerobic conditioning improves one's tolerance to exercise by reducing the ventilatory requirement for any given activity, or simply by improving one's breathing efficiency. People with well-controlled and managed asthma and EIB can engage in regular physical activity as outlined for the general population (ACSM, 2022).

Participants with a pulmonary disease should be educated by their physicians about the early **signs** and symptoms of pulmonary distress and have a written action plan to guide self-management. A written action plan includes emergency phone numbers and actions to take based on symptoms. Participants with asthma should carry rescue medication at all times, especially during outdoor exercise. Participants with pulmonary diseases who are beginning or restarting an exercise program may be hesitant to increase their intensity, but their confidence should increase as they adapt to training and build **self-efficacy** with each successful session. Setbacks are expected, but as long as they become comfortable with their action plan, occasional episodes should not be a permanent deterrent to exercise. Table 12-3 provides steps for managing an asthma attack should symptoms occur. Note that the time to address an asthma episode is when the symptoms (e.g., coughing, wheezing, chest tightness, and difficulty breathing) first appear.

TABLE 12-3
Steps for Managing an Asthma Attack

Rest and Relax
▸ At the first sign of breathing difficulties, the person should STOP and rest for at least 10 minutes. ▸ Make the person feel comfortable and relaxed.
Take Medication
▸ Make sure the prescribed medicine is available and that the person understands how to correctly take the medicine (inhalers require practice).
Drink Warm Liquid
▸ Have the person drink slowly. ▸ Do not allow the person to ingest cold drinks.
Emergency Care
▸ If you have any doubts about the severity of the attack, get medical help immediately. ▸ If the person's lips or fingernails turn blue or if the person exhibits shallow breathing and is focusing all attention on breathing, get medical help immediately.

EXERCISE CONSIDERATIONS FOR PARTICIPANTS WITH ASTHMA

Despite the physiological challenges associated with pulmonary diseases, well-designed and effectively implemented exercise programs can help minimize pulmonary distress symptoms and exacerbations. GFIs should keep the general exercise guidelines presented in Table 12-4 in mind when instructing participants with asthma.

TABLE 12-4
General Exercise Guidelines for Participants with Asthma

Points of Emphasis	▸ Encourage hydration before, during, and after exercise (to keep airways moist). ▸ Have participants use the RPE scale and **dyspnea scale** to monitor exercise intensity.
Modifications	▸ Encourage individuals to utilize an extended warm-up and cool-down. ▸ If pulmonary exacerbations arise before or during exercise, physical activity should be limited, or intensity reduced until symptoms subside. ▸ Encourage frequent rest periods. ▸ Encourage individuals to use diaphragmatic breathing or pursed-lip breathing.
Things to Avoid	▸ Avoid or limit exposure to cold, dry, polluted, or high-allergen environments. ▸ Avoid chlorinated pools, which can trigger an asthmatic event in some individuals.
Additional Precautions	▸ Remind participants to have medication nearby for use in the event of an asthma episode. ▸ Understand the effects of medication on the heart-rate response to exercise (see Table 12-17).

Note: RPE = Rating of perceived exertion

APPLY WHAT YOU KNOW

Breathing Techniques

Pursed-lip breathing has been shown to improve expiratory flow rates and oxygenation in the lungs, and helps to optimize lung function (Lee et al., 2019) and **tidal volume** and reduce respiratory rate in individuals with asthma. The following pursed-lip breathing technique can be used to ease shortness of breath:

- Relax the neck and shoulder muscles.
- Breathe in for two seconds through the nose, keeping the mouth closed.
- Breathe out for four seconds through pursed lips. If this is too long, simply have participants breathe more slowly, but while maintaining a rhythm of breathing out for twice as long as they breathe in (e.g., inhale for one second and exhale for two seconds).

Diaphragmatic breathing can be used to help asthma sufferers improve breathing capacity.

- In the **supine** position, ask participants to place one hand on the abdomen and one hand on the chest and to maintain these positions throughout the duration of the exercise.
- Encourage the participants to slowly inhale and exhale. With the hands in place, they should feel maximal outward movement of the abdomen during the inhale and a return of the abdomen during the exhale. They should also notice that the chest does not move (i.e., does not rise along with the abdomen).
- Once the participant is comfortable in the supine position, they can perform the technique in sitting and standing positions.

Arthritis

Arthritis is a degenerative joint disease and a leading cause of disability, affecting one in four adults, or more than 54 million people in the United States [Centers for Disease Control and Prevention (CDC), 2020a]. By 2040, prevalence is estimated to be over 78 million (CDC, 2018). More than 100 arthritic diseases or chronic conditions have been identified, with the most common types being **osteoarthritis (OA)** and **rheumatoid arthritis (RA)** (ACSM, 2022). The structural changes and symptoms associated with arthritis can lead to activity limitations, making it a contributing factor to the progression of comorbidities such as **diabetes, obesity,** and heart disease (CDC, 2019).

OSTEOARTHRITIS

OA affects approximately 32.5 million people in the United States, or one in seven adults [Osteoarthritis Action Alliance (OAA), CDC, & Arthritis Foundation (AF), 2020]. It is a disease characterized as a degeneration of **synovial fluid,** which over time progresses into a loss of **articular cartilage** and the underlying **subchondral bone.** Articular cartilage provides a protective barrier between bony structures, but it does not have pain

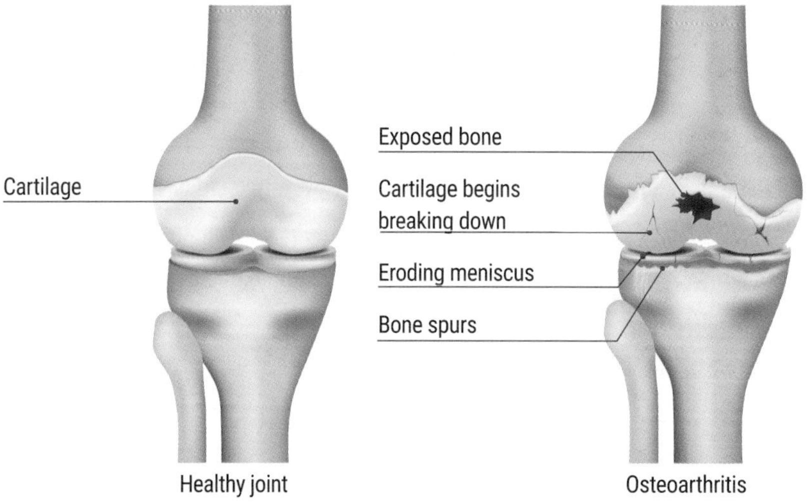

FIGURE 12-1
Injured or degraded cartilage causes painful bone-on-bone interactions affecting mobility, range of motion, and overall function and performance.

receptors. Thus, when cartilage degrades, the bone-on-bone interactions are very painful. Moreover, cartilage has no blood supply, which prevents injured or degraded cartilage from healing (Figure 12-1). Weight-bearing joints of the lower extremity, such as the knee, hip, and lumbar spine, as well as the hands, are most commonly afflicted (OAA, CDC, & AF, 2020). Primary symptoms include localized joint pain, stiffness, swelling, a reduction of **range of motion (ROM), atrophy** of the surrounding muscles, and a feeling that the joint is unstable or loose [National Institutes of Health (NIH), 2019].

EXERCISE CONSIDERATIONS FOR PARTICIPANTS WITH OSTEOARTHRITIS

Due to the decrease in physical **mobility** in individuals with OA, muscle atrophy, ROM limitations, and loss of function are major concerns. Exercise is considered an important component of management for individuals with OA, as it helps to preserve muscle tissue, improve ROM, improve cardiorespiratory fitness, and maintain a healthy body weight. GFIs should keep the general exercise guidelines presented in Table 12-5 in mind when instructing participants with OA.

TABLE 12-5
General Exercise Guidelines for Participants with Osteoarthritis

Points of Emphasis	▸ Perform an adequate warm-up (five to 10 minutes) to ensure joint lubrication and increased elasticity of tissues. ▸ Start with light aerobic exercise to increase systemic blood flow and body temperature. ▸ Dynamic flexibility exercises should be performed to enhance tissue elasticity and further increase joint lubrication. ▸ Perform activation exercises to target specific areas (e.g., knees and hips) during the warm-up and conditioning segment of the class. ▸ Incorporate exercises that relate to activities of daily living, such as sit-to-stand or carrying activities. ▸ Pay attention to each participant's overall posture and joint mechanics and cue proper techniques for ideal joint alignment.

TABLE 12-5 *(continued)*

	▸ Perform an adequate cool-down, gently taking the joints through their ROM. ▸ Teach participants to distinguish between soreness and pain. Soreness, which occurs when people leading a sedentary lifestyle begin an exercise program, is usually located in the muscle, while pain originates in the joint and indicates that the participant may have exercised that joint too strenuously.
Modifications	▸ Reduce volume and intensity if pain is present at higher levels two hours after the exercise session than before the session. ▸ Start with **bilateral** exercises and advance to **unilateral** exercises once strength and technique have been established. ▸ Replace **isotonic** with isometric strengthening exercises for individuals who experience pain, being mindful not to program excessive isometric durations, as hypertension might be a comorbidity in individuals with arthritis. ▸ During strengthening exercise, if pain or swelling appears or persists, reduce load on the affected joint. ▸ Change the body position to avoid pain. For example, adopting a non-weight-bearing position (e.g., sitting or lying prone, supine, or on the side) may be better tolerated than a standing position. ▸ If specific exercises exacerbate joint pain, alternative exercises for the same muscle group and energy system should be considered.
Things to Avoid	▸ Avoid vigorous exercise during acute flare-ups and periods of inflammation. However, gentle ROM exercises are appropriate during these periods. ▸ Do not perform high-impact activities during acute inflammation.
Additional Precautions	▸ Stop exercise if joint pain is too severe. ▸ Water temperatures for aquatic exercise should be between 83 and 90° F (28–32° C) to help relax muscles and reduce pain [Aquatic Exercise Association (AEA), 2020] ▸ Participants should wear appropriate shoes with good shock absorption and stability. ▸ Understand the effects of medication on the heart-rate response to exercise (see Table 12-17).

Note: ROM = Range of motion

Diabetes Mellitus

Diabetes mellitus is one of the most debilitating conditions affecting the U.S. population, ranking as the seventh leading cause of death in the U.S. (CDC, 2020b). Diabetes is often linked to a number of chronic diseases and disabilities, including CVD, hypertension, stroke, amputations, blindness, and kidney failure (CDC, 2020b; CDC, 2020c). Diabetes is a broadly applied term used to denote a complex group of syndromes that result in a disturbance in the body's ability to use **glucose.**

As of 2018, more than 34 million Americans, or more than 10% of the U.S. population, already had diabetes, with rates increasing with age. Approximately 21% of adults living with diabetes (7.3 million people) were not aware they had the condition (CDC, 2020d).

Another 88 million American adults had **prediabetes,** putting them at high risk for developing **type 2 diabetes** at a later date. Unfortunately, only about 15% of those with prediabetes were aware they had the condition (CDC, 2020d). Prediabetes is diagnosed when eight-hour fasting blood glucose levels range between 100 mg/dL and 125 mg/dL. After an eight-hour fast, a glucose level of 126 mg/dL or higher delineates the cutoff for diabetes (American Diabetes Association, 2017).

There are two principal types of diabetes. **Type 1 diabetes** is an autoimmune disease caused by the destruction of pancreatic cells that produce the body's **insulin.** Type 2 diabetes results from **insulin resistance** combined with defective insulin secretion.

TYPE 1 DIABETES

Type 1 diabetes is a serious medical condition that can result in death if not properly treated. A person with this condition must take regular amounts of insulin to sustain a safe amount of glucose in the blood. When insulin is not taken, blood glucose can reach 1,000 mg/dL or higher (normal range after an eight-hour fast is less than 100 mg/dL) and cause the person to go into a diabetic coma. Individuals with type 1 diabetes are insulin-dependent, meaning they must receive periodic doses of insulin. Some people with type 1 diabetes wear an insulin pump that is connected to a catheter under the skin, or they periodically self-administer insulin shots.

TYPE 2 DIABETES

Type 2 diabetes is the most common form of diabetes, affecting over 90 to 95% of all individuals with diabetes. It typically occurs in adults who have **overweight** and is characterized by insulin resistance—a reduced sensitivity of insulin target cells to available insulin, resulting in increased glucose in the blood. Unfortunately, increasing numbers of children are being diagnosed with type 2 diabetes, making the term "adult-onset diabetes" no longer accurate. Unlike those with type 1 diabetes, people with type 2 diabetes are not always prescribed insulin treatment.

Table 12-6 presents a comparison of type 1 and type 2 diabetes.

TABLE 12-6

Comparison of Type 1 and Type 2 Diabetes

Characteristics	Type 1	Type 2
Age of onset	Usually <35 years	Usually >40 years
Clinical onset	Abrupt	Gradual
Family history	Not always	Yes
Body composition	Normal or thin	Usually obese (central type)
Blood insulin levels	Reduced or absent	Normal or increased
Cell insulin resistance	Absent or minor	Present
Treatment for control of hyperglycemia	Insulin, diet, and/or exercise	Weight loss, diet, oral hypoglycemic drugs, or insulin

EXERCISE CONSIDERATIONS FOR PARTICIPANTS WITH DIABETES

Exercise can have a significant effect on lowering blood glucose for all participants and is an essential component of treatment for persons with diabetes. People with diabetes are also encouraged to exercise to gain other benefits, such as a reduction in **body fat** (for those with type 2 diabetes), cardiorespiratory health improvement, muscular fitness improvement, and stress reduction, all of which improve overall health and well-being.

Proper timing of medication administration and nutrient consumption, as well as measuring blood glucose levels before and after exercise, are necessary for safe participation. Consuming too many calories and/or not enough insulin before exercise can cause **hyperglycemia** during exercise, due to excess glucose from the food recently consumed and **fatty acids** and **glycogen** being converted into glucose during exercise, adding to circulating blood glucose levels. **Hypoglycemia** is a dangerous scenario, especially for individuals with type 1 diabetes. It is defined as a blood glucose level lower than 70 mg/dL and is a contraindication for an acute bout of exercise (ACSM, 2022). It can result from low pre-exercise blood glucose levels, too much pre-exercise insulin, or not enough glucose consumption during long-duration physical activity.

People with diabetes should test their blood glucose levels prior to activity; if levels are equal to or below 100 mg/dL, they should consume a small fast-absorbing carbohydrate snack prior to activity, such as juice or a banana. Ideally, participants should adhere to an eating schedule that includes a balance of protein, fats, and low–**glycemic index (GI)** carbohydrates to maintain normal blood glucose levels. Hydration before, during, and after exercise is also very important for participants with diabetes. In fact, one of the classic signs of early hypoglycemia is extreme hunger and/or thirst. In addition, it is prudent to avoid high-intensity activity when blood glucose levels trend toward low levels. Table 12-7 lists the early and late symptoms of hypoglycemia and details how a GFI should best respond if hypoglycemia does occur.

TABLE 12-7
Signs and Symptoms of Hypoglycemia

Early Signs and Symptoms	Late (Severe) Signs and Symptoms
Shakiness	Blurred or impaired vision
Nervousness/anxiety	Confusion
Sweating, chills, clamminess	Slurred speech
Irritability or impatience	Tingling or numbness (in the lips, tongue, and cheek)
Fast heartbeat	Drowsiness
Lightheadedness or dizziness	Seizures
Nausea	Coma
Hunger	Death
Loss of skin color	
Weakness or lack of energy	
Headache	
Clumsiness or coordination problems	
Nightmares or crying out during sleep	

Continued on the next page

TABLE 12-7 (*continued*)

Instructions for a Participant Who Is Experiencing Hypoglycemia (15-15 Rule)
1. Check blood sugar before exercise.
2. If 100 mg/dL or lower, consume 15–20 grams of carbohydrate [e.g., 4 glucose tablets, 1 glucose gel tube, ½ cup of juice or regular soda (not diet), or 1 tablespoon of sugar or honey].
3. After 15 minutes, check your blood sugar again. If it is still below 100 mg/dL, ingest another 15 grams of carbohydrate.
4. Repeat these steps every 15 minutes until your blood sugar is at least 100 mg/dL.
5. Do not start or resume exercise until blood sugar is above 100 mg/dL.

Sources: American Diabetes Association (2021a). *Hypoglycemia (Low Blood Sugar)*. https://www.diabetes.org/healthy-living/medication-treatments/blood-glucose-testing-and-control/hypoglycemia; American Diabetes Association (2021b). *Blood Sugar and Exercise*. https://www.diabetes.org/healthy-living/fitness/getting-started-safely/blood-glucose-and-exercise

EXPAND YOUR KNOWLEDGE

Understanding the Glycemic Index

GI values are based on the blood glucose response to a given food item. High-GI foods break down rapidly, causing a large glucose spike, while low-GI foods are digested more slowly and cause a smaller increase in blood glucose. Table 12-8 provides examples of low-, medium-, and high-GI foods.

TABLE 12-8

Glycemic Index (GI) of Various Foods

High GI ≥70	Medium GI 56–69	Low GI ≤55
White bread	Rye bread	Pumpernickel bread
Corn Flakes	Shredded Wheat	All Bran
Graham crackers	Ice cream	Plain yogurt
Dried fruit	Blueberries	Strawberries
Instant white rice	Refined pasta	Oatmeal

Regular exercise helps reduce CVD and cardiometabolic risk factors, such as mild to moderate hypertension, insulin action and resistance, and glucose metabolism. Also, regular exercise favorably affects the psychological and cognitive health of individuals with diabetes. Table 12-9 provides general guidelines and safety tips for working with participants with diabetes.

TABLE 12-9

General Exercise Guidelines for Participants with Diabetes

Points of Emphasis	▸ Emphasize frequency and duration, as the intensity, frequency, and duration of exercise will depend to a large extent on the severity of the diabetes and the participant's initial fitness level. In general, emphasize frequency and duration over intensity.

TABLE 12-9 (*continued*)

	▸ Ensure that participants understand their own glucose medication management as it relates to exercise. ▸ The timing of exercise in relation to taking insulin and carbohydrate consumption is particularly important for preventing hypo- and hyperglycemia. ▸ For most people with diabetes, optimal pre-exercise blood glucose levels are between 90 and 250 mg/dL.
Modifications	▸ Provide time for participants to monitor their blood glucose levels before, during, and after exercise.
Things to Avoid	▸ Do not perform exercise if blood glucose levels are lower than 70 mg/dL. ▸ Avoid vigorous physical activity if blood glucose levels are above 250 mg/dL.
Additional Precautions	▸ Know the signs and symptoms of hypoglycemia (see Table 12-7). ▸ Encourage self-care for the feet. A common side effect of type 1 diabetes is foot ulcers. Diabetes causes deterioration of the small blood vessels in the feet, diminishing blood flow to these tissues and resulting in foot ulcers. Foot ulcers can last several months or longer, and are exacerbated by high-impact exercise, such as jogging. Discourage participants with foot problems from participating in weight-bearing, jarring exercises such as jogging or racquet sports. ▸ Be aware of the participant's medications and their potential effects on the heart-rate response to exercise (see Table 12-17).

Obesity

Once associated with high-income countries, obesity is now also prevalent in low- and middle-income countries. Worldwide projections by WHO (2018) indicate that 1.9 billion people age 18 years or older have overweight, with approximately 650 million of them having obesity. Often, overweight and obesity are described simplistically as the result of an imbalance between calories consumed (energy intake) and calories expended (energy expenditure). An increased energy intake, without an equal increase in energy expenditure, leads to an increase in weight. Similarly, decreased energy expenditure with no change in energy intake will also result in an energy imbalance and lead to weight gain. While these are contributing variables, obesity is a multifactorial disease involving a complex interplay among environmental, behavioral, genetic, and hormonal factors.

Excess body weight is associated with an increased likelihood to develop heart disease, hypertension, type 2 diabetes, sleep disorders, gallstones, breathing problems, musculoskeletal disabilities, and certain forms of cancer (i.e., endometrial, breast, and colon) (American Cancer Society, 2020). It is also associated with reduced life expectancy and early **mortality** (ACSM, 2022). In addition, obesity has a deleterious effect on the economy of all countries, as it increases the associated costs for treating related diseases.

EXERCISE CONSIDERATIONS FOR PARTICIPANTS WITH OBESITY

Exercise plays an important role in the reduction of excess body weight and in achieving weight stability. Studies have shown a strong dose-response relationship between the amount of exercise performed and maintaining a healthy weight over time and reducing the incidence of obesity and risk of excessive weight gain (U.S. Department of Health & Human Services, 2018). In the absence of concurrent caloric restriction, cardiorespiratory exercise in the range of 150 minutes per week has been associated with modest weight loss [4.4 to 6.6 lb (2.0 to 3.0 kg)], while 225 to 420 minutes per week results in a 11 to 16.5 lb loss (5.0 to 7.5 kg) in studies with durations ranging from 12 to 18 weeks (ACSM, 2009). Individuals seeking weight loss should include exercise as a key component of their programs, and adults with overweight and obesity should initially accumulate more than 150 minutes of moderate-intensity exercise each week and, when possible, more than 225 minutes per week (ACSM, 2022).

The most health benefits come when physically inactive people become moderately active. Making exercise a regular part of one's life can have a major impact on health. The key for GFIs is to support their participants in choosing activities they enjoy and will continue to do until they meet their weight-loss goals and beyond. GFIs should keep the general exercise guidelines presented in Table 12-10 in mind when instructing participants with obesity.

TABLE 12-10

General Exercise Guidelines for Participants with Obesity

Points of Emphasis	▸ The majority of the time exercising should be at a low-to-moderate intensity level to avoid joint stress, injury, and heat intolerance. ▸ To reduce the risk of injury, include the inclusion of cross-training, gradual progression of exercise intensity and duration, and the use of low-impact or non-weight-bearing exercises. ▸ Start with shorter bouts of exercise.
Modifications	▸ For individuals with mobility and/or balance challenges, seated exercise is a good option, as getting up from and down to the floor may be challenging. ▸ Aquatic exercise places less stress on the joints, causes fewer problems with body-temperature regulation, and generates less friction and chafing. It is important, however, to also consider the potential psychological impact of aquatic exercise, as participants with obesity may be self-conscious about their appearance and struggle with body-image issues. ▸ Recumbent cycling may be more comfortable than exercising on a traditional upright bike due the larger seat and reduced balance requirements.
Things to Avoid	▸ Running, jumping, and high-impact types of movement are not recommended. These physical activities may lead to some musculoskeletal problems associated with body weight and impact forces from repeated (and forceful) foot strikes on the ground. ▸ Certain supine exercises may cause breathing difficulty for some participants with obesity (inhibiting the passage of air). ▸ Prudence should be taken in doing too much lunge and squat work because of possible knee and back discomfort and/or injury. ▸ Avoid body-weight exercises performed on an unstable surface due to balance difficulties for some participants.

TABLE 12-10 (*continued*)

Additional Precautions	▸ Individuals with overweight or obesity need high-quality fitness shoes with good shock-absorbing qualities to minimize the chance of exacerbating orthopedic and joint problems. ▸ Skin chafing may occur. Repetitive movements, combined with sweating, can cause skin to rub against skin, producing discomfort and pain. Chafing can be treated with ice packs and over-the-counter ointments such as those used for diaper rash. ▸ Water temperatures for aquatic exercise should be between 80 and 86° F (26.5–30° C) (AEA, 2020). ▸ Be respectful of the physical challenges and emotional struggles faced by participants with obesity.

APPLY WHAT YOU KNOW

Overcoming Weight Bias and Stigma

Given the prevalence of weight bias and stigma in society (Pachankis et al., 2018), GFIs should realize that discussing body weight can be a sensitive issue for many class participants. To ensure a safe and supportive environment, as well as to establish a positive and productive relationship, GFIs must take care to utilize inclusive language that makes participants feel comfortable and valued. Discussing weight should never be done in a way that might humiliate, blame, shame, degrade, or categorize people. This necessitates that GFIs recognize and address their own implicit biases that may unintentionally impact the ability to see each person as being whole, resourceful, and capable of change. The GFI should ask permission to broach the subject of weight and to discuss the topic in a way that is comfortable for the participant (e.g., "What words do you like to use when we talk about weight?"). Utilizing the skills of **motivational interviewing** can be helpful in discussing lifestyle changes in a way that enhances a participant's self-efficacy and demonstrates the GFI's commitment to being a trusted partner in the journey of change (e.g., "What steps do you feel would be best to take to improve your health?"). GFIs should be mindful when speaking about participants with other members of the care team, always utilizing person-first language (e.g., a participant with obesity vs. an obese participant).

Low-back Pain

Low-back pain (LBP) is a non-specific symptom that affects people for a number of reasons, including mechanical problems, excess body weight, injuries, and chronic diseases. LBP causes more disability than any other condition and is the leading global cause of years lived with disability (CDC, 2020e; Wu et al., 2020). Exercise is considered one of the cornerstones of both prevention and treatment of LBP. Cardiorespiratory exercise and exercises designed to enhance lumbar spine stability should be performed on a regular basis, and proper movement mechanics should be emphasized. Maintaining and improving muscle balance across the joints is also particularly important for people with musculoskeletal conditions.

EXERCISE CONSIDERATIONS FOR PARTICIPANTS WITH LOW-BACK PAIN

GFIs should keep the general exercise guidelines presented in Table 12-11 in mind when instructing participants with chronic LBP.

TABLE 12-11

General Exercise Guidelines for Participants with Low-back Pain

Points of Emphasis	▸ Adequately warm up and cool down before and after each class. ▸ Use proper form (exercising in front of a mirror may help). ▸ Maintain neutral posture and an erect torso during any movements. ▸ Perform low- or nonimpact activities. ▸ Focus on core function and fundamental movement patterns. ▸ Utilize more repetitions of less demanding low-back strength and stability exercises to enhance postural endurance and strength.
Modifications	▸ When leaning forward to lift or lower an object, always hinge at the hips and bend the knees.
Things to Avoid	▸ Do not work through pain. ▸ Avoid forward-head positions in which the chin is tilted up. ▸ Avoid hyperextending the spine in an unsupported position. ▸ Avoid extreme ranges of motion, excessive spinal flexion under load, and abrupt twisting movements.
Additional Precautions	▸ Individuals with low-back pain, or a history of low-back pain, should consult with a physician and get specific recommendations for exercise.

APPLY WHAT YOU KNOW

Daily Routine for Enhancing Low-back Health

Because of the high prevalence of low-back pain, GFIs should consider incorporating the movements presented in Figures 12-2 through 12-5 as part of a core conditioning class or during the cool-down segment of other group fitness classes. The following exercises can be used to strengthen the stabilizing musculature of the spine and enhance motor control to ensure that spine stability is maintained in all activities. Keep in mind that these are only examples of well-designed exercises and may not be for everyone—the initial challenge may or may not be appropriate for every individual, nor will the graded progression be the same for all participants. These are simply examples of exercises that challenge the muscles of the torso, improving fluidity of movement and postural stabilization (McGill, 2016). Given that muscular endurance offers protective value to the postural muscles of the spine, gains in strength should not be overemphasized at the expense of endurance.

FIGURE 12-2
Cat-cow

The routine begins with the cat-cow exercise (spine flexion-extension cycles) to improve flexibility and warm the tissue with rhythmic motion. Note that the cat-cow is intended as a motion exercise—not a stretch—so the emphasis is on motion rather than "pushing" at the end ranges of flexion and extension.

Cat position

Cow position

FIGURE 12-3
Modified curl-up
The cat-cow motion exercise is followed by anterior abdominal exercises, in this case the modified curl-up. One important outcome of teaching a modified curl-up is to help participants recognize and maintain a neutral lumbar spine. If a participant has trouble maintaining a neutral lumbar spine, they can place a hand or towel beneath the lower back. Do not allow participants to flatten the back to the floor, as doing so flexes the lumbar spine and increases the loads placed on the discs and ligaments. One knee is flexed but the other leg is straight to lock the pelvis–lumbar spine and minimize the loss of a neutral lumbar posture. Have participants alternate the bent leg (right to left) midway through the repetitions.

FIGURE 12-4
Bird dog
The extensor component consists of the bird dog exercise. Starting with the hands placed directly under the shoulders and the knees directly under the hips, the GFI should instruct participants to find a neutral spine position. Stabilization through the abdominal musculature is needed to ensure consistent neutral spine position while the opposite arm and leg are lifted in unison. If a participant is not ready to stabilize this load, they can begin with lifting the leg or arm only and progress to the full exercise. Holding the position for 5 to 8 seconds for each repetition is recommended to improve muscular endurance before alternating sides.

FIGURE 12-5
Side bridge
The lateral muscles of the torso (i.e., quadratus lumborum and abdominal obliques) are important for optimal stability and are targeted with the side bridge exercise. The beginner level of this exercise involves bridging the torso between the elbow and the knees (a). Once this is mastered and well-tolerated, the challenge is increased by bridging using the elbow and the feet (b). It is important when performing the side bridge exercise to maintain a neutral neck and spine position and not let the hips rotate forward. Holding the position for 5 to 8 seconds for each repetition before alternating sides is recommended to improve muscular endurance.

a. Side bridge

b. Progression

ACE→ MOVER™ METHOD

A New Participant's Concerns About Pain

While a GFI is greeting participants as they arrive for class, a potential new participant stops to introduce themself. They are drawn to the class and would like to be a part of a group when exercising but are not sure if the class is right for them. They state that they would get started right away if it were not for all the pain they constantly experience in their lower back. Realizing there is an opportunity to further connect with and guide this potential new class participant, the GFI asks if they would be willing to stop by later in the day to continue the conversation.

ACE→ ABC APPROACH™

Following is an example of how using the ACE Mover Method™ and the ACE ABC Approach™ can benefit a participant who has been experiencing chronic low-back pain.

Ask: Asking powerful **open-ended questions** helps the GFI gain a better understanding of what class participants want to gain by attending classes and begins the process of uncovering more about this person's experience with pain.

GFI: It was a pleasure speaking with you earlier and I'm glad you were able to come back so that we can continue our conversation. You mentioned earlier that you're interested in attending a group exercise class. What are you hoping to achieve by attending group classes?

Participant: I'm glad I finally worked up the courage to say hello and that you're willing to meet with me. For many years, I've been dealing with chronic low-back pain. I used to lead a more physically active lifestyle but, unfortunately, over the years I have become less and less active to the point that I stopped doing almost any physical activity. Recently, I started to walk for short periods of time, which is what got me passing by your fitness studio. I'm nervous about exercise making my pain worse but if I improve my fitness, socialize with others who are active, and maybe even lose some weight, it may help me to better manage my pain. I guess attending group classes seems like more fun than walking and the idea of exercising with others is appealing.

GFI: Thank you for sharing your journey with pain and physical activity. Your experience with low-back pain over the years has had an impact on your life, to the point that you stopped being physically active. Recently, you have started walking as a way to get some exercise and to see how walking affects your pain. You're interested in attending a group class because it seems fun but are nervous about how exercise might affect your pain levels. What else?

Participant: That really sums it up. I want to be more active and to feel healthier. Managing my pain seems to be the key to unlocking my ability to become more active.

Break down barriers: Ask more open-ended questions to discover any potential barriers or to learn more about barriers already expressed that are getting in the way of becoming more physically active.

GFI: You want to be more physically active but being in pain is preventing you from increasing your activity levels. How does your experience with pain get in the way of your daily life and physical activity?

Participant: Being in pain and the thought of exercising causing more pain is a huge obstacle for me to overcome. Often, when I have days with less pain, I get excited and motivated to exercise and then my fear creeps in and I end up taking no action. I want to feel safe and in control of my pain and want to be able to do the things I enjoy in life without worrying about it. Currently, I sometimes miss work because of the back pain and have also spent entire days lying in bed when it gets really bad. Do you have experience with teaching classes for people in pain? How do they manage this type of fear and apprehension that I am feeling?

GFI: I'm so glad you asked this question! While each person's experience with pain is unique, there are some common themes that emerge. Based on my experience, I can share with you some of the strategies that we use. First, it is important to understand that changing your behavior to become more active is your decision and you can stop at any time if your pain seems to be moving in the wrong direction. Second, we can work together to learn more about the distinction between the pain you are experiencing now and the discomfort that sometimes goes along with exercise. Third, during class, we will use a scale from 0 to 10 for you to rate your level of pain at any point. Using this scale does take some practice, but once you are familiar with it, we will use a rating of 3 as a cut off for knowing when it is time to stop an exercise or move to a different option. While rating your levels of pain is personal, you will not have to face making changes alone. I will be here to support and guide you. Lastly, if you have not yet talked with your doctor about becoming more physically active, it may be a good idea to do so. Your doctor may be able to provide exercise suggestions and recommendations based on your unique health history. Does all of this make sense to you?

Participant: That all sounds terrific! I like the idea of using a scale to rate my pain during classes and adjusting the exercises I am performing based on my level of pain. As you probably expect, some days I simply start out in more pain than others, so using this scale in combination with learning more about the difference between my normal pain and the discomfort from exercise seems like a good idea. I also really like the idea of not being in this alone and that you can help me to adjust movements and exercises based on my pain response. Believe it or not, I actually did recently talk with my doctor, and they were glad to hear that I started walking and encouraged me to become more active. In fact, they did not have any specific limitations or recommendations, but simply encouraged me to do any exercise that does not hurt. The doctor said if an activity does hurt my back, I should find something else to do. My doctor is definitely on board with me becoming more active.

Collaborate: Working together to set goals and identify solutions is the next step now that you have set the stage by increasing awareness of how the participant's low-back pain may be handled in a group exercise setting. The participant has explained why becoming more physically active is important and you have described what your role will be as the GFI. Now, it is time to determine next steps.

GFI: I'm glad to hear that you have already connected with your doctor on this topic. Now that we have discussed your goals and talked more about what exercising in a group setting may be like, what might you imagine as your next step?

Participant: At this point, I'd like to move forward with attending a class and learning more about recognizing and responding to my pain in a group exercise setting. I think trying a class one day next week would be a good next step. Do you think you could help me determine which class may be best for me based on what we have discussed so far?

GFI: Trying a class next week seems like a good next step for you. I will gladly share with you more about the different types of classes we offer, and we can work together to determine which class format might be the most enjoyable for you. I'm looking forward to seeing you in class!

Using the ACE ABC Approach allowed the participant and GFI to engage in a participant-centered conversation. This approach encourages respect and understanding for the participant's feelings, beliefs, and values, while providing reflections to demonstrate that the GFI understands their point of view. Pain is a personal and subjective experience. Using the ACE Mover Method keeps the participant in control by viewing them as the expert on themself and as being resourceful and capable of change.

Special Populations

OLDER ADULTS

Over the past 10 years, the population of older adults (age 65 and older) in the United States has increased from 38.8 million to 52.4 million and is expected to increase to 94.7 million in the year 2060. The growth of the older adult population is moving at a greater rate than that of the total population and the population under age 65 (U.S. Census Bureau, 2021; Administration for Community Living & Administration on Aging, 2020). The increased rate of growth for this population makes offering older adult–specific classes an ideal option, and GFIs are more than likely to have older adults in attendance at their classes. Understanding the needs and unique considerations for older participants is important for creating a safe and effective group exercise experience. Older adults may face debilitating health problems that affect them physically, psychologically, and socially. A GFI can motivate older adults to perform exercises as a way of improving function and slowing age-related changes that typically negatively impact exercise capacity, cognitive and psychological well-being, changes in **body composition,** chronic disease management, risk of physical disability, longevity, and the ability to live an emotionally satisfying life. Exercise programs for older adults should include the same components as those for younger people, with an emphasis on **functional capacity,** mobility, **balance,** strength and **power** development, and bone health. Strength and power training are relevant for older adults to reduce the rate of age-related **sarcopenia,** which is associated with falls and diminished functional capacity (ACSM, 2022).

Exercise Considerations for Older Adults

GFIs should observe the fitness level, mobility limitations, and self-efficacy levels of all class participants, especially older adults. In doing so, a GFI will be able to identify the best approach for maximizing participants' ability and willingness to commit to a lifestyle that includes regular exercise.

Older adults generally suffer losses to multiple senses that impact balance and, consequently, movement efficiency and motor control. Balance, therefore, is the foundational skill to all programming, as it enhances physical performance and contributes to improving the **cognitive domain** and **affective domain** and to building self-efficacy and self-confidence. Core conditioning is a critical component of balance training and must therefore be considered a prerequisite to effective training. High-velocity power training has been shown to elicit meaningful changes in muscle force production, peak power, and muscle contraction speed, and can safely be undertaken with proper instruction and supervision, once an adequate level of fitness is established. High-velocity power training may help improve overall performance and quality of life (Marques, Izquierdo, & Pereira, 2013).

Working with older adults who are frail and possess severe functional and mobility limitations is typically beyond the scope of practice for a GFI (and these individuals are not likely to participate in programs designed for the general population). GFIs should keep the general exercise guidelines presented in Table 12-12 in mind when instructing older adult participants.

TABLE 12-12
General Exercise Guidelines for Older Adults

Points of Emphasis	▸ Include an extended warm-up and cool-down (10 minutes each), as well as activation exercises such as those presented in the "Daily Routine for Enhancing Low-back Health" earlier in this chapter. ▸ Monitor intensity using the dyspnea scale or the RPE scale. ▸ Teach exercises and movement patterns that participants can replicate on their own at home or elsewhere to remain active when they cannot participate in class. ▸ Cognitive exercises, such as catching a tennis ball with one hand, "Simon says," or boxing with a target or mitts may improve reaction time and cognitive function. ▸ If using resistance tubes or bands, coach participants to control the **eccentric** phase, as rapidly "snapping" during the lowering phase can impose excessive **shearing forces** on the elbow joint if performing biceps curls, for example.

Continued on the next page

TABLE 12-12 (*continued*)

	▸ Use music that is appealing to this generation if teaching a dedicated class for older adults. Be mindful of the music and microphone volume, as well as **tempo.**
Modifications	▸ Due to possible physical limitations or orthostatic BP changes, be mindful of older adults' ability to move quickly from the floor to seated or standing positions. ▸ Provide chair-based exercise options for those individuals with balance or mobility issues. ▸ Barefoot balance training, such as in yoga or Pilates classes, can be helpful for improving **proprioception** and tactile response. However, older adults with diabetes or pre-existing podiatric or orthopedic conditions should not train in bare feet unless endorsed by their healthcare provider. ▸ For outdoor formats, such as boot-camp classes that involve running or relay races, allow older adults to complete shorter distances, or offer stationary options such as toe taps on a curb, modified jumping jacks, or step-ups on a stable surface, such as a bench. ▸ For agility exercises, dedicate a specific "lane" in the area for less complex coordination and agility exercises. Even walking backward can be a coordination challenge for some older adults.
Things to Avoid	▸ Avoid the use of excessive equipment due to trip-and-fall hazards. ▸ Due to age-related changes in the eyes, avoid dim lighting in the exercise area.
Additional Precautions	▸ Ask participants at the beginning of each class if they have any limitations they would like to share with the instructor. Consider arriving early enough to class to allow these conversations to occur privately for participants who do not want to share in front of others. ▸ Water temperatures for aquatic exercise should be between 83 and 86° F (28–30° C) for high-intensity exercise and between 86 and 88° F (30–31° C) for low-intensity exercise (AEA, 2020).

Note: RPE = Rating of perceived exertion; BP = Blood pressure

EXPAND YOUR KNOWLEDGE

Exercise Considerations for Participants with Osteoporosis

Osteoporosis a condition characterized by very low bone mass, diagnosed by a **bone mineral density (BMD)** of more than 2.5 standard deviations below the average peak value for normal adults (NIH, 2018). Osteoporosis and low BMD afflicts an estimated 54 million Americans [National Osteoporosis Foundation (NOF), 2017]. The clinical significance of osteoporosis in adults is attributed to increased susceptibility to bone fractures, particularly in older adults, who are prone to **osteoporotic fractures** from falling or injuring themselves by performing ADL such as bending over or lifting objects. Osteoporotic fractures are low-trauma injuries, meaning they occur from a standing height or lower. Overall, the risks for osteoporotic fractures in aging adults are staggering—one in two women and one in four men will break a bone due to osteoporosis after the age of 50 years (NOF, 2017). The short- and long-term consequences of osteoporotic fractures are associated with severe disability, immobility, decreased functional status, poor quality of life, negative self-esteem, and mortality (Dyer et al., 2016).

Weight-bearing cardiorespiratory exercise and muscular training are both beneficial for building and maintaining BMD. Group fitness classes that incorporate these types of activities include, but are not limited to, group strength, dance-based fitness, step training, and treadmill-based classes.

Table 12-13 presents general exercise guidelines for individuals with osteoporosis.

TABLE 12-13

General Exercise Guidelines for Individuals with Osteoporosis

Points of Emphasis	▸ Choose resistance exercises that strengthen the muscles of the hips, such as the squat, leg press, hip extension, hip adduction, knee extension, and hamstrings curl, as well as for the muscles of the spine, such as the back extension, shoulder press, lat pull-down, and seated row. ▸ Choose ROM exercises that improve posture, such as flexibility exercises for the chest, shoulders, hip flexors, calves, and ankles. ▸ Aerobic activity should be weight bearing. ▸ Balance activities should be added to help reduce the risk of falls.
Modifications	▸ Short bouts of activity interspersed with recovery are preferable to long-duration loading. ▸ Multiplanar activity should be encouraged. ▸ Higher loads with fewer repetitions are recommended for bone formation.
Things to Avoid	▸ Avoid explosive movements or high-impact loading if at a high risk for fractures. ▸ If a participant has very low spinal BMD, avoid excessive twisting, bending, or compression of the spine.
Additional Precautions	▸ The intensity of each exercise modality that can be tolerated will vary depending on bone status (i.e., normal, low, or very low BMD), the presence of clinical risk factors for falls, previous fractures, and contraindications to exercise.

Note: ROM = Range of motion; BMD = Bone mineral density

YOUTH

The needs of youth differ from those of adults in that their growth status is an indicator of health. Lack of regular exercise could impact functional development and skeletal and muscular growth. In addition, inactive lifestyles could lead to obesity, which has become an epidemic among youth (Sanyaolu et al., 2019). Sadly, this trend continues to worsen, as children are being diagnosed with lifestyle-related conditions that were once distinctive to adults, such as type 2 diabetes and hypertension. More than 80% of the world's adolescent population is insufficiently physically active, further magnifying the need for public health movements aimed toward youth fitness programs (WHO, 2020a).

Exercise Considerations for Youth

Children's thermoregulatory systems are not as mature as adults. Compared to adults, children have a higher body surface-to-mass ratio and need to devote a large proportion of their **cardiac output** to the skin surface instead of the core in hot conditions. All of these factors contribute to the way children cool their bodies—through dry heat **dissipation** (they sweat less)—whereas adults cool via **evaporation** (Falk & Dotan, 2008). This mechanism allows children to conserve water better than adults. Since children sweat less, caution should be taken when exercising in hot, humid environments because **heat exhaustion** can occur quickly if their core temperature rises faster than their dissipation rate.

For children, muscle-mass increases occurring during growth lead to increased **muscular strength.** Before the onset of puberty, muscular strength can be improved similarly in both males and females through muscular training, whereas during puberty, maturation and **testosterone** levels increase muscle size and strength more significantly among males. There is no evidence that muscular training stunts growth. Therefore, encouraging safe muscular-training practices early will instill good habits for the future. Setting up muscular-training circuits in a circle is an effective way to supervise and coach a group of youth.

GFIs should keep the general exercise guidelines presented in Table 12-14 in mind when instructing youth participants.

TABLE 12-14

General Exercise Guidelines for Youth

Points of Emphasis	▸ Supervise appropriately and use light-weight equipment for safety (e.g., medicine and athletic balls, resistance tubing and bands, suspension straps, stability balls, light dumbbells, gliding discs, and sandbags). ▸ Help children to develop motor skills to run, jump, kick, throw, and perform other basic skills needed to live an active life. ▸ Focus on physical literacy, or developing the ability, confidence, and desire to be physically active. ▸ Incorporate bone-strengthening activities because the greatest gains occur just before and during puberty. ▸ Teach proper breathing techniques. ▸ Encourage frequent fluid consumption before, during, and after exercise. ▸ Encourage communication when feeling tired, fatigued, pain, or discomfort.
Modifications	▸ RPE may be a way to measure exercise intensity for youth over eight years of age, but younger children may not have the cognitive skills to use the RPE scale accurately and consistently. The use of "easy" and "hard" descriptors may be the best option. ▸ To increase **adherence,** gamify exercise sessions (e.g., relay races, scavenger hunts, or dance challenges) and encourage children to use their imaginations when exercising, such as by performing animal-inspired yoga poses.
Things to Avoid	▸ Caution should be taken when exercising in hot, humid environments because heat exhaustion can occur quickly if children's core temperature rises faster than their dissipation rate.
Additional Precautions	▸ Provide proper supervision at all times and focus on exercise technique. ▸ Free weight and body-weight exercises may be preferred over machines and equipment that may not be the right size for children. ▸ Never encourage children to perform single maximal lifts or sudden explosive movements, or to compete with other children while performing muscular training. ▸ Water temperatures for aquatic exercise should be between 83 and 86° F (28–30° C) (AEA, 2020).

Note: RPE = Rating of perceived exertion

PRENATAL AND POSTPARTUM PARTICIPANTS

The potential benefits of a well-designed prenatal exercise program are numerous. Women who exercise during pregnancy may see the following benefits [American College of Obstetricians and Gynecologists (ACOG), 2020; Hinman et al., 2015; Lamina & Agbanusi, 2013; Nascimento, Surita, & Cecatti, 2012; Hall & Brody, 2010; Yeo et al., 2000]:

- Better cardiorespiratory and muscular fitness
- Reduced **fatigue** threshold
- Lower **resting heart rate**
- Higher **$\dot{V}O_2$max**
- Reduced rates of urinary incontinence, low-back pain, **deep vein thrombosis,** pregnancy-induced hypertension, **diastasis recti,** nausea, Cesarean birth, **anxiety,** heartburn, insomnia, leg cramps, and symptoms of **depression**

In terms of fetal health, there is no relationship between mothers who exercise during pregnancy and reduction in birth weight or preterm pregnancies. However, factors such as **ambient temperature** and nutrient availability during exercise can potentially harm the fetus. Therefore, exercising in temperature-controlled areas and eating a snack prior to exercising will promote a safe, healthy exercise experience for mother and baby.

Physical changes during pregnancy may limit some women's ability to exercise. Weight gain recommendations during pregnancy with one baby range from 11 to 40 pounds (5 to 18 kg) depending on the woman's **body mass index,** imposing additional stress on the joints of the back, pelvis, hips, and legs. Over the course of gestation, the mother's growing belly will move upward and out, displacing her **center of gravity** and resulting in low-back discomfort and changes in balance and coordination. Women are also more flexible during pregnancy due to an increase in **relaxin,** a hormone that relaxes ligaments and soft tissues in preparation for childbirth. The combination of joint **laxity** and altered balance and coordination can increase the risk of falls and injuries during pregnancy. Therefore, exercising in a controlled environment with few new situations that require novel or intense physical negotiation and motor skill is ideal.

The content in this section is based on recommendations from the American College of Obstetricians and Gynecologists, U.S. Department of Health & Human Services, and the World Health Organization. Please visit www.ACEfitness.org/Industry-Guidelines to confirm that this is the latest edition of each recommendation. If a newer set of guidelines is available, exam candidates should study that version to ensure they are up to date with the latest industry guidelines.

Exercise Considerations for Pregnant Participants

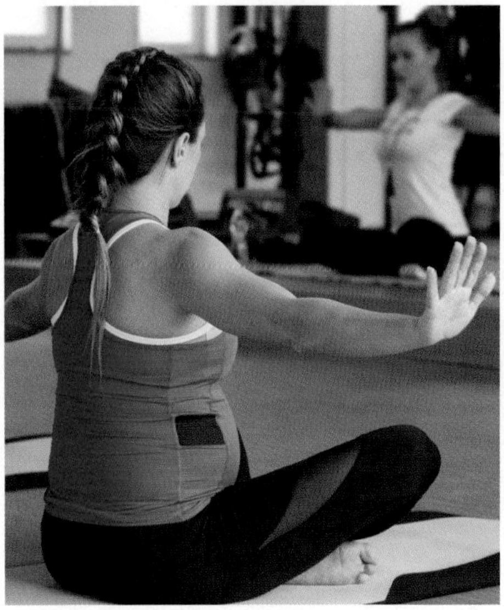

GFIs should learn basic knowledge about the special needs of women during pregnancy and provide modifications when necessary. ACOG (2020) recommends that women with uncomplicated pregnancies engage in moderate-intensity exercise for at least 30 to 60 minutes on at least three to four days per week (up to daily). The U.S. Department of Health & Human Services (2018) and the WHO (2020b) state that during pregnancy healthy women should perform at least 150 minutes per week of moderate-intensity aerobic exercise. GFIs should keep the general exercise guidelines presented in Table 12-15 in mind when instructing participants who are currently pregnant.

TABLE 12-15

General Exercise Guidelines for Participants Who Are Pregnant

Points of Emphasis	▸ Include an extended warm-up and cool-down. ▸ Use the RPE scale and the **talk test** to monitor exercise intensity (e.g., RPE of 9 to 13 on the 6 to 20 scale and can talk comfortably), or maintain an intensity less than 60 to 80% of age-predicted maximal heart rate. ▸ Incorporate exercises for postural muscles (e.g., thighs, hips, trunk, and shoulders). ▸ Adequate hydration and appropriate clothing are essential, as heat dissipation is important throughout pregnancy.
Modifications	▸ Reduce intensity, duration, and frequency over the course of pregnancy if activity is not well tolerated. ▸ In outdoor or treadmill-based classes, walking and running should occur on a flat surface to reduce the risk of falling. ▸ Modify jumping or quick change-in-direction activities due to increased laxity of joints and ligaments.
Things to Avoid	▸ After 20 weeks of gestation, avoid lying in a supine position for long periods. ▸ Avoid hot and humid environments. ▸ Avoid contact or collision activities that may cause loss of balance or trauma to the mother or fetus or increase the risk of falling.
Additional Precautions	▸ Some women may need a snack prior to exercise to help avoid hypoglycemia. ▸ Be aware of warning signs to discontinue exercise, such as vaginal bleeding, amniotic fluid leakage, chest pain, abdominal pain, calf pain or swelling, or regular painful uterine contractions. ▸ Low-back pain during pregnancy is a common experience, so exercise to support low-back health and proper posture should be incorporated. ▸ Water temperatures for aquatic exercise should be between 83 and 85° F (28–29° C) (AEA, 2020).

Note: RPE = Rating of perceived exertion

THINK IT THROUGH

Exercise Modifications for Pregnant Participants

When teaching a group strength training class that includes several participants who are pregnant, what alternative exercise options could you suggest in lieu of a supine abdominal strengthening exercise such as bicycle crunches?

Exercise Considerations for Postpartum Participants

Recovery time post-delivery is individualized, and women who had Cesarean deliveries or medical or surgical complications may require more recovery time. Once the obstetrician-gynecologist authorizes a return to physical activity, the first few months will be devoted to gradually improving maternal fitness, which may include weight loss, restoring pre-pregnancy cardiorespiratory and muscular performance, and regaining a sense of control. GFIs should keep the general exercise guidelines presented in Table 12-16 in mind when instructing postpartum participants who have been cleared to resume exercise.

TABLE 12-16

General Exercise Guidelines for Postpartum Participants

Points of Emphasis	▸ Start slowly and gradually increase the intensity and duration of exercise. ▸ Wear a supportive bra and express milk before exercise to avoid discomfort from engorged breasts. ▸ Select exercises that strengthen major muscle groups. ▸ Drink plenty of water.
Modifications	▸ Women who have had Cesarean deliveries will need extra time before performing abdominal exercises, based on personalized guidelines from the woman's physician.
Things to Avoid	▸ Avoid excessive fatigue. ▸ Avoid dehydration, as good hydration is important for milk production, if nursing.
Additional Precautions	▸ Cease activity if unusual pain is experienced. ▸ Cease activity and seek medical attention if bright red vaginal bleeding occurs that is heavier than a normal menstrual period.

Effects of Common Medications on Heart-rate Response

Prescription medication use is an important consideration when addressing a participant's response to exercise. Substances can alter the biochemistry of the body, which can affect an individual's physiological response to exercise. Moreover, dose response can influence the magnitude of the affects as well. Table 12-17 lists common medication categories and their effects on heart-rate response.

In a group fitness setting, the topic may arise if a participant reports unpredicted or unexpected HR responses during exercise. If this occurs, the GFI can ask the participant if they are taking any medications or using other substances, and refer to this section for more information based on the participant's reply. GFIs should not attempt to diagnose or provide medical advice, but they should use the information in Table 12-17 to make recommendations on how participants can better monitor their intensity if they are taking medication that alters their exercising HR. Any participant taking a prescription medication that could potentially alter their physiological response to exercise should obtain a physician's clearance for physical activity prior to participation.

TABLE 12-17

Effects of Select Substances on Heart-rate Response

Medications	Resting HR	Exercise HR	Exercise Capacity	Comments
Beta blockers	↓	↓	↓ $\dot{V}O_2$max with acute and ↑ with chronic administration	Dose-related response
Angiotensin II receptor blockers (ARBs) and calcium channel blockers (CCBs)	↓ or ↔	↓ or ↔	↔	
Other antihypertensives*	↑, ↔, or ↓	↑, ↔, or ↓	Usually ↔	Many antihypertensive medications are used. Some may decrease, a few may increase, and others do not affect HR. Some exhibit variable and dose-related responses.
Antihistamines	↑	↔	↔ performance and endurance	
Antidepressants and antianxiety medications	↑ or ↔	↑ or ↔		
Stimulants	↑	↑	↑ or ↔ endurance and performance	
Caffeine	↑	↑ or ↔	↑ endurance	
Bronchodilators	↔	↔	↔ $\dot{V}O_2$max; ↑ or ↔ in individuals with COPD	
Alcohol	↔	↔	↓ performance and $\dot{V}O_2$max	Exercise prohibited while under the influence; effects of alcohol on coordination increase possibility of injuries
Nicotine-replacement therapy	↑	↑	↔ or ↓	
Nonsteroidal anti-inflammatory drugs (NSAIDs)			↔ or ↑ performance	

Note: ↑ = increase; ↔ = no significant change; ↓ = decrease; HR = Heart rate; $\dot{V}O_2$max = Maximal oxygen uptake; COPD = Chronic obstructive pulmonary disease

* Many antihypertensive medications can cause positional hypotension, meaning the blood pressure drops when changing positions (sitting to standing). Therefore, a participant may become dizzy if they move too fast after performing abdominal work on the floor.

Note: Many medications are prescribed for conditions that do not require clearance. Do not forget other indicators of exercise intensity (e.g., participant's appearance or rating of perceived exertion).

This table in not intended to be an exhaustive list of all medications and their effects on heart rate. For more information on this topic, refer to American College of Sports Medicine (2022). *ACSM's Guidelines for Exercise Testing and Prescription* (11th ed.). Philadelphia: Wolters Kluwer.

APPLY WHAT YOU KNOW

Intensity Monitoring for Participants Taking Beta Blockers

Beta blockers are commonly prescribed for various cardiovascular disorders, hypertension, and other disorders. This type of medication reduces resting, exercise, and **maximal heart rates (MHR).** Consequently, beta blockers may not allow exercisers to reach **target heart rate (THR)** based on age-predicted MHR. As such, participants should use RPE to monitor intensity. In other words, if a participant is taking a medication that alters the heart's response to exercise, they may actually be working harder than what is reflected by their measured HR. For example, a participant may continue to push beyond a safe limit in an attempt to achieve a specific THR even though the medication will prevent them from being able to achieve it. Using RPE to adjust intensity based on perception will allow appropriate and safe program changes.

ACE UNIVERSITY

If your study program includes ACE University, visit www.ACEfitness.org/MyACE and log in to your My ACE Account to take full advantage of the ACE Group Fitness Instructor Study Program and online guided study experience.

A variety of media to support and expand on the material in this text is provided to facilitate learning and best prepare you for the ACE Group Fitness Instructor Certification exam and a career as a group fitness instructor.

SUMMARY

An increased focus on health and fitness for special populations and those suffering from chronic conditions means that more people within these groups will seek the instruction of knowledgeable health and exercise professionals, including GFIs. Instructors must increase their awareness and apply their knowledge of the unique physical, physiological, cognitive, and emotional needs among these populations. To foster an inclusive environment, GFIs need to design classes that are physically feasible for virtually everyone and encourage gradual progressions as well as appropriate regressions as needed.

REFERENCES

Administration for Community Living & Administration on Aging (2020). *2019 Profile of Older Americans.* https://acl.gov/sites/default/files/Aging%20and%20Disability%20in%20America/2019ProfileOlderAmericans508.pdf

American Cancer Society (2020). *Excess Body Weight: A Major Health Issue in America.* https://www.cancer.org/cancer/cancer-causes/diet-physical-activity/body-weight-and-cancer-risk/health-issues.html

American College of Obstetricians and Gynecologists (2020). Physical activity during pregnancy and the postpartum period, ACOG Committee Opinion No. 804. *Obstetrics and Gynecology,* 135, e178–188.

American College of Sports Medicine (2022). *ACSM's Guidelines for Exercise Testing and Prescription* (11th ed.). Philadelphia: Wolters Kluwer.

American College of Sports Medicine (2009). Appropriate intervention strategies for weight loss and prevention of weight regain for adults. *Medicine & Science in Sports & Exercise,* 41, 2, 459–471.

American Diabetes Association (2021a). *Hypoglycemia (Low Blood Sugar).* https://www.diabetes.org/healthy-living/medication-treatments/blood-glucose-testing-and-control/hypoglycemia

American Diabetes Association (2021b). *Blood Sugar and Exercise.* https://www.diabetes.org/healthy-living/fitness/getting-started-safely/blood-glucose-and-exercise

American Diabetes Association (2017). Classification and diagnosis of diabetes. *Diabetes Care,* 40, S11–S24.

Aquatic Exercise Association (2020). *Aquatic Fitness Programming: Standards and Guidelines.* https://aeawave.org/Portals/0/AEA_Cert_Docs/AEA_Standards_Guidlines_2020.pdf?ver=2019-12-18-131623-417&timestamp=1576696862726

Benjamin, E.J. et al. (2019). Heart disease and stroke statistics – 2019 update: A report from the American Heart Association. *Circulation,* 139, e56–e528.

Cai, H. et al. (2017). Effect of exercise on cognitive function in chronic disease patients: A meta-analysis and systematic review of randomized controlled trials. *Clinical Intervention in Aging,* 12, 773–783.

Centers for Disease Control and Prevention (2020a). *Arthritis.* https://www.cdc.gov/chronicdisease/resources/publications/factsheets/arthritis.htm

Centers for Disease Control and Prevention (2020b). *What Is Diabetes?* https://www.cdc.gov/diabetes/basics/diabetes.html#:~:text=Diabetes%20is%20the%20seventh%20leading,diabetes%20has%20more%20than%20doubled

Centers for Disease Control and Prevention (2020c). *Diabetes and Your Heart.* https://www.cdc.gov/diabetes/library/features/diabetes-and-heart.html

Centers for Disease Control and Prevention (2020d). *National Diabetes Statistics Report: Estimates of Diabetes and Its Burden in the United States.* https://www.cdc.gov/diabetes/pdfs/data/statistics/national-diabetes-statistics-report.pdf

Center for Disease Control and Prevention (2020e). *Acute Low Back Pain.* https://www.cdc.gov/acute-pain/low-back-pain/index.html

Centers for Disease Control and Prevention (2019). *Arthritis: Comorbidities.* https://www.cdc.gov/arthritis/data_statistics/comorbidities.htm

Centers for Disease Control and Prevention (2018). *Arthritis: National Statistics.* https://www.cdc.gov/arthritis/data_statistics/nationalstatistics.html

Dyer, S.M. et al. (2016). A critical review of the long-term disability outcomes following hip fracture. *BMC Geriatrics,* 16, 158.

Falk, B. & Dotan, R. (2008). Children's thermoregulation during exercise in the heat: A revisit. *Applied Physiology, Nutrition and Metabolism,* 33, 2, 420–427.

Hall, C. & Brody, L. (2010). *Therapeutic Exercise: Moving Toward Function* (3rd ed.). Philadelphia: Wolters Kluwer/Lippincott Williams & Wilkins.

Hinman, S.K. et al. (2015). Exercise in pregnancy: A clinical review. *Sports Health,* 7, 6, 527–531.

Ioannidis, J.P. (2018). Diagnosis and treatment of hypertension in the 2017 ACC/AHA guidelines and in the real world. *Journal of the American Medical Association,* 319, 115–116.

Lamina, S. & Agbanusi, E.C. (2013). Effect of aerobic exercise training on material weight gain in pregnancy: A meta-analysis of randomized controlled trials. *Ethiopian Journal of Health Sciences,* 23, 1 59–64.

Lee, W.J. et al. (2019). A comparative study between breathing control and pursed lip breathing among bronchial asthma patients. *International Journal of Advanced Science and Technology,* 28, 16, 1643–1646.

Marques, M., Izquierdo, M., & Pereira, A. (2013). High-speed resistance training in elderly people: A new approach toward counteracting age-related functional capacity loss. *Strength and Conditioning*, 35, 2, 23–29.

McGill, S.M. (2016). *Low Back Disorders* (3rd ed.). Champaign, Ill.: Human Kinetics.

Nascimento, S.L., Surita, F.G., & Cecatti, J.G. (2012). Physical exercise during pregnancy: A systematic review. *Current Opinion in Obstetrics & Gynecology*, 24, 6, 387–394.

National Institutes of Health (2019). *Osteoarthritis*. https://www.niams.nih.gov/health-topics/osteoarthritis#tab-symptoms

National Institutes of Health (2018). *Bone Mass Measurement: What the Numbers Mean*. https://www.bones.nih.gov/health-info/bone/bone-health/bone-mass-measure

National Osteoporosis Foundation (2017). *What Is Osteoporosis and What Causes It?* https://www.nof.org/patients/what-isosteoporosis/

Osteoarthritis Action Alliance, Centers for Disease Control and Prevention, & Arthritis Foundation (2020). *A National Public Health Agenda for Osteoarthritis: 2020 Update*. https://www.cdc.gov/arthritis/docs/oaagenda2020.pdf

Pachankis, J.E. et al. (2018). The burden of stigma on health and wellbeing: A taxonomy of concealment, course, disruptiveness, aesthetics, origin, and peril across 93 stigmas. *Personality and Social Psychology Bulletin*, 44, 4, 451–474.

Quaderi, S.A. & Hurst, J.R. (2018). The unmet global burden of COPD. *Global health, Epidemiology, and Genomics*, 3, e4.

Sanyaolu, A. et al. (2019). Childhood and adolescent obesity in the United States: A public health concern. *Global Pediatric Health*, 6.

U.S. Census Bureau (2021). *A Snapshot of the Fast-Growing U.S. Older Population*. https://www.census.gov/library/stories/2018/10/snapshot-fast-growing-us-older-population.html

U.S. Department of Health & Human Services (2018). *Physical Activity Guidelines for Americans* (2nd ed.). www.health.gov/paguidelines

Whelton, P.K. et al. (2017). 2017 ACC/AHA/AAPA/ABC/ACPM/AGS/APhA/ASH/ASPC/NMA/PCNA guideline for the prevention, detection, evaluation, and management of high blood pressure in adults: A report of the American College of Cardiology/American Heart Association Task Force on Clinical Practice Guidelines. *Journal of the American College of Cardiology*, Nov 7. pii: S0735-1097 (17) 41519-1.

World Health Organization (2021a). *Asthma*. https://www.who.int/news-room/fact-sheets/detail/asthma

World Health Organization (2021b). *Chronic Obstructive Pulmonary Disease (COPD)*. https://www.who.int/news-room/fact-sheets/detail/chronic-obstructive-pulmonary-disease-(copd)

World Health Organization (2020a). *Physical Activity Fact Sheet*. https://www.who.int/news-room/fact-sheets/detail/physical-activity

World Health Organization (2020b). *WHO Guidelines on Physical Activity and Sedentary Behavior*. https://www.who.int/publications/i/item/9789240015128

World Health Organization (2018). *Obesity and Overweight*. https://www.who.int/news-room/factsheets/detail/obesity-and-overweight

Wu, A. et al. (2020). Global low back pain prevalence and years lived with disability from 1990 to 2017: Estimates from the Global Burden of Disease Study 2017. *Annals of Translational Medicine*, 8, 6, 299.

Yeo, S. et al. (2000). Effect of exercise on blood pressure in pregnant women with a history of gestational hypertensive disorders. *Journal of Reproductive Medicine*, 45, 4, 293–298.

SUGGESTED READINGS

American College of Sports Medicine (2016). *ACSM's Exercise Management for Persons With Chronic Diseases and Disabilities* (4th ed.). Champaign, Ill.: Human Kinetics.

Centers for Disease Control and Prevention (2015). *How Much Physical Activity Do Children Need?* www.cdc.gov/physicalactivity/basics/children/

Delgado, J., Barranco, P., & Quirce, S. (2008). Obesity and asthma. *Journal of Investigational Allergology and Clinical Immunology*, 18, 6, 420–425.

Jensen, M.D. et al. (2013). AHA/ACC/TOS guideline for the management of overweight and obesity in adults: A report of the American College of Cardiology/ American Heart Association. *Circulation*, 129, 25 Suppl 2, S102–S138.

Juel, CT-B. et al. (2012). Asthma and obesity: Does weight loss improve asthma control? A systematic review. *Journal of Asthma and Allergy*, 5, 21–26.

SECTION

IV Professional and Legal Considerations

CHAPTER 13

Making Participant Safety a Priority

AMBER LONG, MEd | Executive Director of Wellness & Recreation Services, University of Colorado, Denver; ACE Certified Group Fitness Instructor, Personal Trainer, Health Coach, and Medical Exercise Specialist

IN THIS CHAPTER

LEARNING OBJECTIVES

Upon completion of this chapter, the reader will be able to:

- Describe the common injuries and acute illnesses that could occur in a group fitness setting
- Explain the major risk factors that could increase a participant's incidence of injury or acute illness
- Understand how to prevent and manage common injuries and acute illnesses within the group fitness instructor's scope of practice
- Understand when to activate emergency medical services

ACE UNIVERSITY

If your study program includes ACE University, visit www.ACEfitness.org/MyACE and log in to your My ACE Account to take full advantage of the ACE Group Fitness Instructor Study Program and online guided study experience.

A variety of media to support and expand on the material in this text is provided to facilitate learning and best prepare you for the ACE Group Fitness Instructor Certification exam and a career as a group fitness instructor.

Healthy lifestyle habits, including regular exercise, are associated with numerous benefits and long-term health and wellness outcomes. While the benefits of consistent exercise outweigh the potential risks, exercise professionals must be aware of the possible exercise-related injuries, **signs** and **symptoms** of exercise intolerance, and how to respond to injuries or **acute** illnesses that may occur in group fitness classes.

Recognizing Warning Signs

Safety

ACE Certified Group Fitness Instructors (GFIs) should be able to recognize the observable signs and symptoms that indicate when the safety of class participants may be compromised. In the event a participant does sustain an injury or present signs or symptoms of illness, GFIs must possess the confidence and skillset to respond to emergencies within their **scope of practice.**

> A sign is defined as an objective, *observable* indicator, such as loss of **coordination,** blue lips, or heavy coughing. A symptom, on the other hand, is a subjective sensory indicator that a participant feels, such as dizziness or nausea.

Recognizing the warning signs of **overexertion,** illness, or injury is paramount when leading any fitness class, especially if some participants have health limitations or are new to exercise. Overexertion typically occurs when a person pushes past the limits of their abilities and the energy systems are taxed beyond tolerable levels. Signs and symptoms may include nausea, dizziness, loss of strength, poor and/or unsafe form and technique, vomiting, and, in extreme cases, **rhabdomyolysis.**

While not as serious as overexertion, exercise **fatigue** should also be monitored by the GFI. The most obvious sign of fatigue is improper exercise technique. GFIs should teach participants that the inability to continue performing an exercise correctly is an indication that they should modify the movement. Executing any exercise with improper form could reinforce poor technique, increasing the likelihood that injury could occur presently or again in the future.

EXERCISE DEPENDENCE

While the GFI wants to encourage regular exercise participation, it is important to recognize the signs of **exercise dependence** or addiction that may occur in participants who take the habit of exercise to the extreme. Although it is not recognized as an independent clinical disorder, exercise dependence is a craving for leisure-time physical activity that progresses as excessive exercise behavior and results in physiological (e.g., tolerance) or psychological (e.g., withdrawal) symptoms (Anshel, 2019). Exercise dependence is reported to affect approximately 3 to 5% of the general exercising public, with more prevalence among men than women and affecting more competitive athletes compared to recreational exercisers (Anshel, 2019). If the GFI suspects a participant is exercising to excess, it is important that the GFI express their concerns directly with the participant, using **empathy** and unconditional positive regard. Because exercise dependence is sometimes associated with clinical eating disorders (e.g., anorexia nervosa and bulimia nervosa), it is important to refer to an appropriate mental health professional if an eating disorder is suspected.

APPLY WHAT YOU KNOW

The "Instructor's Eye"

Group fitness programs are typically scheduled with the intent to offer a variety of different exercise classes that might appeal to a large portion of the facility members. In this sense, most schedules are created with apparently healthy individuals in mind and not necessarily those with unique health concerns and needs. Therefore, a GFI must conduct a quick "screening" of participants at the start of every class. Individuals with health limitations may approach a GFI to inquire about the format of the class and to let the instructor know about their limitations and concerns. However, a GFI cannot rely on participants always informing them of their health issues, as some individuals may choose not to disclose personal health information. GFIs should intently watch for warning signs of exhaustion or injury throughout the class. Experience helps instructors develop the "instructor's eye" for recognizing improper mechanics, unsafe movement patterns, and signs of overexertion. Demonstrating the most basic movement first and then providing progressive options will accommodate most participants. GFIs must strive to adapt exercises based on the "in-the-moment needs" of the class. This real-time skill develops as GFIs gain experience and become more observant. The goal is to provide a safe and effective experience for everyone that yields results and healthy habits.

Common Participant Injuries

Exercise-related injuries can range from acute (abrupt) to **chronic** (ongoing). GFIs must be aware of most common injuries and illnesses that could be encountered in class and understand the classic signs and symptoms of each.

The following sections cover some of the most common injuries and acute illnesses a GFI may encounter over the course of their career. Keep in mind that this is not an exhaustive, detailed list of conditions, but rather is intended to reflect potential signs of exercise intolerance, injuries, and medical events that could occur in group fitness classes. In many cases, a GFI will not be able to ascertain the specific ailment (unless they have medical training and licensure within this scope), but recognizing the difference between life-threatening and non-life-threatening situations is critical for participant safety.

EXPAND YOUR KNOWLEDGE

Acute vs. Chronic Injuries

An abrupt onset of injury or medical emergency, such as twisting an ankle, injuring a muscle, or choking on gum, presents immediate symptoms of distress and is categorized as an acute injury. Chronic injuries, illnesses, or medical conditions, such as **tennis elbow** or **type 2 diabetes,** are ongoing. Sometimes, an acute injury can progress into a chronic injury, such as a situation in which slipping on a wet surface and suffering an acute low-back injury leads to chronic back pain. See Chapter 12 for more information on chronic conditions.

MUSCULOSKELETAL INJURIES

Acute musculoskeletal injuries are complex challenges for GFIs, as they can present emergency situations that escalate very quickly, requiring the GFI to remain calm and act swiftly. Table 13-1 highlights several musculoskeletal injuries with which GFIs should be familiar.

TABLE 13-1

Acute Musculoskeletal Injuries

Injury	Description	Signs and Symptoms	Activate EMS?
Sprain	Tearing or overstretching of a ligament, joint capsule, and/or connective tissue. The ankle and knee are common locations for sprains.	Swelling, pain, joint instability, joint stiffness, immobility, and possible discoloration	Possibly, if the person is not able to move to safety and there are no other means to move the person (e.g., along an outdoor trail).
Strain	Tearing or overstretching of a muscle or tendon. Shoulders and hamstrings are common locations for strains.	Swelling, pain, local tenderness, possible discoloration, and loss of strength and ROM	Possibly, if the person is not able to move to safety and there are no other means to move the person (e.g., along an outdoor trail)
Compound fracture	Bone fracture resulting in an open wound	Bony protrusion, bleeding, and possible shock	Yes, especially if there is heavy bleeding
Contusion	A bruise formed from an acute, traumatic blow to the body	Soft tissue hemorrhage, hematoma, and restricted ROM	Possibly, if the person sustains a blow to the head or possible internal bleeding

Note: ROM = Range of motion

Sources: American Council on Exercise (2020). *The Exercise Professional's Guide to Personal Training.* San Diego: American Council on Exercise; Prentice, W.E. (2020). *Essentials of Athletic Injury Management* (11th ed.). New York: McGraw-Hill.

CHRONIC MUSCULOSKELETAL CONDITIONS

Some participants may approach a GFI for advice about a condition that is exacerbated by exercise; however, diagnosing or treating medical conditions is outside the scope of practice for a GFI. Instructors should be prepared to provide exercise options and modifications to help participants perform pain-free exercise. It is important for the GFI to have general knowledge of several common chronic conditions (Table 13-2). Refer to Chapter 12 for more information for working with participants who have health conditions.

In order to accommodate and be inclusive of individuals with chronic musculoskeletal conditions, GFIs must be prepared to modify the class plan. In general, individuals with chronic musculoskeletal conditions benefit from an extended warm-up and cool-down. This strategy allows affected joints, muscles and systems more time to adjust to changing physical demands. In addition, if a participant experiences pain with a particular exercise, GFIs may recommend a modified movement, positioning the body in a different way, or adapting the movement to a single-joint exercise. GFIs should refer participants to a medical professional for more severe or ongoing ailments. In addition, GFIs and participants should always follow the recommendations of the participant's primary care physician. Table 13-2 outlines common chronic musculoskeletal conditions and recommended exercise modifications. Refer to Chapter 12 for a review of additional chronic conditions.

TABLE 13-2

Common Chronic Musculoskeletal Conditions

Condition	Description	Signs and Symptoms	Recommended Modifications
Carpal Tunnel Syndrome	Painful condition of the hand and fingers caused by compression of the median nerve in the wrist	Numbness and tingling in the hands	▸ Stretch the wrist, fingers, and forearm. ▸ Maintain neutral wrist alignment. ▸ Avoid load-bearing wrist flexion and extension. ▸ Change the angle of wrist flexion based on participant comfort.
Tendinitis	Inflammation of a tendon due to overuse	Tenderness, localized or dispersed pain, and loss of strength	▸ When tendons are inflamed, allow time for rest. ▸ Avoid exercises that cause pain. ▸ Perform ROM movements at affected joint(s) to maintain mobility.
Bursitis	Inflammation of a bursa sac near a tendon or joint	Swelling, pain, and some loss of function	▸ Avoid performing one movement or activity for extended periods of time. ▸ Progress intensity and load slowly. ▸ Focus on proper posture and ROM.
Plantar fasciitis	Inflammation of the plantar surface of the foot	Pain and tightness under the foot that may worsen with weight bearing	▸ Avoid high-impact exercises (e.g., running and jumping) during flare-ups. ▸ Stretch the feet and toes before and after exercise. ▸ Strengthening exercises might be suggested by a physician or physical therapist.
Shin splints (medial tibial stress syndrome)	Pain or inflammation of the soft tissue(s) along the shin bone from repetitive loading	Bone and soft-tissue tenderness, and pain during and after activity	▸ Reduce or avoid high-impact exercises (e.g., running and jumping) during flare-ups.

TABLE 13-2 (*continued*)

Condition	Description	Signs and Symptoms	Recommended Modifications
Iliotibial (IT) band friction syndrome	Inflammatory overuse condition in which the IT band (connective tissue) rubs against the lateral femoral epicondyle (outside of the knee)	Pain, burning, or tightness during running, cycling, or multidirectional movements along the outside of the knee	• Avoid aggravating activities (e.g., lying on the affected side and prolonged walking and running), if pain is present. • Focus on exercises that strengthen the hip and gluteal muscles.
Patellofemoral pain syndrome	Lateral deviation of the patella during knee extension that causes painful contact between the patella and femur	Tenderness, pain, swelling, and discomfort during activity	• Avoid exercises that compress the patella against the femur (e.g., high-impact activities, repetitive stepping, and kneeling, moves with deep knee flexion).
Impingements	When a muscle, tendon, or nerve pinches between bony structures; common areas are the shoulder and the spine	Local pain and tenderness, burning sensation, loss of range of motion and mobility, and muscle weakness	• Avoid exercises that place stress or pressure on the affected area. • Shoulder impingement: Avoid overhead movements, upright rows, and triceps dips, which place stress on the shoulder. • Recommend the participant rest the affected area and provide alternative movement options.

Note: ROM = Range of motion

SOFT-TISSUE INJURIES

Wounds such as a **laceration** (cut), **puncture** (hole), **avulsion** (skin tearing off), and **abrasion** (scrape) are injuries that result from an acute trauma to the skin. Signs and symptoms may include bleeding, pain, and exposure of bone, soft tissue, and, in extreme cases, internal organs. If the injury results in heavy, uncontrolled bleeding, EMS should be activated immediately.

THINK IT THROUGH

Supporting a Participant after an Injury

Individuals who are injured must deal with the mental and emotional impacts that a physical injury may create. After an injury, a healthcare provider may recommend that the participant temporarily reduce or eliminate exercise. This can be especially upsetting to individuals who were regularly active prior to the injury. Some participants might try to convince a GFI to allow them to participate in a class before their injuries have gone through the appropriate stages of healing or prior to medical clearance for physical activity. How would you handle someone who requests that you step outside your professional scope of practice and allow them to participate in your class before they have been cleared for exercise?

ACE→ MOVER™ METHOD

A Participant Coping with Injury

One day, you see one of your regular participants, who has not been to class all week. You wave hello and notice that they seem a little down, so you walk over to ask how they are doing. The participant lets you know that they recently hurt their shoulder while doing yardwork and have been diagnosed with a muscle strain. The participant says that their shoulder hurts most when they raise their arm overhead, they are experiencing a loss of strength in the injured shoulder, and that it feels tender when touched. They are very concerned about losing all the progress they have made over the past year since they can no longer exercise consistently. After asking the participant if they have time to talk more about their injury and goals, you both decide to move to a quiet location to continue the conversation.

Following is an example of how the ACE Mover Method™ and ACE ABC Approach™ can be used to help a participant stay focused on their health-related goals while recovering from an acute musculoskeletal injury.

ACE→ ABC APPROACH™

Ask: Asking powerful **open-ended questions** helps to gain a better understanding of what specific goals the participant has and how their injury may impact the progress they have been making.

GFI: You mentioned that you are concerned about losing the progress you've achieved over the past year. What specifically are you hoping to achieve by maintaining your exercise plan?

Participant: This injury really could not have come at a worse time, as things are very busy at work and at home. I've been adhering to my exercise program and making healthy changes to my diet. My goal has been to attend group classes three days per week and complete at least 150 minutes of physical activity each week. In addition, I've been trying new recipes, packing healthy lunches and snacks for work, and have replaced all of my soda intake with water and other zero-calorie beverages. I've been really motivated lately—that is, until I hurt my shoulder.

GFI: Thank you for sharing with me more about the progress you've made, your goals, and how this injury may impact your ability to maintain the work you've been doing to make additional progress. What did your doctor tell you about being physically active while recovering from your injury?

Participant: My doctor told me that I should avoid movements that cause pain in my shoulder. As of now, this means not reaching overhead or applying too much pressure directly on my shoulder. My doctor did mention that I can exercise as tolerated, but what is the point if I can't fully move my arm? I don't want to make my injury worse.

Break down barriers: Ask open-ended questions to learn more about the barriers the participant is facing because of their injury.

GFI: You want to maintain your physical-activity levels and exercise participation, but don't want to make your injury worse. How is your injury preventing you from being physically active?

Participant: Well, as I mentioned earlier, my doctor told me that I should not do movements that cause me to be in pain, so that means limiting the way I move my right arm. In all the classes I attend, the arms seem so heavily involved and I don't think I can participate.

GFI: What about the physical activity you perform outside of class? How is that impacted by your injury?

Participant: Outside of class, I primarily walk to accumulate my 150 minutes of physical activity each week, but I should probably not exercise at all until my injury is healed, right?

GFI: Great question! Based on the information you've shared with me about the specific recommendations from your doctor, it sounds like you should restrict arm movements on your injured side, but that you can also continue to exercise as tolerated. You can also follow up with your doctor if you think having more specific guidelines and recommendations would be helpful. You are correct that you want to limit moving your shoulder, but you can still benefit from being physically active even during this time of recovery. Do you have any other questions?

Participant: What about the group classes? There is so much arm movement that takes place and I don't want to be in pain.

GFI: I don't want you to be in pain either. The great thing about exercise is that it can take place in a variety of ways and can involve your entire body. Typically, in situations where a class participant is managing an injury, I adjust the exercises used in the class by providing options to allow for an inclusive experience for all participants. For example, let's say the class is doing a plank exercise and this position hurts your shoulder. I can offer you another option for targeting your core musculature that does not put as much stress on your shoulder. Together, we can find creative ways to maintain your class participation while minimizing or even avoiding pain. Does that make sense?

Participant: That does make sense! I appreciate that you are willing to find solutions with me to help me to maintain my exercise routine. Thank you!

Collaborate: Working together with the participant, it is now time to set goals and decide on next steps. Barriers have been identified, information has been shared, and now it is up to the participant to decide how they would like to move forward.

GFI: We have discussed a lot of information in a short period of time, and I am thankful that you stopped to chat with me today. How do you think you will move forward?

Participant: When we first started talking today, I was thinking I needed to put my goals and exercise plan on hold until my shoulder was 100% better. Now that you have planted the seed of continuing to exercise while avoiding painful movements, I'm excited to continue while recovering and being mindful to avoid positions that may cause pain. Starting this week, I would like to attend a class and see how we can work together to decide on exercise options that allow me to get in a good workout while also protecting my injured shoulder. If this goes well, then I see no reason not to exercise!

GFI: Attending a class this week and exploring other exercise options seems like a good next step for you. What else?

Participant: I think I was wanting to put everything on hold because I was feeling discouraged. However, knowing that I'll still exercise is motivating me to continue with my walking, which does not really involve or hurt my shoulder. I also see no reason why I can't continue trying new recipes and bringing healthy food to work.

GFI: It sounds like you feel comfortable with your next steps. I look forward to seeing you in class this week and hearing more about the progress you are making and how your recovery is going.

In this scenario, the GFI uses a series of open-ended questions and reflective listening to help a participant refocus on their goals during a time of injury. GFIs will encounter participants who have sustained injuries and it is important to work with them, when appropriate, to maintain their exercise participation in a safe and effective manner. While some injuries may require complete rest and the guidance of medical professionals and physical therapists, it is crucial to understand the extent of an injury, what limitations or recommendations have been provided, and how the participant would like to move forward. The ACE Mover Method and ACE ABC Approach can be used to uncover this necessary information in a way that respects the participant's **autonomy** and keeps them in control of deciding on how they would like to move forward.

Medical Emergencies

Knowing basic injury and illness management and when to activate emergency medical services (EMS) is within the scope of practice for a GFI. In fact, it is imperative for ensuring participant safety. The following section outlines medical emergencies that a GFI may encounter while teaching classes. GFIs must understand the signs and symptoms associated with medical emergencies in order to make swift decisions regarding the activation of emergency medical services.

Activating EMS should be reserved for serious situations. For all other situations, GFIs should respond while staying within their scope of practice by providing **cardiopulmonary resuscitation (CPR),** using an **automated external defibrillator (AED),** and implementing their first-aid training. ACE requires all GFIs to successfully complete adult CPR and AED training and encourages first-aid training prior to taking the ACE Group Fitness Instructor Certification Exam. Once certified, GFIs must maintain adult CPR/AED certification in order to renew their ACE certification every two years.*

CARDIORESPIRATORY EMERGENCIES

Cardiorespiratory emergencies, during which a participant is experiencing difficulty breathing or may not be breathing at all, require immediate activation of EMS. GFIs should be familiar with the signs and symptoms of the conditions outlined in Table 13-3 and be prepared to take action should one of these emergency situations arise.

TABLE 13-3
Cardiorespiratory Emergencies

Condition	Description	Signs and Symptoms	Activate EMS?
Heart attack	Caused by an obstruction or blockage of blood flow to the heart	Pain in the chest, arms, back, neck, or jaw; labored or difficulty breathing; nausea; anxiety; lightheadedness; sweating; fatigue; and syncope	Yes
Exercise-induced bronchoconstriction	Swelling, inflammation, or narrowing of the airways that inhibits breathing	Irregular or labored breathing or wheezing, sweating and paleness, excessive throat clearing, coughing for no apparent reason, anxious appearance, and breathing with pursed lips	Yes, if the person is not able to relieve the symptoms with medication and especially if breathing becomes labored or the person loses consciousness
Choking	When an object obstructs the airway	Coughing, loss of speech, pale or blueish skin, and syncope	Yes, and the EMS can be called off if the object becomes dislodged

Sources: American Council on Exercise (2020). *The Exercise Professional's Guide to Personal Training.* San Diego: American Council on Exercise; Prentice, W.E. (2020). *Essentials of Athletic Injury Management* (11th ed.). New York: McGraw-Hill.

CEREBROVASCULAR EMERGENCIES

Cerebrovascular emergencies such as **strokes, concussions,** and **seizures** can be serious and life-threatening. Table 13-4 provides an overview of the common signs and symptoms that should prompt the GFI to activate EMS.

---

*Obtaining and maintaining AED certification is only applicable to regions that allow non-healthcare providers to practice life-saving maneuvers. The American Council on Exercise does not supersede regional or federal laws on this statute. Therefore, this AED requirement will be waived for GFIs who live in regions that prohibit non-healthcare professionals from using AEDs.

TABLE 13-4
Cerebrovascular Emergencies

Condition	Description	Signs and Symptoms	Activate EMS?
Stroke	Cerebrovascular emergency caused by a lack of blood supply and oxygen to the brain	Numbness in the arms, legs, or face; confusion; trouble speaking; dizziness; loss of vision, balance, or coordination; drooping on one side of the face; and loss of consciousness	Yes
Concussion	Trauma-induced alteration of mental status resulting from a direct blow to the head	Blurred vision, dizziness, drowsiness, loss of consciousness, loss of orientation, nausea, memory problems, sensitivity to noise and light, seeing stars, ringing in the ears, and vomiting	Yes, if loss of consciousness occurs
Seizures	Changes in brain activity that can cause mild to severe convulsions	Convulsions, syncope, loss of coordination, clenching of the jaw, and loss of bladder and/or bowel function	Yes

Sources: American Council on Exercise (2020). *The Exercise Professional's Guide to Personal Training*. San Diego: American Council on Exercise; Prentice, W.E. (2020). *Essentials of Athletic Injury Management* (11th ed.). New York: McGraw-Hill.

EXPAND YOUR KNOWLEDGE

Safety

The Signs and Symptoms of Stroke

The brain controls various body functions, so symptoms of a stroke depend on what area of the brain is affected. Typical effects of a stroke include facial droop, weakness or paralysis of the body, vision problems, memory loss, and speech or language problems.

The GFI should be aware of the warning signs of a stroke:

- Sudden numbness or weakness of the face, arms, or legs
- Sudden confusion or trouble speaking or understanding others
- Sudden trouble seeing in one or both eyes
- Sudden walking problems, dizziness, or loss of **balance** and coordination
- Sudden severe headache with no known cause

The acronym FAST (which stands for facial drooping, arm weakness, speech difficulties, and time to call emergency services) serves as a mnemonic to help GFIs recognize and respond to the needs of a participant having a stroke.

METABOLIC EMERGENCIES

Low blood sugar attributed to the physiological effects of exercise, known as exercise-induced **hypoglycemia,** can occur in group fitness participants. Signs and symptoms may include dizziness, confusion, hunger, headache, pale skin, sweating, anxiety, weakness, and poor coordination. At the onset of these symptoms, participants should stop activity and check **glucose** levels, if possible, then obtain treatment as soon as possible (e.g., medication, juice, or glucose tabs). Facility first-aid kits should include glucose tablets. EMS may need to be activated if these symptoms worsen.

For participants with diabetes, dangerously low blood sugar levels can result in severe hypoglycemia, characterized by worsening of the signs and symptoms of hypoglycemia with possible loss of consciousness (see Chapter 12). EMS should be activated immediately if severe symptoms of hypoglycemia occur. GFIs should never try to give an unconscious participant anything by mouth (e.g., sugar), as doing so could compromise the individual's airway.

PREGNANCY-RELATED EMERGENCIES

While there are numerous benefits associated with exercising during pregnancy, including reduced prenatal discomforts, faster recovery from labor, and reduced incidence of postpartum **depression,** there are potential risks of which GFIs should be aware. Prolonged or high-intensity exercise, for example, can lead to hypoglycemia, so it is important to ensure adequate caloric intake prior to exercise and limit the exercise session length and intensity to minimize risk [American College of Obstetricians and Gynecologists (ACOG), 2020]. If a person who is pregnant experiences the signs and symptoms of hypoglycemia, such as dizziness, confusion, hunger, headache, pale skin, weakness, and poor coordination, GFIs should pay close attention and monitor the participant. EMS may need to be activated if symptoms do not subside. Individuals who experience a hypoglycemic event while pregnant should consume food and/or drinks containing easily digestible sugar sources (e.g., fruit, candy, juice, or sports drink) as soon as possible to stabilize their blood sugar, and contact their obstetrician-gynecologist or other obstetric care provider.

Pregnancy-related emergencies that require immediate activation of EMS include both labor and vaginal bleeding, which could indicate miscarriage. Miscarriage is the spontaneous loss of pregnancy in which bleeding, extreme cramping, inability to stand, nausea, vomiting, and dizziness may occur.

Strategies for Preventing Common Injuries

It can be a challenging task to create an environment in which participants can achieve their varied fitness goals, while addressing each person's individual needs to ensure everyone's safety. GFIs must have knowledge of risk factors associated with injuries, methods for prevention, and appropriate modifications for specific limitations.

Safety

The injury-related responsibilities of GFIs are to:

- Prevent injury by carefully planning and delivering safe exercise classes
- Ensure the exercise environment is free of potential hazards

- Provide **regressions** and adaptations for participants with movement limitations
- Address acute injuries that may occur during a class

Execution of these responsibilities is challenging because participants attending a group fitness class have a wide variety of exercise goals, backgrounds, and physical strengths or limitations. It is the job of a GFI to encourage participants to work within their own individual limits and to inform participants that they ultimately have control over their workout intensity (see Chapter 4). The instructor is teaching the class for the participants' workout, not their own, and should appropriately set the intensity of the class by example. GFIs should demonstrate multiple exercise options, and then continue to perform the variation that is most appropriate for the majority of class participants. It is important to remember that the risk of a musculoskeletal injury occurring or being aggravated is always present during exercise. Therefore, a primary objective for a GFI is to provide a safe environment for all participants. Success is dependent on understanding musculoskeletal injuries, their causes, and exercise contraindications for participation.

RISK FACTORS AND PREVENTION

The risk of in-class injuries and medical emergencies can be higher when the environment poses extrinsic risk factors. In addition, class participants may possess personal or intrinsic risk factors. GFIs can help reduce or mitigate these risks by eliminating some of the extrinsic factors, as introduced in Chapter 4, and provide modifications for those who may possess intrinsic risk factors.

Tables 13-5 and 13-6 provide an overview of the most common group fitness–related intrinsic and extrinsic factors and how a GFI can respond and reduce the risks when possible.

TABLE 13-5

Intrinsic Risk Factors in Group Fitness

Intrinsic Risk Factor	GFI Prevention/Course of Action
Pre-existing injuries, ailments, and conditions (including age and any of the conditions described in Table 13-2)	▸ Increase the duration of the warm-up and cool-down. ▸ Provide regressions to ROM, intensity, complexity, and duration of exercise. ▸ Offer exercises that do not involve the affected body part(s). ▸ Participants with known cardiovascular, metabolic, or renal disease, or those experiencing signs or symptoms of such disease, should receive medical clearance prior to increasing physical-activity levels and intensity. For those already exercising regularly, medical clearance is recommended before progressing to vigorous intensity exercise if it is known they have the condition.

TABLE 13-5 (*continued*)

Intrinsic Risk Factor	GFI Prevention/Course of Action
Body composition that is either above or below recommended levels	▸ Suggest lower-impact exercises. ▸ Demonstrate basic movements before progressing intensity and complexity. ▸ If an eating disorder or exercise addiction is suspected, a GFI should approach the participant with empathy and provide professional guidance about healthy exercise habits and body weight and refer them to a healthcare provider.
Deconditioned	▸ Increase the duration of the warm-up and cool-down. ▸ Provide options for fewer repetitions and sets, and shorter exercise bouts. ▸ Provide RPE recommendations periodically so participants can learn to self-monitor. ▸ Offer frequent breaks and active recovery opportunities.
Strength or flexibility imbalances	▸ Limit ROM by reducing the amount of joint movement required to achieve the exercises(s). ▸ Begin with dynamic flexibility movements and end with static stretches. ▸ Offer props such as yoga blocks, bolsters, and stretch straps for support. ▸ Help participants distinguish between pain and discomfort through supportive cueing.

Note: ROM = Range of motion; RPE = Rating of perceived exertion

TABLE 13-6
Extrinsic Risk Factors in Group Fitness

Extrinsic Risk Factor	GFI Response/Course of Action
Complexity, intensity, speed, and type of movement	▸ Allow participants to master the foundational exercise before advancing to movements that demand more coordination, speed, and conditioning. ▸ GFIs should always demonstrate the foundational layers first and then provide advanced progressions. ▸ GFIs should perform and model the exercise variation that would best suit beginners and deconditioned individuals to help them feel more comfortable and successful in the class experience.
Number of repetitions and sets	▸ Create a balanced class plan that takes into account muscular balance and appropriate repetition, set, and rest schemes to build muscular fitness safely for all participants. ▸ Avoid an excessive number of repetitions. ▸ When performing core-supported exercises (e.g., planks and bent-over rows), provide frequent breaks from maintaining the exercise posture.

Continued on the next page

TABLE 13-6 *(continued)*

Extrinsic Risk Factor	GFI Response/Course of Action
Surface	▸ Consider adapting the class plan based on the floor surface (e.g., hardwood, concrete, carpet, or grass). ▸ Perform lateral movements cautiously on carpeted or uneven surfaces. ▸ Reduce high-impact activities on hard surfaces, like concrete. ▸ Provide appropriate progression opportunities when using stability tools (e.g., balls, pads, and balance discs). Always provide a stable, solid exercise surface option. ▸ Ensure the surface is free of slip or trip hazards.
Footwear	▸ Recommend cross-training shoes for group fitness. Running shoes lack lateral support, but many group fitness classes incorporate running; therefore, a hybrid shoe, such as a cross-trainer, is suitable for short distances. ▸ For dance classes, participants should wear shoes with lateral support and minimal tread on the sole to avoid friction during turns, as this friction can lead to ankle, knee, or hip injuries.
Fatigue	▸ Suggest hydration breaks. ▸ Create active recovery opportunities by targeting different energy systems. ▸ Be aware of the signs of fatigue, such as reduced coordination, balance, speed, and acuity, which can lead to an acute injury. ▸ Reduce the intensity or discontinue the activity for the day when signs of fatigue are present.
Equipment	▸ Use equipment according to the manufacturer's instructions. Utilizing equipment in ways that the manufacture did not recommend will present physical risk to the participants and legal risk to the instructor. ▸ Do not utilize homemade equipment for public use, as the quality, safety, and applicability of such equipment has not been validated or deemed reliable by authoritative safety testing organizations. This leaves the GFI liable to legal implications in the event of injury to the participant.
Climate/temperature	▸ Recommend athletic clothing based on the environment. Clothing should be breathable while providing protection from the elements. ▸ Exercise indoors on days with extreme temperatures or humidity. ▸ Understand contraindications of exercising in hot, humid environments (e.g., heated group fitness studio environments or outdoors) for some populations (see Chapter 12). ▸ Encourage frequent fluid intake and extend the warm-up and cool-down periods.
Air quality	▸ Avoid outdoor exercise on high alert days. Environmental pollution or allergens can affect the cardiorespiratory response to exercise. The U.S. Environmental Protection Agency posts alerts and information about air quality in hundreds of U.S. and Canadian cities (www.airnow.gov).

MINIMIZING RISK THROUGH INSTRUCTIONAL STRATEGIES

Symptoms of many musculoskeletal injuries or wounds include pain, swelling, loss of motion and strength, reduced functional capacity, and bleeding. These symptoms are present in various degrees and combinations in most injuries. Acute injuries are the result of an immediate trauma. Chronic injuries are developed gradually from repeated stress over time. Chronic and acute injuries can be caused by any number of factors, including footwear, flooring or exercise surface, equipment, movement execution, class intensity, and frequency of participation. It is important for GFIs to consider injury-prevention efforts within instructional strategies.

Preventing or managing injuries while staying within the scope of practice for a GFI can be summarized by a few key concepts and guidelines (Anderson & Barnum, 2022; Prentice, 2020):

Safety

- Include a format-specific warm-up and cool-down.
- Monitor environmental and outdoor exercise space conditions to ensure safe participation.
- Limit motion and stretching to a pain-free range and intensity.
- Gradually increase the intensity of activity during the conditioning segment, with work added in small increments.
- Focus on technique and proper form.
- Assess the appropriateness of jumping, especially box jumps and other plyometric-type techniques.
- Load closed-kinetic-chain exercises, such as squats and lunges, according to the tolerance of the joints (including the back).
- Avoid extreme **range of motion (ROM).**
  - Avoid excessive **flexion** for knee injuries.
  - Provide modifications for overhead activities, such as avoiding full extension of the arms and positioning the shoulders more toward the front of the body (i.e., in the **scapular plane,** where the shoulder is positioned between the **sagittal plane** and the **frontal plane,** approximately 30 degrees anterior to the frontal plane) (Figure 13-1).
- Check equipment for proper fit. Repetitive movements, like cycling, can cause inflammation of the soft tissues if the equipment is improperly fit to the exerciser (see Chapter 8).

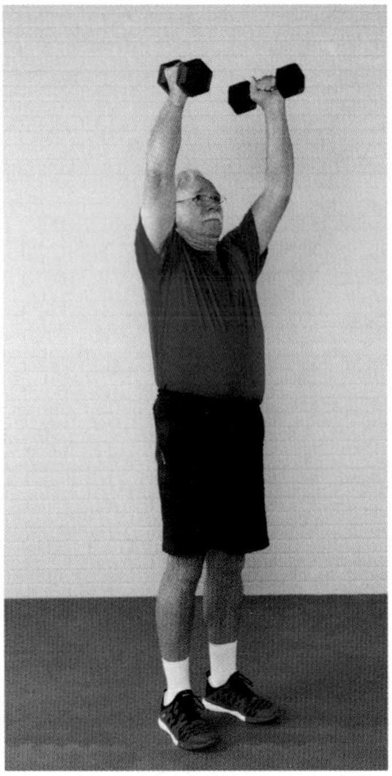

FIGURE 13-1
Overhead press in the scapular plane

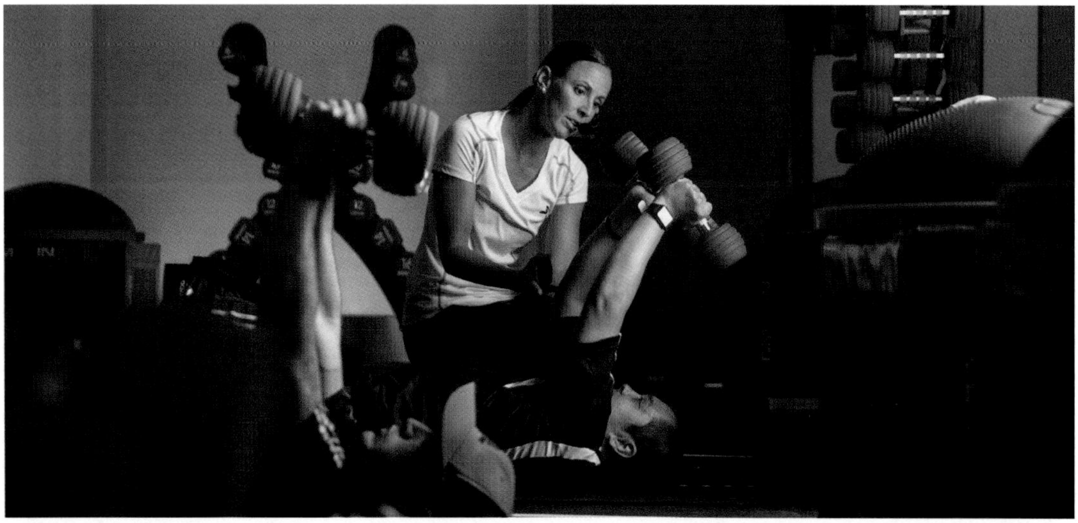

UNDERSTANDING FACILITY POLICIES AND PROCEDURES

While some emergency situations are unavoidable, the best approach is to be prepared. The American Heart Association (AHA) and American College of Sports Medicine (ACSM) publish guidelines for fitness facilities that involve pre-screening members, having adequate staffing, and establishing emergency policies. A fitness facility can take the following steps to minimize the risk of injuries (ACSM, 2014; Balady et al., 1998):

- Fitness staff should hold current certifications accredited by the National Commission for Certifying Agencies (NCCA) or equivalent in their specialty areas (e.g., personal training, group fitness instruction, or lifeguarding). If a staff member works with special population groups such as seniors, youth, or prenatal or postpartum women, additional training for working safely and effectively with that population is recommended.
- Record and track all employees' CPR, AED, first aid, and fitness certification information, including the issuing organization, issue date, certification number, and expiration date.
- Many states now have laws that require health clubs to have at least one AED on the premises. Visit the Sudden Cardiac Arrest Foundation's website (www.sca-aware.org) for an updated listing.
- Facilities should screen new members to identify those who may need medical clearance before becoming physically active by using a simple screening questionnaire such as the **Physical Activity Readiness Questionnaire for Everyone (PAR-Q+)** (www.eparmedx.com). Collecting and maintaining this information is typically not the responsibility of a GFI, but it is important to understand the significance and necessity of this information. The PAR-Q+ can help to identify individuals who need medical clearance or require modifications to their exercise programs. This tool can also help identify the need for additional qualified staff members if there are a number of at-risk participants (ACSM, 2014; Balady et al., 1998).
- Fitness facilities should establish a method of notifying participants about the risk of injury associated with exercise, such as having new members sign **informed consent** forms. Additionally, fitness facilities should have participants complete

preparticipation health screening forms and obtain medical clearance when necessary, as determined by the participant's current physical-activity levels; known cardiovascular, metabolic, or renal disease; and the presence of signs or symptoms of such disease (ACSM, 2022).

Safety

The fitness center should take responsibility for minimizing any additional risks by ensuring the following (ACSM, 2014; Balady et al., 1998):

- Adequate staffing and supervision
- Cleanliness to minimize the transfer of bloodborne pathogens or other bodily fluids that could spread disease or cause infection
- Clear walkways and pathways to emergency exits
- Adequate ventilation and air movement
- Hand sanitizer stations
- Adequate lighting
- Nonslip surfaces around showers and pools
- Caution signs for wet floors and other hazards (for example, "No Diving" signs at the shallow end of the pool)
- Regular maintenance and repair of equipment
- A clean drinking water supply
- Fire/smoke alarms installed
- Limiting the number of people in the building and in group fitness classes to avoid overcrowding
- First-aid kits that are kept in convenient locations and assigned to someone to restock on a regular basis
- Phones that can be easily accessed with emergency numbers posted nearby
- Establishing and practicing an emergency action plan that includes what documentation should be kept, the location of emergency equipment (first-aid kits and AEDs), how to use the land lines, emergency exits, and accessible emergency routes.

Incident Management and Emergency Response

Acute injuries need to be handled quickly, but with caution, as participant safety is paramount. A GFI should apply the first-aid and emergency response actions learned from their primary emergency training, and refer the participant to an appropriate healthcare provider when an injury is serious enough (e.g., an individual who is unable to walk after twisting an ankle during agility exercises or who feels sudden shoulder pain and weakness after swinging a kettlebell). Injuries that result in heavy bleeding, airway obstruction, labored or loss of breathing, symptoms of **shock,** or unconsciousness are scenarios that necessitate immediate activation of EMS.

If an acute injury occurs, the GFI may need to assist with early intervention, which often includes medical management (Kaminski et al., 2013). The acronym RICE (rest or restricted activity, ice, compression, and elevation) describes a common early-intervention strategy for many acute injuries. In the following example, an ankle injury has taken place.

R	I	C	E
REST OR RESTRICTED ACTIVITY	**ICE**	**COMPRESSION**	**ELEVATION**
Avoid weight-bearing activity until cleared by a physician.	Ice should be applied every hour for 10 to 20 minutes until the tendency for swelling has passed.	This involves placing a compression wrap on the area to minimize local swelling.	Elevation of the ankle 6 to 10 inches above the level of the heart will help control swelling. This is done to reduce hemorrhage, inflammation, swelling, and pain.

Example created based on information in Kaminski, T.W. et al. (2013). National Athletic Trainers' Association position statement: Conservative management and prevention of ankle sprains in athletes. *Journal of Athletic Training*, 48, 4, 528–545.

First-aid training is highly recommended for GFIs to educate themselves about wound care, precautions to avoid exposure and transmission of diseases, and how to secure the area until emergency services arrive. Such training may even be required in order to work at certain facilities. Organizations such as the American Red Cross and the American Heart Association possess core competency in this category. Accordingly, CPR, AED, and first-aid training are not delivered in this textbook, and GFIs must complete these trainings through a reputable provider of their choosing.

Managing life-threatening situations—such as loss of consciousness, obstruction of the airway, impaired breathing or circulation, convulsions, severe bleeding, or apparent shock—take precedence over all other injuries. A GFI's first reaction in a critical situation should be to activate EMS and then assess what emergency care can be rendered, such as CPR, defibrillation with an AED, or locating the victim's medication (e.g., inhaler). In some cases, rescue services will provide emergency care directions over the phone until first responders arrive.

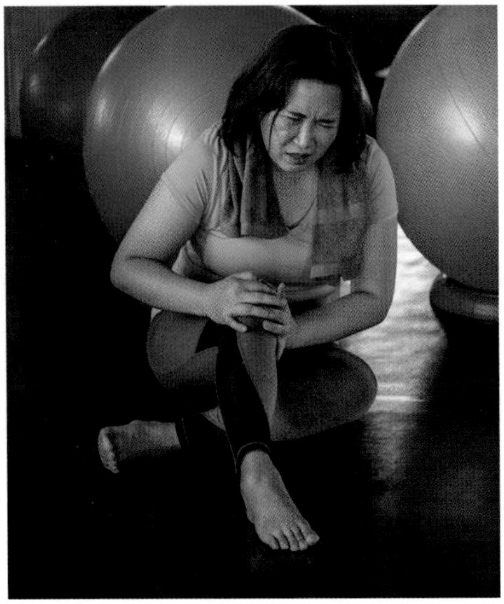

It is appropriate for a GFI to call in any emergency responders if they are unsure of how to handle a situation. However, a GFI should not call if there is not a true emergency, as doing so can delay response time to true emergencies and incur unnecessary costs. For non-emergencies, call the appropriate agency or the emergency contact if available.

CPR, AED, and first-aid certifications provide training and education to understand various medical circumstances and courses of action to take during a medical emergency. It is important to remember that the diagnosis and treatment of injuries is outside the scope of practice for the GFI.

Regardless of the safety measures provided, some injuries are going to occur on occasion during fitness activities. When someone is injured, it is necessary for the GFI to file an accident report at the facility. ACSM (2019) suggests that accident/incident reports should be approved by legal counsel before use and should include the following information:

- Day, date, and time of incident
- Location of incident
- Person(s) involved in the incident
- Witnesses to the incident
- Staff responding to the incident
- Details of incident
- Actions taken by staff
- Outcomes of the incident

Accident reports should be kept on file, according to the statute of limitations where the organization resides. If the person was injured in a formal class setting, it may also be helpful to file a class outline or lesson plan with the accident report. In addition, a yearly review of injuries can be helpful in reducing accidents causing injuries to participants.

If a GFI collects medical information about a participant following an incident or accident, the victim's information must be kept confidential and only shared with management or medical providers. The **Health Insurance Portability and Accountability Act (HIPAA)** of 1996 is a federal law that protects a victim's privacy by putting the individual in control of who has access to their health and medical records. Therefore, accident and incident reporting documents must be stored in a locked area. See Chapter 14 for more information on participant confidentiality.

ACE UNIVERSITY

If your study program includes ACE University, visit www.ACEfitness.org/MyACE and log in to your My ACE Account to take full advantage of the ACE Group Fitness Instructor Study Program and online guided study experience.

A variety of media to support and expand on the material in this text is provided to facilitate learning and best prepare you for the ACE Group Fitness Instructor Certification exam and a career as a group fitness instructor.

SUMMARY

GFIs have several responsibilities to ensure a safe exercise experience for participants. They must:

- Reduce injury risk by carefully planning and delivering every exercise class
- Provide appropriate exercise modifications for participants with injury or chronic condition limitations
- Respond to acute injuries or emergencies that may occur during a class
- Ensure proper documentation of illness or injury that occurs during a class

Although the diagnosis and treatment of injuries is outside the scope of practice for GFIs, all exercise professionals should have knowledge and understanding of chronic and acute conditions that may occur in a group fitness setting. In addition, GFIs must be able to respond to medical emergencies that can arise during group fitness classes. GFIs should learn to recognize medical emergencies and know when it is necessary to activate EMS.

REFERENCES

American College of Obstetricians and Gynecologists (2020). Physical activity during pregnancy and the postpartum period, ACOG Committee Opinion No. 804. *Obstetrics and Gynecology*, 135, e178–188.

American College of Sports Medicine (2022). *ACSM's Guidelines for Exercise Testing and Prescription* (11th ed.). Philadelphia: Wolters Kluwer.

American College of Sports Medicine (2019). *ACSM's Health/Fitness Facility Standards and Guidelines* (5th ed.). Champaign, Ill.: Human Kinetics.

American College of Sports Medicine (2014). *ACSM's Resource Manual for Guidelines for Exercise Testing and Prescription* (7th ed.). Philadelphia: Wolters Kluwer/Lippincott Williams & Wilkins.

American Council on Exercise (2020). *The Exercise Professional's Guide to Personal Training*. San Diego: American Council on Exercise.

Anderson, M.K. & Barnum, M.G. (2022). *Foundations of Athletic Training: Prevention, Assessment, and Management* (7th ed.). Philadelphia: Wolters Kluwer.

Anshel, M.H. (Ed.) (2019). *APA Handbook of Sport and Exercise Psychology: Vol. 2. Exercise Psychology*. Washington, D.C.: American Psychological Association.

Balady, G.J. et al. (1998). AHA/ACSM Scientific Statement: Recommendations for cardiovascular screening, staffing, and emergency policies at health/fitness facilities: A Joint Position Statement by the American College of Sports Medicine and the American Heart Association. *Circulation*, 97, 2283–2293.

Kaminski, T.W. et al. (2013). National Athletic Trainers' Association position statement: Conservative management and prevention of ankle sprains in athletes. *Journal of Athletic Training*, 48, 4, 528–545.

Prentice, W.E. (2020). *Essentials of Athletic Injury Management* (11th ed.). New York: McGraw-Hill.

SUGGESTED READINGS

Myers, C. (2019). *How to Work Around Your Clients' Injuries*. https://www.acefitness.org/education-and-resources/professional/certified/january-2019/7165/how-to-work-around-your-clients-injuries/

Nitschke, E. (2017). *How to Work with Clients Who Have Chronic Conditions*. https://www.acefitness.org/education-and-resources/professional/expert-articles/6385/how-to-work-with-clients-who-have-chronic-conditions/#:~:text=Encourage%20regular%20and%20consistent%20aerobic,exercise%20session%20to%2030%20minutes.

Price, J. (2014). *Understanding and Alleviating Plantar Fasciitis*. https://www.acefitness.org/education-and-resources/professional/prosource/april-2014/3766/understanding-and-alleviating-plantar-fasciitis/

Stull, K. (2021). *Carpal Tunnel Syndrome Stretches: Corrective Exercise for the Wrist*. https://blog.nasm.org/fitness/carpal-tunnel-syndrome-corrective-exercise-programming-wrist

Wang, Z.R., & Ni, G.X. (2021). Is it time to put traditional cold therapy in rehabilitation of soft tissue injuries out to pasture? *World Journal of Clinical Cases*, 9, 17, 4116–4122.

CHAPTER 14

Legal Guidelines and Professional Responsibilities

MARK S. NAGEL, EdD | Professor, Sport and Entertainment Management Department, University of South Carolina

IN THIS CHAPTER

LEARNING OBJECTIVES

Upon completion of this chapter, the reader will be able to:

- Identify ways to stay current through ongoing education and training in order to safely and effectively instruct participants
- Understand important legal terms—including liability, negligence, standard of care, copyright, and trademark—and how each relates to a career in the fitness industry
- Describe a group fitness instructor's responsibilities related to health screening, instruction, supervision, facilities, equipment, and transportation
- Explain the appropriate use of legal forms, including waivers, informed consents, and agreements to participate
- Describe the differences between an independent contractor and employee

ACE UNIVERSITY

If your study program includes ACE University, visit www.ACEfitness.org/MyACE and log in to your My ACE Account to take full advantage of the ACE Group Fitness Instructor Study Program and online guided study experience.

A variety of media to support and expand on the material in this text is provided to facilitate learning and best prepare you for the ACE Group Fitness Instructor Certification exam and a career as a group fitness instructor.

To provide safe and effective classes in which both participants and the instructor are protected legally, ACE Certified Group Fitness Instructors (GFIs) must understand the fundamental professional and business-related concerns that pertain to the group fitness environment. This chapter offers guidance to help instructors navigate the legal aspects of a career in the health and fitness industry.

Legal Framework

Although most people who teach or administer group fitness programs have received training in exercise instruction, often their knowledge of the law related to their profession is limited. With the continual evolution of the health and fitness industry, GFIs must develop and maintain an understanding of basic legal concepts that apply to the field in which they practice. This chapter is not meant to prepare GFIs to become attorneys but will help them recognize applicable legal issues and communicate more effectively with attorneys. From employment status and **copyright** law to insurance coverage and **risk management,** learning how these concepts apply to the group fitness setting will help minimize the risk of injury to participants, decrease the potential for litigation (i.e., the pursuit of legal action), and mitigate potential damages.

Although the chapter goes into detail on legal issues related specifically to the fitness industry, the most important legal considerations for a GFI are fairly straightforward:

- Everything that is done must be explainable and defendable.
- If it does not follow common sense, do not do it.
- If there is any doubt about the potential safety of an activity, do not engage in it.
- Legal standards change, so it is important to stay abreast of local, state, and federal guidelines.
- A small fee with an attorney and an insurance consultant early is more effective than a series of large fees later.

In many legally detrimental situations that have occurred, the exercise professional could have avoided significant legal problems if they had simply remained mindful of the aforementioned considerations.

THINK IT THROUGH

Considering Legal Questions

How much time do you spend thinking about the law and its impact upon your career as a GFI? What specific legal-related questions do you have that pertain to your profession? Compile a list of questions or concerns that you plan on discussing with a lawyer with expertise in the fitness industry.

LIABILITY AND NEGLIGENCE

The term **liability** refers to responsibility. Legal liability concerns the responsibilities recognized by a court of law. Every GFI who stands in front of a class maintains the responsibilities of recognizing the capacities of, and setting limitations on, participants before they begin and as they continue throughout an exercise program. They also have the added responsibility of ensuring that the facilities and equipment are appropriate and safe before beginning any exercise activity. Although health and exercise professionals simply cannot avoid liability, liabilities may be reduced through adherence to the appropriate **standard of care** and the implementation of certain risk-management principles.

The responsibilities arising from the relationship between the GFI and the participant produce a legal expectation, commonly referred to as the standard of care. This means that the quality of services provided in a fitness setting is commensurate with current professional standards.

Negligence is usually defined as "failure to act as a reasonable and prudent person would act under a similar circumstance." For the GFI, this definition has two important components. The first deals specifically with actions. "Failure to act" refers to acts of omission as well as acts of commission. In other words, a GFI can be successfully sued for not doing something that should have been done—such as not adequately preparing a safe exercise environment—as well as for doing something that should not have been done—such as forcing a participant to continue exercising when they clearly were exhausted and/or injured. The second part of the definition of negligence pertains to the appropriateness of the action in light of the standard of care, or a "reasonable and prudent" professional standard. In a lawsuit, the court would ask the question, "What would a reasonable, competent, and prudent GFI do in a similar situation?" If other qualified instructors would have acted similarly under the same circumstances, a court would probably not find an instructor's action negligent.

To legally substantiate a charge of negligence, four elements must be shown to exist (Wong, 2010):

- *Duty:* The **defendant** (person being sued) had a duty to protect the **plaintiff** (person filing the suit) from injury.
- *Breech:* The defendant breeched their duty or, stated differently, failed to exercise the standard of care necessary to perform that duty.
- *Injury (proximate cause):* Such failure was the proximate cause of the plaintiff's injury.
- *Damages:* The injury caused damage to occur to the plaintiff.

APPLY WHAT YOU KNOW

Negligence Example

A GFI is leading a **high-intensity interval training (HIIT)** class in which a participant badly sprains their ankle while following instructions for a series of high-impact exercises. The movement sequence that directly involved the injury consisted of an excessive number of jump squats. If the participant sues the instructor for negligence, the following questions and answers would likely be discussed in court:

- *Was it the instructor's duty to provide proper instruction?* Yes, instructors of group fitness classes have a duty to their participants to provide proper instruction.

- *Was that duty satisfactorily performed?* Performing an excessive number of repetitions of a high-intensity, high-impact exercise like jump squats is not usually advocated by group fitness instructors, indicating that the standard of care was likely violated.
- *Was the instructor's failure to provide safe instruction the direct cause of the injury?* The plaintiff will likely successfully argue that the injury was directly caused by the excessive repetition of the movement.
- *Did actual damages occur?* The plaintiff's doctor will certainly testify that an injury occurred and, at a minimum, damages involving medical care will be sought.

Areas of Responsibility

The duties assigned to health and exercise professionals vary from one position to another and from organization to organization. Five major areas of responsibility are presented in this section: health screening, instruction, supervision, facilities and equipment, and transportation. Each area poses unique questions that are important to every certified instructor. ACE's Code of Ethics is helpful in guiding the actions of all health coaches and exercise professionals (see the Appendix).

HEALTH SCREENING

An exercise professional's responsibility begins when a new participant walks in the door. Most prospective participants will be apparently healthy individuals interested in improving their personal health and fitness. Others, however, may not have exercised in years or may have various health/medical conditions that affect their safety while participating in physical activity. Although most GFIs are not responsible for health screening, it is recommended that facility personnel conduct a preparticipation screening for each participant to determine and document the need for medical clearance based on any existing conditions, **signs** and **symptoms** of underlying metabolic, cardiovascular, or renal disease, and current physical-activity levels that might affect safe performance in an exercise program (see Chapter 4).

The screening procedure should be valid, simple, cost- and time-efficient, and, most importantly, appropriate for the target population. Screening questionnaires should ideally be interpreted and documented by qualified staff to limit the number of unnecessary medical referrals and avoid barriers to participation. In many cases, the health-history form may indicate that certain individuals should not be participating in certain forms of physical activity or should only participate to a certain level of exertion.

Instructors have been charged with negligence for not accurately assessing available information that could have prevented an injury. Every fitness facility should establish policies and procedures to ensure that each participant's personal history and medical information are taken into account.

Health Screening Guidelines

Each participant beginning a fitness program should receive a thorough screening. In many facilities and programs, this screening will be performed by someone other than the GFI. Specific risk-management criteria may include the following:

- Evaluation is conducted prior to participating in exercise. If a potential exercise participant asks to "try out a workout and get the health screening done later," that person should not be permitted to engage in any activities until they have submitted the proper health-screening forms.
- Screening methods concur with national guidelines (such as those recommended by the American Council on Exercise, American College of Sports Medicine, and American Heart Association).

INSTRUCTION

To conduct a safe and effective exercise class, GFIs are expected to provide instruction that is both adequate and proper. Adequate instruction refers to the amount of direction given to participants before and during activity that is both sufficient and understandable. For example, an instructor who asks a class to perform a complex exercise without first demonstrating how to do it properly (act of omission) could be found negligent if a participant performs the exercise incorrectly and is injured as a result (proximate cause). Proper instruction, on the other hand, is factually correct and reflects what a reasonable, prudent instructor would provide in the same situation. In other words, an instructor may be liable for a participant's injury resulting from an exercise that was not demonstrated or was demonstrated improperly (act of commission), or from an unsafe exercise that should not have been included in a group fitness class based on the GFI's standard of care.

In the courtroom, the correctness of instruction is usually assessed by an expert witness who describes the proper procedures for conducting the activity in question. Therefore, the instructional techniques used by a GFI should be consistent with professionally recognized standards. Proper certification from a program accredited by the National Commission for Certifying Agencies (NCCA) or a comparable third-party accreditor of certification programs, as well as appropriate documentation of training (e.g., degrees and continuing education), can enhance a GFI's competence in the eyes of a court, should they ever be charged with negligence.

In addition to providing adequate and proper instruction, GFIs should be careful not to diagnose or suggest treatment for injuries. This includes not only those injuries sustained in class, but also those injuries that occur during other activities. When participants ask for medical advice regarding injuries, GFIs must refer them to the appropriate medical provider. In general, only physicians and certain other healthcare providers are allowed to diagnose and treat injuries.

APPLY WHAT YOU KNOW

Considerations When Offering Advice

Even providing advice that may seem like "common sense" to the GFI can result in potential legal problems, especially when the participant is not familiar with typical injury rehabilitation.

Consider the following situation: When a participant sprained their ankle during a group fitness class, the instructor told them to go home and ice the ankle to reduce the swelling. Because the ice made the injury feel much better, the participant kept their foot in ice water for two hours. As a consequence, several of their toes later had to be amputated because of frostbite.

While this example may be extreme, it serves as a valuable warning, as the instructor could have avoided this unfortunate situation. In an instance like this, the best approach would be for the GFI to provide specific instructions (both written and verbal) on the first-aid procedures recommended by the American Heart Association or the American Red Cross and suggest that if the injury did not respond well, then the participant should seek the advice of a physician.

Instruction Guidelines

A GFI must provide instruction that is both "adequate and proper." To fulfill this standard of care, the following criteria would apply to instruction:

- Instructions or directions provided to participants prior to, and during, activity are sufficient and understandable.
- The GFI conforms to the standard of care (what a reasonable and prudent instructor would provide in the same situation).

SUPERVISION

The GFI is responsible for supervising all aspects of a class. The standards that apply to supervision are the same as those for instruction: adequate and proper. A prerequisite to determining adequate supervision is the ratio of participants to instructors. A prudent instructor should allow a class to be only as large as can be competently monitored. The participant:instructor ratio will, of course, vary with activity, facility, and type of participant. An exercise class of 30 may be appropriate in a large yoga studio, but too big for a Pilates reformer class. Adequate and proper supervision may be different for a class of seasoned participants than for a class of novice exercisers.

With the proliferation of online fitness activities, "proper supervision" is undergoing reassessment. Traditional, in-person classes provide the instructor an easier opportunity to view and assess the progress of each participant through a concerted examination of the exercise environment. The online class environment makes it more difficult for an instructor to observe the progress, and potential incorrect form or even distress, of each participant, since the participants may appear small on a computer screen, if their cameras are even turned on. Though this is an evolving area of law, GFIs teaching classes in an online environment should ensure that their desktop, laptop, phone, or other electronic delivery device has a high-resolution camera and fully functioning microphone so that the instructor can be seen and heard and any participant desiring to ask a question can attract the attention of the GFI. In addition, GFIs should always do the following at the beginning of, and/or consistently throughout, the class:

- Remind participants that the instructor cannot monitor all of their movements in the same manner as they could in an in-person class, and that the participant needs to monitor their own progress and slow down and rest if needed. Participants should also be reminded not to put themselves in physical distress and to inform the GFI if they are having concerns.
- Remind participants that for some exercise movements, they may need to stop their activity to observe the instructor's demonstration. Participants should not strain their necks to constantly watch the instructor's feed, particularly if activities involve the participant exercising on the ground in a **prone** position (e.g., yoga or stretching classes).
- Provide additional time after demonstrating a movement for participants to begin the exercise. In some cases, participants may need to adjust their body positioning and/or the position of their electronic device/camera before transitioning from one exercise to another. In some cases, the number of class exercises/movements and/or transitions from one activity to another may need to be lowered when teaching classes in an online environment rather than in-person.

Given the online environment, GFIs may need to spend some time investigating and practicing the use of various computers, cameras, camera positions (e.g., on a tripod and focused vertically or horizontally), and microphones. In addition, the distance that the GFI stands/sits from the camera for optimal viewing may be different for various types of classes and exercises.

Certainly, the teaching of online classes is likely to continue to expand in prevalence and GFIs should be aware of the potential risks and benefits of delivering classes in this manner. Having patience is especially important, as even if the GFI may have extensive online experience, not all participants will have that same level of familiarity.

In situations where a class may be taught "on demand" rather than live with potential instructor feedback as an element of the class, the GFI needs to be especially focused on providing adequate instruction. A class delivered from a pre-recorded session removes the element of instructor supervision, so an emphasis should be placed on providing even more time for demonstration and additional reminders in the recorded session for participants to observe proper form and to rest as needed. Because of the lack of access to direct communication with the instructor, the video must provide sufficient demonstration and reminders for safety that the GFI would provide in a "live class."

Supervision Guidelines

GFIs must perform their supervisory duties in accordance with the following professionally devised and established guidelines:

- Continuous supervision is provided in immediate proximity to the participant to ensure safety.
- Larger groups are supervised from the perimeter of the exercise area to ensure all participants are in full view of the instructor.
- Specific supervision is employed when the activity merits close attention to an individual participant.
- As supervision standards for teaching in the online environment are still being established and modified, the GFI must remain appraised of developments in this area.

FACILITIES AND EQUIPMENT

Safety is the basic issue for a fitness facility. Instructors should continually inspect the environment and ensure that it is free from unreasonable hazards and that all areas of the facility are appropriate for the specific type of activity to be conducted in that area. For example, dance-based fitness and martial arts classes require a floor surface that will cushion the feet, knees, and legs from inordinate amounts of stress (see Chapter 6).

Some facilities provide locker rooms and showers for participants to use. These areas must be sanitary and the floors must be textured to reduce accidental slipping. Although most GFIs are not responsible for designing and maintaining the fitness facility, any potential problem the GFI detects should be reported and corrected as soon as possible. Until a correction is made, appropriate signs should be clearly posted to warn participants of the unsafe conditions, and access to the area should be restricted.

In some cases, a GFI may be assigned to teach in an area of the fitness facility that is unsafe or inappropriate for the activity. Under these circumstances, a prudent instructor would refuse to teach and would document that decision in writing to club or studio management so that constructive action may be taken.

For a program that uses exercise equipment, the legal concerns center primarily on selection, installation, maintenance, and repair. Equipment should meet all appropriate safety and design standards in the industry. If the equipment has been recently purchased from a competent manufacturer and is maintained properly, these standards will probably be met.

GFIs should instruct each participant regarding equipment safety. In addition, each instructor should be required to examine the equipment before each use and report any problems immediately.

Facility and Equipment Guidelines

The central focus is whether the environment is free from unreasonable hazards. Examples of risk-management criteria include the following:

- The floor surface is appropriate for each activity.
- Lighting is adequate for performance of the skill and for supervision.
- Entrances and exits are well marked.
- An appropriate temperature (not too hot or too cold) is maintained in the room.

In terms of equipment, the legal concerns center primarily on selection, maintenance, and repair. A risk-management plan should examine the following points:

- Equipment selected meets all safety and design standards within the industry.
- Assembly of equipment follows manufacturers' guidelines.
- A schedule of regular service and repair is established and documented.
- Caution is exercised in relation to recommending equipment.
- Homemade equipment is avoided.

In cases where a class is taught online, the instructor should remind participants to ensure their workout area is clear of any potential hazards and that their environment is conducive to exercise (e.g., the room has a comfortable temperature and proper ventilation and the participant is wearing appropriate shoes and clothing). The instructor should also remind participants to only use proper equipment that is designed specifically for the activities that will take place during the session. Online environments present challenges for the instructor in determining what equipment a participant may be utilizing, but they should remind the participants of the need for maintaining a safe environment while they access the class remotely.

TRANSPORTATION

In most cases, transportation of participants is not a concern for the GFI. Participants are expected to arrive and depart from the facility by arranging their own transportation (or they will participate online). However, in some instances, an activity that is scheduled "off-site" may involve the GFI helping to transport participants. This offers potential legal concerns for the GFI, whether they do this as a mandated part of their work for a fitness facility or if they volunteer to help participants.

If the GFI is asked to transport participants by their employer, they should make sure that the employer's insurance covers the GFI for this type of activity. Ideally, the employer will provide written requirements for the GFI to complete this task so that if something were to occur, the GFI would be able to produce documentation as to the specific requirement to transport class participants. If the GFI desires to transport participants of their own volition, they should understand that their standard **professional liability insurance** policy may not cover them while driving (since it is not within a GFI's **scope of practice**) and their standard automobile insurance policy may not cover injuries (and resulting damages awarded through litigation) for their passengers, since those passengers were transported for a business purpose. Ultimately, it is good practice to avoid transporting participants, but if the situation arises, the GFI should make special arrangements to ensure they are covered for potential injuries for themselves and their passengers.

Transportation Guidelines

- Providing transportation to participants is typically not advisable since it is not part of the core functions of a GFI.
- If a GFI who is an employee is requested by their employer to provide transportation for participants, they should confirm that request in writing.
- Specific insurance clauses in professional liability and automobile liability policies may need to be secured before transporting participants.

Implementation of a Risk-management System

There are risks to any activity, but exercise programs carry certain special risks due to the physical movement and exertion often required. Typical risk-management practices in health and fitness involve evaluating the severity of risks and then the likely occurrence of those risks. Some risks of injuries that are minor will be accepted, as things like sprains and strains can certainly occur during exercise. To eliminate all risks of minor injuries would require no physical exertion of any kind, which obviously is not an option for the GFI and their participants. Other activities that have high risk (such as severe cardiovascular distress) but low occurrence can be transferred to the participant and/or an insurance carrier. Risks that are low but could occur often in a specific scenario (such as having participants do wide-moving exercises that take them from one side of a room to another in a limited space) can be mitigated by altering the choice of exercise to better match the environment.

Since physical activity involves a number of potential issues, every GFI should contemplate the potential risks of the various activities they will employ. Identifying and evaluating those risks is a key component of an effective risk-management system. In most cases, a good risk-management system will involve the following five steps:

- *Risk identification:* This step involves the specification of all risks that may be encountered in the areas of instruction, supervision, facilities, equipment, and transportation.
- *Risk evaluation:* The GFI must review each risk, with consideration given to the probability that the risk could occur and, if it does occur, the conceivable severity. Table 14-1 can be used to assess the identified risks.
- *Selection of an approach for managing each risk:* Several approaches are available to the GFI for managing and reducing the identified risks:
    - *Avoidance:* Remove the possibility of danger and injury by eliminating the activity.
    - *Transfer:* Move the risk to others through **waivers,** insurance policies, etc.
    - *Reduction:* Modify the risks by removing or altering part of the activity.
    - *Retention:* Often, there are risks that will be retained, especially if the removal of the risk would eliminate a potential benefit (e.g., no risks will occur if exercise is eliminated, but then no health benefits can be accrued).

The recommended approach for extreme risks is to avoid the activity completely. Risks that fall into one of the high categories can be managed either through insurance or viable actions to reduce the likelihood of occurrence or severity of outcome. Reduction is also the preferred method for addressing risks in the medium category, while risks with low impact can be retained. Remember, for any choice regarding risk management, a potential court proceeding will assess if the GFI acted as a reasonable and prudent professional would in similar circumstances.

- *Implementation:* Institute the plan.
- *Evaluation:* Continually assess the outcome of risk-management endeavors. The standard of care regarding some risks may change over time. Therefore, risk-management approaches may need to be altered.

TABLE 14-1

Evaluating Risk Based on Frequency and Severity

Severity of Injury or Financial Impact	Frequency of Occurrence		
	High or Often	Medium or Infrequent	Low or Seldom
High or Vital	Avoid	Avoid or transfer	Transfer
Medium or Significant	Avoid or transfer	Transfer, reduce, or retain	Transfer, reduce, or retain
Low or Insignificant	Retain	Retain	Retain

GFIs should constantly search for methods to make the environment safer for their participants. Periodically reviewing programs, facilities, and equipment to evaluate potential dangers allows the GFI to decide the best way to minimize potentially costly injuries.

WAIVERS, INFORMED CONSENTS, AND AGREEMENTS TO PARTICIPATE

An important element of being a successful exercise professional is utilizing proper techniques and tools to limit the risk of injury to participants and to reduce the risk of liability for the instructor. Within the health profession, three documents are often utilized to assist with potential legal concerns arising from exercise and associated activities. Each serves a specific purpose, and one may be more appropriate to utilize than the others in various situations and locations.

The staff members of many facilities attempt to absolve themselves of liability by having all participants sign a liability waiver to release the instructor and fitness center from all liability associated with the conduct of an exercise program and any resulting injuries. Waivers transfer the risk of injury to the participant. Waivers typically include some of the language of an **informed consent** form (letting participants know of the dangers of physical activities) and an **agreement to participate** form (expressly stating that the participant freely agrees to engage in the program) but include a specific clause that states that the signer agrees not to sue the GFI.

Specific language in a waiver can be recognized differently in various jurisdictions. In some cases, "universal" waivers have been of little value because the courts in some states have enforced the specific wording of the waiver under their own state laws. What may be legal and properly worded in one state may not apply in another state. Further, some states do not formally recognize waivers (O'Malley, 2019). Every waiver needs to specifically mention that negligence on the part of the instructor or fitness center is waived if the waiver is to be effective. Therefore, waivers must be clearly written and include statements to the effect that the participant waives all claims to damages, even those caused by the negligence of the instructor or fitness center.

Waivers are typically governed by state law, so if an online class is to be conducted, the location of the participant is of utmost importance. An instructor may conduct a class in one state while a participant is in another state, necessitating that the participant signs a waiver that is appropriate for the state in which they reside. It is critical that an attorney who is experienced in specific state law regarding the fitness industry be consulted when crafting waivers and other participation documents.

A sample waiver is presented in Figure 14-1.

FIGURE 14-1
Sample waiver

I, ______________________________, by attending group fitness classes, have agreed to voluntarily participate in an exercise program, including, but not limited to, cardiorespiratory, muscular, and flexibility training under the guidance of [name of group fitness instructor and/or business]. I hereby stipulate and agree that I am physically and mentally sound and currently have no physical conditions that would be aggravated by my involvement in an exercise program. I have provided verification from a licensed physician that I am able to undertake a general fitness-training program.

I understand and am aware that physical-fitness activities, including the use of equipment, are potentially hazardous activities. I am aware that participating in these types of activities, even when performed properly, can be dangerous. I agree to follow the verbal instructions issued by the group fitness instructor. I am aware that potential risks associated with these types of activities include, but are not limited to: death, fainting, disorders in heartbeat, serious neck and spinal injuries that may result in complete or partial paralysis or brain damage, serious injury to virtually all bones, joints, ligaments, muscles, tendons, and other aspects of the musculoskeletal system, and serious injury or impairment to other aspects of my body, general health, and well-being.

I understand that I am responsible for my own medical insurance and will maintain that insurance throughout my entire period of participation with [name of group fitness instructor and/or business]. I will assume any additional expenses incurred that go beyond my health coverage. I will notify the [name of group fitness instructor and/or business] of any significant injury or change in health status that requires medical attention (such as emergency care, hospitalization, etc.).

[name of group fitness instructor or business] or I will provide the equipment to be used in connection with workouts, including, but not limited to, benches, dumbbells, barbells, and similar

Continued on the next page

FIGURE 14-1
(continued)

items. I represent and warrant any and all equipment I provide for training sessions is for personal use only. [name of group fitness instructor or business] has not inspected my equipment and has no knowledge of its condition. I understand that I take sole responsibility for my equipment. I acknowledge that although [name of group fitness instructor and/or business] takes precautions to maintain the equipment, any equipment may malfunction and/or cause potential injuries. I take sole responsibility to inspect any and all of my or [name of group fitness instructor and/or business]'s equipment prior to use.

Although [name of group fitness instructor and/or business] will take precautions to ensure my safety, I expressly assume and accept sole responsibility for my safety and for any and all injuries that may occur. In consideration of the acceptance of this entry, **I, for myself and for my executors, administrators, and assigns, waive and release any and all claims against [name of group fitness instructor and/or business] and any of their staff, officers, officials, volunteers, sponsors, agents, representatives, successors, or assigns and agree to hold them harmless from any claims or losses, including but not limited to claims for negligence for any injuries or expenses that I may incur while exercising or while traveling to and from training sessions.** These exculpatory clauses are intended to apply to any and all activities occurring during the time for which I have contracted with [name of group fitness instructor and/or company].

I represent and warrant I am signing this agreement freely and willfully and not under fraud or duress.

HAVING READ THE ABOVE TERMS AND INTENDING TO BE LEGALLY BOUND HEREBY AND UNDERSTANDING THIS DOCUMENT TO BE A COMPLETE WAIVER AND DISCLAIMER IN FAVOR OF [name of group fitness instructor and/or business], I HEREBY AFFIX MY SIGNATURE HERETO.

____

Participant's name (please print clearly)

_______________________________ Date: ____________

Participant's signature

____

Participant's address

_______________________________ Date: ____________

Parent/guardian signature (if applicable)

_______________________________ Date: ____________

Group fitness instructor's signature

Note: This document has been prepared to serve as a guide to improve understanding. Group fitness instructors should not assume that this sample form will provide adequate protection in the event of a lawsuit. Please see an attorney before creating, distributing, and collecting any agreements to participate, informed consent forms, or waivers.

Though a waiver is the most powerful written tool in protecting a GFI and/or a fitness facility from potential liability, some fitness centers require the signing of an informed consent form before allowing people to participate in unique, structured physical activities. While this document has many similar components to most waivers, it does not ask the participant to waive their right to sue. In states where waivers are recognized, a general waiver may be utilized for most physical activities, and specific informed consent forms may also be signed when unique programs, activities, or assessments are first implemented. In other states, the informed consent form is needed since waivers are not formally recognized. Regardless of the presence of a waiver, the informed consent form is used to make the dangers of a program or assessment procedure known to the participant and thereby provide an additional measure of defense against lawsuits.

Obtaining informed consent is very important because GFIs need participants to understand activities and appreciate associated dangers. The following should be an automatic procedure for every person who begins an exercise program:

- Inform the participant of the exercise program and explain the purpose of its activities.
- Provide a thorough and unbiased written explanation.
- Inform the participant of the risks involved in the program, along with the possible discomforts.
- Inform the participant of the benefits expected from the program.
- Solicit questions regarding the testing procedure or exercise program and give unbiased answers to these inquiries.
- Inform the participant that they are free, at any time, to discontinue participation.
- Obtain the written consent of each participant.

In most cases, an informed consent form signed before participating for the first time will cover all fitness activities for that participant. However, in special cases where a "test" may be conducted, an additional informed consent form may be utilized (Figure 14-2). Additional informed consent forms are sometimes utilized by GFIs and/or fitness centers when collecting data to analyze for tracking health and fitness improvements. Collected data may be shared either publicly or anonymously to track progress made since baseline measures were first collected. Subsequent informed consent forms should not only inform the participant of the unique aspects of the test, but also remind them that their participation is voluntary and, if applicable, indicate potential alternatives that may be more advantageous to them.

FIGURE 14-2
Sample informed consent form

CARDIORESPIRATORY FITNESS TEST

Informed Consent for Exercise Testing of Apparently Healthy Adults
(without known heart disease)

Name ____

1. Purpose and Explanation of Test

I hereby consent to voluntarily engage in an exercise test to determine my cardiorespiratory fitness. It is my understanding that the information obtained will help me evaluate future physical activities and sports activities in which I may engage.

Before I undergo the test, I certify that I am in good health and have had a physical examination conducted by a licensed medical physician within the past ________ months. Further, I hereby represent and inform the facility that I have accurately completed the pre-test health-history questionnaire or interview presented to me by the facility staff and have provided correct responses to the questions as indicated on the health-history form or as supplied to the interviewer. It is my understanding that I will be interviewed by a physician or other person prior to my undergoing the test who will in the course of interviewing me determine if there are any reasons that would make it undesirable or unsafe for me to take the test. Consequently, I understand that it is important that I provide complete and accurate responses to the interviewer and recognize that my failure to do so could lead to possible unnecessary injury to myself during the test.

The test that I will undergo will be performed on a motor-driven treadmill or bicycle ergometer with the amount of effort gradually increasing. As I understand it, this increase in effort will continue until I feel and verbally report to the operator any symptoms such as fatigue, shortness of breath, or chest discomfort that I may experience. It is my understanding and I have been clearly advised that it is my right to request that a test be stopped at any point if I feel unusual discomfort or fatigue. I have been advised that I should, immediately upon experiencing any such symptoms or if I so choose, inform the operator that I wish to stop the test at that or any other point. My wishes in this regard shall be absolutely carried out.

During the test itself, it is my understanding that a trained observer will monitor my responses continuously and take frequent readings of blood pressure, the electrocardiogram, and my expressed feelings of effort. I realize that a true determination of my exercise capacity depends on progressing the test to the point of fatigue.

Once the test has been completed, but before I am released from the test area, I will be given special instructions about showering and recognition of certain symptoms that may appear within

Initial: _____

FIGURE 14-2
(continued)

the first 24 hours after the test. I agree to follow these instructions and promptly contact the facility personnel or medical providers if such symptoms develop.

2. Risks

It is my understanding and I have been informed that there exists the possibility of adverse changes during the actual test. I have been informed that these changes could include abnormal blood pressure, fainting, disorders of heart rhythm, stroke, and very rare instances of heart attack or even death. Every effort, I have been told, will be made to minimize these occurrences by preliminary examination and by precautions and observations taken during the test. I have also been informed that emergency equipment and personnel are readily available to deal with these unusual situations should they occur. I understand that there is a risk of injury, heart attack, stroke, or even death as a result of my performance of this test, but knowing those risks, it is my desire to proceed to take the test as herein indicated.

3. Benefits to Be Expected and Alternatives Available to the Exercise Testing Procedure

The results of this test may or may not benefit me. Potential benefits relate mainly to my personal motives for taking the test (e.g., knowing my exercise capacity in relation to the general population, understanding my fitness for certain sports and recreational activities, planning my physical conditioning program, or evaluating the effects of my recent physical habits). Although my fitness might also be evaluated by alternative means (e.g., a bench step test or an outdoor running test), such tests do not provide as accurate a fitness assessment as the treadmill or bike test, nor do those options allow equally effective monitoring of my responses.

4. Confidentiality and Use of Information

I have been informed that the information that is obtained from this exercise test will be treated as privileged and confidential and will consequently not be released or revealed to any person without my express written consent or as required by law. I do, however, agree to the use of any information for research or statistical purposes so long as same does not provide facts that could lead to the identification of my person. Any other information obtained, however, will be used only by the facility staff to evaluate my exercise status or needs.

5. Inquiries and Freedom of Consent

I have been given an opportunity to ask questions about the procedure. Generally, these requests, which have been noted by the testing staff, and their responses are as follows:

____

____

Initial: ______

Continued on the next page

FIGURE 14-2
(continued)

I further understand that there are also other remote risks that may be associated with this procedure. Despite the fact that a complete accounting of all remote risks is not entirely possible, I am satisfied with the review of these risks, which was provided to me, and it is still my desire to proceed with the test.

I acknowledge that I have read this document in its entirety or that it has been read to me if I have been unable to read same.

I consent to the rendition of all services and procedures as explained herein by all facility personnel.

Date ______________________________

Participant's Signature ______________________________

Witness' Signature ______________________________

Test Supervisor's Signature ______________________________

Modified with permission from Herbert, D.L. & Herbert, W.G. (2002). *Legal Aspects of Preventive, Rehabilitative, and Recreational Exercise Programs* (4th ed.). Canton, Oh.: PRC Publishing. Pages 467–470.

Note: This document has been prepared to serve as a guide to improve understanding. Group fitness instructors should not assume that this sample form will provide adequate protection in the event of a lawsuit. Please see an attorney before creating, distributing, and collecting any agreements to participate, informed consent forms, or waivers.

Figure 14-3 provides an example of an agreement to participate form, which is designed to protect the GFI from a participant claiming to be unaware of the potential risks of physical activity. An agreement to participate is not typically considered a formal contract, but rather serves to demonstrate that the participant was made aware of the "normal" outcomes of certain types of physical activity and willingly assumed the risks of participation. Typically, the agreement to participate form is utilized for "class" settings and should detail the nature of the activity, the potential risks to be encountered, and the expected behaviors of the participant. This last consideration is important, as the participant recognizes that they may need to follow instructions while participating.

When preparing legal documents, every exercise professional should consult with an attorney who has experience and expertise in state and local laws regarding fitness participation.

Regardless of jurisdiction or unique situation, participants should be required to sign a waiver, informed consent, and/or agreement to participate before they enter a gym and/or begin any exercise program. There have been instances of gyms and/or GFIs allowing participants to "turn in their forms later" but then the participant has been injured while participating and the lack of legal paperwork has hindered the defense to negligence lawsuits. Each of the aforementioned legal documents is designed to protect the GFI and the fitness facility by informing the participant of dangers and then transferring the risks of participation to the participant by their **assumption of risk.** Even in jurisdictions where

FIGURE 14-3
Sample agreement to participate

"I, ______________________, have agreed to participate in a series of group fitness classes including, but not limited to, high-intensity interval training, weight training, stationary bicycling, and the use of various aerobic-conditioning machinery offered by [name of group fitness instructor and/or business]. I am aware that participating in these types of activities, even when completed properly, can be dangerous. I agree to follow the verbal instructions issued by the group fitness instructor. I am aware that potential risks associated with these types of activities include, but are not limited to, death, serious neck and spinal injuries that may result in complete or partial paralysis or brain damage, serious injury to virtually all bones, joints, ligaments, muscles, tendons, and other aspects of the musculoskeletal system, and serious injury or impairment to other aspects of my body, general health, and well-being.

Because of the dangers of participating, I recognize the importance of following the group fitness instructor's instructions regarding proper techniques and training, as well as other organization rules.

I am in good health and have provided verification from a licensed physician that I am able to undertake a general fitness-training program. I hereby consent to first aid, emergency medical care, and admission to an accredited hospital or an emergency care center when necessary for executing such care and for treatment of injuries that I may sustain while participating in an exercise-training program.

I understand that I am responsible for my own medical insurance and will maintain that insurance throughout my entire period of participation with [name of group fitness instructor and/or business]. I will assume any additional expenses incurred that go beyond my health coverage. I will notify [name of group fitness instructor and/or business] of any significant injury or change in health status that requires medical attention (such as emergency care, hospitalization, etc.).

Signed ______________________

Printed Name ______________________

Phone Number ______________________

Address ______________________

Emergency Contact ______________________

Contact Phone Number ______________________

Insurance Company ______________________

Policy # ______________________

Effective Date ______________________

Name of Policy Holder ______________________

Note: This document has been prepared to serve as a guide to improve understanding. Group fitness instructors should not assume that this sample form will provide adequate protection in the event of a lawsuit. Please see an attorney before creating, distributing, and collecting any agreements to participate, informed consent forms, or waivers.

waivers are not formally recognized, having the participant sign paperwork that indicates they know and assume the risks of participation can be a powerful defense in a lawsuit.

The documents referenced and presented in this chapter are designed to serve as a guide to improve understanding. GFIs should not assume that any example included will provide adequate protection in the event of a lawsuit. Please see a local attorney before creating, distributing, and collecting agreements to participate, informed consent forms, and/or waivers. Regardless of jurisdiction or type of activity, it is sound practice to have every participant complete a waiver, informed consent, and/or agreement to participate and a preparticipation health screening before beginning any exercise program.

THINK IT THROUGH

Participation without Signing a Waiver

Before beginning the first session of a six-week boot-camp series, you ask new participants to complete a preparticipation health screening and sign a liability waiver. One participant says that they do not want to sign any paperwork before "trying out the class" and is very excited to just get started. What potential issues might arise if you do not require the participant to sign the waiver?

Liability Insurance

Even after taking precautions by transferring some of the risk of exercise to the participants, it is important for GFIs to be aware of the importance of insurance. The need for insurance is always present, but as GFIs and their businesses become more financially successful, the importance of insurance increases. Insurance protection provides some peace of mind, as GFIs can feel secure knowing that if someone were to be injured as a result of their actions or if a meritless lawsuit were to occur, insurance coverage would be adequate to compensate that individual for their losses.

In general, GFIs should not assume that any of their typically established personal insurance (e.g., auto and home) extends to their professional activities. GFIs need to secure professional liability insurance that is specifically designed to cover work within the health and fitness industry. The selected liability insurance policy should cover personal injuries that can occur as a result of an exercise session. Injured participants may sue not only for medical expenses, but also for a variety of other compensation, such as lost wages from being unable to work and pain and suffering. ACE recommends retaining at least $1 million in coverage, as medical expenses can easily cost hundreds of thousands of dollars. In some instances, a higher liability coverage amount may be advisable.

The American Council on Exercise has established a relationship with a reputable insurance carrier that specializes in insuring professionals within the fitness industry. Visit https://www.acefitness.org/education-and-resources/professional/liability-insurance for more information.

GFIs must understand the specific insurance needs that may arise given the location of the exercise activities. In each policy, a **rider**—a special addition to typical policy provisions—will explain specific details regarding when and where the insurance policy applies. In cases where GFIs will work outside of a fitness center, it is imperative that the insurance carrier is aware of the professional activities that will occur. In most cases, outdoor classes will require insurance (typically at higher rates) that specifically covers the GFIs for these locations. The proliferation of online health and fitness activities has necessitated a reexamination of professional liability insurance. GFIs teaching online should ensure their policies cover this type of class format. For GFIs who own their own businesses, insurance should be retained that covers potential problems with the facility as well as the instruction and supervision of the GFI.

EXPAND YOUR KNOWLEDGE

Understanding an Umbrella Policy

Most insurance agents now recommend that professionals purchase an **umbrella liability policy,** which provides added coverage for all of the other insurance (e.g., auto, home, and professional liability) that a person may have in place. For example, if a GFI was sued and the judgment exceeded their professional liability coverage, the umbrella policy would cover the insurance shortfall. When purchasing an umbrella policy, GFIs should be sure that it covers professional activities associated with group fitness instruction. In addition, every liability policy should be examined to ensure that it covers the GFI while working in various locations (e.g., fitness center, outdoors, and online).

Other Legal Considerations

GFIs are providers of a special service. As a result, they must be familiar with the specific aspects of the law that are most frequently encountered in the conduct of their business.

CONTRACTS

Health and exercise professionals must have an adequate knowledge of legal contracts to perform tasks, get paid, and avoid costly legal battles with participants and/or facilities. Some GFIs will want to work as individuals not affiliated with one particular club, while others may want to be employed by a club or fitness center.

Whatever the nature of the work arrangement, a GFI must be aware of the essentials of contract law. Basic contract law indicates that the following elements are necessary to form a binding contract:

- *An offer and acceptance:* Mutual agreement to terms
- *Consideration:* An exchange of items of value
- *Legality:* Does not involve illegal action
- *Capacity:* Such as majority age (typically 18 years of age in the United States) and mental competency

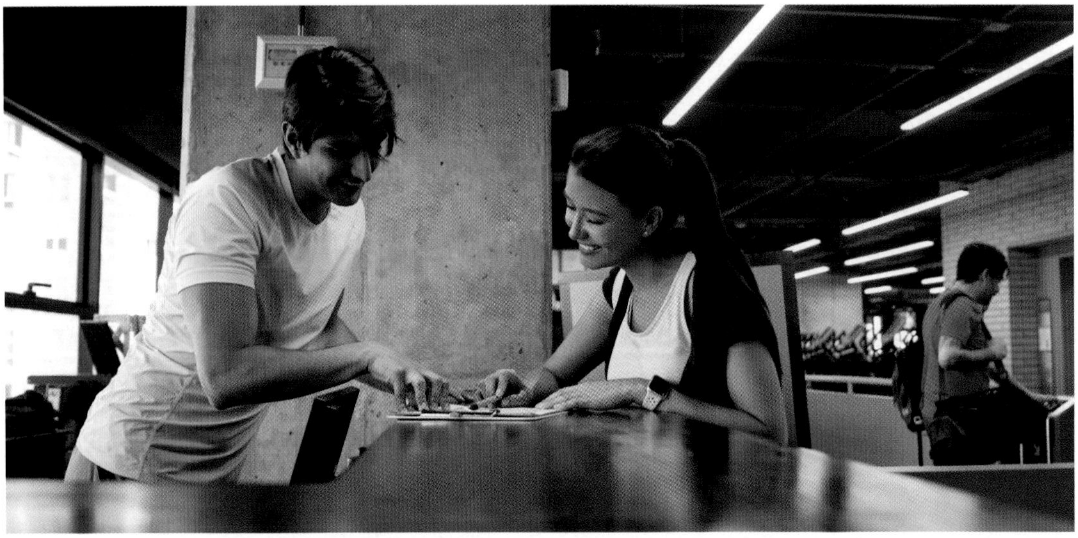

The general considerations that should be addressed in contracts for use with participants, as well as contracts between health and exercise professionals and clubs for which they intend to work, should include the following:

- *Identification of the parties:* GFI and participant/club
- *Description of the services to be performed:* Group fitness instruction and consultation
- *Compensation:* An agreed upon wage or fee per hour, day, month, or class, and payment method
- *Confidential relationship:* Agreement by each party not to divulge personal or business information gained through the relationship
- *Business status:* Confirmation of employment status
- *Term and termination:* Express definition of the length of the contract and the conditions under which termination is allowed by either party

EMPLOYMENT STATUS

Another prominent concern for many health and exercise professionals deals with employment status: **independent contractor** versus **employee.** Both of these terms can apply to those who work in a fitness center. However, only the independent contractor status applies to self-employed GFIs working independently from a club. Most clubs still require independent contractors hired by the club to follow facility rules and to provide proof of liability insurance.

In some instances, owners of fitness centers or clubs have used the term independent contractor to describe employees. Club owners are often motivated to hire independent contractors in place of regular employees because the facility does not have to provide training, offer medical or other benefits, arrange for social security withholding, or pay into worker's compensation or unemployment funds for independent contractors.

A legal dichotomy exists between regular employees and independent contractors. Most commonly, courts have considered a variety of questions or "tests" to determine if the business relationship in question between a club and a health and exercise professional is that of a regular employee or an independent contractor. These tests can include:

- *The extent of control that, by agreement, the employer can exercise over the details of the work:* The existence of a right to control is indicative of an employer–employee relationship.
- *The method of payment, whether by time or by the job:* Generally, those persons scheduled to be paid on a regular basis at an hourly or weekly rate have been considered employees. Conversely, those paid in a single payment for services rendered have more easily qualified as independent contractors.
- *The length of time for which the person is employed:* Individuals hired for short periods of time (a few days or weeks) have more often been seen as independent contractors, whereas employment periods that extended upward of a full year have been ruled as establishing an employer–employee relationship.
- *The skill required for the provision of services:* When the worker needs limited or no training because of the specialized or technical skills that the employer intends to utilize, the worker will likely be viewed as an independent contractor. Conversely, if an employer provides training to a recently hired individual, that person will more than likely be judged to be an employee.
- *Whether the person employed is in a distinct business or occupation:* If a worker offers services to other employers or clients, a status of independent contractor would probably be found. If, however, the worker only intended to provide services for one employer and failed to offer the services to others as an independent business, the employee status will likely be found.
- *Whether the employer or the worker provides the equipment:* Independent contractors typically provide and/or utilize their own equipment.
- *Whether the work is a part of the normal business of the employer:* Court rulings have favored classifying individuals as regular employees when services rendered are integral to the business of the employer. Supplemental, special, or one-time services are more likely to be provided by independent contractors.
- *Whether the work is traditionally performed by a specialist in similar businesses:* Employers and employees must examine their field of business to gain an understanding of current practices and align themselves with the prevailing trends.
- *The intent of the parties involved in the arrangement:* The courts will attempt to enforce intent of the parties at the time the agreement was executed. If a professional thought that they were hired as an independent contractor, as did the club, it would influence the court's determination, though not guarantee a legal outcome. A clear understanding of the arrangement is critical but may not completely guarantee how the relationship is perceived by the courts. This is particularly important in some states that have recently made it more difficult to classify a worker as an independent contractor, especially if the worker engages in activities that are a normal part of the businesses' usual activities (California Department of Industrial Relations, 2021; Myers, Bhuiyan, & Roosevelt, 2019).

The process of determining employment status is marked by careful analysis of the facts and the weighing of interpretations on both sides of the issue. All of the issues addressed in this list have been used in court cases dealing with this matter, each with varying degrees of authority. It is, therefore, imperative that all health and exercise professionals and club owners understand and examine these factors when initiating agreements.

For more specific information on the legal aspects surrounding the independent contractor versus employee issue, consult the guidelines published by the Internal Revenue Service (www.irs.gov).

Regardless of status as an employee or independent contractor, GFIs need to be aware of a small, but growing trend of facilities asking or even mandating that employees not work for other facilities. In some cases, facilities have made a condition of hiring that a contract be signed limiting the GFI's ability to work for another entity. On the surface, these contracts are designed to prevent the GFI from aiding a competitor and to prevent the GFI from becoming "overworked" and not capable of performing to their maximum ability with their primary employer. However, depending on the unique circumstances and jurisdiction of the facility, such contractual requests may be illegal. When presented with such a "restrictive" contract, the GFI should examine the potential compensation provided by the facility. Their financial commitment to the GFI may warrant signing an agreement that limits the GFI's alternative employment or independent contractor options. However, in other cases, the compensation offered may be too low to enable the GFI to maintain a living wage. In those cases, communication should occur and a full discussion of the parameters of the restrictive agreement should be considered before signing. If such a contract is legal and is agreed to, both parties should ensure they adhere to its tenets. From a GFI's perspective, the restrictive elements of the contract should end when the business relationship concludes and there should not be any "**restrictive covenant**" upon completion that limits the GFI's ability to seek work opportunities elsewhere when their relationship with the first facility is concluded.

EXPAND YOUR KNOWLEDGE

When Is an Hour Not an Hour?

GFIs are often hired to teach classes that last a specific period of time. However, in some cases, GFIs are expected or mandated to spend considerable amounts of time before and after classes actively engaged in talking with participants, conducting assessments, and cleaning. Even though a facility may only pay for the "teaching time," given the nature of the GFI's relationship with the fitness facility, in some jurisdictions, these "added responsibilities" must be compensated. Even in cases where the employment contract does not require the added compensation, litigation and settlements have resulted in situations in which fitness facilities have failed to "properly" pay their exercise professionals for these duties (Norfleet, 2020; Dominic, 2017). Though this is largely an unsettled area of state and federal law, the increasing number of lawsuits have prompted many facilities to better explain their expectations, and payment schedules, for exercise professionals. GFIs should communicate with fitness facilities about the expectations and compensation for their performance. If they are required to complete extensive pre- and post-class responsibilities without pay, they should potentially consult with an attorney about the legality of their relationship.

COPYRIGHT LAW

One of a GFI's major legal responsibilities is compliance with copyright law. All forms of commercially produced creative expression are protected by copyright law, but music is the area most pertinent to instructors. This has become an extremely important issue with the availability of downloadable music. Simply stated, almost all musical compositions that one can hear on the radio or television or buy from music outlets online are owned by artists and studios and are protected by federal copyright law. An instructor who creates a playlist of various downloaded songs they have purchased online and then uses that music in a for-profit exercise class—legally speaking, a **public performance**—is in violation of copyright law.

To be able to use copyrighted music in an exercise class, one must obtain a performance license from one of the major **performing rights societies**—the **American Society of Composers, Authors and Publishers (ASCAP), Broadcast Music, Inc. (BMI),** or the **Society of European Stage Authors and Composers (SESAC).** These organizations vigorously enforce copyright law for their memberships and will not hesitate to sue a health club, studio, or freelance instructor who plays copyrighted music without a license. They may also provide options for exercise professionals to use their music in order to maximize their artists' exposure and revenue.

Accordingly, most clubs and studios obtain a **blanket license** for their instructors. The license fees for the clubs are determined by the number of participants who attend classes each week, the number of speakers used in the club, or whether the club has a single- or multifloor layout.

GFIs who teach as independent contractors at several locations and/or who use their own music may have to obtain their own licenses. They should check with the clubs where they teach to see if each club's blanket license covers their classes. One viable option for instructors is to buy licensed music made specifically for fitness classes, where the copyright holder expressly permits the original music to be used in class. Another option common for pre-choreographed classes is for clubs to buy "packaged" group fitness programs where all of the advertising, music, and instructor training are provided, and the fitness center is allowed to use the name brand of the program in its advertising.

Professional liability insurance will usually not cover an instructor for copyright infringement claims or offer protection in suits involving **libel, slander, invasion of privacy,** or **defamation of character.** These sorts of actions may be considered intentional **torts** and are not typically covered.

The proliferation of online fitness classes has resulted in the need to update music licenses to adhere to the new environment. GFIs need to ensure that they are licensed to utilize music not only for in-person classes but also in the online group exercise environment. Importantly, even if one has secured a license to use protected music in an online class, the delivery mechanism can impact the ability to exercise the license. Many social media sites such as Facebook and YouTube have mechanisms to detect and potentially mute copyrighted music (Golden, 2021). It is not advisable to deliver an online fitness class through a platform that may automatically silence music without warning.

EXPAND YOUR KNOWLEDGE

Obtaining Copyright Protection

Some GFIs may want to obtain copyright protection for certain aspects of their own work, including the following:

- *Choreographic work:* If an instructor creates more than a simple routine, and publicly distributes (through a dance notation system), performs, or displays the choreography, it can be copyrighted.
- *Books, videos, and films:* If a choreographed work by an instructor is sold to a publisher, video distributor, or movie studio, that business entity will own the copyright for the material and the instructor will be compensated with either an advance or a certain portion of the proceeds (royalties), or both. Through negotiation with the producing or distributing company, the instructor may be able to retain certain rights to the material.
- *Compilations of exercise routines:* If an instructor makes an original sequence of routines (i.e., a **compilation**), it may be protected by copyright and licensed to others for a book, video, film, or other presentation form.
- *Graphic materials:* If an instructor creates pictures, charts, diagrams, informational handouts, or other graphic materials for instructional aides or promotional material, these too may be copyrighted.

For copyright information or applications, visit www.copyright.gov.

TRADEMARKS

Though it is important for GFIs to protect their developed intellectual property, it is also imperative that instructors respect the intellectual property of others. Many businesses operate in the fitness industry and their unique names, logos, slogans, and other intellectual property cannot be utilized for commercial purposes without their express written consent. For example, Zumba is a popular company, and as such many participants are familiar with the corporate name and the class format they have created. GFIs, or the health and fitness facilities for which they work, cannot advertise their classes

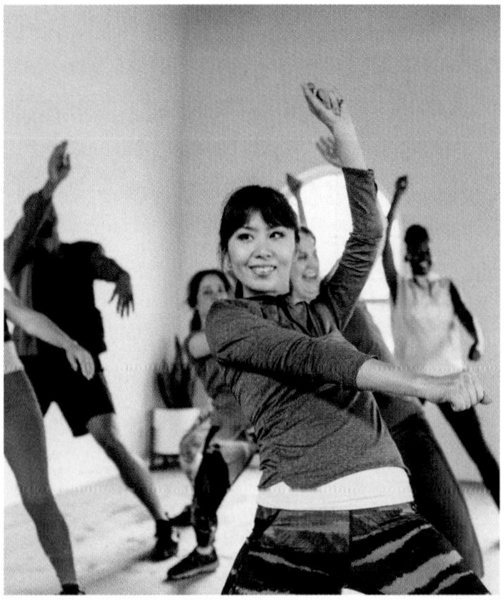

as "Zumba" or "Zumba-like" unless they have successfully completed the Zumba instructor training course and have created the appropriate contractual relationship with Zumba that grants permission to utilize the protected Zumba name.

During the Covid-19 pandemic, a number of exercise professionals who had secured licenses to teach specific "branded" classes (e.g., Zumba, Spin, and Body Pump) in fitness facilities converted to teaching online classes. Even though many of the licensing agreements prohibited such delivery, in some cases companies were lax in their enforcement of these intellectual property violations given the severe lifestyle changes that everyone was forced to endure. GFIs who were licensed to deliver trademarked classes in a fitness facility but not in an online environment should be vigilant in their observation and adherence to updated protocols as they are announced by companies.

SHARED-USE SPACE

There is a growing trend in the health and fitness industry to hold workouts in public settings. Often, this means GFIs are holding classes in an outdoor area rather than a controlled, indoor environment. Prior to conducting any form of exercise, the GFI must research the jurisdiction of the potential workout area to determine what is legal to undertake. Often, it is illegal to instruct participants on public beaches, parks, or trails, even if the class offered is donation-based or not-for-profit. It is the GFI's responsibility to know the local laws prior to using these areas.

Once a "legal" outdoor area has been identified and selected for a class offering, the GFI should be sure to understand the potential dangers of the environment before leading a class for participants. The GFI should also review the weather forecast for potential likelihood of thunderstorms, extreme temperatures, and other potentially dangerous inclement weather. If the weather forecast is deemed acceptable for outdoor exercise, the GFI should inspect the workout area before each class to identify any unusual dangers, as discussed in Chapter 11.

Before undertaking any outdoor or public-space classes, the GFI should consult their insurance policies to ensure such activities are covered. In addition, a consultation with an attorney may provide insights to better assess the legal ramifications of conducting classes away from a fitness center.

AMERICANS WITH DISABILITIES ACT

Health and exercise professionals can be affected by a variety of legislative mandates. One of the laws that affects the profession is the **Americans with Disabilities Act,** which became law in 1992. Modeled after the Civil Rights Act, it prohibits discrimination on the basis of disability. The law provides for equal treatment and equal access to programs for disabled Americans. The act extends provisions to all areas of public accommodation, including businesses such that all participants, regardless of disability, are guaranteed access to all programs and spaces within the facility. Therefore, it is essential that GFIs make sure that their buildings, equipment, and programs are available to persons with disabilities. Employers must also provide reasonable accommodations for employees with disabilities, including adjusted workstations and equipment as necessary.

Therefore, whether a person with a disability is an employee or a participant, steps must be taken to ensure that the professional and business environment is one that respects the dignity, skills, and contributions of that individual.

ENSURING PARTICIPANT CONFIDENTIALITY

When working in the health and fitness industry, GFIs are often exposed to sensitive personal information. Material provided on health screening forms as well as conversations with participants may reveal personal information that should always remain confidential. In order to protect participants' personal data, all individual information should remain secured, away from public access. This may require the GFI to store health screening forms and waivers in a locked file cabinet to prevent unrestricted access. Also, though it may be seen by most as a positive, GFIs must be careful not to share a participant's personal health success story with other participants. Often, "innocent" mistakes are made when a GFI shares a person's weight-loss achievements or other health advancements. Sharing of personal information can not only be against the wishes of a participant but may also potentially be against the law. GFIs should acquire express, written consent from a participant before divulging any participant information. With the proliferation of social media, many GFIs should remember that photos of individual or group fitness activities should remain out of the public domain, just like private participant information. Though some state and local laws differ by jurisdiction, photos identifying individual class participants should not be shared or utilized as marketing tools without the consent of the identified participants. In most cases, permission to utilize photos can be obtained when participants first attend the class and provide their preparticipation health screening information and signed waiver.

EXPAND YOUR KNOWLEDGE

Are State and Local Licenses a Part of the Future?

Since the 1970s, most government entities have believed that third parties would provide the best and most flexible initial and ongoing training to support the health and fitness profession and provide clients and participants with an optimal experience. However, in the first 20 years of the 21st century, a number of states strongly considered adding state license requirements to different areas of the fitness industry (e.g., personal training and group fitness instruction). In most cases, those proposals were not implemented, as the benefits to the government (e.g., higher fees generated and greater control of the industry) were not seen as the best course of action. Though Washington, D.C., enacted a limited accreditation and registration system in 2013, most states largely abandoned the idea until recently (Bedosky, 2018). A number of prominent state politicians have reintroduced the idea of a state licenses for the fitness industry. Given the potential impact of these types of laws (i.e., no license means a person has no ability to work), GFIs should note the potential political activity in the city, county, and state where they work and adhere to any updated regulations.

ACE Professional Practices and Disciplinary Procedures

The ACE Professional Practices and Disciplinary Procedures are intended to assist and inform ACE Certified Professionals, candidates for ACE certification, and the public of the ACE Application and Certification Standards relative to professional conduct and disciplinary procedures. ACE may revoke or otherwise take action with regard to the application or certification of an individual in the case of:

- Ineligibility for certification
- Irregularity in connection with any certification examination
- Unauthorized possession, use, access, or distribution of certification examinations, score reports, trademarks, logos, written materials, answer sheets, certificates, certificant or applicant files, or other confidential or proprietary ACE documents or materials (registered or otherwise)
- Material misrepresentation or fraud in any statement to ACE or to the public including, but not limited to, statements made to assist the applicant, certificant, or another to apply for, obtain, or retain certification
- Any physical, mental, or emotional condition of either temporary or permanent nature, including, but not limited to, substance abuse, which impairs or has the potential to impair competent and objective professional performance
- Negligent and/or intentional misconduct in professional work, including, but not limited to, physical or emotional abuse, disregard for safety, or the unauthorized release of confidential information
- The timely conviction, plea of guilty, or plea of *nolo contendere* ("no contest") in connection with a felony or misdemeanor that is directly related to public health and/or fitness instruction or education, which impairs competent and objective professional performance. These include, but are not limited to, rape,

sexual abuse of a participant, actual or threatened use of a weapon of violence, and the prohibited sale, distribution, or possession with intent to distribute of a controlled substance.

- Failure to meet the requirements for certification or recertification

ACE has developed a three-tiered disciplinary process of review, hearing, and appeals to ensure fair and unbiased examination of alleged violation(s) of the Application and Certification Standards in order to determine the merit of allegations and impose appropriate sanctions as necessary to protect the public and the integrity of the certification process.

THINK IT THROUGH

Legal Requirements of the Fitness Industry

Given the nature of physical activity and the continual evolution of legal standards, what will you do to remain up to date regarding the legal requirements of your profession? What resources can you utilize to not only maintain, but enhance your understanding of the law and its impact on the fitness industry?

ACE UNIVERSITY

If your study program includes ACE University, visit www.ACEfitness.org/MyACE and log in to your My ACE Account to take full advantage of the ACE Group Fitness Instructor Study Program and online guided study experience.

A variety of media to support and expand on the material in this text is provided to facilitate learning and best prepare you for the ACE Group Fitness Instructor Certification exam and a career as a group fitness instructor.

SUMMARY

No group fitness class, regardless of how well it is designed and implemented, can completely avoid all potential participant injuries. In an attempt to reduce injuries to participants and minimize the potential legal complications, GFIs and facility management would be wise to adhere to the following guidelines:

- Obtain ongoing professional education and guided practical training under a qualified professional and maintain current certification from a certification program accredited by the NCCA, or comparable accrediting body.
- Design and instruct classes that reflect current professional standards and guidelines.
- Formulate and enforce policies for the conduct of the class in accordance with professional recommendations, including obtaining documents from prospective participants such as a signed waiver prior to attending class.

- Establish and implement adequate and proper procedures for supervision in all segments of the class.
- Post safety regulations in the facility and ensure that they are rigidly enforced by supervisory personnel.
- Keep the facility free from hazards and maintain adequate free space for class activities.
- Routinely inspect all equipment and facilities and report any potential hazards promptly.
- Formulate policies and guidelines for emergency situations, rehearse the procedures, and require all instructors to have current first-aid, **cardiopulmonary resuscitation (CPR),** and **automated external defibrillator (AED)** training and certification.

By applying these recommendations, GFIs can help reduce the probability of injury to participants and limit potential legal liability. Should legal action result from an injury, the facts of the case would be examined to determine whether negligence was the cause. A properly trained, competent, and certified GFI conducting a program that was in accordance with current professional standards would probably prevail.

All GFIs should remember that professional standards in the health and fitness field are continually changing. It is the responsibility of the GFI to remain aware of pertinent legal developments in the industry in addition to keeping abreast of the latest health and fitness research and updated standards and guidelines. By understanding professional and legal responsibilities, GFIs can develop and offer group fitness classes in a way that participants enjoy while limiting instructor liability.

REFERENCES

Bedosky, L. (2018). *The Future of Personal Training May Be in Regulation, Certification and Integration.* www.clubindustry.com/trends/future-personal-training-may-be-regulation-certification-and-integration

California Department of Industrial Relations (2021). *Independent Contractor versus Employee.* www.dir.ca.gov/dlse/faq_independentcontractor.htm

Dominic, A. (2017). *Life Time Fitness Reaches $940,000 Settlement with Trainers in Wages Lawsuit.* www.clubindustry.com/news/life-time-fitness-reaches-940-000-settlement-trainers-wages-lawsuit

Golden, N. (2021). *How to Run an Online Group Fitness Class.* https://blog.afaa.com/how-to-run-online-group-fitness-class

Herbert, D.L. & Herbert, W.G. (2002). *Legal Aspects of Preventive, Rehabilitative, and Recreational Exercise Programs* (4th ed.). Canton, Oh.: PRC Publishing.

Myers, J., Bhuiyan, J., & Roosevelt, M. (2019). *Newsom Signs Bill Rewriting California Employment Law, Limiting Use of Independent Contractors.* https://www.latimes.com/california/story/2019-09-18/gavin-newsom-signs-ab5-employees0independent-contractors-california

Norfleet, N. (2020). *Life Time Faces Lawsuit over Alleged Unpaid Fitness Instructor Hours.* https://www.startribune.com/life-time-faces-lawsuit-over-alleged-unpaid-fitness-instructor-hours/571451862/

O'Malley, M. (2019). *Is Your Gym's Waiver Unnecessary? It Should Be.* www.ihrsa.org/improve-your-club/is-your-gyms-waiver-unnecessary-it-should-be/

Wong, G.M. (2010). *Essentials of Sport Law* (4th ed.). Westport, Conn.: Praeger.

SUGGESTED READINGS

Cotton, D.J. & Wolohan, J.T. (2021). *Law for Recreation and Sport Managers* (8th ed.). Dubuque, Iowa: Kendall Hunt.

Pitt, A. (2020). *Tips for Taking and Teaching Virtual Fitness Classes.* https://aladygoeswest.com/tips-for-taking-and-teaching-virtual-fitness-classes/

ACE® Code of Ethics

ACE Certified Professionals are guided by the following principles of conduct as they interact with clients/participants, the public, and other health and exercise professionals.

ACE Certified Professionals will endeavor to:

- Provide safe and effective instruction
- Provide equal and fair treatment to all clients/participants
- Stay up to date on the latest health and fitness research and understand its practical application
- Maintain current CPR and AED certification and knowledge of first-aid services
- Comply with all applicable business, employment, and intellectual property laws
- Maintain the confidentiality of all client/participant information
- Refer clients/participants to more qualified health or medical professionals when appropriate
- Uphold and enhance public appreciation and trust for the health and fitness industry
- Establish and maintain clear professional boundaries

PROVIDE SAFE AND EFFECTIVE INSTRUCTION

Providing safe and effective instruction involves a variety of responsibilities for ACE Certified Professionals. Safe means that the instruction will not result in physical, mental, emotional, or financial harm to the client/participant. Effective means that the instruction or coaching has a purposeful, intended, and desired effect toward the client's/participant's goal. Great effort and care must be taken in carrying out the responsibilities that are essential in creating a positive and enjoyable exercise experience for all clients/participants.

Preparticipation Health Screening

ACE Certified Professionals should have all potential clients/participants complete an industry-recognized health-screening tool to ensure safe and enjoyable exercise participation. If significant risk factors or signs and symptoms suggestive of chronic disease are identified, refer the client/participant to a physician or primary healthcare practitioner for medical clearance and guidance regarding which types of assessments, activities, or exercises are indicated, contraindicated, or deemed high risk. If an individual does not want to obtain medical clearance, it may be prudent to have that individual sign a legally prepared document that releases you and the facility in which you work from any liability related to any injury that may result from exercise participation or assessment. Once the client/participant has been cleared for exercise and you have a full understanding of the client's/participant's health status and medical history, including their current use of medications, a formal risk-management plan for potential emergencies must be prepared and reviewed periodically.

Assessments

The main objective of a health and fitness assessment is to establish the client's/participant's current health and fitness levels in order to design an appropriate exercise program. Explain the risks and benefits of each assessment and provide the client/participant with any pertinent instructions. Prior to conducting any type of assessment, the client/participant must be given an opportunity to ask questions and read and sign an informed consent. The types and order of assessments are dictated by the client's/participant's health status, fitness level, symptoms, and/or use of medications. Remember that each assessment has specific protocols and only those within your scope of practice should be administered. Once the assessments are completed, evaluate and discuss the results objectively as they relate to the client's/participant's health condition and goals. Educate the client/participant and emphasize how an exercise program will benefit the client/participant.

Program Design

You must not prescribe exercise, diet, or treatment, as doing so is outside your scope of practice and implies ordering or advising a medicine or treatment. Instead, it is appropriate for you to design exercise programs that improve components of physical fitness and wellness while adhering to the limitations of a previous injury or condition as determined by a certified, registered, or licensed allied health professional. Because nutritional laws and the practice of dietetics vary in each state, province, and country, understand what type of basic nutritional information is appropriate and legal for you to disseminate to your client/participant. The client's/participant's preferences, and short- and long-term goals, as well as current industry standards and guidelines, must be taken into consideration as you develop an engaging and realistic program to facilitate desired physical activity, behavior change, and other health and fitness outcomes. Provide as much detail for all exercise parameters such as frequency, intensity, type of exercise, duration, volume, progression, and termination points.

Program Implementation

Do not underestimate your ability to influence the client/participant to become active for a lifetime. Be sure that each class or session is well-planned, sequential, and documented. Instruct the client/participant how to safely and properly perform the appropriate exercises and communicate this in a manner that the client/participant will understand and retain. Each client/participant has a different learning curve that will require different levels of attention, learning aids, and repetition. Supervise the client/participant closely, especially when spotting or cueing is needed. If supervising a group of two or more, ensure that you can supervise and provide the appropriate amount of attention to each individual at all times. Ideally, the group will have similar goals and will be performing similar exercises or activities. Position yourself so that you do not have to turn your back to any client/participant performing an exercise.

Facilities and Non-Facility Spaces

Although the condition of a facility, or non-facility, space may not always be within your control, you are still obligated to ensure a hazard-free environment to maximize safety. If you notice potential hazards in the exercise space, communicate these hazards to the client/participant and/or the facility management. For example, if you notice that the clamps that keep the weights on the barbells are getting rusty and loose, it would be prudent of you to remove them from the training area and alert management that immediate repair is required.

Equipment

Obtain equipment that meets or exceeds industry standards and utilize the equipment only for its intended use. Arrange exercise equipment and stations so that adequate space exists between equipment, participants, and foot traffic. Schedule regular maintenance and inspect equipment prior to use to ensure it is in proper working condition. Avoid the use of homemade equipment, as your liability is greater if it causes injury to a person exercising under your supervision.

PROVIDE EQUAL AND FAIR TREATMENT TO ALL CLIENTS/PARTICIPANTS

ACE Certified Professionals are obligated to provide fair and equal treatment for each client/participant without bias, preference, or discrimination against gender, ethnic background, age, national origin, basis of religion, or physical disability.

The Americans with Disabilities Act protects individuals with disabilities against any type of unlawful discrimination. A disability can be either physical or mental, such as epilepsy, paralysis, HIV infection, AIDS, a significant hearing or visual impairment, intellectual disability, or a specific learning disability. ACE Certified Professionals should, at a minimum, provide reasonable accommodations to each individual with a disability. Reasonable simply means that you are able to provide accommodations that do not cause you any undue hardship that requires additional or significant expense or difficulty. Making an existing facility accessible by modifying equipment or devices, assessments, or training materials are a few examples of providing reasonable accommodations. However, providing the use of personal items or providing items at your own expense may not be considered reasonable.

This ethical consideration of providing fair and equal treatment is not limited to behavioral interactions with clients/participants, but also extends to exercise programming and other business-related services such as communication, scheduling, billing, cancellation policies, and dispute resolution.

STAY UP TO DATE ON THE LATEST HEALTH AND FITNESS RESEARCH AND UNDERSTAND ITS PRACTICAL APPLICATION

Obtaining an ACE certification required you to have broad-based knowledge of many disciplines; however, this credential should not be viewed as the end of your professional development and education. Instead, it should be viewed as the beginning or foundation. The dynamic nature of the health and fitness industry requires you to maintain an understanding of the latest research and professional standards and guidelines and their impact on the design and implementation of exercise programming. To stay informed, make time to review a variety of industry resources such as professional journals, position statements, trade and lay periodicals, and correspondence courses, as well as to attend professional meetings, conferences, and educational workshops.

An additional benefit of staying up to date is that it also fulfills your certification renewal requirements for continuing education credit (CEC). To maintain your ACE Certified status, you must obtain an established amount of CECs every two years. CECs are granted for structured learning that takes place within the educational portion of a course related to the profession and presented by a qualified health or exercise professional.

MAINTAIN CURRENT CPR AND AED CERTIFICATION AND KNOWLEDGE OF FIRST-AID SERVICES

ACE Certified Professionals must be prepared to recognize and respond to heart attacks and other life-threatening emergencies. Emergency response is enhanced by training and maintaining skills in cardiopulmonary resuscitation (CPR) and using automated external defibrillators (AEDs), which have become more widely available. An AED is a portable electronic device used to restore normal heart rhythm in a person experiencing a cardiac arrest and can reduce the time to defibrillation before emergency medical services (EMS) personnel arrive. For each minute that defibrillation is delayed, the victim's chance of survival is reduced by 7 to 10%. Thus, survival from cardiac arrest is improved dramatically when CPR and defibrillation are started early.

COMPLY WITH ALL APPLICABLE BUSINESS, EMPLOYMENT, AND INTELLECTUAL PROPERTY LAWS

As an ACE Certified Professional, you are expected to maintain a high level of integrity by complying with all applicable business, employment, copyright, and intellectual property laws. Be truthful and forthcoming with communication to clients/participants, coworkers, and other health and exercise professionals in advertising, marketing, and business practices. Do not create false or misleading impressions of credentials, claims, or sponsorships, or perform services outside of your scope of practice that are illegal, deceptive, or fraudulent.

All information regarding your business must be clear, accurate, and easy to understand for all potential clients/participants. Provide disclosure about the name of your business, physical address, and contact information, and maintain a working phone number and email address. So that clients/participants can make an informed choice about paying for your services, provide detailed information regarding schedules, prices, payment terms, time limits, and conditions. Cancellation, refund, and rescheduling information must also be clearly stated and easy to understand. Allow the client/participant an opportunity to ask questions and review this information before formally agreeing to your services and terms.

Because employment laws vary in each city, state, province, and country, familiarize yourself with the applicable employment regulations and standards to which your business must conform. Examples of this may include conforming to specific building codes and zoning ordinances or making sure that your place of business is accessible to individuals with a disability.

The understanding of intellectual property law and the proper use of copyrighted materials is an important legal issue for all ACE Certified Professionals. Intellectual property laws protect the creations of authors, artists, software programmers, and others with copyrighted materials. The most common infringement of intellectual property law in the fitness industry is the use of music in an exercise class. When commercial music is played in a for-profit exercise class, without a performance or blanket license, it is considered a public performance and a violation of intellectual property law. Therefore, make sure that any music, handouts, or educational materials are either exempt from intellectual property law or permissible under laws by reason of fair use, or obtain express written consent from the copyright holder for distribution, adaptation, or use. When in doubt, obtain permission first or consult with a qualified legal professional who has intellectual property law expertise.

MAINTAIN THE CONFIDENTIALITY OF ALL CLIENT/PARTICIPANT INFORMATION

Every client/participant has the right to expect that all personal data and discussions with an ACE Certified Professional will be safeguarded and not disclosed without the client's/participant's express written consent or acknowledgment. Therefore, protect the confidentiality of all client/participant information such as contact data, medical records, health history, progress notes, and meeting details. Even when confidentiality is not required by law, continue to preserve the confidentiality of such information.

Any breach of confidentiality, intentional or unintentional, potentially harms the productivity and trust of your client/participant and undermines your effectiveness as an exercise professional or health coach. This also puts you at risk for potential litigation and puts your client/participant at risk for public embarrassment and fraudulent activity such as identity theft.

Most breaches of confidentiality are unintentional and occur because of carelessness and lack of awareness. The most common breach of confidentiality is exposing or storing a client's personal data in a location that is not secure. This occurs when a client's/participant's file or information is left on a desk, or filed in a cabinet that has no lock or is accessible to others. Breaches of confidentiality may also occur when you have conversations regarding a client's/participant's performance or medical/health history with staff or others and the client's/participant's first name or other identifying details are used.

Post and adhere to a privacy policy that communicates how client/participant information will be used and secured and how a client's/participant's preference regarding unsolicited mail and email will be respected. When a client/participant provides you with any personal data, new or updated, make it a habit to immediately secure this information and ensure that only you and/or the appropriate individuals have access to it. Also, the client's/participant's files must only be accessed and used for purposes related to health and fitness services. If client/participant information is stored on a personal computer, restrict access by using a protected password. Should you receive any inquiries from family members or other individuals regarding the progress of a client/participant or other personal information, state that you cannot provide any information without the client's/participant's permission. If and when a client/participant permits you to release confidential information to an authorized individual or party, utilize secure methods of communication such as certified mail, sending and receiving information on a dedicated private fax line, or email with encryption.

REFER CLIENTS/PARTICIPANTS TO MORE QUALIFIED HEALTH OR MEDICAL PROFESSIONALS WHEN APPROPRIATE

It is vitally important that ACE Certified Professionals refer their clients/participants to a more qualified professional (e.g., physician, physical therapist, registered dietitian, psychologist, or attorney) when warranted. Doing so not only benefits your clients/participants by making sure that they receive the appropriate attention and care, but also enhances your credibility and reduces liability by defining your scope of practice and clarifying what services you can and cannot reasonably provide.

Knowing when to refer a client/participant is, however, as important as choosing to which professional to refer. For instance, when a client/participant complains of symptoms of muscle soreness or discomfort or exhibits signs of fatigue or lack of energy, it is not an absolute indication to refer your client/participant to a physician. Because continual referrals such as this are not practical, familiarize and educate yourself on expected signs and symptoms, taking into consideration the client's/participant's fitness level, health status, chronic disease, disability, and/or background as they are screened and as they begin and progress with an exercise program. This helps you better discern between emergent and non-emergent situations and know when to refuse to offer your services, continue to monitor, and/or make an immediate referral.

It is important that you know the scope of practice for various health professionals and which types of referrals are appropriate. For example, some states require that a referring physician first approve visits to a physical therapist, while other states allow individuals to see a physical therapist directly. Only registered or licensed dietitians or physicians may provide specific dietary recommendations or diet plans; however, a client/participant who is suspected of an eating disorder should be referred to an eating disorders specialist. Refer clients/participants to a clinical psychologist if they wish to discuss family or marital problems or exhibit addictive behaviors such as substance abuse.

Network and develop rapport with potential allied health professionals in your area before you refer clients/participants to them. This demonstrates good will and respect for their expertise and will most likely result in reciprocal referrals for your services and fitness expertise.

UPHOLD AND ENHANCE PUBLIC APPRECIATION AND TRUST FOR THE HEALTH AND FITNESS INDUSTRY

The best way for ACE Certified Professionals to uphold and enhance public appreciation and trust for the health and fitness industry is to represent themselves in a dignified and professional manner. As the public is inundated with misinformation and false claims about fitness products and services, your expertise must be utilized to dispel myths and half-truths about current trends and fads that are potentially harmful to the public.

When appropriate, mentor and dispense knowledge and training to less-experienced exercise professionals and health coaches. Novice exercise professionals and health coaches can benefit from your experience and skill as you assist them in establishing a foundation based on exercise science, from both theoretical and practical standpoints. Therefore, it is a disservice if you fail to provide helpful or corrective information—especially when an individual, the public, or other exercise professionals or health coaches are at risk for injury or increased liability. For example, if you observe an individual using momentum to perform a strength-training exercise, the prudent course of action would be to suggest a modification. Likewise, if you observe an exercise professional in your workplace consistently failing to obtain informed consents before clients/participants undergo fitness testing or begin an exercise program, recommend that they consider implementing these forms to minimize liability.

Finally, do not represent yourself in an overly commercial or misleading manner. Consider the exercise professional who places an advertisement in a local newspaper stating: "Lose 10 pounds in 10 days or your money back!" It is inappropriate to lend credibility to or endorse a product, service, or program founded upon unsubstantiated or misleading claims; thus a solicitation such as this must be avoided, as it undermines the public's trust of exercise professionals and health coaches.

ESTABLISH AND MAINTAIN CLEAR PROFESSIONAL BOUNDARIES

Working in the fitness profession requires you to come in contact with many different people. It is imperative that a professional relationship be maintained with all clients/participants. Exercise professionals and health coaches are responsible for setting and maintaining the boundaries between a working relationship and friendship with their clients/participants. To that end, ACE Certified Professionals should:

- Never initiate or encourage discussion of a sexual nature
- Avoid touching clients/participants unless it is essential to instruction. When essential, ask for permission first.
- Inform clients/participants about the purpose of touching and find an alternative if the client/participant objects
- Discontinue all touching if it appears to make the client/participant uncomfortable
- Take all reasonable steps to ensure that any personal and social contacts between themselves and their clients/participants do not have an adverse impact on the client–personal trainer, client–coach, or participant–instructor relationship

If you are unable to maintain appropriate professional boundaries with a client/participant (whether due to your attitudes and actions or those of the client/participant), the prudent course of action is to terminate the relationship and, perhaps, refer the client/participant to another professional. Keep in mind that charges of sexual harassment or assault, even if groundless, can have disastrous effects on your career.

Abrasion A scraping away of a portion of the skin or mucous membrane.

Action The stage of the transtheoretical model of behavior change during which the individual is actively engaging in a behavior that was started less than six months ago.

Active listening Mode of listening in which the listener is concerned about the content, intent, and feelings of the message.

Activities of daily living (ADL) Activities normally performed for hygiene, bathing, household chores, walking, shopping, and similar activities.

Acute Descriptive of a condition that usually has a rapid onset and a relatively short and severe course; opposite of chronic.

Add-in strategy See Part-to-whole teaching strategy.

Adenosine triphosphate (ATP) A high-energy phosphate molecule required to provide energy for cellular function. Produced both aerobically and anaerobically and stored in the body.

Adherence The extent to which people follow their plans or treatment recommendations. Exercise adherence is the extent to which people follow an exercise program.

Aerobic system The process for meeting energy requirements from the combustion of carbohydrates and fats in the presence of oxygen.

Affective domain One of the three domains of learning; involves the learning of emotional behaviors.

Agility The ability to rapidly and accurately change the position of the body in space; a skill-related component of physical fitness.

Agonist The muscle directly responsible for observed movement; also called the prime mover.

Agreement to participate Signed document that indicates that the client or participant is aware of inherent risks and potential injuries that can occur from participation.

Ambient temperature The temperature of the surrounding air; room temperature.

American Society of Composers, Authors and Publishers (ASCAP) One of two performing rights societies in the United States that represent music publishers in negotiating and collecting fees for the nondramatic performance of music.

Americans with Disabilities Act Civil rights legislation designed to improve access to jobs, workplaces, and commercial spaces for people with disabilities.

AMRAP An acronym used to describe a type of training based on performing "as many rounds (or repetitions) as possible." This format of training refers to performing as many repetitions of a single exercise or rounds of a workout routine as possible in a given amount of time.

Angina A common symptom of coronary artery disease characterized by chest pain caused by an inadequate supply of oxygen and decreased blood flow to the heart muscle; an early sign of coronary artery disease. Symptoms may include pain or discomfort, heaviness, tightness, pressure or burning, numbness, aching, and tingling in the chest, back, neck, throat, jaw, or arms; also called angina.

Antagonist The muscle that acts in opposition to the contraction produced by an agonist (prime mover) muscle.

Anterior Anatomical term meaning toward the front. Same as ventral; opposite of posterior.

Anticipatory cue A cue that tells participants what the next move will be and when to perform that movement; often includes a countdown of repetitions.

Anxiety A state of uneasiness and apprehension; occurs in some mental disorders.

Articular cartilage Cartilage covering the ends of the bones inside diarthrodial joints; allows the ends of the bones to glide without friction.

Associative stage of learning The second stage of learning a motor skill, when performers begin to master the fundamentals and can concentrate on skill refinement.

Assumption of risk A person freely elects to engage in an activity after being made aware of the potential risks of participation and may in advance relieve another person or party of potential legal obligation to act toward them with due care.

Asthma A chronic inflammatory disorder of the airways that affects genetically susceptible individuals in response to various environmental triggers such as allergens, viral infection, exercise, cold, and stress.

Atherosclerosis A specific form of arteriosclerosis characterized by the accumulation of fatty material on the inner walls of the arteries, causing them to harden, thicken, and lose elasticity.

Athletic trainer A healthcare professional who collaborates with physicians and specializes in providing immediate intervention when injuries occur and helping athletes and clients in the prevention, assessment, treatment, and rehabilitation of emergency, acute, and chronic medical conditions involving injury, impairment, functional limitations, and disabilities.

Atrophy A reduction in muscle size (muscle wasting) due to inactivity or immobilization.

Automated external defibrillator (AED) A portable electronic device used to restore normal heart rhythms in victims of sudden cardiac arrest.

Autonomous motivation Engaging in an activity out of free will and the desire to do so.

Autonomous stage of learning The third stage of learning a motor skill, when the skill has become habitual or automatic for the performer.

Autonomy The capacity of a rational individual to make an informed, un-coerced decision. Regulation by the self.

Avulsion A wound involving forcible separation or tearing of tissue from the body.

Balance The ability to maintain the body's position over its base of support within stability limits, both statically and dynamically; a skill-related component of physical fitness.

Baroreceptors A sensory nerve ending that is stimulated by changes in pressure, as those in the walls of blood vessels.

Base of support The areas of contact between the feet and their supporting surface and the area between the feet.

Beats Regular pulsations that have an even rhythm and occur in a continuous pattern of strong and weak pulsations.

Bilateral Affecting both the right and left sides of the body.

Bilateral training Exercise that targets both sides of the body simultaneously (e.g., body-weight squat or barbell chest press).

Biomechanics The mechanics of biological and muscular activity.

Blanket license A certificate or document granting permission that varies and applies to a number of situations.

Blood pressure (BP) The pressure exerted by the blood on the walls of the arteries; measured in millimeters of mercury (mmHg) with a sphygmomanometer.

Body composition The makeup of the body in terms of the relative percentage of fat-free mass and body fat; a health-related component of physical fitness.

Body fat A component of the body, the primary role of which is to store energy for later use.

Body mass index A relative measure of body height to body weight used to determine levels of health, from underweight to extreme obesity.

Bone mineral density (BMD) A measure of the amount of minerals (mainly calcium) contained in a certain volume of bone.

Broadcast Music, Inc. One of two performing rights societies in the U.S. that represent music publishers in negotiating and collecting fees for the nondramatic performance of music.

Carbohydrate The body's preferred energy source. Dietary sources include sugars (simple) and grains, rice, potatoes, and beans (complex). Carbohydrate is stored as glycogen in the muscles and liver and is transported in the blood as glucose. Each gram of carbohydrate contains four calories.

Cardiac output The amount of blood pumped by the heart per minute; usually expressed in liters of blood per minute. Cardiac output = Heart rate x Stroke volume.

Cardiopulmonary resuscitation (CPR) A procedure to support and maintain breathing and circulation for a person who has stopped breathing (respiratory arrest) and/or whose heart has stopped (cardiac arrest).

Cardiorespiratory endurance The capacity of the heart, blood vessels, and lungs to deliver oxygen and nutrients to the working muscles and tissues during sustained exercise and to remove metabolic waste products that would result in fatigue; a health-related component of physical fitness.

Cardiorespiratory fitness The ability to perform large muscle movement over a sustained period; related to the capacity of the heart-lung system to deliver oxygen for sustained energy production. Also called cardiorespiratory endurance or aerobic fitness.

Cardiorespiratory system The cardiovascular (heart, blood, and blood vessels) and respiratory (airway and lungs) systems working together to obtain and circulate vital compounds such as oxygen and nutrients to the entire body.

Cardiovascular disease (CVD) A general term for any disease of the heart, blood vessels, or circulation.

Center of gravity The point around which all weight is evenly distributed; also called center of mass.

Central nervous system The brain and spinal cord.

Certificant An individual who has earned a certification.

Choreography The art of designing sequences of movements.

Chronic Descriptive of a condition that persists over a long period of time; opposite of acute.

Chronic disease Any disease state that persists over an extended period of time.

Chronic obstructive pulmonary disease (COPD) A condition, such as asthma, bronchitis, or emphysema, in which there is chronic obstruction of air flow.

Cognitive distortion Unproductive thought process that can paralyze a client or participant when making a positive and lasting behavioral change.

Cognitive domain One of the three domains of learning; describes intellectual activities and involves the learning of knowledge.

Cognitive stage of learning The first stage of learning a motor skill when performers make many gross errors and have extremely variable performances.

Command style of teaching A teaching style in which the instructor makes all decisions about rhythm, posture, and duration while participants follow the instructor's directions and movements.

Competence Having the necessary ability, knowledge, or skill to do something successfully; one of the three basic psychological needs that influence motivation, according to self-determination theory.

Compilations Original, copyrightable sequences or a program of dance steps or exercise routines that may or may not be copyrightable individually.

Concentric A type of isotonic muscle contraction in which the muscle develops tension and shortens when stimulated.

Concussion A type of traumatic brain injury caused by a bump, blow, or jolt to the head or by a hit to the body that causes the head and brain to move rapidly back and forth.

Contemplation The stage of the transtheoretical model of behavior change during which the individual is weighing the pros and cons of behavioral change.

Controlled motivation Doing a task with a sense of pressure, demand, or coercion.

Coordination The ability to process and execute appropriate actions or motor responses with proper sequence (timing) and magnitude to produce smooth, flowing movement; a skill-related component of physical fitness.

Copyright The exclusive right, for a certain number of years, to perform, make, and distribute copies and otherwise use an artistic, musical, or literary work.

Coronary artery disease See Coronary heart disease (CHD).

Coronary heart disease (CHD) The major form of cardiovascular disease; results when the coronary arteries are narrowed or occluded, most commonly by atherosclerotic deposits of fibrous and fatty tissue; also called coronary artery disease (CAD).

Creatine phosphate A storage form of high-energy phosphate in muscle cells that can be used to immediately resynthesize adenosine triphosphate (ATP).

Creatine phosphate system See Phosphagen system.

Cultural competence The ability to communicate and work effectively with people from different cultures.

Decisional balance One of the four components of the transtheoretical model of behavior change. A choice-focused technique that can be used when coaching with neutrality, devoting equal exploration to the pros and cons of change or a specific plan.

Deep vein thrombosis A blood clot in a major vein, usually in the legs and/or pelvis.

Defamation of character A false statement about someone that harms their reputation.

Defendant The party in a lawsuit who is being sued or accused.

Depression 1. The action of lowering a muscle or bone or movement in an inferior or downward direction. 2. A condition of general emotional dejection and withdrawal; sadness greater and more prolonged than that warranted by any objective reason.

Diabetes See Diabetes mellitus.

Diabetes mellitus A disease of carbohydrate metabolism in which an absolute or relative deficiency of insulin results in an inability to metabolize carbohydrates normally.

Diaphragmatic breathing A deep, relaxing breathing technique that helps chronic obstructive pulmonary disease (COPD) patients improve their breathing capacity.

Diastasis recti A separation of the recti abdominal muscles along the midline of the body.

Diastolic blood pressure (DBP) The pressure in the arteries during the relaxation phase (diastole) of the cardiac cycle; indicative of total peripheral resistance.

Dissipation A loss of energy such as occurs during the cooling of the body in the open air, or the conversion of mechanical energy into heat.

Distal Farthest from the midline of the body, or from the point of origin of a muscle.

Diversity The practice or quality of including or involving people from a range of different social or ethnic backgrounds and of different genders, sexual orientations, etc.

Downbeat The regular strong pulsation in music occurring in a continuous pattern at an even rhythm.

Dyspnea Shortness of breath; a subjective difficulty or distress in breathing.

Dyspnea scale A subjective score that reflects the relative difficulty of breathing as perceived by the participant during physical activity, with 0 reflecting no shortness of breath and 4 representing the most severe or intense dyspnea ever experienced.

Eccentric A type of isotonic muscle action in which the muscle lengthens against a resistance when it is stimulated; sometimes called "negative work" or "negative reps."

Electrocardiogram (ECG) A recording of the electrical activity of the heart.

Elicit-provide-elicit An approach to providing information in which the exercise professional first asks permission to do so. When permission is granted, the professional follows with an open-ended question to understand what the client or participant knows already (elicit). The professional follows with a small amount of highly relevant information (provide) and then checks back with the client or participant to assess understanding and the response to the information (elicit).

EMOM An acronym that stands for "every minute on the minute." A type of interval training indicating that a predetermined number of repetitions must be completed in one minute. If the repetitions are completed before the minute ends, the participant may rest until the next minute begins.

Empathy The extent to which a professional communicates an accurate understanding of the client or participant's perspectives and experiences; most commonly manifested as reflection.

Emphysema An obstructive pulmonary disease characterized by the gradual destruction of lung alveoli and the surrounding connective tissue, in addition to airway inflammation, leading to reduced ability to effectively inhale and exhale.

Employee A person who works for another person in exchange for financial compensation. An employee complies with the instructions and directions of their employer and reports to them on a regular basis.

Equity The quality of being fair and impartial.

Evaporation The process by which molecules in a liquid state (e.g., water) spontaneously become gaseous (e.g., water vapor).

Exercise dependence A state in which physical activity is extreme in frequency and duration, relatively resistant to change, and is associated with an irresistible impulse to continue exercise despite injury, illness, or fatigue.

Exercise evaluation A process of evaluating an exercise or movement based on its effectiveness and safety.

Exercise-induced bronchoconstriction (EIB) The narrowing of the airways causing difficulty moving air out of the lungs during exercise. Caused by the loss of heat, water, or both from the airways during exercise when quickly breathing in air that is drier than what is already in the body. Symptoms typically appear within a few minutes after exercise begins and may continue for 10 to 15 minutes after a workout is complete.

Extension The act of straightening or extending a joint, usually applied to the muscular movement of a limb.

External cue A cue that directs the exercisers attention outward, toward the environment and the outcome of the movement. Used to enhance performance and increase movement effectiveness.

Extrinsic motivation Motivation that comes from external (outside of the self) rewards, such as material or social rewards.

Fat An essential nutrient that provides energy, energy storage, insulation, and contour to the body. Each gram of fat contains nine calories.

Fatigue The decline in ability of a muscle to generate force.

Fatty acid A long hydrocarbon chain with an even number of carbons and varying degrees of saturation with hydrogen.

Feedback An internal response within a learner; during information processing, it is the correctness or incorrectness of a response that is stored in memory to be used for future reference. Also, verbal or nonverbal information about current behavior that can be used to improve future performance.

Femoral anteversion A congenital condition in which the femur is rotated inward (medially).

Fiber Carbohydrate chains the body cannot break down for use and which pass through the body undigested.

First ventilatory threshold (VT1) Intensity of aerobic exercise at which ventilation starts to increase in a nonlinear fashion in response to an accumulation of metabolic by-products in the blood.

Flexibility The range of motion available at a joint or the degree of tissue extensibility available at a joint; a health-related component of physical fitness.

Flexion The act of moving a joint so that the two bones forming it are brought closer together.

Follow-up cue A specific cue that helps a participant improve performance by correcting form or enhancing the exercise by providing specific, tangible, and immediate feedback. May also include progressions and regressions.

Frontal plane A longitudinal section that runs at a right angle to the sagittal plane, dividing the body into anterior and posterior portions.

Functional capacity The maximum physical performance represented by maximal oxygen consumption.

Gait The manner or style of walking.

Glucose A simple sugar; the form in which all carbohydrates are used as the body's principal energy source.

Glycemic index (GI) A ranking of carbohydrates on a scale from 0 to 100 according to the extent to which they raise blood sugar levels.

Glycogen The chief carbohydrate storage material; formed by the liver and stored in the liver and muscle.

Glycolysis The breakdown of glucose or of its storage form glycogen.

Glycolytic anaerobic system The energy pathway that uses glycogen to produce power, but not quite as much or as quickly as the creatine phosphate system.

Green exercise Exercise performed in natural environments.

Ground reaction force The force exerted by the ground on a body in contact with it.

Health belief model A model to explain that people's emotions and ideas about illness, prevention, and treatment may influence health-related behaviors and decisions about changing (or not changing).

Health Insurance Portability and Accountability Act (HIPAA) Enacted by the U.S. Congress in 1996, HIPAA requires the U.S. Department of Health and Human Services (HHS) to establish national standards for electronic health care information to facilitate efficient and secure exchange of private health data. The Standards for Privacy of Individually Identifiable Health Information ("Privacy Rule"), issued by the HHS, addresses the use and disclosure of individuals' health information—called "protected health information"—by providing federal protections and giving patients an array of rights with respect to personal health information while permitting the disclosure of information needed for patient care and other important purposes.

Health perception An individual's perception of their relative level of wellness and illness.

Healthy Mediterranean-Style Dietary Pattern One of three USDA Food Patterns featured in the *Dietary Guidelines for Americans;* modified from the Healthy U.S.-Style Dietary Pattern to more closely reflect dietary patterns that have been associated with positive health outcomes in studies of Mediterranean-style diets.

Healthy U.S.-Style Dietary Patterns One of three USDA Food Patterns featured in the *Dietary Guidelines for Americans;* based on the types and proportions of foods Americans typically consume, but in nutrient-dense forms and appropriate amounts.

Healthy Vegetarian Dietary Pattern One of three USDA Food Patterns featured in the *Dietary Guidelines for Americans;* modified from the Healthy U.S.-Style Dietary Pattern to more closely reflect dietary patterns reported by self-identified vegetarians.

Heart rate (HR) The number of heartbeats per minute.

Heart-rate reserve (HRR) The reserve capacity of the heart; the difference between maximal heart rate and resting heart rate. It reflects the heart's ability to increase the rate of beating and cardiac output above resting level to maximal intensity.

Heat exhaustion The most common heat-related illness; usually the result of intense exercise in a hot, humid environment and characterized by profuse sweating, which results in fluid and electrolyte loss, a drop in blood pressure, lightheadedness, nausea, vomiting, decreased coordination, and often syncope (fainting).

High-intensity interval training (HIIT) An exercise strategy alternating periods of short, intense anaerobic exercise with less-intense recovery periods.

High-low A class format that combines both low-impact and high-impact movements into one class.

Hyperextension Extension of an articulation beyond anatomical position.

Hyperflexion Flexion of an articulation beyond anatomical position.

Hyperglycemia An abnormally high content of glucose (sugar) in the blood.

Hypertension High blood pressure, or the elevation of resting blood pressure to 130/80 mmHg or greater.

Hypertonic 1. Having extreme muscular tension. 2. Having a solute concentration that is greater than the concentration of human blood.

Hypoglycemia A deficiency of glucose in the blood commonly caused by too much insulin, too little glucose, or too much exercise where glycogen stores become depleted. Most commonly found in those with insulin-dependent diabetes and characterized by symptoms such as fatigue, dizziness, confusion, headache, nausea, or anxiety.

Inclusion The practice or policy of providing equal access to opportunities and resources for people who might otherwise be excluded or marginalized, such as having physical or mental disabilities or belong to other minority groups.

Independent contractor A person who conducts business on their own on a contract basis and is not an employee of an organization.

Informed consent A written statement signed by a client or participant prior to testing that informs them of testing purposes, processes, and all potential risks and discomforts.

Instructional cue A cue used to set up and execute an exercise by focusing on the most important aspects of the exercise, such as posture/alignment, safety considerations, range of motion, and speed of movement.

Insulin A hormone released from the pancreas that allows cells to take up glucose.

Insulin resistance An inability of muscle tissue to effectively use insulin, where the action of insulin is "resisted" by insulin-sensitive tissues.

Integumentary system The largest system of the body forming a physical barrier between the internal and external environment. Made up of the epidermis, dermis, and hypodermis, it functions to protect the internal environment, regulate temperature, maintain cellular fluid, detect stimuli, and synthesize vitamin D.

Internal cue A cue that directs the exercisers' attention inwardly, toward their own body and movement process. This type of cue is especially helpful for beginners and may enhance motor learning and kinesthetic awareness.

Intrinsic motivation Motivation that comes from internal states, such as enjoyment or personal satisfaction. The enactment of a behavior because it is consistent with personal goals and values.

Invasion of privacy An unjustifiable intrusion upon another's right to privacy.

This can occur not only by the revelation of private information, but also by the improper use of one's name, likeness, or other personal attribute without their permission.

Ischemia A decrease in the blood supply to a bodily organ, tissue, or part caused by constriction or obstruction of the blood vessels.

Isometric A type of muscular contraction in which the muscle is stimulated to generate tension but little or no joint movement occurs.

Isotonic A type of muscular action where the muscle is stimulated to develop tension and joint movement occurs. Eccentric and concentric muscle actions are isotonic.

Joint capsule A ligamentous sac that surrounds the articular cavity of a freely movable joint.

Kinesthetic awareness The perception of body position and movement in space.

Kinetic chain The concept that joints and segments have an effect on one another during movement.

Kyphosis Posterior curvature of the spine, typically seen in the thoracic region.

Laceration A jagged, irregular cut or tear in the soft tissues, usually caused by a blow. Because of extensive tissue destruction, there is a great potential for contamination and infection.

Lateral Away from the midline of the body, or the outside.

Laxity Lacking in strength, firmness, or resilience; joints that have been injured or overstretched may exhibit laxity.

Layering A method of choreography wherein the instructor starts with a base move and then layers on one new element at a time.

Lever length The distance from the joint (axis of rotation) to the tendon insertion point (motive force lever arm), or the distance from the joint to the load (resistance lever arm). Shortening the resistance lever length or lengthening the motive lever length makes it possible to lift a load with less tension.

Liability Legal responsibility.

Liability insurance Insurance for bodily injury or property damage resulting from general negligence.

Libel A published false statement that is damaging to a person's reputation.

Ligament A strong, fibrous tissue that connects one bone to another.

Linear progression Consists of one movement that transitions into another without cycling sequences.

Lipid The name for fats used in the body and bloodstream.

Lordosis Excessive anterior curvature of the spine that typically occurs at the low back (may also occur at the neck).

Maintenance The stage of the transtheoretical model of behavior change during which the individual is incorporating the new behavior into their lifestyle and has been doing so for more than six months.

Matching In choreography, where one exercise ends, another starts.

Maximal heart rate (MHR) The highest heart rate a person can attain. Sometimes abbreviated as HRmax.

Maximal oxygen uptake ($\dot{V}O_2max$) The maximum capacity for the body to take in, transport, and use oxygen during maximal exertion; a common indicator of physical fitness. Also called aerobic capacity.

Medical nutrition therapy Disease management through nutritional diagnostic, therapy, and counseling services provided by a registered dietitian or nutrition professional.

Mending In choreography, stringing two exercises or movements together.

Mineral An inorganic substance needed in the diet in small amounts to help regulate bodily functions.

Mirroring In group fitness classes, the practice of an instructor facing the class while teaching movements so that the participants can make direct eye contact with the instructor and see a "mirror image," rather than looking at the instructor's back.

Mobility The degree to which an articulation is allowed to move before being restricted by surrounding tissues or structures.

Monounsaturated fat A type of unsaturated fat (liquid at room temperature) that has one open spot on the fatty acid for the addition of a hydrogen atom (e.g., oleic acid in olive oil).

Mortality The death rate; the ratio of deaths that take place to expected deaths.

Motivation The psychological drive that gives purpose and direction to behavior.

Motivational cue A cue that enhances the overall experience, fosters enjoyment, and encourages participants to give stronger effort.

Motivational interviewing A person-centered conversation style that encourages clients and participants to honestly examine beliefs and behaviors, and that motivates them to make a decision to change a particular behavior.

Motor learning The process of acquiring and improving motor skills.

Motor skill The degree to which movements using agility, balance, and coordination are executed.

Motor unit A motor nerve and all of the muscle fibers it stimulates.

Muscular endurance The ability of a muscle or muscle group to exert force against a resistance over a sustained period of time; a health-related component of physical fitness.

Muscular fitness Having appropriate levels of both muscular strength and muscular endurance.

Muscular strength The maximal force a muscle or muscle group can exert during contraction; a health-related component of physical fitness.

Musculoskeletal system Body system composed of the skeleton and skeletal muscles that allows, supports, and helps control human movement.

Myocardial infarction (MI) An episode in which some of the heart's blood supply is severely cut off or restricted, causing the heart muscle to suffer and die from lack of oxygen. Commonly known as a heart attack.

Myocardium Muscle of the heart.

National Commission for Certifying Agencies (NCCA) Part of the Institute for Credentialing Excellence (I.C.E.), the NCCA establishes standards for the accreditation of certification programs to help ensure the health, welfare, and safety of the public.

Negligence Failure of a person to perform as a reasonable and prudent professional would perform under similar circumstances.

Neuromuscular efficiency The ability of the neuromuscular system to allow muscles that produce movement and muscles that provide stability to work together synergistically as an integrated functional unit.

Neuromuscular system The nervous and muscular systems, which work together to control, direct, and allow movement of the body.

Noncommunicable diseases (NCD) A medical condition or disease that is noninfectious and non-transmissible among people.

Nutrient A component of food needed by the body. There are six classes of nutrients: water, minerals, vitamins, fats, carbohydrates, and protein.

OARS A tool used to explore a client or participant's values; stands for open-ended questions, affirmations, reflections, and summarizing.

Obesity An excessive accumulation of body fat. Usually defined as more than 20% above ideal weight, or over 25% body fat for men and over 32% body fat for women; also can be defined as a body mass index of ≥30 kg/m^2 or a waist girth of >40 inches (102 cm) in men and >35 inches (89 cm) in women.

Occupational therapist A healthcare provider specializing in treatments that help people who suffer from mentally, physically, developmentally, or emotionally disabling conditions to develop, recover, or maintain daily living and work skills that include improving basic motor functions and reasoning abilities.

Omega-3 fatty acid An essential fatty acid that promotes a healthy immune system and helps protect against heart disease and other diseases; found in egg yolk and cold-water fish and shellfish like tuna, salmon, mackerel, cod, crab, shrimp, and oyster. Also known as linolenic acid.

Open-ended question A question that offers the client or participant broad latitude and choice in how to respond.

Orthostatic hypotension A drop in blood pressure associated with rising to an upright position.

Osteoarthritis A degenerative disease; characterized by pain and stiffness in the joints. Most common form of arthritis.

Osteoporosis A disorder, primarily affecting postmenopausal women, in which bone mineral density decreases and susceptibility to fractures increases.

Osteoporotic fracture Bone fracture that occurs in individuals with compromised bone mass density; most common at the spine, hip, and wrist.

Outcome goal A goal that can be assessed via a measured outcome [e.g., weight loss of 5 pounds (2.3 kg)].

Overexertion Pushing oneself past the point of volitional control or exceeding the limits of one's abilities.

Overload The principle that a physiological system subjected to above-normal stress will respond by increasing in strength or function accordingly.

Overtraining syndrome The result of constant intense training that does not provide adequate time for recovery; symptoms include increased resting heart rate, impaired physical performance, reduced enthusiasm and desire for training, increased incidence of injuries and illness, altered appetite, disturbed sleep patterns, and irritability.

Overuse injury An injury caused by activity that places too much stress on one area of the body over an extended period.

Overweight A term to describe an excessive amount of weight for a given height, using height-to-weight ratios.

Oxidative system The body's most complex energy system, which generates energy by disassembling fuels with the aid of oxygen and has a very high energy yield.

Palpitation A rapid and irregular heartbeat.

Part-to-whole teaching strategy A teaching strategy involving breaking a skill down into its component parts and practicing each skill in its simplest form before placing several skills in a sequence.

Patching In choreography, adding an additional movement between two exercises or movements for a seamless transition.

Pedagogy Method and style of education, including the study and practice of how best to teach.

Perceived seriousness An individual's feelings regarding the severity associated with developing an illness or disease. This is one of the four constructs of the health belief model.

Perceived susceptibility An individual's perception of the risk of personal vulnerability to illness or disease. This is one of the four constructs of the health belief model.

Performance license A license obtained from a performing rights society that allows someone to use copyrighted music in an exercise class.

Performing rights society An organization to which the copyright or publisher assigns the nondramatic performing rights in a musical composition.

Peripheral arterial disease Any disease caused by the obstruction of large peripheral arteries, which can result from atherosclerosis, inflammatory processes leading to stenosis, an embolism, or thrombus formation.

Phosphagen system A system that transfers chemical energy from the breakdown of creatine phosphate to regenerate adenosine triphosphate (ATP). At the onset of activity, or with an increase in intensity, the immediate energy needs are met by the phosphagen system.

Phrase 32 counts of music; composed of four segments of eight beats each.

Physical Activity Readiness Questionnaire for Everyone (PAR-Q+) A brief, self-administered medical questionnaire recognized as a safe pre-exercise screening measure for low-to-moderate (but not vigorous) exercise training.

Plaintiff A party who brings a suit against another party in a court of law.

Planes of motion The conceptual planes in which the body moves; called the sagittal, frontal, and transverse planes; often used to describe anatomical movement.

Plantar flexion Distal movement of the plantar surface of the foot; opposite of dorsiflexion.

Plyometrics High-intensity movements, such as jumping, involving high-force loading of body weight during the landing phase of the movement that take advantage of the stretch-shortening cycle.

Polyunsaturated fat A type of unsaturated fat (liquid at room temperature) that has two or more spots on the fatty acid available for hydrogen (e.g., corn, safflower, and soybean oils).

Posterior Toward the back or dorsal side.

Postural hypotension See Orthostatic hypotension.

Posture The arrangement of the body and its limbs.

Power The capacity to move with a combination of speed and force; a skill-related component of physical fitness.

Practice style of teaching A teaching style that provides opportunities for individualization and includes practice time and individualized instructor feedback.

Precontemplation The stage of the transtheoretical model of behavior change during which the individual is not intending to change within the next six months

Prediabetes The state in which some but not all of the diagnostic criteria for diabetes are met (e.g., blood glucose levels are higher than normal but are not high enough for a diagnosis of diabetes).

Preparation The stage of the transtheoretical model of behavior change during which the individual is getting ready to make a change.

Prime mover A muscle responsible for a specific movement. Also called an agonist.

Process goal A goal a person achieves by doing something, such as completing an exercise session or attending a talk on stress management.

Professional liability insurance Insurance that protects an exercise professional against negligence or failure to perform as a competent and prudent professional would under similar circumstances.

Progression 1. The systematic process of applying overload. For example, in resistance training, more resistance is added to progress the training stimulus. 2. Offering participants options for increasing the intensity or complexity of an exercise or movement.

Pronation Internal rotation of the forearm causing the radius to cross diagonally over the ulna and the palm to face posteriorly.

Prone Lying flat, with the anterior aspect of the body facing downward.

Proprioception Sensation and awareness of knowing where one's body or body part is in space.

Protein A compound composed of a combination 20 amino acids that is the major structural component of all body tissue; one of the macronutrients found in a variety of animal and plant sources and helps to clot blood; balance bodily fluids; contract and build muscles; transport oxygen, vitamins, minerals, and fats around the body; and fight infections. Each gram of protein contains four calories.

Proximal Nearest to the midline of the body or point of origin of a muscle.

Psychomotor domain One of three domains of learning; comprised of physical movement, coordination, and use of the motor skill.

Public performance Playing a recording of a copyrighted musical composition at a place where a substantial number of persons outside of a normal circle of a family and its social acquaintances are gathered.

Puncture A piercing wound from a sharp object that makes a small hole in the skin.

Pursed-lip breathing A breathing technique that increases the amount of air taken in through the damaged tissues of the lungs (e.g., in COPD patients) and reduces the incidence of dyspnea.

Range of motion (ROM) The number of degrees that an articulation will allow one of its segments to move.

Rapport A relationship marked by mutual understanding and trust.

Rating of perceived exertion (RPE) A scale, originally developed by noted Swedish psychologist Gunnar Borg, that provides a standard means for evaluating a participant's perception of exercise effort. The original scale ranged from 6 to 20; a revised category ratio scale ranges from 0 to 10.

Reaction time The amount of time required to respond to a stimulus; a skill-related component of physical fitness.

Recovery heart rate The number of heartbeats per minute following the cessation of vigorous physical activity. As cardiorespiratory fitness improves, the heart rate returns to resting levels more quickly.

Registered dietitian A food and nutrition expert who has met the following criteria: completed a minimum of a bachelor's degree at a U.S. or regionally accredited university, or college and coursework accredited by the Accreditation Council for Education in Nutrition and Dietetics (ACEND); completed an ACEND-accredited supervised practice program; passed a national examination; and completed continuing professional education requirements to maintain registration. Also called a registered dietitian nutritionist.

Regression Offering participants options for decreasing the intensity or complexity of an exercise or movement.

Rehearsal move A movement typically performed during the warm-up in a group fitness class that mimics an upcoming conditioning exercise and helps prepare the neuromuscular system for increased intensity.

Relatedness A sense of belonging and connectedness with others; one of the three basic psychological needs that influence motivation, according to self-determination theory.

Relaxin A hormone of pregnancy that relaxes the pelvic ligaments and other connective tissue in the body.

Repetition-reduction teaching strategy Teaching strategy involving reducing the number of repetitions that make up a movement sequence.

Restrictive covenant A clause in a contract that restricts a company, employee, or other pertinent party to a contract from engaging in certain actions during and/or after a set period of time subsequent to a contract's completion.

Resting heart rate The number of heartbeats per minute when the body is at complete rest; usually counted first thing in the morning before any physical activity.

Reversibility The principle of exercise training that suggests that any improvement in physical fitness due to physical activity is entirely reversible with the discontinuation of the training program.

Rhabdomyolysis The breakdown of muscle fibers resulting in the release of muscle fiber contents into the circulation. Some of these are toxic to the kidney and frequently result in kidney damage.

Rheumatoid arthritis (RA) An autoimmune disease that causes inflammation of connective tissues and joints.

Rhythm A strong, regular, repeated pattern of movement or sound.

Rider Specific additions to a standard insurance policy.

Risk management Minimizing the risks of potential legal liability.

Sagittal plane The longitudinal plane that divides the body into right and left portions.

Sarcopenia Decreased muscle mass; often used to refer specifically to an age-related decline in muscle mass or lean-body tissue that may result in diminished muscle strength and functional performance.

Saturated fat A fatty acid that contains no double bonds between carbon atoms; typically solid at room temperature and very stable.

Scapular plane A shoulder angle about halfway between the sagittal plane and the frontal plane, which represents approximately 30–45 degrees of shoulder flexion. This angle is in line with the orientation of the scapula as it rests naturally against the rib cage and helps protect the shoulder joint during overhead movements.

Scoliosis Excessive lateral curvature of the spine.

Scope of practice The range and limit of responsibilities normally associated with a specific job or profession.

Second ventilatory threshold (VT2) A metabolic marker that represents the point at which high-intensity exercise can no longer be sustained due to proton accumulation causing acidosis.

Sedentary Describing any waking behavior characterized by a low level of energy expenditure [less than or equal to 1.5 metabolic equivalents (METs)] while sitting, reclining, or lying.

Seizure A sudden attack of illness, especially a stroke or an epileptic fit, that typically involves spasms or convulsions.

Self-check style of teaching A teaching style that relies on individual performers to provide their own feedback.

Self-determination theory A psychological theory suggesting that people need to feel competent, autonomous, and connected to others in the many domains of life.

Self-efficacy One's perception of their ability to change or to perform specific behaviors (e.g., exercise).

Self–myofascial release The act of rolling one's own body on a round foam roll or other training tool, massaging away restrictions to normal soft-tissue extensibility.

Shared-use agreement A legal document that allows public and private property owners to broaden access to their underutilized facilities for community use.

Shearing force Any force that causes slippage between a pair of contiguous joints or tissues in a direction that parallels the plane in which they contact.

Shock A life-threatening condition that occurs when the body is not getting enough blood flow.

Sign An objective, observable indicator that the safety of an individual may be compromised, such as loss of coordination, blue lips, or heavy coughing.

Simple-to-complex teaching strategy Advanced teaching strategy that treats a sequence of movement patterns as a whole, teaching small changes (adding small amounts of complexity) to progressively challenge the exercise participant.

Slander A false spoken statement that is damaging to a person's reputation.

Slow-to-fast teaching strategy Teaching strategy used to allow participants to learn complex movement at a slower pace, emphasizing proper placement or configuration of a movement pattern (e.g., teaching a movement at half-tempo).

SMART goal A properly designed goal; SMART stands for specific, measurable, attainable, relevant, and time-bound.

Social support The perceived comfort, caring, esteem, or help an individual receives from other people.

Society of European Stage Authors and Composers (SESAC) A performing rights organization designed to represent songwriters and publishers and their right to be compensated for having their music performed in public.

Spatial awareness Being aware of oneself in space along with other objects in the immediate surroundings.

Specificity Exercise training principle explaining that specific exercise demands made on the body produce specific responses by the body; also called exercise specificity.

Speed Rate of movement; a skill-related component of physical fitness.

Sprain A traumatic joint twist that results in stretching or tearing of the stabilizing connective tissues; mainly involves ligaments or joint capsules, and causes discoloration, swelling, and pain.

Stability Characteristic of the body's joints or posture that represents resistance to change of position.

Stages-of-change model A lifestyle-modification model that suggests that people go through distinct, predictable stages when making lifestyle changes: precontemplation, contemplation, preparation, action, and maintenance. The process is not always linear.

Standard of care Appropriateness of a health coach or exercise professional's actions in light of current professional standards and based on the age, condition, and knowledge of the client or participant.

Steady-state exercise A state of aerobic exercise in which the intensity remains consistent, as opposed to alternating between higher and lower intensities.

Strain A stretch, tear, or rip in the muscle or adjacent tissue such as the fascia or tendon.

Stroke A sudden and often severe ischemic attack due to blockage of an artery into the brain.

Subchondral bone Bone structure that lies under articular cartilage and contains marrow.

Supination External rotation of the forearm (radioulnar joint) that causes the palm to face anteriorly.

Supine Lying face up (on the back).

Sway-back A long outward curve of the thoracic spine with a backward shift of the trunk starting from the pelvis.

Symptom A subjective sensory indicator that a person feels that indicates that an individual may be compromised, such as dizziness or nausea.

Synovial fluid A thick fluid produced by the synovial membrane that nourishes articular cartilages and lubricates joint surfaces.

Systolic blood pressure (SBP) The pressure exerted by the blood on the vessel walls during ventricular contraction.

Talk test A method for measuring exercise intensity using observation of respiration effort and the ability to talk while exercising.

Target heart rate (THR) Number of heartbeats per minute that indicates an appropriate exercise intensity levels for each individual; also called training heart rate. Usually expressed as a percentage of maximal heart rate.

Telemetry The use of instruments to record electrical signals from within the body, such as a heartbeat.

Tempo The rate of speed of music, usually expressed in beats per minute.

Tendinitis Inflammation of a tendon.

Tennis elbow Pain on the outside of the elbow at the attachment of the forearm muscles; lateral epicondylitis.

Testosterone In males, the steroid hormone produced in the testes; involved in growth and development of reproductive tissues, sperm, and secondary male sex characteristics.

Three-dimensional cueing The process of delivering multiple pieces of information simultaneously, all while addressing the three learning styles (i.e., verbal, visual, and kinesthetic).

Tidal volume The volume of air inspired per breath.

Torsion The rotation or twisting of a joint by the exertion of a lateral force tending to turn it about a longitudinal axis.

Tort A civil wrong, other than breach of contract, that causes a claimant to suffer loss or harm.

Trans fat An unsaturated fatty acid that is converted into a saturated fat to increase the shelf life of some products.

Transtheoretical model of behavior change (TTM) A theory of behavior that examines one's readiness to change and identifies five stages: precontemplation, contemplation, preparation, action, and maintenance. Also called the stages-of-change model.

Transverse plane Anatomical term for the imaginary line that divides the body, or any of its parts, into upper (superior) and lower (inferior) parts. Also called the horizontal plane.

Triglyceride Three fatty acids joined to a glycerol (carbon and hydrogen structure) backbone; how fat is stored in the body.

Type 1 diabetes Form of diabetes caused by the destruction of the insulin-producing beta cells in the pancreas, which leads to little or no insulin production; generally develops in childhood and requires regular insulin injections; formerly known as insulin-dependent diabetes mellitus (IDDM) and childhood-onset diabetes.

Type 2 diabetes Most common form of diabetes; typically develops in adulthood and is characterized by a reduced sensitivity of the insulin target cells to available insulin; usually associated with obesity; formerly known as non-insulin-dependent diabetes mellitus (NIDDM) and adult-onset diabetes.

Umbrella liability policy Insurance that provides additional coverage beyond other insurance such as professional liability, home, automobile, etc.

Unilateral Affecting one side of the body at a time.

Valsalva maneuver Forced expiration against a closed glottis to compress the contents of the thoracic and abdominal cavity causing an increased intrabdominal and intrathoracic pressure.

Vegan A person who does not consume any animal products, including dairy products such as milk and cheese, eggs, and may exclude honey.

Vegetarian A person who does not eat meat, fish, poultry, or products containing these foods.

Vestibular system Part of the central nervous system that coordinates reflexes of the eyes, neck, and body to maintain equilibrium in accordance with posture and movement of the head.

Visual system The series of structures by which visual sensations are received from the environment and conveyed as signals to the central nervous system.

Vitamin An organic micronutrient that is essential for normal physiologic function.

$\dot{V}O_2$max See Maximal oxygen uptake ($\dot{V}O_2$max).

$\dot{V}O_2$reserve ($\dot{V}O_2$R) The difference between $\dot{V}O_2$max and $\dot{V}O_2$ at rest; used for programming cardiorespiratory exercise intensity.

Waiver Voluntary abandonment of a right to file suit; not always legally binding.

INDEX

Figures, tables, and boxes are indicated by f, t, and b, respectively, following the page number.

A

C

F

G

H

I

M

N

O

P

Q

R

S

U

V

W

Y

Z